The Wisdom of Trees

SUNY series in Environmental Philosophy and Ethics

J. Baird Callicott and John van Buren, editors

The Wisdom of Trees
Thinking Through Arboreality

Edited by

David Macauley and Laura Pustarfi

Published by State University of New York Press, Albany

© 2025 State University of New York

All rights reserved

Printed in the United States of America

No part of this book may be used or reproduced in any manner without written permission. No part of this book may be stored in a retrieval system or transmitted in any form or by any means including electronic, electrostatic, magnetic tape, mechanical, photocopying, recording, or otherwise without the prior permission in writing of the publisher.

Links to third-party websites are provided as a convenience and for informational purposes only. They do not constitute an endorsement or an approval of any of the products, services, or opinions of the organization, companies, or individuals. SUNY Press bears no responsibility for the accuracy, legality, or content of a URL, the external website, or for that of subsequent websites.

EU GPSR Authorised Representative:
Logos Europe, 9 rue Nicolas Poussin, 17000, La Rochelle, France
contact@logoseurope.eu

For information, contact State University of New York Press, Albany, NY
www.sunypress.edu

Library of Congress Cataloging-in-Publication Data

Names: Macauley, David, editor. | Pustarfi, Laura, 1986– editor.
Title: The wisdom of trees : thinking through arboreality / edited by David Macauley and Laura Pustarfi.
Description: Albany : State University of New York Press, [2025] | Series: SUNY series in environmental philosophy and ethics | Includes bibliographical references and index.
Identifiers: LCCN 2024049504 | ISBN 9798855802702 (hardcover : alk. paper) | ISBN 9798855802726 (ebook)
Subjects: LCSH: Trees—Philosophy. | Forests and forestry—Moral and ethical aspects. | Environmental ethics. | Human-plant relationships.
Classification: LCC SD387.E78 W96 2025 | DDC 174/.96349—dc23/eng/20250131
LC record available at https://lccn.loc.gov/2024049504

Contents

List of Illustrations   ix

Acknowledgments   xi

Foreword   xiii
    Joan Maloof

Introduction: The Wisdom of Trees   1
    David Macauley and Laura Pustarfi

Trees as Beings

Interstice: Redwood   31

1   Arboreality: Trees as Ontologically Valuable Beings   35
    Laura Pustarfi

2   In the Beginning She Was a Redwood: Rethinking Ontology through an Ecofeminist Materialism   55
    Kimberly Carfore

The Language of Trees

Interstice: The Forest   77

3   Speaking Trees: The Language of Nature and Arboreal Communication   79
    Luke Fischer

4 The Silence of Primeval Forests   103
    Daniel O'Dea Bradley

Thinking (Like) Trees

Interstice: Arborescence   133

5 Vegetal Imagination: Schelling and Whitehead as Exemplars
    of Marder's Plant-Thinking   137
    Matthew David Segall

Trees and Time

Interstice: Rings   157

6 "Old Trees Hold Memory": Aboriginal Australian Perspectives
    on Memory, Trauma, and Witnessing in the Arboreal World   161
    John Charles Ryan

7 Birth and Death in Trees   183
    Alphonso Lingis

The Place and Ecology of Trees

Interstice: Banyan   193

8 The Place of Trees: Taking Trees over the Edge   195
    Michael Marder and Edward S. Casey

9 Organisms and Environments: What Alexander von Humboldt
    Learned from Trees   213
    Dalia Nassar

Trees and Aesthetics

Interstice: Cypress   241

| 10 | Thirteen Ways of Looking at a Tree: Appreciating the Beauty of the Arboreal World
David Macauley | 243 |
| 11 | Do Trees Sing?
David Rothenberg | 291 |

Trees and Ethics

Interstice: Apple		303
12	The Ponderosa Pines of Gold Creek: Discerning Arboreal Values for an All-Too-Human World *James Hatley*	307
13	Wise Trees: Exemplars in the Arts of East Asia *Mara Miller*	327

Legal and Political Trees

Interstice: Eucalyptus		369
14	Philosophers with a Peculiarly Instructive Aversion toward Trees *Sam Mickey*	371
15	Trees as Legal Persons *Eric W. Orts*	389

Afterword: The Sequoia Archipelago *Don Hanlon Johnson*	415
Suggestions for Further Reading	419
Contributors	427
Index	435

Illustrations

Figure I.1	Armstrong Redwoods State National Reserve, Guerneville, California.	30
Figure 2.1	Grandmother Redwood.	56
Figure 2.2	Redwood celery.	64
Figure 2.3	Grandmother and kin.	65
Figure I.2	Forest in winter, near Zürich, Switzerland.	76
Figure I.3	Rooted at home, St. Petersburg, Florida.	132
Figure I.4	Redwood cross-section, Big Sur, California.	156
Figure 6.1	Mulga (*Acacia aneura*) in Central Australia.	162
Figure 7.1	Woman in a white dress lying on the ground in the forest.	183
Figure 7.2	Tree burial, Kambira Village, Tana Toraja.	189
Figure I.5	Banyan with child, St. Petersburg, Florida.	192
Figure I.6	Cypress, Barcelona, Spain.	240
Figure 11.1	Sonogram made from David Haskell's ultrasonic ponderosa pine sounds, beyond the range of human hearing.	295
Figure I.7	A cat in an apple tree, Arcata, California.	302
Figure 12.1	Ponderosa pines.	308
Figure 13.1	Buddhist monk Myōe Shōnin meditating in a tree.	331

Figure 13.2	*Enjoying the Moon in a Riverside Cottage*, Ike no Taiga, 1765.	333
Figure 13.3	*Murasaki Shikibu writing the* Tale of Genji *at Ishiyama-dera (Temple), overlooking a garden beneath pine trees*.	333
Figure 13.4	Pine trees at Itsukushima Shrine (c. 693), temple and palace of the Taira (Heike) family, Miyajima, Hiroshima Prefecture, 2003.	334
Figure 13.5	Bamboo grove at the Suzhou Museum designed by I. M. Pei + Pei Architects, Suzhou, China, 2006.	335
Figure 13.6	*Early Spring* by Guo Xi (1020–1090).	340
Figure 13.7	*Landscape for Zhao Yipeng*, after Tang Yin (Chinese, 1470–1524).	341
Figure 13.8	*The Orchid Pavilion Gathering*, Yamamoto Jakurin (1721–1801).	342
Figure 13.9	*Wang Xizhi Watching Geese*, Qian Xuan (1239–1301), Chinese, ink painting with color, c. 1295.	343
Figure 13.10	*Peach Blossom Spring*, Zhang Hong, Chinese, dated 1638.	351
Figure 13.11	*Hawk-Eagle in a Pine Tree*, Soga Nichokuan (act. C. 1625–1660).	352
Figure 13.12	*Bamboo in the Wind*, Yi Jeong (artist name Taneun, 1541–1626).	355
Figure I.8	Eucalyptus, El Cerrito, California.	368
Figure A.1	Don Hanlon Johnson.	417

Acknowledgments

Both of us would like to thank Michael Rinella, the copy editor, and the production staff at SUNY Press for their assistance, encouragement, and patience in seeing this book through to its completion. We also thank the multiple contributors of chapters to this volume, along with the authors of a foreword and afterword, for working with us in assembling the collection. We are grateful to two anonymous peer reviewers for their constructive feedback and suggestions for improving the manuscript. Finally, we would like to extend gratitude to the trees in each of our locales, as well as those globally represented in these pages

David Macauley would like to thank Laura Pustarfi for working closely, thoughtfully, and enthusiastically with him on the volume from its inception to its conclusion. He also thanks Penn State University for the institutional support he received, including from the staff at the Brandywine campus library. Lastly, he would like to acknowledge the International Association for Environmental Philosophy (IAEP) and the Comparative and Continental Philosophy Circle (CCPC) for allowing him to present shorter versions of his chapter on the aesthetics of trees at their respective annual conferences.

Laura Pustarfi thanks David Macauley for the initial idea for this volume, the inspiration to bring a panel and presentations on trees to multiple conferences, and the dedicated collaboration to bring the volume through to completion. She would like to especially thank the trees of both Tilden Park in Berkeley and Crane Creek Park in Sonoma County, California. She also thanks Don Hanlon Johnson, Janis Phelps, Cathy Coleman, Maria Mangini, and Keith Williams for scholarly encouragement and her family along with Jacob Coverstone for their ongoing support.

Foreword

Joan Maloof

What are trees, really, and how should we interact with them? Are they merely commodities—endlessly useful to humans and other organisms—or are they sentient beings worthy of reverence?

There are many, many words in this volume, all aimed at exploring the riddle of the tree. The trees have no idea what we are saying. We are using words to try to bridge the distance between *us* and *them*. Instead of an *us* and a *them*, could there be a *we*? Some Indigenous groups called trees the "Standing People." What did they know that we are just now learning?

The beautiful blue, white, and green planet we call home has gone from being 46 percent covered in trees to 31 percent covered. This decline is entirely due to the actions of our own species, and it has not stopped. Beyond measuring forest cover, the trees that exist on Earth now are, on average, smaller and younger than they were five hundred years ago. Again, we know why. The authors here realize that it is past time to get serious about what this really means. What is it about humans and the cultures we have created that makes this possible?

"Would we *be* different if there were no trees left standing?" asks one of the contributors to this volume. It is a question worth asking since trees are given so little status. Is this because we can't hear them yelp? In the town where I live it is illegal to kick a dog, but it is perfectly legal for landowners to kill every single tree in their yard by cutting them to the ground. Likely, it is the same in your town.

By way of example, I'd like to tell you about an old-growth forest not too far from my home. One day I strolled through the shady forest admiring the huge oaks, ancient pines, towering tulip-poplars, and massive beech trees. A gentle stream ran through the center of the forest. Flitting jewel-winged damselflies added a bit of magic to the scene. Birdsong decorated the air. I caught a glimpse of a little ovenbird flying from the base of one of the beech trees. I took a few steps forward and bent down to put my hand on the smooth toe of the tree, so I could look closer into the small, dark hollow from which the bird had emerged. There I could see a tiny, perfectly made nest holding four eggs. I don't have to tell you how much that meant to me. I know that you, too, would be moved.

Could we call this beech a Mother Tree?

The forest was both lovely and serene. I felt small, surrounded as I was by tree arms silently turning sunlight into solid matter. But the beauty was encircled by sorrow because most of the trees had rings spray-painted around their trunks—indicating they had been chosen for cutting. If trees have a language, they were saying the same thing we would say if we bore such a mark: "I want to live. I do not consent to being killed."

The two of us who were trying to save the forest needed a name for it, and we ended up calling it Foster's Forest after the ninety-two-year-old man who had recently bought it and ordered it cut. (In case you were wondering, and felt ready to give him an excuse, he did not need the money.) While naming the forest after the new owner might seem like knee-jerk colonial toponymy, it was less heartbreaking than calling it Ovenbird's Beech Grove—especially considering what happened next.

I didn't feel more *tree* when I was in that forest; I felt more human. Sadly, we couldn't save it. Foster was determined to have the trees cut, and the mill owner was happy to comply. Neither one of the men had a relationship with the trees in that forest. As far as I could tell, neither one had ever spent any time among those trees. They didn't know how important that beech tree was to that ovenbird—and the generations of ovenbirds who had come before it. No laws can stop even the oldest and most beautiful forests from being cut if they are on private land.

There was a good market for the big timbers that would come from the oaks and the pines, but what about the tulip-poplars and the beech trees? When I asked, I learned that the tulip-poplars were destined to be made into coffins, which would then be buried in the ground. So, we turn live trees into dead trees to decompose along with our dead bodies. There are many living trees in cemeteries, but there are many dead ones too that you cannot see.

And the beautiful beech? They would be transformed into construction mats: strong platforms to hold equipment so it won't sink in the mud. The mats might hold backhoes for digging out soil for a new highway, or cranes for putting up large electrical transmission towers, or—the irony—they might be used to support logging trucks. Oh, how I wish the trees were useless!

We will always rely on trees, and I love wood floors, too, but do the uses above show "respect for their lives," as editor Pustarfi recommends? I think not. Especially not for the ancient trees standing since before our parents were born, and their parents too, and our parents' parents' parents. The trees may be wise, but in this case the men were not.

In North America we inherited—or took—a land filled with abundant large trees. Of the nearly two hundred countries across the planet, the United States is in the top five in terms of forest cover. Has this abundance inured us to their destruction?

I hear myself asking so many questions, but I am not alone. There are 244 question marks in this volume, not including my own. Perhaps that is where we start: just asking the right questions. Another step taken in this volume is acquainting ourselves with the terms and ideas used to discuss our relationships to the vegetal world: phytophobia, phytophilia, arborophobia, and many others.

The heartbreak is real. That alone should tell us something. When I returned after the cut, there was no shade, no birdsong, no damselflies. The soil, now exposed, was crisscrossed by deep patterns from industrial-sized tires. I put my hand on a pale, flat, fragrant stump. This tree was not just a *thing*—it was a being. *You existed*, I tell it, *and now you do not*. I'm sorry.

These trees held memories in their arboreal bodies. Memories of sunny days—so many of them, waxing and waning as the year progressed—and memories of the frightening storms when neighbors shattered. And now the memory of them lives in me. In some way maybe they do still exist, like the pines and plums in the ancient Japanese artworks.

Humans have often made the "other" inhuman so that we feel we can kill in innocence. The treatment of enslaved Africans is one egregious example of this process, but many other instances from other regions and eras abound. These killings went unpunished. It was the same for domestic animals. But now those of other races, religions, and even species are offered protection under the law. These changes came slowly, and partially in response to philosophical reflection. Today we are examining trees in this same way. Are they individuals? Do they deserve protection, or at least consideration?

Whatever we decide, the trees cannot run away.

Cue the timpani drums. Maybe the song of the tree is its final crashing climax as it falls. We certainly hear the crash if we are nearby, and if we are not near, all other living things with a tympanic membrane hear it.

We are witnesses. May this volume become a portal to a new relationship with *tree*. As Jim Hatley notes in his essay, "Whoever they are, they exceed us."

In mass, in age, and likely in other ways too.

Introduction

The Wisdom of Trees

DAVID MACAULEY AND LAURA PUSTARFI

> Tree. One of the most potent monosyllables in our tongue. A word that roots far into the ground of our human being. Tree of life. Tree of knowledge. World Tree. Tree of the cross . . . it is one of those fundamental nouns—like mother or father—each of which ramifies into a whole tree of language in itself. Already, in the dim forest of Indo-European, its trunk was sturdily in place before it branched out into Sanskrit *dāru* meaning a kind of pine, in Greek *dóru* meaning wood or a spear, into Old Irish *daur* and Welsh *drewen* meaning an oak, into Russian *drevo* and Swedish *trād* and old English *treo*(w).
>
> —Seamus Heaney, Irish poet

Listening to Trees

In recent years, we have not only been discovering the many wondrous and reliable ways that trees contribute to our languages, lives, and cultures but also how they support and commune with each other through subterranean fungal networks—the "Wood Wide Web," as it is widely known through the research of forest ecologist Suzanne Simard and others.[1] Listening to and learning from trees and forests is now decisive for both our own survival and the continued flourishing of the natural world. In his highly acclaimed novel *The Overstory*, Richard Powers calls attention to this development with poetic verve:

> We found that trees could communicate, over the air and through their roots. Common sense hooted us down. We found that trees take care of each other. Collective science dismissed the idea. Outsiders discovered how seeds remember the seasons of their childhood and set buds accordingly. Outsiders discovered that trees sense the presence of other nearby life. That a tree learns to save water. That trees feed their young and synchronize their masts and bank resources and warn kin and send out signals to wasps to come and save them from attacks.

Powers then adds a speculative flourish:

> Here's a little outsider information, and you can wait for it to be confirmed. A forest knows things. They wire themselves up underground. There are brains down there, ones our own brains aren't shaped to see. Root plasticity, solving problems and making decisions. Fungal synapses. What else do you want to call it? Link enough trees together, and a forest grows aware.[2]

The very meaning of philosophy of course involves the love and pursuit of wisdom. However, this passionate and once perennial search has arguably declined or been attenuated and displaced over time, along with the broad and profound ties between philosophy and the natural environment. In the ancient world, wisdom was a paramount concern and linked closely to the highest of goals and purposes in life. Stories, art, myth, and philosophy explored the ways through which a deep reflection on human experience and the earth could provide meaning, knowledge, and practical guidance about how to lead a good life. In the modern and contemporary eras, the place of wisdom within philosophy and related fields has tended to play second or even third fiddle to other ideas and interests, including truth, logic, knowledge, power, and language.

Thus, associating wisdom with—or attributing it to—trees and forests might understandably raise a few eyebrows. One sense of this connection, though, simply recognizes that we ourselves can find insight and even enlightenment by spending time with and learning from the wooded world. Wisdom is the fruit we might obtain through listening closely and long to trees and other earthly beings. A second, more contentious sense of the linkage suggests that trees themselves may embody a form of wisdom. The attribution of this trait and virtue to trees—or the discovery of it within the world's forests—both reasonably relativizes the notion and moves it away from a sole and singular province in the human mind.

This view suggests that phenomena like perception, experience, agency, intelligence, knowledge, and awareness might exist in degrees or as part of a continuum marked by distinctions, gradations, and differences. In this regard, we speak sensibly at times of the wisdom of the body, the wisdom of the heart, the wisdom of the child, and the wisdom of places.[3] We extend wisdom beyond a narrow philosophically enforced domain and acknowledge both that sharply drawn boundaries between the human and more-than-human worlds may be more permeable and fluid than formerly thought and that other beings may reveal a form of sapience, a way of knowing acquired through evolutionary adaption. As this volume hopes to show, there is much wisdom to be gained by us from understanding the many ecological services, quiet strength and resilience, and deep beauty of the arboreal realm.

References are widespread in world literature to the wisdom humans receive from trees along with the virtues that trees and other plants themselves may possess. Ancient trees have been referred to regularly as "sages" in the East. Ralph Waldo Emerson once proclaimed, "Wise are ye, O ancient woods! Wiser than man."[4] Novelist Marcel Proust declared, "We have nothing to fear and a great deal to learn from trees, that vigorous and pacific tribe which without stint produces strengthening essences for us, soothing balms, and in whose gracious company we spend so many cool, silent, and intimate hours."[5] Hermann Hesse pronounced that trees "are wiser than we are, as long as we do not listen to them. But when we have learned how to listen to trees, then the brevity and the quickness and the childlike hastiness of our thoughts achieve an incomparable joy."[6] Nietzsche, too, spoke of the need to "start with the 'sagacity' of plants" in the re-evaluation of all values.[7] Both William Blake's remark, "A fool sees not the same tree that a wise man sees," and Rabindranath Tagore's reminder, "The one who plants trees, knowing that he will never sit in their shade, has at least started to understand the meaning of life," underscore these broad associations as well.[8]

In the scholarly world, Simard selected "Discovering the Wisdom of the Forest" as the subtitle for her influential book, *Finding the Mother Tree* and has written about how the forest is "wired for wisdom;" the "overwhelming wisdom of the elders, the firs and ponderosas;" and the "beauty of [a dying forest's] hard wiring that passed wisdom to the next generation" of trees.[9] Historian Jared Farmer has likewise explored the importance of "elderflora" and the value of ancient trees, which are respected and honored widely across diverse cultures.[10] And philosopher Michael Marder has examined "plant-thinking" and "the wisdom of plants" in his bellwether works.[11] As we learn more about the capacities of trees, qualities such as humility (from *humilis*, of the ground), patience, perseverance, sharing, and good community membership are increasingly connected with—even if metamorphically—the plant kingdom and forests as well.

One key dimension of the bond between wisdom and trees concerns time. Trees are living witnesses to the evolutionary forces and complex biological activity on Earth. We get an apt sense of this truth in viewing a large cross section of an old tree—like one in the Museum of Natural History in New York, those in the "Trees of Mystery" forests in Northern California, or the artistic renderings by Tiffany Shlain in her Dendrofemonology series—when tree rings are marked with corresponding dates in human history that carry us back in time through the invention of the printing press, Chaucer's literary works, the Crusades, the Holy Roman Empire, the Viking discovery of America, and beyond. Trees in fact are some of the longest-lived organisms on earth. Dendrochronologists—biologists who specialize in dating trees—determine tree longevity by examining wood core samples, counting rings on cut trees, and engaging in radiocarbon dating and historical estimation. Trees grow from the living cambium layer under the bark by adding cells to both the exterior bark and interior wood, which reveals the rings visible in a cross section of the trunk. These rings, while not always annually regular, are particular enough to provide not only the age of the tree but also information about the surrounding ecology and climate.[12] Famously, one of the oldest trees ever found, Prometheus, a bristlecone pine in California's Inyo National Forest, was felled in 1964 by a young dendrochronological researcher, who discovered too late that his study subject boasted 4,844 rings.[13] An older, living Great Basin bristlecone pine was subsequently located in 2012 and dated at 5,062 years.[14]

In addition to individual trees like the bristlecone pine, clonal trees, which can duplicate themselves, may be much older. A diminutive Norway spruce found on a Swedish mountain has been dated to over 9,550 years old at its roots, although the visible portion of the tree is approximately six hundred years old. Almost unbelievably, a clonal quaking aspen in Colorado called Pando has roots that are at least eighty thousand years old, with some scientists claiming the tree could be over a million years old given the stability of local environmental conditions. This genetically individuated organism has more than forty-seven thousand stems, covers an area of 106 acres, and weighs over 6,600 tons, making them one of the largest organisms on the planet.[15] Trees like the aspen also raise questions about arboreal identity, and whether what we perceive on the surface as one stem is an individual tree. Some trees in fact can grow new stems from the trunk of an older tree, leaving a ring where the initial tree once stood. This is common in redwoods, with one exemplary ring comprising forty-five trunks and measuring seventeen by fifteen meters in circumference.[16] Is this successive ring one tree or multiple? This kind of conundrum opens many others, especially philosophical issues of identity and difference.[17]

The Arboreal World

Trees are not just generally older than humans, they are also very different from us in their existence as sessile, modular beings. These woody, perennial plants form the backbone of forest ecology, providing habitats for mammalian, avian, amphibian, and insect species. Their roots connect soil systems, their trunks verticalize water, and their canopies create hidden worlds in the sky. We know them as photosynthesizers, tasked with transforming sunlight into sugars and sustenance for themselves and other forest occupants. They offer an exchange for the air we breathe as one of their many contributions to planetary cycles.

We evolved as a species in the shade of trees, built societies in the openings of forests, and created economies, art, and stories with and within arboreal boughs. Forests are fundamental to human cultures. Vast stands of trees, and their clearing, helped to establish the ground of most civilizations. Trees form our homes and the pages of our books, and they are incorporated widely into our consumer products, including even toothpaste. They provide us with innumerable edibles, including fruits and nuts, as well as a source for medicinal knowledge. Trees have been locations for civic assemblies, shelters for weddings, and markers for both birth and death. Beyond the woods, affluent neighborhoods congregate trees in parks and gardens, along streets, and in yards to heighten property appeal. These trees afford habitats and beautify communities, impacting positively our health and psychology.[18] Notably, less affluent urban regions are often relatively devoid of trees and green spaces, a sad social commentary on the landscape.[19]

Trees inspire creativity and excite fears. They appear in myth, story, poem, and song in guises from primordial characters to archetypal divinities. Religious iconography and lore make use of trees and the woods in origin stories and throughout religious practice. Trees appear as vessels for spiritual wisdom, as subjects of praise, and as loci of mystical experience. Far beyond the mundane, the forest can be a place of heightened beauty or deep chthonic terror, and it can issue into a sublime experience for the romantically inclined, leading to poetic insights. Trees appear as figures in fairy tales and folklore, and they are a primary metaphor in world literature. The visible structure of a tree lends itself to hierarchy, and it helps to form a symbolic configuration for our philosophical, cultural, and scientific thought.

Trees are pervasive phenomena, and few cultures are absent of their influence. Western civilization was built from forests, and trees continue to be deeply intertwined with our lives even when we are unaware of their presence. But what exactly is a tree? This question, while seemingly simple, has given rise to many possible answers and remains contested among biologists. Some botanists rely upon a Wittgensteinian concept of family resemblance in terms of what a constitutes a tree. They point, for example, to the juridical definition of English judge Lord Denning, who proclaimed, "Anything that one would ordinarily call a tree is a 'tree.'"[20] While most of us recognize a tree upon encountering one, this approach is ultimately inadequate.

Trees are distinguished biologically from bushes and other plants. They are also differentiated linguistically in many Western languages, classified socially by their status and economic value, mythologically and religiously by their beauty or function, and metaphorically by their use in scientific, literary, or philosophical models and frameworks. In contemporary botany, a tree is generally a plant over twenty feet in height with a self-supporting, woody stem that lives for more than a year. While most people identify trees as tall, woody, green things rooted in the ground, scientists have taken pains to categorize and catalogue the earth's sylvan communities. Even a brief glance at a field guide will reveal that defining trees is no easy task given the diversity of leaf configurations, bud shapes, bark textures, and mature forms. There are as many as one hundred thousand tree species on Earth in several families, and the oldest date back more than 390 million years, as compared to three hundred thousand years for *homo sapiens*.[21] Some species, such as tree ferns, do not exhibit a typical woody stem yet are still widely considered trees, while others, such as bamboo and banana, possess no woody stem and are not viewed as trees by many botanists.

The disparate functions of an individual tree, even of the average variety, are quite striking. Trees, of course, use photosynthesis to make oxygen and generate energy out of light through the cells in their leaves. One beech tree can produce enough oxygen to support ten humans for an entire year. Large trees possess hundreds of thousands of leaves, and a mature American elm has up to five million.[22] Some trees can even adjust their leaves or the cells within their leaves to gather more needed light. Trees require enormous amounts of water for transpiration, but they can also limit fluid loss during droughts. In the rainforest, trees may lose up to twelve hundred liters of water each day, while in the desert they can restrict loss to as little as twenty-five milliliters.[23] Biologists, however, still do not fully understand the way trees lift water from the ground to the highest leaves up the great length of the trunk.

Trees flourish across the earth in most terrestrial ecosystems and often thrive within proximity of each other. Over three trillion individual trees exist on the planet, or almost four hundred trees to each human person on Earth, as of a 2015 estimate.[24] Ecologically, trees are interconnected with other plants, fungi, insects, birds, and animals in a dizzying array of relationships. Like the microbiomes of humans, trees live symbiotically with a multitude of organisms throughout their bodies. Forests provide critical habitat for other species, becoming homes and sources of food for wildlife and other plants. Forests also provide an untold number of ecosystem services worldwide, including carbon storage, oxygen production, and the ability to lower the albedo of the planet.

Scientists are only now beginning to understand the many ways in which trees and plants seem to exhibit a sense of intelligence and agency. Plants are now known to possess photoreceptors akin to sight, chemical stimuli that approximate smell, tactile senses that parallel feeling, vibrational sensations similar to hearing, perception of gravity that allows movement, and storage of past information analogous to memory.[25] Forests also function as an organism—or, perhaps more fittingly, a super-organism—and biologists, ecologists, and foresters are providing new insights about how trees interact as a larger biotic community.[26]

Trees in short are some of the most impressive entities on earth. They are both the tallest and most voluminous organisms known on the planet. Both records are held by Californian specimens: the tallest is a redwood, and the most voluminous is a sequoia. Hyperion, located in a secret grove in Redwood National Park, was measured at almost 380 feet in 2006, with four other local redwoods towering 370 feet or higher. The largest individual tree is a giant sequoia in Sequoia National Park called General Sherman. The 275-foot-tall general has an estimated volume of 52,500 cubic feet and an estimated weight of 650 tons for the trunk alone.[27] These incredible behemoths far exceed in size other currently living entities, and their magnitudes can be difficult to grasp with our Earth-bound imaginations.

Philosophy in the Forest

In quiet but significant ways, trees have been part of philosophical traditions and conversation around nature, wisdom, beauty, enlightenment, and truth for centuries. In the West, we find Plato's plane tree in the *Phaedrus* dialogue and his olive tree in the Academy grove where he taught. We encounter Aristotle's oak tree and the *telos* of the acorn, Augustine's pear tree from which he plundered fruit, and Newton's epiphanic apple tree. Later, we read of Sartre's anxious reflections on chestnut tree roots in *Nausea*, Jung's World Tree as *axis mundi*, Buber's interaction with a tree in terms of an I–Thou relationship, Heidegger's *Holzwege* and meditations on wood paths, forest clearings, and rootedness, as well as Deleuze and Guattari's critique of the tree via the rhizome. In the East, we can point to Buddha's Bodhi Tree, the Cosmic Tree of Hinduism, the "Useless Tree" in Zhuangzi, the Uncarved Block (樸) in the *Tao Te Ching*, and the many appearances of trees in Zen haiku, among other outcroppings.

There is, nevertheless, a philosophical fork in the Western woods. One path has tended to marginalize trees or denigrate their role and value. The other has slowly embraced or perhaps discreetly engaged them, following in the line of Theophrastus, student of both Plato and Aristotle who treated plants on their own terms rather than in comparison to humans and animals.[28] Trees and plants appear throughout the Western philosophical lineage often as a polar reference to humanity.[29] They are invoked as common philosophical examples and metaphors throughout this tradition, including Plato's discussion of humans as upside-down plants with our souls rooted in heaven and Merleau-Ponty's meditations on the trees outside of his window to illuminate the Cartesian *cogito*.

More recently, figures in the emerging interdisciplinary field of critical plant studies, such as Matthew Hall, Monica Gagliano, Michael Marder, and

Luce Irigaray, have revisited ideas of plants in philosophy, literature, and the sciences to rethink classical and modern divisions between human and non-human beings. The work of philosopher Marder has been especially influential. In books such as *Plant Thinking*, *The Philosopher's Plant*, *Time is a Plant*, and *Plants in Place*, Marder examines the ethical and ontological exclusion of vegetal life in Western thought, providing a way to consider and appreciate plants in their unique orientations and existence as they grow perpetually outward into the world. Deliberation about the status of plants is part of a broader "nonhuman turn" and "posthuman theory" that has been occurring in intellectual discourse, one that includes work in animal studies, ecological literary criticism, the treatment of elemental phenomena such as water, air, earth, stone, and fire, and increasingly artificial intelligence and artificial life.[30]

Several new theories seek to explain both our lack of attention to plants and our love for them: plant blindness and phytophobia as well as phytophilia and arborphilia. The idea of plant blindness was introduced by educator James Wandersee and biologist Elizabeth Schussler. Noticing that school children tend to prefer studying animals to plants, they describe plant blindness as the inability to recognize or appreciate plants in human and non-human environments and "the misguided anthropocentric ranking of plants as inferior to animals and thus, as unworthy of consideration."[31] They offer several reasons for this conceptual oversight, including a widespread lack of deep knowledge about plants, the perceived homogeneity of plant kinds, the absence of observable movement by plants, and our seeming over-familiarity with them. As a possible response to this problem, they call for additional plant study in early biology curricula.[32]

Philosopher Matthew Hall argues that plant blindness as well as zoocentrism, the centering of animals within our society, is an affliction of the Western mind and does not appear in all cultures. He claims the reasoning offered by Wandersee and Schussler assumes a physiological foundation, and he speculates instead that excluding plants from our spheres of concern is "a cultural-philosophical attitude" primarily in the West.[33] Somewhat similarly and without the ableism of the term "plant blindness," Michael Marder regards the West's "widespread conceptual allergy to vegetable life" as an intellectual phytophobia, a concept that he contrasts with phytophilia.[34] Phytophobia, in which trees and plants are ignored, backgrounded, or homogenized, however, may be more than just an intellectual bias. A recent study by two psychologists showed that infants were reluctant to touch plants or items that looked like plants, which they label as inanimate, compared to other phenomena, whether familiar or unfamiliar, artificial or naturally occurring.[35] The conclusions of this study suggest an evolutionary basis for the difference. Although the psychologists do not use the term "phytophobia," their work shows a differentiation in response at early ages between plants and other entities that points to a fear of the former.

By contrast, phytophilia involves the love of plants, a condition that appears in the writings of a few philosophical biographies and much more commonly in literature and poetry.[36] Relatedly, religious studies scholar Bron Taylor characterizes arborphilia as "friendly or loving feelings toward trees," noting religious, historical, and imaginative examples of tree love.[37] Both extremes may influence our actions toward arboreal neighbors. Phytophobia and the ignorance of trees is much more common, and that may be a reason why it is difficult for some of us to understand that trees and plants are strongly affected by anthropogenic environmental change. Those who are phytophilic or arborphilic may be more attuned to conservation efforts. Either way, trees have typically suffered from the environmental crisis in pronounced and lasting ways.

Trees in Troubled Times

In 1940, German playwright Bertolt Brecht spoke of the "dark times" that many people in the world were experiencing and the deep desire and corresponding need for comforting wisdom. In a poem entitled "An die Nachgeborenen" ("To Those Born Later"), he asked, "What kind of times are they, when / A talk about trees is almost a crime / Because it implies silence about so many horrors?"[38] Brecht, of course, was concerned about the war and other perils ravaging Europe, but he seemed to imply that conversation about seemingly quotidian and other-than-human matters such as trees was a form of luxury and a distraction from justice that we could ill afford.[39] Many decades afterward, however, American poet Adrienne Rich offered a belated response to Brecht's query in a poem she called "What Kind of Times are These." Rich wrote: "There's a place between two strands of trees where the grass grows uphill / . . . And I won't tell you where it is, so why do I tell you / anything? Because you still listen, because in times like these / to have you listen at all, it's necessary / to talk about trees."[40] Indeed, in our current alarming era of unprecedented heat, drought, deforestation, weather extremes, and loss of biodiversity, not to speak of—and listen to—trees is both irresponsible and dangerous.

While there exists a vast and diverse set of species, trees are an immensely valuable and instructive subject upon which to focus and reflect since they are prevalent throughout the globe and are affected greatly by the environmental crisis. Trees thrive within both forest systems and urban landscapes, and also serve as an exemplar and archetype of a perennial plant. Trees are used instrumentally by humans and are intertwined in our lives in both overt and covert ways. They have, however, often been backgrounded in Western culture and characterized as mere resources for lumber, medicine, and recreation, among other uses.[41] At the same time, they are frequently idealized or framed as beautiful objects to be admired in the landscape. Both views unfortunately may miss engaging with trees as beings in their own right and thereby ignore other possible understandings of and relationships with them that are potentially available, and valuable, to us.

We have increasingly developed ruthless mechanisms and systems of resource extraction that have led to and magnified environmental destruction, deforesting the planet in the process. Forests, however, are carbon sinks and by sequestering carbon they counter anthropogenic climate change, which as a planet-wide crisis, urgently requires response.[42] Human activities are extinguishing animal and plant species and razing the woods at astounding rates. Impacts on global forests are intertwined with cultural systems of domination and colonialization, which in turn are connected to the intellectual and religious traditions that fostered and continue to support narrowly anthropocentric perspectives. The way we view trees, especially in Western culture, is representative of larger trends and tendencies about which we need to be aware and responsive, too.

Although thinkers, writers, and scientists have been sounding an alarm for decades, ecological degradation continues to worsen and expand. Our current planetary challenges, particularly the rapidly changing climate, are generating new ways of thinking about our impact on the Earth. We have likely moved into a new geologic epoch characterized by human-born changes: the Anthropocene.[43] Environmental disasters are presenting us with emerging problems that do not conform to our previous experiences or expectations, putting us under duress to find novel solutions. While technology and scientific knowledge have advanced rapidly, the scope of the crisis continues to outpace both our technical abilities and political will.

Contemporary forests are marked both by global devastation and regenerative powers. Michael Marder, drawing on Giorgio Agamben's notion of *homo sacer*, has advanced the term *arbor sacra*: "a creature that is either barely alive or not deemed alive at all and that at any moment may be chopped down without care for the future."[44] Given current rates of deforestation, it might be said that in most parts of the world trees are now viewed as *arbor sacra* with their only "crime" as that of usefulness to humans. Deforestation due to population increases and economic demands, of course, is not uncommon throughout human history. But what is becoming clearer are the interconnections between forests and human well-being, especially regarding health and social affluence, along with the ties to planetary threats such as climate change and species extinction.

While humans have always had complex relationships with the forest that entailed clearing large swaths of trees, over the last seventy years deforestation has increased greatly worldwide, particularly in the tropics, in what geographer Michael Williams calls "The Great Onslaught."[45] He explores political, economic, technological, and demographic reasons for this increase in intensity of deforestation:

> The main causes of contemporary deforestation seem simple enough and easily isolated. From time immemorial it has been expanding population numbers and increased technological abilities to promote change that has placed people in competition with all other life forms for the remaining niches in the world. More land goes into cultivation, shifting agriculture is extended, fallows are shortened, and more livestock are grazed more intensively. Timber extraction and fuelwood gathering are promoted, as are technological innovations. It is a simple land use problem . . . but more recently the simple central facts of numbers, affluence, and technology have been augmented by other leading or underlying causes . . . the realization that deforestation is a complex and multifaceted process operating at various scales, in various places, and with a multiplicity of variables augmenting and sometimes even cancelling its impact, has induced other researchers to attempt a more holistic and global explanation.[46]

These underlying causes involve the complexities of increasing globalization, as forests continue to be central yet often unnamed players and "protagonists" in global dramas.

The Food and Agricultural Organization (FAO) of the United Nations has been compiling data and reporting on global forests since 1948. According to their Global Forest Resources Assessment in 2020, the most recent report available, slightly more than 31 percent of total land area worldwide is forested, which is just over four billion hectares.[47] In this regard, the FAO defines a forest as "land spanning more than .5 hectares with trees higher than 5 meters and a canopy cover of more than 10 percent, or trees able to reach these thresholds *in situ*."[48] Another recent report, "Mapping Tree Density at a Global Scale," published in the prestigious journal *Nature*, used updated global ground measures and satellite imagery to arrive at a figure of three trillion trees existing on the planet. The authors of that report conclude that almost half of Earth's trees have been removed without replacement since the beginning of human civilization.[49] Even though the loss has been stemmed to some degree in Asia, Europe, Oceania, and North America, the total area deforested each year remains extensive. Africa and South America continue to experience most of the contemporary forest disappearance.[50] Reasons for this trend vary, but the causes include the expansion of agricultural lands, the increase in ranching and pasture generation, widespread fuelwood gathering, and intensive logging, along with the pressures of international trade.[51]

Philosophical Branches

The very ideas within philosophy of who might count as a person and who might possess agency, display intelligence, embody worth, or express beauty have traditionally been shaped or even determined by human frameworks, or at best, by more-than-human perspectives that include non-human animals. Underlying this point is an issue that many contributors to this book engage: whether and how we can reconsider the ways in which trees enter our estimations of value—both to ourselves and to other living kinds. In this volume—the first collection to wed philosophy specifically with trees—we bring into discussion arboreal thinking as it is informed by phenomenology, natural history, and ecological science, with a particular emphasis on both continental philosophy and the environmental humanities.

Trees are not simply complex beings because they provide a vast array of ecological services to a host of living organisms, including our all-too-human selves; rather, they are also uniquely capable of entwining our ways of knowing the world with their own modes of existence. In this manner, they might possibly become our mentors or models for building a more sustainable and inclusive world, an idea well known in some Indigenous traditions. Biologist Robin Wall Kimmerer, speaking of her Potawatomi ancestors and community, says, "The trees, especially, we recognize as our teachers."[52] If their instruction is to be acknowledged and shared widely, philosophers, as well as other thinkers and writers, must reorient the conversation about why trees matter, how they can best be protected, our obligations to them, and even what or who they are.

Through a series of diverse chapters, we show how a new and emerging understanding of trees encourages a revisioning of philosophical categories, a reconceptualization with ecological and social implications for human interactions with them and the forests in which they reside. These contributions investigate the ontological, epistemological, ethical, political, and aesthetic dimensions of arboreality, focusing on issues related to time, mind, truth, memory, being, beauty, goodness, wisdom, personhood, and death. While these chapters represent varied and pluralistic perspectives of the arboreal world, we recognize that some voices may not be expressed in the pages that follow. We hope this volume opens opportunities for further conversation and dialogue regarding arboreal philosophy from writers, artists, and environmentalists.[53]

The volume commences with two investigations of the ontology of trees. Ontology treats the very nature of what it means to be and to exist. With trees, ontological questions can be raised, for example, about whether they are discrete individual entities, fields of being, non-human persons, natural objects, or nodes in a vast incarnate network. Laura Pustarfi explores the ontological status of trees through a perspective inspired by the work of phenomenologist Maurice Merleau-Ponty. She argues for valuing trees as significant living beings due to their capacities for agency, intelligence, and relationality. Kimberly Carfore follows this discussion by making a case for rethinking arboreal ontology through a viewpoint informed by ecofeminist materialism. She draws on the writings of Luce Irigaray, Val Plumwood, and Suzanne Simard to develop a relational perspective of trees guided by storytelling and her own wilderness experiences.

Poet Howard Nemerov has written, "Before you can learn the trees / you have to learn the language of trees."[54] Luke Fischer shows his conversancy with this language, setting forth a nuanced view of arboreal expression and tree communication. Along the way, Fischer builds on the thought of European Romantics, especially Goethe and Novalis. He develops the notion of a gestural language in nature that reveals the capacities of trees through poetic modes of understanding. By contrast, Daniel Bradley investigates and thoughtfully celebrates the relative silence of conifer forests. He engages the philosophy of Irigaray and Emmanuel Levinas as well as forest ecology and eco-phenomenology to critique what he considers to be a modern bias against darkness and silence.

Plant-thinking and intelligence are at the heart of recent dialogue and debate in critical plant studies circles. Matthew Segall enters this discussion by engaging Michael Marder's views on vegetal metaphysics through a consideration of the philosophies of Alfred North Whitehead and Friedrich Schelling. He examines the process thought of these two figures in terms of speculative imagination, which he characters as plant-like in approach.

The temporality and place of trees are the foci of the next group of contributions. John Ryan looks in depth at the role of memory in trees, particularly through the lens of Aboriginal Australian narratives containing arboreal wisdom. He shows that trees are both important agents and bearers of memory as well as living witnesses to ecological trauma. According to Ryan, understanding these reserves of memory better enables us to accept dendrophilia, "a love for trees as wise fellow-beings in all their forms." Alphonso Lingis also takes up the theme of time in reflecting upon the lives and deaths of trees within the broader context of evolution and life on earth. He addresses the interdependency of organisms and their relationships to trees in or upon which many beings are born and die, including some human babies in Indonesia.

Michael Marder and Edward Casey collaborate to develop a detailed phenomenology of the places of trees. They show how trees shape and are shaped by the places in which they grow. In doing so, they focus on the interlaced edges of these plants with soil, atmosphere, and other trees. And they elaborate on a host of relevant place-based and edge-bound distinctions, including arborescence, site, boundary, branching, clearing, directionality, lateralizing, and locality, recognizing that trees not only *have* places but *are* places. Dalia Nassar also looks closely at the topic of place construed as "environment" through the work of German geographer, naturalist, and explorer Alexander von Humboldt. She investigates and articulates Humboldt's early ecological insights into trees and the dynamic bilateral relationships he discovered between organisms and their surroundings—in short, the ways that trees are not only receptively changed by their contexts but also actively transform the environments in which they reside. Nassar underscores the importance of this collaborative interdependence—expressed through plant forms—for establishing and understanding ecology as a discipline and responding to ecological challenges.

We close the volume with a reflection on value issues, taking up in turn the aesthetic, ethical, political, and legal dimensions of trees. While a large amount of research has been conducted on forests, very little work has focused on the aesthetic qualities of trees themselves despite the great numbers of people lured to the woods and wilderness. David Macauley identifies and articulates thirteen interrelated approaches to appreciating trees and forests, including those that focus on evolution, function, use, holism, emotion, sensual qualities, storytelling, sacredness, ambience, and imagination, among others. He develops and defends a view that combines scientific and cognitive elements with more participatory and sensually engaged features to best capture the wide range of arboreal beauty and the diversity of human encounters with trees. David Rothenberg in turn draws on his background as both a philosopher and musician to explore the question of whether trees emit sounds, make music, or even sing. As he has done elsewhere with birds, whales, and bugs, he listens closely to trees to discover what we might learn from the wonderous natural world.

Regarding ethical issues, James Hatley writes of discerning arboreal values through encounters and moral "entanglement" with ponderosa pines on an annual pilgrimage into the woods. He draws on a range of thinkers and writers along with his own experiences in the forest to speak of the ways that trees are connected intimately with flowing water, landscape, naming, fire, language, and other living creatures. In the process, he points to the power of storytelling and ethnography to evoke ecological and more-than-human ties. Mara Miller alternatively delves deeply into and extols the virtues of "wise trees" in eastern cultures, especially in Japan and China. She considers their expressions, representations, and meanings as they appear in ancient art, philosophy, and literature and thereby helps to define and defend the moral wisdom and beauty of the arboreal world.

Legal and political matters come to the fore in the next two chapters. Sam Mickey raises questions about the "peculiarly instructive aversion" of selected philosophers toward trees. He looks critically at the views of Socrates, Sartre, and Deleuze/Guattari. Mickey concludes with an edifying comparison of the "useless tree" of the Chinese Daoist philosopher, Zhuangzi. In the next contribution, Eric Orts takes up the question of whether trees might reasonably possess or be granted legal rights. He discusses Christopher Stone's landmark article, "Should Trees Have Standing?"

and argues that the legal category of "persons" is flexible enough to include individual trees as well as other organisms. Finally, Don Hanlon Johnson contributes an afterword to the volume as he meditates on the magisterial California redwoods and sequoias, the tallest trees that have ever lived, and what he has learned about them during time spent in Japan.

Family Trees

There is clearly an evolutionary and corporeal kinship between humans and trees. As upright beings, we evolved in similar landscapes with our crowns in the air and our limbs rooted on the soiled land—"human" derives from "humus," meaning of the earth. Our families and kin both extend deeply into a shared past and reach broadly across the planet's surface. Our histories and genealogies are indelibly intertwined in many intriguing ways through origin stories such as the biblical "Genesis" to forest fairy tales and from Ovid's imaginative *Metamorphoses* to the real-life wanderings of Johnny Appleseed.

In 1748, French philosopher, physician, and enlightenment materialist Julien Offray de La Mettrie, author most famously of *L'homme machine* (*Machine Man*), published *L'Homme-plante* (*Man as Plant*), a short work in which he compared the workings of the human body with the organization of plants to show the uniformity of the vegetable and animal kingdoms. La Mettrie wrote:

> In our species, as in plants, there is a main root and capillary roots. One is formed by the reservoir of the lumbar region and the thoracic canal, and the other by the lacteal veins. Everywhere we see the same uses and the same functions. Food is carried by these roots throughout the whole of the organised body . . . the lungs are our leaves, which replace this organ in vegetals as in us the organ replaces the leaves we lack. If the plant's lungs have branches it is in order to multiply their extent so that as a result more air enters them; which means that vegetals, and trees in particular, breathe more comfortably.[55]

More recently, archetypal theorist and analyst Carl Jung has called attention to the symbolic and psychological associations between trees and humans, pointing out that like trees—which he viewed as the embodiments of meaning in life—we are rooted in depth and darkness and that some of us need shadows as well as light to mature. In 1954, Jung wrote a lengthy study of the tree archetype entitled "The Philosophical Tree." There, he pointed out that "If a mandala may be described as a symbol of the self seen in cross-section, then the tree would represent a profile view of it: the self depicted as a process of growth."[56] "Why not go into the forest for a time, literally?," he once wrote to a colleague. "Sometimes a tree tells you more than can be read in books."[57]

Both editors of this volume have developed close relationships with trees that commenced early in their lives. In fact, it's probably fair to say that parts of our respective identities or elected affinities are bound with forests and wooded lands. I (David) grew up along the Susquehanna River outside of Bloomsburg, a sleepy college town in rural northeastern Pennsylvania.[58] Some of my most vivid childhood recollections and formative experiences involve trees, forests, and wood. Cherry, apple, and pear trees punctuated my family's backyard and supplied us with fruit when the bugs or birds didn't get to it first, while willow and maple trees offered us strategic perches upon which to survey the neighborhood or erect arboreal forts, including a two-tiered structure with sliding board, "bat pole," and tent top roof. Our brick house contained a fireplace, a potbelly stove, and later a wood-burning stove. We also had a fireplace in an outdoor pavilion and constructed a fire pit close to the river. Keeping the vestal flame alive necessitated cutting down trees selected by the forest service for culling in spring, splitting wood in the summer months, and then stacking it and hauling it inside in autumn and winter.

Wood from trees was present in other less noticeable but significant ways, too. My grandfather worked regularly with this material. On birthdays and Christmas, he would gift my siblings and me wooden mallets, coasters, and paperweights that he had lathed or carved from rich brown oak, bird's-eye maple, and light-hued poplar. When I split logs and dried stumps for the fireplace, I enjoyed applying the repetitive rhythmic strokes of a sharp, wood-handled axe and sledgehammer to the timber or to a metal wedge lodged within it, as I learned to read and follow the lead of the grain. A smattering of carpentry skills I acquired from my father through helping to remodel a house, build a deck, and frame a dormer—as well as by making an occasional towel rack in shop class or a small vehicle for a pinewood derby—also taught me about the peculiar textures and nuances of the substance.

Trees and forests have been part of my life in many other ways: camping in the woods during years as a Boy Scout; raking leaves in the backyard each autumn as a child and jumping joyfully through the accumulated piles; walking sections of the tree-laden Appalachian Trail; playing Frisbee golf on a beautiful course set in the Redwoods of Humboldt County in northern California; long-distance training runs on the wooded trails of Scandinavia, Bali, and Greece; and spending time in the cloud forests of Costa Rica and Columbia as well as the rainforests in the Peruvian Amazon.

Additional experiences come to mind as I reflect on the subject: climbing sixty feet high into a towering pine to find a sequestered spot during an adolescent game of hide and seek; taking a family photo with my siblings, parents, nephews, and niece as we perched in a great banyan tree in St. Petersburg, Florida; driving a car through a giant Redwood along the coast of California and crawling into a burned-out trunk of one north of that location; parading through the woods outside Tübingen, Germany, with two friends while in graduate school as we each pretended to be one of three great colleagues—Hegel, Schelling, and Hölderlin—who lived in the city together; writing a forest fairy tale about how the trees rescued themselves from an environmental disaster;[59] and feeling melancholic during my youth when the family next door cut down a healthy tree in their backyard for reasons I could not fathom.

More recently, my neighbors and I planted a weeping snow cherry that bursts into snow-white petals each spring, marking the divide between our properties but also giving us a common living entity for which to care. I also now run regularly in the Woodlands Cemetery of West Philadelphia, an urban necropolis and arboreal oasis full of stony graves anchored by craggy trees growing above the gravestones and shooting their outstretched limbs into the sky like *Vrksasana*, the dynamic tree pose I practice in my yoga classes.

I have a fondness, too, for hardwood floors and once spent a week tearing up old tiles and tacky carpet in a New York apartment to reach the original flooring, which I then sanded down and stained. I work on an old wooden roll-top desk, and when I write I am usually surrounded by a "grove" of books. Each of these things—the grainy floor of the "forest" beneath, the broad supporting "limbs" of my desk, and the ascending "trunks" of bookcases around me—tends to mitigate a severed connection with trees and even to delight me at times with a very latent scent of wood or the imaginative experience of the woods. On top of this, I live in a residential section of Philadelphia that bespeaks, like many towns across the country, the ties with trees in its street names: Larchwood, Hazel, Cedar, Spruce, Chestnut, Locust, and Pine.

On my university campus, we have been exploring the possibility of establishing a fifty-acre arboretum with walking trails, benches, binoculars for bird watching, and activities designed to better connect place with pedagogy. Toward this end, I regularly lead students on walks in the woods or to nearby Tyler Arboretum, and I am always surprised to learn how unusual this kind of outing is for them. Some students admit to having never been to a forest, just as many of them have never visited a farm, gone camping, or floated in a body of water larger than a chlorinated pool. They may be experiencing something like what Richard Louv calls "nature deficit disorder" in his book *Last Child in the Woods*. This is unfortunate because forests offer a place of learning and mystery; they can provide an outdoor course in botany, ecology, and natural history; and they encourage encounters with philosophical wonder, the depths of time, and the intoxicating puzzle of beauty.

Similar to David, I (Laura) had impactful connections with trees and plants early in life. When I was a young child, a peach tree lived prominently outside one of my first homes in Georgia (lands of the Hitchiti and Muscogee people), teaching me how delicious and edible fruits grow slowly from spring to summer. A few years later, I spent mornings and afternoons in the car to and from an elementary school some distance away from home, and I fondly tried to memorize the particular pattern of pine trees that zipped by along the Tennessee highway (lands of the Cherokee, Yuchi, and Shawnee people). Middle grades back in Georgia (lands of the Muscogee people), though across the state, found me often walking home through the back doors of the school building, across the parking lot, and into the thin strip of woods that surrounded a trickling creek. I was able to use a fallen tree to traverse the water, testing my footing and balance, before crossing a road and hiking up to the back porch of my home.

During high school, I was also likely to steal away into the interstitial spaces between the built neighborhoods, buildings, and roads. Now in Northern Virginia (lands of the Patawomeck people), I encountered in my upper-middle-class neighborhood a small woodland between those homes already completed, new construction, and a major highway. This tiny utopia, likely something around two acres unsuitable for building, was home to many trees. The creek revealed wagon wheel marks, and a particular path through the woods led upwards to a clearing, perched above a major highway, that disclosed secret bushes of wild blackberries in the summer months, a sacred spot that I reluctantly shared with friends. By the time I left high school and that home, the neighbors had also developed a connection with the wood, and a walking path had been installed. Though my memories do not include specific trees, the trunks and boughs of the trees in this place held the boundaries of a location preserved due to its inefficiency for human homesites.

At the College of Charleston in South Carolina (lands of the Kusso and Sewee people), I was surrounded by large live oak trees. The majesty of these trees in the Cistern Yard and lining walkways was ever-present, and their roots were the reason for the "Charleston shuffle"—students and tourists tripping regularly over the raised bricks and cobblestones throughout the campus and downtown. The activism of a fellow graduate of the college has stayed with me since my time in Charleston. To protect the trees surrounding the magnificent Angel Oak on Johns Island from development, Samantha Siegel spent years beginning in 2008 petitioning, gathering support, and arguing for the importance of the ecological community around the centuries-old live oak. The planned 150-foot buffer was terribly inadequate to protect the tree. Siegel says of the Angel Oak, "When you're standing at the base of the tree, you see the world through the eyes of a child again . . . You understand how connected the world is."[60] Though I was not involved at the time, the campaign and Siegel's insistence on the arboreal community surrounding the Angel Oak continued to fascinate me.

The trees and plants of the San Francisco Bay Area greeted me as I moved toward further study. Graduate school allowed me to delve more deeply into my scholarly interests with trees, and I am grateful for the intellectual freedom and faculty support that I found at the California Institute of Integral Studies in the Philosophy, Cosmology, and Consciousness program as well as the Ecology, Spirituality, and Religion program. The cypress trees in both Pacifica and on the lawn at the Esalen Institute, the oak woodland punctuated by eucalyptus groves in the East Bay and southern Sonoma County, and the redwoods along the coastal fog corridor became regular forums for my connection to individual trees and roaming with my thoughts or with similarly intentioned friends. I became aware that my relationship to the land was predicated on colonially occupied territory and that any writing about my connections with trees required acknowledgment that San Francisco, Pacifica, and the East Bay are occupied Ohlone land, the Esalen Institute is occupied Esselen land, and Sonoma is occupied Coast Miwok and Southern Pomo land. This acknowledgment is especially important as I think and write about trees. As former U.S. Poet Laureate Joy Harjo shares in her poem, "Speaking Tree," "I have heard trees talking, long after the sun has gone down: / *Imagine what would it be like to dance close together / In this land of water and knowledge . . . / To drink deep what is undrinkable.*"[61]

Trees, and my relationships with specific trees, grew as my scholarly work came into focus and my research deepened. The trees themselves are not philosophical study subjects but are collaborators in writing of arboreality. A particular coast redwood tree in the Berkeley hills allowed for reflection both of their bifurcated trunk and deep into their roots that plunged into a creek. A specific Monterey pine overlooking a popular visitor's spot anchored my regular hikes and runs. These trees and many others became my companions as I thought deeply about tree and human relationships both personally and globally. My routines included visits to the county parks in all seasons and weather when I had time to linger and when I needed to move quickly along the path through the trees. These two trees exist in a regional park in a wealthy Bay Area city, and I was privileged to have such easy access to see them regularly, including walking several miles uphill to the park during the height of the pandemic shutdown when driving was discouraged. Each visit inspires reflection on how the being of the living tree both remains the same and appears differentiated in my perception depending on my approach, my location nearby, and my own observations. This ongoing attention is the basis for relating to a more-than-human being such as a tree, just as attention is the foundation of any relationship.

Planting the Future

In the opening line of a poem entitled "Place," the influential American poet W. S. Merwin once confessed, "On the last day of the world I would want to plant a tree."[62] In a similar vein, there is a Chinese proverb to the effect that twenty years ago is the best time to plant a tree, while the second-best time to do so is now. What both remarks fittingly underscore are the arboreal ties that exist across historical eras and the importance of trees in securing a sustainable future for the earth. If one plants an elm, oak, or redwood seedling, for example, in the present moment, most of the benefits to human individuals or the ecological community will not likely accrue in one's lifetime; nevertheless, it is still vital to undertake this sowing.

Somewhat paradoxically, it may be the case that we need to appreciate the past to fully value and plan for the future. Doing so helps us to better grasp and respect continuity across large spans of time. Our gratitude for what others, including non-humans, have contributed or sacrificed in bygone ages might encourage our generosity toward those who have not yet arrived or been born. At the same time, there is a countervailing idea and imaginative adage that "We do not inherit the earth from our ancestors, we borrow it from our children."[63] In other words, we need to think and act as stewards of the forests, mountains, estuaries, seas, and rivers for future generations who will either enjoy the fruits of our well-intentioned work or bear the burdens of our neglect and poor decisions. As novelist Richard Powers puts it succinctly, "What you make from a tree should be at least as miraculous as what you cut down."[64]

Despite the many challenges, there is much we can still do at both the personal and public policy levels to preserve trees and protect forests. Restoration, resistance, and reclamation are broad watchwords to keep in mind. Saving old-growth and mature forests, native trees, and ancient groves should be primary goals. Early childhood environmental education and the direct exposure of youth to the woods will encourage emotional and cognitive connections with trees and build upon a more innate sense of biophilia. Establishing additional arboreta and supporting sustainable eco-tourism may help, too. Urban trees and forests also require attention since much of the world's population now live in cities.

In terms of environmental policy, debt relief or debt trade for economically struggling nations with large forests containing high densities of biodiversity should be considered by wealthy countries in North America and Europe. Land and forest policy must be focused on more than just timber and resource management to include protection and expansion of wilderness areas, roadless regions, and national or state parks. The construction and maintenance of the Svalbard Global Seed Vault in Norway, which stores more than a million seed samples, including many forest tree species from cultures around the world, serves as a long-term "doomsday" backup gene bank and is a great example of planning ahead that might stimulate similar ambitious undertakings.

We need to draw as well upon sources of artistic imagination and inspiration. From the photographs of trees by Ansel Adams and the ephemeral earthworks composed of leaves and wood by Andy Goldsworthy to the tree sculptures by Olga Ziemska and the arboreal-themed poems of Robert Frost and Seamus Heaney, beautiful, interesting, and original depictions of the wooded realm help us to appreciate forests and see trees in fresh ways. Thoreau once remarked, "Though I do not believe a plant will spring up where no seed has been, I have great faith in a seed. Convince me that you have a seed there, and I am prepared to expect wonders."[65] It is up to us to plant, nurture, and cultivate a vast variety of seeds—both literal and figurative—so that the earth and its great chorus of inhabitants might conceivably enjoy the many marvels that will emerge from them in the future.

Notes

1. Suzanne W. Simard, David A. Perry, Randy Molina, Melanie D. Jones, Daniel M. Durall, and David D. Myrold, "Net Transfer of Carbon between Ectomycorrhizal Tree Species in the Field," *Nature* 388, no. 6642 (Aug. 7, 1997): 579–82.

2. Richard Powers, *The Overstory* (New York: W. W. Norton and Company, 2018), 453.

3. Nietzsche writes, "There is more wisdom in your body than in your deepest philosophy" in *Thus Spoke Zarathustra*; Henry Miller titles one of his books, *The Wisdom of the Heart*; balasana (child's pose) in yoga is also known as "wisdom pose;" and ethnographer-linguist Keith Basso argues that "wisdom sits in places" in his work of this name.

4. Ralph Waldo Emerson, "Woods, A Prose Sonnet," in Harry Thomas, ed., *Poems about Trees* (New York: Alfred A. Knopf, 2019), 30.

5. Marcel Proust, *Pleasures and Regrets* (London: Peter Owen Publishers, 2002), 165.

6. Hermann Hesse, *Wandering: Notes and Sketches*, trans. James Wright (J. Cape, 1972), quoted in "The Marginalian" blog: www.themarginalian.org/2012/09/21/hermann-hesse-trees

7. Friedrich Nietzsche, *The Will to Power*, trans. Walter Kaufman and R. J. Hollingdale (New York: Vintage Books, 1968), section 660, 349.

8. William Blake, "Proverbs of Hell" in *The Marriage of Heaven and Hell* (Victoria, BC, Canada: Mint Editions, 2020), 12.

9. Suzanne Simard, *Finding the Mother Tree: Discovering the Wisdom of the Forest* (New York: Knopf, 2021).

10. Jared Farmer, *Elderflora: A Modern History of Ancient Trees* (New York: Basic Books, 2022).

11. Michael Marder, *Plant-Thinking: A Philosophy of Vegetal Life* (New York: Columbia University Press, 2013).

12. Peter A. Thomas, *Trees: Their Natural History*, 2nd ed. (Cambridge: Cambridge University Press, 2014), 62.

13. Eric Rutkow, *American Canopy: Trees, Forests, and the Making of a Nation* (New York: Scribner, 2012), 2–3.

14. "Rocky Mountain Tree-ring Research," Oldlist. www.rmtrr.org/oldlist.htm. Accessed May 1, 2018.

15. Jeffrey B. Mitton and Michael C. Grant, "Genetic Variation and the Natural History of Quaking Aspen," *Bioscience*, 46, no. 1 (Jan. 1996): 27.

16. Thomas, *Trees*, 303.

17. A poem about the ginkgo by Goethe is illustrative, wherein he inquires of the tree's leaf, "Is it but one being single / Which as same itself divides? / Are there two which choose to mingle / So that each as one now hides?" Goethe's creative answer is, "I have found a sense that's true: / Is it not my songs' suggestion / That I'm one and also two?" Johann W. Goethe, "Ginkgo Biloba," trans. J. Whaley. For a copy of the original poem, see Siegfried Unseld, *Goethe and the Ginkgo* (Chicago: University of Chicago Press, 2003).

18. For example, one famous study showed that viewing green space, particularly trees, from a window after surgery may improve recovery times. See Ulrich, "View through a Window May Influence Recovery from Surgery," *Science* (April 27, 1984), 420–421.

19. Bill M. Jesdale, Rachel Morello-Frosch, and Lara Cushing, "The Racial/Ethnic Distribution of Heat Risk-Related Land Cover in Relation to Residential Segregation," *Environmental Health Perspectives* 121, no. 7 (Jul. 1, 2013): 811–17.

20. Andrew Hirons and Peter A. Thomas, *Applied Tree Biology* (Hokoken, NJ: Wiley-Blackwell, 2018), 15.

21. Thomas, *Trees*, 1–4.

22. Thomas, *Trees*, 13.

23. Thomas, *Trees*, 19.

24. T. W. Crowther et al., "Mapping Tree Density at a Global Scale," *Nature* 525 (Sept. 2015): 201–5.

25. Daniel Chamovitz, *What a Plant Knows: A Field Guide to the Senses* (New York: Farrar, Straus, and Giroux, 2012).

26. Peter Wohlleben, *The Hidden Life of Trees: What They Feel, How They Communicate—Discoveries from a Secret World* (Vancouver, Canada: Greystone Books, 2016), 244.

27. Thomas, *Trees*, 207–8.

28. Theophrastus, *Enquiry into Plants and Minor Works on Odours and Weather Signs*, trans. Arthur Hort (New York: G. P. Putnam's Sons, 1916).

29. Matthew Hall, *Plants as Persons: A Philosophical Botany* (Albany, NY: SUNY Press, 2011), 17–35.

30. See, for example, Richard Grusin, ed., *The Nonhuman Turn* (Minneapolis: University of Minnesota Press, 2015).

31. James H. Wandersee and Elisabeth E. Schussler, "Preventing Plant Blindness," *The American Biology Teacher* 61, no. 2 (Feb. 1, 1999): 82.

32. Wandersee and Schussler, "Preventing Plant Blindness," 84, 86.

33. Hall, *Plants as Persons*, 6.

34. Michael Marder, *The Philosopher's Plant: An Intellectual Herbarium* (New York: Columbia University Press, 2014), xiv.

35. Annie E. Wertz and Karen Wynn, "Thyme to Touch: Infants Possess Strategies that Protect them from Dangers Posed by Plants," *Cognition* 130, no. 1 (Jan., 2014): 44–49.

36. Michael Marder and Patrícia Vieira, "Writing Phytophilia: Philosophers and Poets as Lovers of Plants," *Frame: Journal of Literary Studies* 26, no. 2 (2013): 39–55.

37. Bron Taylor, "Aborphilia and Sacred Rebellion," *Journal for the Study of Religion, Nature, and Culture* 7, no. 3 (2013): 239–42.

38. Bertolt Brecht, "To Those Born Later"(*An die Nachgeborenen*), *The Collected Poems of Bertolt Brecht*, trans. and eds., Tom Kuhn and David (New York: W. W. Norton, 2019), 734–36.

39. A similar criticism was leveled at the photographer Ansel Adams during the dust bowl era and the breadlines in which people waited. Some critics thought he was ignoring human poverty and hunger because he was focusing on mountains, rocks, and trees. Adams's response was that he was exploring the nature and beauty of deeper time.

40. Adrienne Rich, "What Kind of Times are These" in *Collected Poems: 1950-2012* (W. W. Norton, 2018), 291.

41. Val Plumwood, *Feminism and the Mastery of Nature* (New York: Routledge, 1997), 48–57.

42. Gordon B. Bonan, "Forests and Climate Change: Forcings, Feedbacks, and the Climate Benefits of Forests," *Science* 320, no. 5882 (June 13, 2008): 1444–49; and Josep G. Canadell and Michael R. Raupach, "Managing Forests for Climate Change Mitigation," *Science* 320, no. 5882 (June 13, 2008): 1456–57.

43. Donna Haraway, *Staying with the Trouble: Making Kin the Chthulucene* (Durham, NC: Duke University Press, 2016), 44–47.

44. Marder, *The Philosopher's Plant*, 98.

45. Michael Williams, *Deforesting the Earth: From Prehistory to Global Crisis* (Chicago: University of Chicago Press, 2003), 421.

46. Williams, *Deforesting the Earth*, 425–26.

47. Food and Agricultural Organization of the United Nations, *Global Forest Resources Assessment: Main Report 2020 (Rome 2020)*, xi.

48. Food and Agricultural Organization of the United Nations, *FRA 2020: Terms and Definitions* (Rome 2020), 7.

49. Crowther et al., "Mapping Tree Density at a Global Scale," 1.

50. FAO, *Global Forest Resources Assessment 2020*, xii.

51. Williams, *Deforesting the Earth*, 459.

52. Robin Wall Kimmerer, *Braiding Sweetgrass: Indigenous Wisdom, Scientific Knowledge, and the Teachings of Plants* (Canada: Milkweed Editions, 2013), 18.

53. See "Further Reading" at the back of this volume for suggestions about other voices on trees.

54. Howard Nemerov, "Learning the Trees," in Harry Thomas, ed., *Poems about Trees* (New York: Alfred A. Knopf, 2019), 223.

55. Julien Offray de La Mettrie, *Man as Plant* in *Machine Man and Other Writings*, translated and edited by Ann Thomson (Cambridge, UK: Cambridge University Press, 1996), 78.

56. C. G. Jung, *Alchemical Studies*, edited and translated by Gerhard Adler and R. F. C. Hull in *The Collected Words of C.G. Jung*, Vol. 13 (Princeton, NJ: Princeton University Press, 1967), 251ff.

57. Carl Jung, *Carl Jung, Letters*, Vol. 1, quoted in Meredith Sabini, ed., *The Earth has a Soul: The Nature Writings of C.G. Jung* (Berkeley, CA: North Atlantic Books, 2002), 6. On trees as "direct embodiments of the incomprehensible meaning of life," 29.

58. These personal reflections draw upon and extend an earlier description I composed in David Macauley, *Elemental Philosophy: Earth, Air, Fire, and Water as Environmental Ideas* (Albany, NY: SUNY Press, 2010).

59. David Macauley, "Fabulism: A Sort of Forest Fantasy" in Macauley, *Flights of Philosophical Fancy* blog. https://davidmacauley2003.wordpress.com/2020/01/04/fabulism-a-sort-of-fantasy

60. Stratton Lawrence, "Samantha Siegel's Relentless Resolve to Protect the Angel Oak." *Charleston City Paper*, February 3, 2010. https://charlestoncitypaper.com/2010/02/03/samantha-siegels-relentless-resolve-to-protect-the-angel-oak

61. Joy Harjo, "Speaking Tree," in *Conflict Resolution for Holy Beings: Poems* (New York: W. W. Norton & Company, 2017): 118–19.

62. W. S. Merwin, "Place" in Thomas, *Poems about Trees*, 104.

63. This quote is often attributed to Native Americans, though the origin is obscure. Similar quotes have been variously attributed to Oscar Wilde, Wendell Berry, and David Brower.

64. Powers, *The Overstory*, 464.

65. Henry David Thoreau, *Faith in a Seed*, ed., Bradley P. Dean (Washington, DC, 1993), xvii.

Trees as Beings

Figure I.1. Armstrong Redwoods State National Reserve, Guerneville, California.
Source: Courtesy of Laura Pustarfi.

Interstice

Redwood

Walking, I can almost hear the redwoods beating. And the oceans are above me here, rolling clouds, heavy and dark. It is winter and there is smoke from the fires. It is a world of elemental attention, of all things working together, listening to what speaks in the blood. Whichever road I follow, I walk in the land of many gods, and they love and eat one another. Suddenly all my ancestors are behind me. Be still, they say. Watch and listen. You are the result of the love of thousands.

—Linda Hogan, *Dwellings*

The redwoods, once seen, leave a mark or create a vision that stays with you always . . . They are not like any trees we know, they are ambassadors from another time.

—John Steinbeck, *Travels with Charley*

Trees are the tallest organisms known on the planet, with coast redwood trees (*Sequoia sempervirens*) as the superlative tree species. Hyperion, a tree located in a secret grove in Redwood National Park, California, measures at almost 380 feet, with four other local redwoods rising 370 feet or more. Some redwoods grow new stems from the trunk of an older tree, leaving a ring of trees where the initial tree once stood, with one exemplary ring comprising forty-five trunks and measuring seventeen by fifteen meters in circumference. Because these tall trees can continue to reproduce from small shoots of a dying or dead tree, they might live for millennia through their genetically identical offspring.

Redwoods are an endangered species due to threats from development, logging, and drought caused by climate change, registering only 5 percent old growth compared to extant forests. The redwood is found only on the western coast of the United States, though a related tree, the dawn redwood (*Metasequoia glyptostroboides*) is native to China. Dawn redwoods have softer, brighter green leaves, a more ruddy rose-colored bark, and grow only a fraction of the height of their more famous kin.

Redwoods are considered charismatic megaflora, or trees that evoke strong feelings in humans, and they have inspired activists to work toward preservation of them. In California, Julia Butterfly Hill found herself 180 feet high in a redwood named Luna, living there for more than two years in the late 1990s in an effort to conserve the area from logging. A small expanse around Luna was eventually saved, though the tree itself was later vandalized but survived. In *The Overstory*, a fictionalized group of activists work similarly to protect redwood trees with two characters, Nick and Oliva, sitting in one named Mimas for several months. While the fictional tree was cut down, the novel has galvanized new interest in trees and forests.

The trees in the photo at the opening of this Interstice are in Armstrong Redwoods State National Reserve near Guerneville, California. This grove has recently been inducted into the Old-Growth Forest Network, a system of exceptional forests across the United States. Old-growth redwood forests are quiet, almost silent places, with the soft duff underfoot dampening most sound. The trees tower impossibly above, fading into the distant sky in a puff of small, waxy leaves. Few such leaves, however, are visible from the forest floor, and those that can be seen have dark green spikes, occasionally with brilliant, bright new growth at the tips or diminutive cones in anticipation of the next generation. Some of these redwoods are living, hollow towers, their heartwood ravaged by fire, rotted away, or otherwise destroyed while leaving the living cambium layer under the growing bark. When such giants tip to the forest floor in a death bow, the fall can expose the shallow maze of roots that interlocks with other nearby trees. One particular tree in the park possesses a mass of entwined roots soaring above human visitors. Outside of the forest, even small stands of redwoods are impressively tall as the air turns damp and the temperature drops under their branches.

What it means "to be" is one of the most perennial, vexing, and significant philosophical questions. Through their immense height, age, and size, redwood trees make a claim upon us to recognize their status as magnificent and majestic living entities who deserve respect and protection. They even seem to possess an individuality and distinct character—a kind of "person-ality" as long-lived witnesses to the landscape. Redwoods also raise issues related to our understandings of time, personhood, place, beauty, and non-human legal rights, topics explored elsewhere in this volume.

The following section addresses the ontology of trees and inquires into arboreal being. Laura Pustarfi makes the case for considering trees as ontologically valuable beings with intelligence, relationality, and agency. Kim Carfore, in turn, develops a materialist ecofeminist ontology in collaboration with a tree she calls Grandmother Redwood.

—Laura Pustarfi

1

Arboreality

Trees as Ontologically Valuable Beings

LAURA PUSTARFI

> If I am to recognize this tree as a tree, then beneath this acquired signification, the momentary arrangement of the sensible spectacle must begin afresh—as if at the origin of the vegetal world—to sketch out the individual idea of this tree.
>
> —Maurice Merleau-Ponty

The table I sit at, made of rough boards, is a forest picnic table. The colors of the wood grains gleam in the afternoon light like the flight feathers of a hawk. I run my hand along them, catching my fingers on each ring, every year of life taking a millisecond's pause before allowing for exploration of the next one. Though this table is no longer part of a living tree, the glints and glamor on the surface remind me that this is a *body* comparable to my own. This body is dismembered, parted, like a skeleton scaffold. Moving from vertical tree to a horizontal table takes a being in a milieu and hews them into a part of the human order, worldmaking from body to body. The violence enacted upon trees—such as the one that became this table—occurs not in the making of a table, not even in the taking of the tree from the forest, but in the cutting and taking *alone*, as if there were no *one* to take from. This one—this being—is felt and is present by its life. A tree is a living being, understandable over the course of years, not minutes, hours, or even days. How can our quick-witted human consciousness comprehend the seemingly vast time scale and relative stillness of these beings, which build an inner fortress one sheath of cells at a time?

Maurice Merleau-Ponty reminds us that, "it is precisely my body that perceives the other's body and finds there something of a miraculous extension of its own intentions, a familiar manner of handling the world." He goes on to say, "this only establishes another living being, and not yet another man [sic]," a feat which requires for him, as for others, language and dialogue.[1] This familiarity of a body touching and connecting with other bodies occurs not only between humans but between living beings more broadly. The possibility of embodied recognition of life, which we humans have the luxury of articulating, is what gives ground to our understanding of ontological reality and force to our ethical intuitions. Once a tree is felled, its body becomes highly useful to us. This table as a wooden body continues to exist in relationship to my own physical body, and its position and form change my movements through place and space, creating different experiences depending on the ways human hands or machines have shaped that body.[2] The body of the tree, in the form of this table where I sit, establishes the possibilities for my felt experience and is designed such that my comfort allows for the withdrawal of my own material body, which then gives way to intellectual activity. The table continues to participate in what Merleau-Ponty terms the flesh of the world, *la chair du monde*—this tree as table is an essential partner in my writing process. Although formed and shaped, the wood evokes the living body it once was, and this informs my own experience, including the composition of this essay.

Our current ecological situation compels us to ask why we humans in the Western world have such a destructive relationship with trees. I choose to focus on the Western philosophical and cultural tradition in part because it is my own intellectual and personal lineage. Beginning with Plato and Aristotle, trees and plants have been construed as ontologically inferior to both animals and humans.[3] This view of trees has indirectly encouraged and allowed Western consumers in particular to rely upon disposable wood and tree products, as well as other items that depend on forest clearing, and pressured industry and governments to respond to this demand with increasing worldwide deforestation. This instrumental relationship is founded on the ontological superiority of humans, which values trees and plants as mere resources for human use. However, these assumptions mask the intelligence, agency, and relationality present in trees and forests, and it is these qualities that characterize their ontological and ethical significance.

The term *arboreality* is a deliberate reference to the Latin word for tree, *arbor*, and the notion of reality—that is, what exists in the world. This concept addresses the issues raised by a philosophy of trees, including unique ontological questions about our descriptions of reality within the Western paradigm. While trees and plants do not have individuality in the way humans and animals do, trees are boundaried individual entities with their cambium, or living cells, between the bark and wood. Arboreality is not an uncommon term in the botanical and biological sciences, and it is typically used to describe a species' interaction with trees in their habitat. Through a modified articulation of arboreality that integrates an interdisciplinary humanities perspective, I intend to open new possibilities for thinking about human relationships with our arboreal neighbors.

As philosopher Luce Irigaray suggests, "We must learn how to look at a tree, not to perceive its present form in order to re-present it mentally and fix it by naming it. Rather, we must gaze at its being as living and changing."[4] Using Merleau-Pontian phenomenology along with research in the field of plant signaling and behavior,[5] I will discuss arboreal intelligence, relationality, and agency and explore three additional issues relevant to arboreal ontology: language, personhood, and consciousness. Further, I will consider some ethical implications of such capacities as well as ways to move toward more respectful relationships between trees and humans. Arboreal intelligence, relationality, and agency point, in turn, toward viewing trees as ontologically valuable non-human beings.

Thinking of Trees

Ideas of being throughout the Western tradition have hinged to a great degree on Cartesian self-reflection and Kantian rationality or autonomy as the peaks of existential experience. When rationality, however, is the primary measure of value, then humans are usually the only beings considered worthy of ontological and ethical significance. This narrow framework in essence places humanity at the top of an ontological hierarchy, bestowing metaphysical and moral privileges upon us alone. Along with the possible inclusion of animals, this view encourages and attempts to legitimate an instrumental relationship with trees and plants wherein their being is construed as inferior to ours and such that they exist primarily for human use and enjoyment. If, however, trees possess an ontological value independent of—or even interdependent with—humanity, what might that mean for our relationships with them?

Trees inhabit a very different way of being in the world than we humans, and yet our supposed ontological superiority is premised on anthropocentric assumptions that they and other plants presumably lack. Ontological value is not at odds with the concept of intrinsic value, that entities have value in themselves rather than solely through relations or use potential. Philosophers including Holmes Rolston III, J. Baird Callicott, and Tom Regan have explored intrinsic value within environmental ethics, though there are challenges to the concept, including a lack of focus on relations, metaphysical complexity regarding value, and pragmatist considerations.[6] As Rolston states, "the deeper ethic is that a sequoia has age, size, persistence resisting fire, insects, disease, an integrity, a good of its own, intrinsic value."[7] Intrinsic value remains important to the conversation regarding non-human value and is analogous with my purpose in a limited way. However, I have chosen here to focus on ontological value because I am concerned with the being of trees and plants and our human relationships with them.

While present-day industrial activities might imply the opposite, there is no widespread scientific disagreement that rooted, growing trees are beings, or living entities. Although trees and plants are often compared to or contrasted with nonliving entities, each tree is autopoietic, or self-maintaining, growing and developing of their own accord into their mature form. Some philosophers have argued for plant minds based primarily on these autopoietic and adaptive capacities, claiming that life is sufficient for a version of mind that includes perception, memory, and agency.[8] A challenge posed for many thinkers, and stemming from Aristotelian roots, lies in a tree's lack of spatial movement and lack of human language, an absence of traits which has been used to justify denying trees an ontological value that would occasion a relationship based on respect rather than instrumentalism. Trees and plants are arguably concerned with being-ness and maintaining or defending their existence in a way that is wholly different than humans.[9] Living beings tend toward life, nutritive growth, and procreation, which is a vital expression of their existence. While there are many arboreal capacities that could occasion the need for such an ontological re-valuation, I will focus on three: intelligence, relationality, and agency in trees.

Arboreal Intelligence

Intelligence involves the capacity to assess the environment and choose from among alternatives and possibilities. Assessing the environment requires awareness, or a basic perception of one's surroundings, as well as memory of the past and the capacity to learn from prior experience. Because of its current use by plant scientists and plant studies scholars, I choose here to speak of intelligence rather than cognition, sentience, or a neologism.[10] In the human realm, intelligence has been formalized with the use of Intelligence Quotient, or I.Q. testing, and is apparent in the flurry of research and development around artificial intelligence and machine learning.

Some plant researchers, like botanist Anthony Trewavas, draw on experiments with learning, communication, and memory to argue for plant intelligence, which might be defined broadly as "adaptively variable behavior during the lifetime of the individual."[11] Learning requires both having a goal and a way to assess errors in the journey toward the goal. Plants seem to meet both these requirements as they grow or when they are deprived of a primary resource such as water. For example, *Arabidopsis thaliana*, a member of the mustard family, has root caps that grow toward humidity when water is scarce. Communication is necessary for the network of cells and modular parts of an individual plant to respond to external stimuli. Experiments have shown plants communicate between their various parts when faced with either removal of a given part or with resource scarcity by focusing their growth away from the inflicted damage. Plants also appear to exhibit memory, which refers to the ability to retrieve and use relevant information from past experience to respond to current situations. Memory has been displayed, for example, with light sensitivity when plants appear to remember or recall a pattern even after it is no longer present. Trees in a forest also position leaves to maximize limited light availability.[12] While memory is typically associated with the existence of a mind, the relevant evidence for plant intelligence calls for an updated understanding of our conceptions of this faculty. (See also the essay by John Charles Ryan on arboreal memory and trauma in Aboriginal Australia in this volume.[13])

Trees and plants seem to be intelligent in the ways they attend to their environment and react in complex and adaptive manners. Some of these behaviors are perceptible to human observers, like the patterns of branches reaching for sunlit openings and the brilliant colors of flowers and fruit calling to animal symbionts. These are finely honed ways trees interact with their surroundings. To reference another example, ecologists have found that mountain birch trees which suffered attacks by moths possess an immunological memory similar to that of animals.[14] Other studies offer additional evidence of plant intelligence such as those headed by biologist and interdisciplinary scholar Monica Gagliano showing *Mimosa pudica*'s memory and learning. Gagliano, who insists on the term "plant cognition," is best known for her work on this plant (also known as shy plant, sensitive plant, and touch-me-not), a common, flowering species named for its propensity to fold its leaves when disturbed. Gagliano and her co-researchers experimented on *Mimosa pudica* by dropping the plant several feet numerous times until it no longer closed its leaves in reaction to the fall. The same plant continued to remember the drop and did not react when dropped after periods of one day, six days, and twenty-eight days following the initial training. This behavior, habituation, is a simple form of memory, and Gagliano's experiment demonstrates that plants possess both the ability to learn and a type of memory. The authors suggest calcium signaling in the cell network operates as the way in which these capacities function in plants.[15] While not focused on trees directly, Gagliano's studies with *Mimosa pudica* have advanced thinking about plant intelligence and therefore may also apply to arboreal intelligence.

Of course, humans will always measure more highly than trees and plants in intelligence on anthropocentric scales. If some trees in fact possess intelligence, that calls into question conceptions of our own supposedly unique faculties. What does intelligence mean if it is disconnected from rational mentation? Recognizing plant intelligence requires us to consider other ways of knowing that exist outside traditional philosophic and scientific understandings. Without delving into the complex field of epistemology, it can be said that knowledge systematizes intelligence developed and acquired over time. Though we possess measures and formulas for engaging the sphere of *knowledge*, we often overlook the value and significance of *wisdom* in the West, as detailed in the introduction to this volume. As our understanding of plant intelligence develops and deepens, it alters not just our view of trees. Trees arguably possess their own forms of intelligence, and perhaps even wisdom, that matter within the sylvan realm and are independent of Western intellectual standards. That we continue to see these beings, along with the intelligence exhibited by other non-humans, as unworthy of the term further underscores our deep anthropocentrism and sense of exceptionalism.

Arboreal Relationality

Of the three arboreal capacities presently being explored, relationality is the easiest to perceive with human senses or faculties. Relationality describes connections to other beings, whether symbiotic or not. In our perceptions, we can experience the external relationship of a tree with the birds and mammals that call them home, the insects that view them as dinner, and their place within the greater forest or environment, whether urban, agricultural, or otherwise. Trees also exhibit familial-type relations as well. Forest ecologist Suzanne Simard's work shows how Hub or Mother trees provide nutrients to other trees based on their kinship. Simard has studied tree communication through fungal networks. The mycorrhizal, or collaborative, relationship between trees and fungi facilitates exchange of chemicals around a forest and helps ward off unwanted insect attacks.[16] She has promoted the idea of hub or Mother Trees that share water, carbon, nitrogen, and other nutrients with their kin trees, and she notes, "a single elder Douglas fir tree, for example, can be connected to hundreds of other trees, either of the same or different species, by the sheer magnitude of its massive root system and diverse fungal community."[17] Simard's maps and diagrams of forest networks reveal the profound and complex interconnections between trees in the forest and the importance of the fungal webs to this network. This research shows that trees are constantly transmitting both nutrients and information in deeply entwined relationships with both other trees and fungi in ways that were unimaginable to prior conceptions of a tree or forest.

Entomologist and ecologist Richard Karban and ecologist Kaori Shiojiri studied discernment in plants for a sense of "self" and "non-self" in sagebrush and found that plants make this distinction through chemical signals and use this information to respond cooperatively against attacks from plant eaters.[18] Karban uses terms like "kin" and "relatives" to refer to plant recognition, and he shows that sagebrush responds differently to more closely related plants, suggesting as well that some may even have personalities.[19] Drawing in part on this research, forest biologist Altaf Hussain and team studied lodgepole pine trees in Jasper National Park in Alberta Canada. They found that following a beetle attack, the pines emitted volatile organic compounds that warned related (rather than unrelated) trees, thus displaying both communication and kin recognition in these pines.[20]

Trees and plants also exist in close relationships with humans, not only economically but socially through forests and forest products as well as imaginatively through both metaphor and myth. Trees have created meeting places under their boughs, formed the walls of homes and ships, provided sustenance and raw materials for consumption and other uses, delineated parks, been fashioned into musical instruments, and appeared in religious and literary works. How does recognizing arboreal relationality impact our understanding of human relationality? We already think deeply about our formal and informal relationships to other humans. However, our connections to non-human beings and ecological systems in the West need to be reconsidered as we come into greater awareness of the ecological crisis and the destruction our current relationships are enabling. Since we are always in direct and indirect relationships with trees and other non-humans, the task and project ahead involve shifting both our consciousness and our actions toward relationships that value and respect non-human others as well as our societies and cultures.

Arboreal Agency

Agency, or intentional action, likely depends on intelligence (discussed above) as well as the capacity to act decisively rather than merely respond to one's environment. Arboreal agency is by far the most difficult quality to understand for human beings. Trees operate on such different time scales from us that we might need to spend decades or even a full lifetime in close association with them to perceive this capacity in action. Some scientific studies, however, show that plants are arguably making what might be considered choices in their behavior. Some researchers suggest trees are making decisions imperceptible to humans, such as when hub trees offer fungi and other trees nutrients and water through their roots or, in plants, when *Mimosa pudica* no longer closes their leaves after learning an action will not be harmful to them. The research on plant decision making points toward the possibility of a form of plant and tree autonomy.[21] Like humans, trees are constrained by the shape of their bodies and the places or situation in which they live, but they appear to choose how they use their resources in terms of growth, reproduction, cooperation, and defense. Though the findings exhibit agential action, critics and skeptics still often claim this is automated responsiveness rather than agency. In the end, more research is undoubtedly needed to support the argument for full vegetative agency.

Agency, however, may be akin to what philosopher Michael Marder calls in plants "non-conscious intentionality,"[22] an inversion of Levinas's concept of non-intentional consciousness, and this form of intentionality offers meaning even in the absence of consciousness. He calls this, "a kind of 'thinking before thinking,' an inventiveness independent from instinctual adaptation and from formal intelligence."[23] He uses the concept of intentionality to grant plants an ontological grounding while acknowledging their distinctions like rootedness and modularity and works from this to build his theory. He suggests addressing plants as they are, and intentionality becomes the forefront activity of his philosophy. Similarly, recognizing agency and decision-making capacity in plants and trees is critical to reconsidering vegetal or arboreal ontology. Marder denies that attributing plants autonomy or individuality is ontologically necessary, and instead claims the argument does more violence to plants by "forcing plants into the mold of appropriative subjectivity."[24]

The full force of the capacities of intelligence, relationality, and agency are not completely apparent to ordinary human perception. Even a careful observer of trees will land at the same basic ontological conclusions given by Aristotle. To a narrow view of rational consciousness, trees seem to be stationary, living entities that grow and change throughout the seasons and years, though in relationship to other plants, fungi, animals, and humans. This is due in part to our different time and size scales, where some trees live thousands of years and much of the action occurs underground or in the canopy. In this way, a phenomenological analysis of trees is insufficient and must be bolstered by other approaches and methods. This is where recent scientific findings are essential for reconsidering arboreal ontology.

Language, Personhood, and Consciousness

Language, personhood, and consciousness are three topics of concern to the conversation regarding arboreal ontology as well. Each of these subjects is highly dependent on how the concept in question is defined, developed, and understood, and the debate can be quite contentious. In general, although the use of these terms is often fraught with human associations, expanding their meanings to include plants highlights similarities rather than differences and gives articulation to the new behavioral research until better terminology is found.[25]

First, while humans use symbolic language, the current plant signaling and behavior research, some of which was discussed in the previous section, points toward the conclusion that we can no longer reasonably say plants do not communicate or share meaning in a way that resembles language.[26] The distinction between language and communication is widely debated, and the research on plants adds complexity to the dialogue. Gagliano, along with her colleague Mavra Grimonprez, propose that plants themselves may have language. They suggest that plants possess language that "is primarily (as currently understood) a silent language of shapes, colors, and scents."[27] Gagliano notes, "Breaking this silence calls for a truly 'cross-cultural' dialogue—a full immersion into the ecological context and beingness of humans, plants, as well as other non-human organisms with whom we share a common world."[28] Sylvan language, often mediated by chemicals or nutrients, is one arena that most humans seem not to have a means of understanding, although conversation is happening around us all the time when we are in a forest. Merleau-Ponty avers, following Paul Valéry, that "Language is everything, since it is the voice of no one, since it is the very voice of the things, the waves, and the forests."[29] Key to intelligent plant language is the claim that there is meaning inherent in the communication, as Luke Fischer elegantly explores in this volume.[30] Through this potential language, trees are exhibiting a sense of intellect through constant exchange that recent research is only beginning to understand.

Second, the idea of personhood frequently brings with it rights and responsibilities, thus why the American legal system, among others, has bestowed personhood onto corporations. Philosopher Matthew Hall argues for the personhood of plants and ethical action based on this view. Hall's conception of a specifically vegetal personhood stems from Indigenous and animistic views, including Aboriginal Australia, North American groups, Māori, and European paganism. Using the phrase "other-than-human persons" following Irving Hallowell and referring to animistic paradigms, he states, "personhood is a crucial, all-pervading concept—for as persons, plants are recognized as volitional, intelligent, relational, perceptive, and communicative beings."[31] As persons, trees and plants have awareness, relationships, and responsibilities in community with humans and other beings. Hall proposes that plants are autonomous subjects worthy of human ethical treatment and respect, which due to their personhood must be included in moral consideration. He advocates reducing unnecessary waste of plant lives and overconsumption, as well as restoration practices that directly impact plant flourishing.[32] Hall further proposes a relational concept of plant personhood as an "overarching category of being."³³ Critically, Hall does not claim that an ethical relationship toward plants disallows any use, instead advocating a respectful relationship with plant persons.

What would be the implications of vegetal and therefore arboreal personhood? This question highlights the tenuous edges of sylvan and human relationships, as we can only answer this question from the human situation, conferring what we deem proper for arboreal persons.³⁴ Considering its alterity, vegetal personhood must be differentiated from human and other personhood, since we cannot say that a tree has a basic right to life or bodily integrity because we must take some trees for our livelihoods and well-being. We could say that it is a human responsibility to arboreal persons that we will only take trees as needed and employ sustainable practices rather than engaging in clearcutting. Taking into account varying identity, where a single stem may be a clone of a much larger entity or a cutting of a tree may become its own entity, granting arboreal or forest personhood may necessitate the woodcutter to plant another tree when one is cut down. The language of personhood further illuminates our relationships to our arboreal neighbors, yet the concept and idea includes legal attachments and challenges. While this is only beginning to be addressed by the legal field, providing a precedent for tree personhood could be an initial step toward larger societal changes. Eric Orts takes up this issue later in this volume, suggesting efficiency when use is unavoidable and respect for the ecological value of forests is critical.³⁵

Third, I propose we cannot know if trees are conscious, have self-consciousness or awareness of being aware, or if they possess interior experience.³⁶ Based on their behavior, we can arguably consider them intelligent, agential entities, selecting among possibilities for their best livelihood, and we can reasonably argue that they have a world that they create which is largely inaccessible to humans as our world is likely inaccessible to them. They are clearly relational beings in their ecological connections both to other trees as well as plant and animal entities in both forest and urban environments. They also communicate between themselves and local fungi, although their language is yet untranslated.

However, some scientists have proposed that trees and plants may possess a form of consciousness. For example, a highly cited study reviewed plants' reaction to anesthetics, which researchers had previously thought required a central nervous system to elicit an effect. A research team led by bioscientist Ken Yokawa tested several plant species including *Mimosa pudica*, pea plants, and garden cress both by exposing them to anesthetic gases through their leaves and liquids through their roots. The *Mimosa pudica* lost its ability to close its leaves when disturbed, and the pea plant ceased growing in a rotational movement for several hours. The authors even suggest that garden cress plants, "represent an ideal in aims to illuminate the elusive mechanisms underlying both anesthetics and the phenomenon of consciousness" and propose they could be used to study and test human anesthesia.[37] Biologist František Baluška and botanist Stefano Mancuso support claims for plant consciousness, stating, "As the awareness of environment is, in essence, consciousness and sentience, it can be suggested that plant-specific consciousness is essential for sensory aspects of plant life as well as for adaptation and survival via plant-specific learning based on memories and predictions. This new view of plants, including the still speculative concept of the plant-specific consciousness, is supported by our recent study showing that diverse anesthetics prevent plant movements via blockage of action potentials."[38] Here, however, consciousness is used to mean awareness, rather than an awareness of being aware. Given current research, we cannot know for certain if trees and plants are self-aware. Because of our Western lineage of thought that values collectively held proofs, reason, and evidence, I hesitate to offer any claim for plant consciousness, though I leave open this possibility. This does not preclude animist or panpsychist views, which are beyond the scope of this work. This agnosticism on plant consciousness also circumvents, for now, questions around whether plants have minds, especially without a brain or nervous system, and what this might mean about states of interiority in plants.

Though considering trees as linguistic communicators, as persons, and as conscious beings is an important exercise toward revisioning arboreal ontology, there is more scientific and philosophical research to be performed to affirm or refute the possible faculties of language and consciousness, and more discussion is needed in legal and philosophical spheres regarding arboreal and vegetal personhood. However, the capacities that trees do exhibit and that are supported by current research are sufficient to reconsider arboreal value and reassess our relationships with trees.

Ontological Value

The existence of arboreal intelligence, relationality, and agency might serve as an alarm to or warning to us that our ontological categories are awry—too fixed and inflexible. The emergent understanding of trees and plants points toward engaging vegetal and arboreal ontology on its own terms. Arboreal intelligence shows that trees are aware, learn, and remember; arboreal relationality indicates that trees recognize themselves and their kin; and arboreal agency reveals that trees can choose among many possibilities. Recognizing this shift away from classical and modern ontology requires rethinking our actions toward trees and plants. These vegetal capacities support the argument for the ontological value of trees as living beings who—at the very least—deserve our respect in the form of acknowledgment and gratitude.

Recognizing trees as ontologically valuable beings calls into question our own concepts of human ontology. We must reconsider ourselves and our own nature or being, no longer claiming to be at the apogee of ontological expression. Our capacities are among the many ontologically valuable qualities in the world, rather than the only worthwhile ones. Who are we, then, if not the most superior beings? Instead of fearing ontological repositioning, this call for reorganization highlights how much is available for us to learn in relation to other beings. We are the only creatures who problematize being itself, as far as we know. And yet, the more receptive we are to the potentiality of other life forms, the less exceptional we seem and the closer we come to Thomas Berry's notion of a "communion of subjects."[39]

Our own being is interconnected and entangled with the non-human world, as our ecological crisis makes clear. Our embodied perceptions can confirm and deepen this insight. We evolve and develop within embodied situatedness, and the global changes we are rapidly catalyzing are changing more than the landscape. We are always in complex relationships with others around us, including plants. If we lose trees, will we also lose ourselves? Would we *be* different if there were no trees left standing? As we push the forest clearing to the ends of the earth, we may soon find out. Our relationships with non-humans, especially trees, remind us that we live in large-scale systems and communities beyond our full comprehension. Not solely due to our own needs, but rather also because trees are ontologically valuable beings, should we act more ethically and respectfully toward the forests—and their inhabitants—that populate the earth.

Arboreal Ethics

Revisioning an arboreal ontology and thus human ontology leads directly to questioning how humans should interact ethically with trees and plants.[40] Our lives depend on taking theirs; in Whitehead's words, "life is robbery," though "the robber requires justification."[41] Acknowledging arboreal value calls for an ethic that takes into account the needs of trees as well as our human interconnection with them while also justifying our need to depend on them for both our lives and livelihoods.[42] This however does not mean that eating, building, or heating our homes are unethical activities. My intent is not to propose a fully developed vegetal ethic, but to uncover some of the unique issues trees and plants pose to Western ethics and to point toward resources for more fully thinking through respectful relationships with them.

While some thinkers on animal ethics argue that humans should not eat, experiment on, or use animals in other harmful ways, plants are ethically problematic in a different manner. Even a fruitarian diet, eating only the fruits and nuts a plant would typically discard, does not address the use of tree products for building and fuel. While human life is contingent on taking arboreal life, there are ways trees and plants are used instrumentally that do not kill them and, in fact, are sometimes even beneficial to the species, such as when we eat fruits intended for long-distance seed distribution. Many of us intuitively feel that clear-cutting, which indiscriminately fells trees, is wrong, and maintain that sustainable forestry is a good that increases the thriving of the trees and the forest ecosystem. But this also is complex. In some cases, burning a forest regularly may avert a greater, more damaging fire later, killing many plants and animals in the process. In other cases, sustainable forestry removes trees and allows neighboring ones to thrive or suggests planting a monocrop tree farm that reduces ecological resilience. It is notable, too, that religious and philosophical perspectives that are staunchly nonviolent often encourage or require vegetarian diets. An ethical stance toward trees may not necessarily be based on a complete absence of harm toward them but instead on use that shows respect for their lives. Rather than broadly taking trees for human use, respectful taking may include harvesting from trees in ways that does not kill them and causes them the least harm, abstaining from using products from highly endangered trees, and reusing existing items rather than creating from newly taken trees.

We need not develop a wholly novel ethical approach. Here is where Western thought can respectfully find insights and advice in non-appropriative ways from other cultures with different relationships with plants and other non-humans. Some of these philosophies include Indigenous traditions, as well as religious and animistic systems, such as contemporary paganism. Robin Wall Kimmerer, biologist and enrolled member of the Citizen Potawatomi Nation in North America, speaks of ethics in relation to Indigenous North American Potawatomi black ash basket makers like master basket maker John Pigeon. Kimmerer recounts:

> Traditional harvesters recognize the individuality of each tree as a person, a nonhuman forest person. Trees are not taken, but requested. Respectfully, the cutter explains his purpose and the tree is asked permission for the harvest. Sometimes the answer is no. It might be a cue in the surroundings—a vireo nest in the branches, or the bark's adamant resistance to the questioning knife—that suggests a tree is not willing, or it might be the ineffable knowing that turns him away. If consent is granted, a prayer is made and tobacco is left as a reciprocating gift. The tree is felled with great care so as not to damage it or others in the fall. Sometimes a cutter will make a bed of spruce boughs to cushion the landing of the tree. When they finish, John and his son hoist the log to their shoulders and begin the long walk home.[43]

For Potawatomi basket makers, the one-to-one respectful relationship includes both consent and reciprocation as well as asking for what is needed to receive an answer. The act of killing itself is done with careful intention to respect the gift of life. Kimmerer also suggests a new pronoun, ki, or plural kin, for more-than-human others. Ki is derived from the Anishinaabe word *aki*, meaning land or Earth, and acknowledges relationship and respect.[44] In contemporary paganism, stemming from place-based traditions in Europe, trees and plants agentially offer gifts and may retaliate against careless or disrespectful humans by "swip[ing] the momentarily impolite or careless cutter on a calm and windless day."[45] This animist perspective encourages attention and consideration when interacting with or harvesting from trees and plants. While this brief overview discusses only two examples, these traditions and others offer models which could be ethically formative if approached respectfully.[46]

While there is much more work to be done to fully articulate an arboreal or vegetal ethic, we can be sure that our planetary rates of deforestation and the impacts of climate change are not in line with ethical action toward plants. The ontological value of trees and plants provides one more reason among many others to change actions that are accelerating the anthropogenic environmental crisis.

Conclusion

Life is given to us that we may recognize and respect other life. When we peer into the eyes of another human, we see the depths that might reveal a shared sense of being. Without eyes, trees reveal to us their being on the tips of their leaves as the spring growth shows new green, through the wooden rings of their many years, and through our own bodies when we imbibe their leaves, liquids, and roots. The possibility of embodied recognition of life on the earth, which we humans have the luxury of articulating, is what gives ground to our understanding of ontological reality and force to our ethical intuitions. Arboreality is a metaphysical position in which non-humans, like trees and other plants, as beings with a sense of intelligence, relationality, and agency, while very different from us, are no less ontologically valuable. In his later work, Merleau-Ponty calls the "thickness of the flesh" between bodies "their means of communication."[47] This connection between us and others, including trees, speaks to the need for that communication, which can appear as acknowledgment and gratitude, the beginnings of respect for the more-than-human world.

While a plastic desk would also support my hand as I write, my attention to the wooden table where I sit settles me, my eyes tracing the textures and shapes within the wood grains. We often value wood, especially solid wood furniture, over plastic, metal, and glass, as evidenced by the pricing. Of course, there are many ways to use a tree without death, either with harm or without harm, from taking the fruits, nuts, or downed branches to tapping into the living trunk for saps and resins. And yet, these actions still represent a use of the body of the tree. In such relational moments between humans and trees, there are industrial ways of doing that efficiently interact to get the most possible from the thing, and there are options that treat the tree as worthy of respect. This respect is presupposed by acknowledging the being and value of trees and their distinct capacities which we are just beginning to understand from a Western perspective. Recognizing trees as ontologically valuable within an emerging framework of arboreality might inspire new thinking not just about trees but also about our own species, our relationships with more-than-human beings, and the consequences of environmental degradation. Further, recognizing trees and plants as ontologically important requires re-evaluating our own significance on the earth at the supposed pinnacle of an ontological hierarchy and the very hierarchical frame itself.

Notes

1. Maurice Merleau-Ponty, *Phenomenology of Perception*, trans. by Donald A. Landes (New York: Routledge, 2012), 370.
2. For another phenomenological perspective on wood, see Galen A. Johnson, "Forest and Philosophy: Toward an Aesthetics of Wood," *Environmental Philosophy* 4, no. 1–2 (2007): 59–76.
3. For a detailed treatment of ancient Greek thought on plants, see Matthew Hall, "The Roots of Disregard: Exclusion and Inclusion in Classical Greek Philosophy," in *Plants as Persons: A Philosophical Botany* (Albany, NY: SUNY Press, 2011), 17–35.
4. Luce Irigaray and Michael Marder, *Through Vegetal Being: Two Philosophical Perspectives* (New York: Columbia University Press, 2016), 49.
5. See review articles including František Baluška and Stefano Mancuso, "Individuality, Self and Sociality of Vascular Plants," *Philosophical Transactions of the Royal Society B* 376, no. 1821 (Feb. 8, 2021): 20190760, doi:10.1098/rstb.2019.0760; Daniel A. Chamovitz, "Plants are Intelligent; Now what?" *Nature Plants* 4, no. 9 (2018): 622–23, doi:10.1038/s41477-018-0237-3; Monica Gagliano, Charles Abramson, and Martial Depczynski, "Plants Learn and Remember: Let's Get Used to It," *Oecologia* 186, no. 1 (2018): 29–31, doi:10.1007/s00442-017-4029-7; and Tony Trewavas, "Plant Intelligence: An Overview." *BioScience* 66, no. 7 (July 1, 2016): 542–51. doi:10.1093/biosci/biw048
6. See Katie McShane, "Why Environmental Ethics Shouldn't Give up on Intrinsic Value." *The Ethics of the Environment* (2017): 59–77. https://doi.org/10.4324/9781315239897-5
7. Holmes Rolston, III, *A New Environmental Ethics: The Next Millennium for Life on Earth* (New York: Routledge, 2012), 100–1.
8. Chauncey Maher, *Plant Minds: A Philosophical Defense* (New York: Routledge, 2017), 120.
9. Paco Calvo, "What Is It Like to Be a Plant?," *Journal of Consciousness Studies* 24, no. 9–10 (2017): 205–27.
10. Biologist Richard Firn and others argue against using the term intelligence for plants, claiming the argument for vegetal intelligence is based, problematically, in thinking about plants as individuals and instead suggest a neologism. Richard Firn, "Plant Intelligence: An Alternative Point of View," *Annals of Botany* 93 (2004): 345.
11. Anthony Trewavas, "The Foundations of Plant Intelligence," *Interface Focus* 7 (2017): 2. http://dx.doi.org/10.1098/rsfs.2016.0098.
12. Trewavas, "The Foundations of Plant Intelligence," 6–8.
13. John Charles Ryan, "'Old Trees Hold Memory': Aboriginal Australian Perspectives on Memory, Trauma, and Witnessing in the Arboreal World," in *The*

Wisdom of Trees: Thinking Through Arboreality, eds. David Macauley and Laura Pustarfi (Albany, NY: SUNY Press, 2025), Chapter 6.

14. Teija Ruuhola, Juha-Pekka Salminen, Sanna Haviola, Shiyong Yang, and Markus J. Rantala, "Immunological Memory of Mountain Birches: Effects of Phenolics on Performance of the Autumnal Moth Depend on Herbivory History of Trees," *Journal of Chemical Ecology* 33, no. 6 (2007): 1160–76. doi:10.1007/s10886-007-9308-z

15. Monica Gagliano, Michael Renton, Martial Depczynski, and Stefano Mancuso, "Experience Teaches Plants to Learn Faster and Forget Slower in Environments Where it Matters," *Oecologia* 175, no. 1 (May 1, 2014): 63–72. For a narrative description of this research, see Monica Gagliano, *Thus Spoke the Plant: A Remarkable Journey of Groundbreaking Scientific Discoveries and Personal Encounters with Plants* (Berkeley, CA: North Atlantic Books, 2018), 55–71.

16. See Suzanne W. Simard, David A. Perry, Randy Molina, Melanie D. Jones, Daniel M. Durall, and David D. Myrold, "Net Transfer of Carbon between Ectomycorrhizal Tree Species in the Field," *Nature* 388, no. 6642 (Aug. 7, 1997): 579–82, doi:10.1038/41557; and Monika A. Gorzelak, Amanda K. Asay, Brian J. Pickles, and Suzanne W. Simard, "Inter-Plant Communication through Mycorrhizal Networks Mediates Complex Adaptive Behaviour in Plant Communities," *AoB Plants* 7 (May 15, 2015): plv050. doi:10.1093/aobpla/plv050

17. Suzanne Simard, "The Mother Tree," in *The Word for World is Still Forest*, eds. Anna-Sophie Springer and Etienne Turpin (Berlin: K. Verlag, 2017), 66–67.

18. Richard Karban, Kaori Shiojiri, Satomi Ishizaki, William C. Wetzel, and Richard Y. Evans, "Kin Recognition Affects Plant Communication and Defence," *Proceedings of The Royal Society* (2013): 280.

19. Richard Karban, Patrick Grof-Tisza, and Charline Couchoux, "Consistent Individual Variation in Plant Communication: Do Plants have Personalities?" *Oecologia* 199, no. 1 (2022): 129–37. doi:10.1007/s00442-022-05173-0

20. Altaf Hussain, Jean C. Rodriguez-Ramos, and Nadir Erbilgin, "Spatial Characteristics of Volatile Communication in Lodgepole Pine Trees: Evidence of Kin Recognition and Intra-Species Support," *The Science of the Total Environment* 692 (Nov. 20, 2019): 127–35. doi:10.1016/j.scitotenv.2019.07.211

21. Hall, *Plants as Persons*, traces theories of plant autonomy to Theophrastus (30–35), Jainism (80–90), and some Indigenous philosophies (101–17).

22. Marder, *Plant-Thinking: A Philosophy of Vegetal Life* (New York: Columbia University Press, 2013), 154.

23. Marder, *Plant-Thinking*, 154. Marder draws on Bergson's notion of creative activity, identifying both life and consciousness with this concept, and he implies a dormant thinking or potentate thinking in his description of nonconscious intentionality.

24. Marder, *Plant-Thinking*, 55.

25. Even research scientists find usefulness in using anthropomorphic terms for plant capacities in private dialogue. See Natasha Myers, "Conversations on Plant Sensing: Notes from the Field," *NatureCulture* (2015): 35–66.

26. Richard Karban, *Plant Sensing and Communication* (Chicago: University of Chicago Press, 2015).

27. Monica Gagliano and Mavra Grimonprez, "Breaking the Silence—Language and the Making of Meaning in Plants," *Ecopsychology* 7, no. 3 (September, 2015): 147.

28. Gagliano and Grimonprez, "Breaking the Silence," 150.

29. Maurice Merleau-Ponty, *The Visible and the Invisible*, trans. Alphonso Lingis, ed. Claude Lefort (Evanston, IL: Northwestern University Press, 1968), 155.

30. Luke Fischer, "Speaking Trees: The Language of Nature and Arboreal Communication," in *The Wisdom of Trees: Thinking Through Arboreality*, eds. David Macauley and Laura Pustarfi (Albany, NY: SUNY Press, 2025), Chapter 3.

31. Hall, *Plants as Persons*, 100.

32. Hall, *Plants as Persons*, 163–69.

33. Matthew Hall, "In Defence of Plant Personhood," *Religions* 10, no. 5 (2019): 1–12. https://doi.org/10.3390/rel10050317

34. Legal scholar Christopher Stone famously published "Should Trees Have Standing?—Toward Legal Rights for Natural Objects" in 1972. In his article, Stone argues for legal rights for trees, other non-humans, and ecosystems on the basis that many groups of humans have not historically had legal rights but now do, and he suggests that if a non-human or ecosystem is harmed, a human friend could seek guardianship and redress in the court system. Christopher D. Stone, "Should Trees have Standing?: Toward Legal Rights for Natural Objects," *Southern California Law Review* 45 (1972): 450–501.

35. See Eric Orts in this volume as well as the Rights of Nature Movement. Eric Orts, "Trees as Legal Persons," in *The Wisdom of Trees: Thinking Through Arboreality*, eds. David Macauley and Laura Pustarfi (Albany, NY: SUNY Press, 2025), Chapter 15.

36. A critical text dealing with the issue of whether or not an outside observer can infer interior experience and consciousness in another being is Thomas Nagel, "What Is It Like to Be a Bat?" *The Philosophical Review* 83, no. 4 (Oct., 1974): 435–50.

37. K. Yokawa, T. Kagenishi, A. Pavlovic, S. Gall, M. Weiland, S. Mancuso, and F. Baluška, "Anesthetics Stop Diverse Plant Organ Movements, Affect Endocytic Vesicle Recycling and ROS Homeostasis, and Block Action Potentials in Venus Flytraps," *Annals of Botany* (Dec. 11, 2017), 8.

38. František Baluška and Stefano Mancuso, "Plant Cognition and Behavior: From Environmental Awareness to Synaptic Circuits Navigating Root Apices,"

in *Memory and Learning in Plants*, ed. František Baluška, Monica Gagliano and Guenther Witzany (New York: Springer, 2018), 54.

39. Thomas Berry, *Evening Thoughts: Reflecting on Earth as Sacred Community*, ed. Mary Evelyn Tucker (San Francisco: Sierra Club Books, 2006), 17.

40. Marder similarly makes a connection between ontological questions and ethical implications, particularly in regard to non-human beings including animals and plants. See Marder, *Plant-Thinking*, 2.

41. Alfred North Whitehead, *Process and Reality*, ed. David Ray Griffin and Donald W. Sherburne (New York: The Free Press, 1978), 105.

42. Precedents for ethical treatment of trees include James Russell Lowell, "Humanity to Trees," *The Crayon* 4, no. 3 (1857): 96; J. L. Arbor, "Animal Chauvinism, Plant-regarding Ethics and the Torture of Trees," *Australasian Journal of Philosophy* 64, no. 3 (1986): 335–39; and Stone, "Should Trees have Standing?," 450–501. Also see "The Dignity of Living Beings with Regard to Plants: Moral Consideration of Plants for their Own Sake" (Berne, Switzerland: Swiss Federal Ethics Committee on Non-Human Biotechnology ECNH, 2008).

43. Robin Wall Kimmerer, *Braiding Sweetgrass: Indigenous Wisdom, Scientific Knowledge, and the Teachings of Plants* (Canada: Milkweed Editions, 2013), 144.

44. Robin Wall Kimmerer, "The Covenant of Reciprocity," in *The Wiley Blackwell Companion to Religion and Ecology*, ed. John Hart (Hoboken, NJ: John Wiley & Sons Ltd., 2017), 376–77.

45. Graham Harvey, *Animism: Respecting the Living World*. 2nd ed. (London: Hurst & Company, 2017), 103.

46. See especially Eduardo Kohn, *How Forests Think: Towards an Anthropology Beyond the Human* (Berkeley: University of California Press, 2013) and David Haberman, *People Trees: Worship of Trees in Northern India* (New York: Oxford University Press, 2013) among many others.

47. Merleau-Ponty, *The Visible and the Invisible*, 135.

2

In the Beginning She Was a Redwood
Rethinking Ontology through an Ecofeminist Materialism

KIMBERLY CARFORE

The title of this chapter is a play off of French philosopher Luce Irigaray's piece, "In the Beginning, She Was." The idea for this chapter began as an epiphany sparked in the presence of "Grandmother Redwood"—a two-thousand-year-old, old-growth Redwood tree located in Jack London State Park in Glen Ellen, California. My first encounter with her occurred when I took my Environmental Studies class on a hike to witness one of the few remaining old-growth redwoods left. The goal of this chapter is to rethink ontology as relational utilizing an ecofeminist framework. In order to do so I bridge Irigaray with ecofeminist philosopher Val Plumwood to develop a materialist ecofeminist ontology.

With a focus on the material world, I offer an analysis of beginnings as unspoken relationality before *logos*. According to Irigaray, in the beginning was "nature, woman, or Goddess."[1] She demonstrates how "the forgetting of her" occurs as male-centered concepts of beginnings forget that the beginning of their world is the always-already material world of a woman. An ontological "backgrounding" of her creates the material conditions for thinking to occur. In other words, in order for thought to begin, for philosophy to start, a material and ontological "backgrounding" of her has already occurred.[2] Consider Nietzsche's phrase: "Supposing that Truth is a woman—what then? Is there not ground for suspecting

Figure 2. 1. Grandmother Redwood. *Source*: Courtesy of Kimberly Carfore.

that all philosophers, in so far as they have been dogmatists, have failed to understand women?"[3] To understand does not mean to colonize with conceptual frameworks. It is an understanding that avoids dogma preventing her expression.

Grounding my analysis in ecology, I compare feminist philosophical insights of relational ontology to the groundbreaking scientific work of Suzanne Simard in *Finding the Mother Tree*. Since language (specifically *logos* and logic) can oftentimes capture and suffocate feminine unspoken relational wisdom, I lean on French feminist Irigaray to maintain openness to the mystery. In this way concepts do not co-opt but rather leave open the space for Sophia (wisdom gendered feminine) to arrive. I offer my experience encountering "Grandmother Redwood" as a pillar throughout the chapter to ground my analysis of an ecofeminist relational ontology in the material world. As ontology has been ontotheology, I close with the poetry of Carol Lynn Pearson to demonstrate how the ideal and real are always tied to the material, specifically through the concept of God.

Encountering "Grandmother Tree"

In her presence, a stillness washes over me; a silence emerges within the cavern of my heart. This silence is not nothing. It is a definite *something*—a pressure from within. A force. Not a weight pressing on my chest from the outside. Rather, it is a force pressing outward from within. This resonance calls for me to notice, to pay attention. Her being demands respect, not in the way an authority figure would instill a top-down fear—I should respect this other because I fear the consequences. Rather, I experience an awe with a bit of trembling, and I wonder about her existence. This reverence is palpably experienced, yet she has not "said" a word. She demands for me to stand up straight, pay attention, and cultivate right-mind simply from being in her presence.

What is it about her that evokes one's attention and reverence? Perhaps it is her arms reaching for the sky, outstretched for some mysterious reason. They sag from age, or perhaps from the weight of gravity. Local experts say she was perhaps struck by lightning, causing irregularities in her growth, including her large "candelabra" branch.[4] She doesn't look like other trees. She is not straight and narrow but tall and broad. Her multiple large branches grow outward instead of upward.

While I can exhaust myself trying to find exactly which qualities are the ones that make her unique, this method assumes that only her uniqueness makes her worthy of reverence. However, the experience of reverence isn't the result of me witnessing her specific characteristics. It is not something I can point to, name, categorize, or comprehend. It is her *je ne sais quoi*—the unnamable quality of her experienced reverence in our face-to-face encounter. I can only describe this as a subject-to-subject experience that moves beyond words.

Irish philosopher Edmund Burke states, "There is something so overruling in whatever inspires us with awe . . . There lies the qualities of beauty, either dead and unoperative [sic], or, at most, exerted to mollify the rigor and sternness of the terror which is the natural concomitant of greatness."[5] If I am in awe, it is partly because she is great. And she is great partly because I am terrified of her, or of that which created her. Fear and awe are two sides of the same coin. For German philosopher Rudolph Otto, the experience of both fear and awe is an experience with the *mysterium tremendum et fascinans*—an encounter with the numinous. The *mysterium tremendum et fascinans* includes three elements: (1) "awefulness" which includes both awe and terror, fascination and fear; (2) "overpoweringness" or majesty, where the encounter with the Holy includes both being attracted to the majesty and repelled from it; and (3) encountering the numinous includes a sense of energy or urgency.[6] It calls for you to respond with responsibility. If I truly feel her and fear her, I fear existence without her.

Her mystery making me stand in awe and wonder is not some transcendent mystery. It bridges transcendence with immanence. I wonder, why is she the only old-growth redwood left standing? What happened to the others? Are there other old-growth redwoods in existence? If so, where are they? After doing a bit of research by asking local park rangers, educators, naturalists, and historians, I discovered that it was her peculiarity that allowed her to survive. Susan St. Marie, Director of Program and Volunteer Management at Jack London State Park, informed me, "The tree has logging notches indicating it was planned to be cut down. The tree was likely preserved because it has a large candelabra branch which would probably have made for undesirable lumber."[7] She was "a bit gnarly" and "too much hassle" to cut down.[8]

Her undesirability and uselessness were what saved her. Being undesirable and useless are not characteristics most modern women seek to adopt. We are socialized to be desirable in our beauty (nature) and useful through our caretaking behaviors (nurture). Hearing the phrases, "gnarly" and "too much hassle" reminds me of the first American female presidential candidate Hillary Clinton being called a "nasty woman" by her opponent Donald Trump in the 2016 election. Oftentimes going against stereotypical femininity, in other words, redefining for oneself who a woman is, or what her nature is, threatens others' comfortable categories of "femininity," and "woman." Perhaps this discomfort signals important nuance in the emergence of being.

In the spirit of being "too much hassle" and a "nasty woman," I offer a truth that I actively repress as I compose this chapter. In the time it took for me to write this paragraph, over one hundred football fields of trees were lost.[9] Will the practice of writing this chapter translate into benefiting actual sentient beings? Will this benefit be worth the sacrifice of the lives of trees through paper?

Rethinking Ontology as a Woman

To begin speaking as a woman philosopher on femininity is an impossible task. To define herself, for herself, is an ongoing task, one that involves trial and error, mimicry, and "strategic essentialism."[10] I agree with Catherine Malabou: "To speak of the feminine as a 'philosopher' requires a revisiting of ontology and biology."[11] This is because concepts such as "woman," "nature," and "the unconscious" have been defined for us, before us, by men. They have built the foundations of philosophy from their perspectives. We, as women, become as having been defined by male concepts. He defines, and she fits into these concepts, not as individual choice, but as societal expectation, unconscious bias, and modes of economic survival.

The identity of a woman philosopher forces us to rethink being because, "To claim that the feminine can be expressed in the form of a concept is to allow oneself to be caught up again in a system of 'masculine' representations."[12] To think within these frames of representation, "women are trapped in a system of meaning which serves the auto-affection of the (masculine) subject."[13] What would it look like if women plunged into the depths of truth and became from there? As the depths of truth have been defined by men as "the unconscious," this has become both her home and her cage. What if she had the time, space, support, and economic resources to become herself, defining herself for herself? And what if this was in support and partnership of other women, men, and the natural world?

Perhaps within "the unconscious"—her cage and her home—is the fecund potential for new beginnings. For Irigaray, she *is* the unconscious as it consists of the "repressed/censured feminine element of history."[14] In a sense, creatively appropriating the concept of the unconscious could be her liberation. If she (as defined by him) belongs to the unconscious—the repressed elements of history—is she imprisoned there as long as patriarchy structures her reality? The problem lies in representation. If her being is the repressed, fluid elements of history, is creating a concept to define herself for herself harboring the potential for her liberation? Or does she immediately become other than herself, through representation—which has been historically masculine?

By navigating these questions, the woman philosopher navigates the territories of time and space, the here and the beyond. A concept transcends time and space as it harbors the potential to change laws, affect consciousness, structure families and economies, in and across historical time periods. Consider patriarchal laws that have lasted for over five thousand years. Even when they violate bodies in the here and now, causing injustices that humans are aware of and disagree with, we remain somewhat powerless as they continue to structure reality. Concepts exist in a transcendent, symbolic realm as somewhat untouchable entities.

One of the most untouchable patriarchal concepts is the metaphysical masculine element known as God in the West. Questioning the gendered aspect of God is considered blasphemous, so feminine dimensions of metaphysics remain repressed in the unconscious. As noted earlier, concepts structure economies, laws, and policies, and in this way the symbolic realm and the material world are inextricably intertwined. They do not exist separately from one another but rather inform and reform the material world through economic and social systems. Consider Mary Daly's phrase: "if God is male, then the male is God."[15] If he is the signifier, she will always be the signified. Therefore, rethinking the gendered nature of ontology without replicating his nature and role as signifier is important.

I propose that rethinking ontology through an affirmation of sexual difference includes rethinking the gendered nature of a Western God as well as philosophical Absolutes. Claims to abstract universalities prevent experiences of both desire and repulsion—inter-actions and intra-actions—in-between living beings in the here and now. As Irigaray and Michael Marder state, when these "energetic impetuses are not used as they ought to be used" we lose perception as it is lived, resulting in destruction to others and ourselves.[16] For both philosophical Absolutes and a universal male God, experience with alterity (otherness) is filtered through perceptual frameworks. Raw experience becomes impossible.

In terms of ontological claims, "Instead of saying: the world is born from her, and from my relation with her, the Western philosopher says: there is Being, there are beings, which is, or are, given without anyone who gives."[17] All humans are materially born of a woman, and so far science hasn't encroached on this universality. Sexual difference is key here because her biology—womb, amniotic fluid, placenta, and breasts—create the conditions for life. Female biology is tied to female ontology. Saying "there is Being, there are beings" separates one from their relations, forgetting that the conditions of our being are always already Her.

Toward an Ecofeminist Relational Ontology: Unpacking the Logic of Colonization

In this chapter I revisit ontology through an ecofeminist lens posing an ecofeminist philosophy of sexual difference. Ecofeminists draw connections—theoretical, social, historical, and symbolic—between the domination of women by men, and the domination of nature by humans. Ecofeminism is an umbrella term to cover multiple approaches, forms, and roles ecofeminists can take on.[18] They can be activist or academic, religious or secular, radical ecofeminist, cultural ecofeminist, ecowomanist, male, female, or nonbinary ecofeminists. One need not identify as female to ascribe to the philosophy of ecofeminism. Attending to the "logic of colonization" is attending to the way oppression has been enacted theoretically, symbolically, and historically.

Philosopher Val Plumwood points out that it is the same underlying logic—the "logic of colonization"—that justifies the domination of man over woman and human over nature.[19] In this way, the oppression of women is tied to the destruction of nature. An ecofeminist framework offered by Plumwood offers an intersectional framework demonstrating how the logic of colonization enacts systems of oppression across race, class, gender, ethnicity, to name a few. It works by creating value-laden hierarchical dualisms, where those categories on the top are valued over those on the bottom. According to Plumwood, a dualism is "the process by which contrasting concepts (for example, masculine and feminine gender identities) are formed by domination and subordination and constructed as oppositional and exclusive."[20] Examples of dualisms include male/female, reason/emotion, human/nature, reason/matter (physicality).[21] Those categories on the left have historically been valued over those categories on the right. This logic has justified the oppression of categories on the right (subordinate) by categorical concepts on the left (superior).

The logic of colonization works by linking concepts and categories based on association.[22] Plumwood calls the associations of dualisms "linking postulates."[23] An example of this is according to the traditional philosophical Western framework commencing with Plato, trees are not intelligent, nor do they communicate.[24] According to this logic, intelligence belongs to the category of reason (superior) and belongs to beings with higher forms of intelligence, which is exclusive to reasoning and rationality (humans). Trees belong in the category of nature (subordinate), and therefore trees are subordinate to humans, and this attitude justifies their domination and destruction.

Linking postulates creates the symbolic order, which translates into philosophy, unconscious bias, socioeconomic organization, and law. Consider the example: Mother Nature and Father Time where the symbolic imagination genders certain characteristics and concepts. Women get clumped with nature, assuming characteristics like reproduction, immanence, and bondage that assume a lower status to be controlled by culture through production, transcendence, and freedom—tied to masculinity.

The gendered dualism Mother Earth/Father Time is tied to the rise of modern science, the connection strengthened by Francis Bacon, dubbed the Father of Modern Science. He wrote a book called *The Masculine Birth of Time*, where he defined knowledge before him as effeminate.[25] This "effeminate" knowledge *was* to Bacon, traditional ecological knowledge, and in this way perpetuated the subordination of both women and nature. In the 1600s, amidst the "birth of masculine time," numerous women practicing ecological science were labeled as witches and burned at the stakes. A witch wasn't connected to the devil, she was tied to the land. But it was this connection to land and ecological communities that prevented the full adoption of patriarchal science because it threatened progress in the service of capital.

Economic progress in the service of capital shaped perceptions of both women and wilderness. Consider the term "virgin forest," which describes an untouched forest containing valuable and desirable lumber. While Grandmother Redwood was useless to seventeenth-century lumberjacks, the not-so-fortunate redwood highlighted in Susan Griffin's "Timber" was too straight and too proper to be left alone.[26] Within the socioeconomic patriarchal system, social and economic roles were defined by men to serve men and masculinity.

The rise of patriarchal science is directly tied to the "death of nature" and the "forgetting of her."[27] The forgetting of her was not merely symbolic, but She as relationality, interconnection, and ecology—including ecological knowledge—has been forgotten through the genocide of Native Americans and the burning of witches, both holders of ecological knowledge and wisdom traditions. This forgetting was not accidental; rather, it has been an active forgetting, an ongoing erasure. Certain aspects of Indigenous, ecological, and feminine wisdom and knowledge were erased through the destruction of those bodies who carried that knowledge.

But resistance remains in the subordinate as an "ineffaceable 'remains.'"[28] In this "remains" is a "kernel of resistance . . . with the strength of a new beginning."[29] This new beginning is the affirmation of our "relational reality."[30] It is the practice of ecology. Patriarchal science is *not* normative science, and rethinking science outside patriarchal objectivity is key. According to ecofeminist Carolyn Merchant, "Ecology has been a subversive science in its criticism of the consequences of uncontrolled growth associated with capitalism, technology, and progress."[31] Indigenous knowledge is scientific, Earth systems are participatory, humans and nature are interconnected.

The work of women in science is highlighting participatory and interconnected aspects of nature.[32] Suzanne Simard's groundbreaking work on trees demonstrates that mother trees feed their offspring and kin through underground mycorrhizal networks connecting, communicating, and transmitting nutrients.[33] Knowledge of this harbors the potential to transform modern forestry practices. The groundbreaking work of primatologist Jane Goodall has redefined the traditional scientific method, which utilized objectivity as its main mode of inquiry. Rather, for Goodall, empathy was an important tool for developing relationships with chimpanzees allowing her access to their community. Without empathy—subject to subject connection—she would have remained an outsider to the chimpanzees.

Other examples of women offering different perspectives to the scientific community highlighting interconnection, participation, and relationality include Nobel Prize–winning scientist Barbara McClintock who studied genetics in corn and discovered "jumping genes." She described her scientific method as having a "feeling for the organism"—another example of using empathy as scientific method. This feeling for the organism requires an openness to "let it come to you" to "hear what the material has to say to you."[34] In this method, subjectivity informs objectivity, and the two are inextricably intertwined. Evolutionary biologist Lynn Margulis also utilized relationality in her groundbreaking science when she overturned the modern concept of the emergence of life on Earth through her serial endosymbiotic theory. She discovered that through "symbiogenesis" bacteria formed more complex forms of life. Life didn't emerge from nothing. Rather, complex life forms developed through symbiotic relationships with simpler forms of life.

More recently in the field of ornithology, scientists previously thought that only male birds sang. Female ornithologists recently discovered that female birds also sing.[35] Discoveries like these support the inclusion of more diverse people and perspectives into science. While most women were excluded from university education until the nineteenth century, allowing her access opens perspectives to include feminine metaphors to gain insight into scientific truths. Perhaps evolution doesn't occur solely as Darwin claimed: through survival of the fittest. There is also survival of the most cooperative. I agree with theologian Belden Lane, in that "survival-of-the-most-collaborative is what carries the day more often in the natural world."³⁶ There are just as many examples of cooperation in nature but there aren't enough people who see the world through this perspective, foregrounding it as normative.

In this way, in the beginning was not separation from Her but rather the affirmation of relationship with her, including affirmation of the between-us in the here and now as well as the always already. This is where the material existence of Grandmother Redwood can help us reimagine a relational ontology. Standing before her, I could imagine the root systems and mycorrhizal networks communicating with and feeding each other, with the help of Suzanne Simard's work. Using these relational metaphors and frameworks, I can see the forest, a place I've been to many times, in a new light. I can see how second-growth redwoods are relational as they grow together from the base like a celery stalk.

Figure 2.2. Redwood celery. *Source*: Courtesy of Kimberly Carfore.

Figure 2.3. Grandmother and kin. *Source*: Courtesy of Kimberly Carfore.

About 80 percent of Redwoods grow in circles called "fairy rings."[37] These "cathedral trees" emerge from, and are nourished by, dead trees.[38] It reminds me of how human families often surround grandparents during holidays or family reunions. As they age, they remain the central hub of the family, nourishing their kin with traditional food, drink, and wisdom.

Finding Mother Tree, Finding Mother God

The act of finding operates under the premise that something has been lost, has gone missing, or that it has never existed in the first place. In this section I analyze the term "finding" as it appears in both Suzanne Simard's *Finding the Mother Tree*, and Carol Lynn Pearson's book of poetry—*Finding Mother God*. Finding is an "act of sustaining, supporting, or providing the necessities of life."[39] For Simard, a forest ecologist, she is searching for the mother tree as it is the not-yet. For Pearson, author and artist, it is Mother God who has gone missing. These two women use intuition and imagination—two legitimate modes of inquiry that have also been feminized and disregarded as scientific.

For both, finding this missing aspect of existence is an act of healing. Pearson states, "Our world suffers the pain of her absence" whereby the act of finding her is affirming a partnership ethic in this world.[40] Simard affirms that when she began researching the mother tree, she "poured everything [she] had into becoming a sleuth of what it takes to heal the natural world."[41] And in the search for truth, "the trees have shown [her] their perceptiveness and responsiveness, connections and conversations."[42] If we learn to listen, and rediscover how to perceive, perhaps we can find a piece of ourselves in the process.

Most of us have stopped talking to trees, plants, and animals. The logic of colonization assumes that only humans are capable of speech, language, and intelligence. This attitude causes us to suffer "species loneliness," forgetting not only Her but also the intelligence that surrounds us in the natural world at any given moment.[43] Just as in any relationship, if you stop talking to them, they stop talking to you. Perhaps the same has happened both with Mother God and the Mother Tree.

If Mother (I use Mother to conflate Mother God with Mother Tree) has been actively erased, suppressed, oppressed, and repressed, how do we find her? I turn to womanist theologian Delores Williams for insight, specifically her concept of "wilderness experience," which is a symbolic term representing "survival intelligence" that kicks in when a woman is to "make a way out of . . . no way."[44] Williams's creation of this concept is used to describe Black women's post-antebellum experience in the United States. I want to preserve its specificity here, but I do see it as a helpful concept searching for missing Mother. I propose that when we as a human species find the Mother Tree, we will find Mother God. In the meantime, we wander in the dark. It is like spelunking when your headlamp runs out of batteries. (This is why being on the trail and getting lost can cultivate rich inner experience, as long as we avoid near-death experiences.) Learning to navigate the panic and learning to survive in the wild, the first rule of survival is always to stay calm.

What would a Mother God look like? Is it even possible to conceptualize Mother God? Perhaps the feminine par excellence, in other words a metaphysical feminine known as Mother God, doesn't exist, and cannot exist, because it isn't in her nature to exist representationally. Perhaps her existence is encountered—it is lived and experienced. Once it becomes representational, she is lost. Perhaps it is through encountering her ontological difference that opens onto the third space. She is not his binary opposite (passive to his active, nurture to his nature), but rather, encountering her alterity opens complexity. This is why the term "the wild" or "wildness" are helpful to describe her as the third space: where transcendence and immanence meet and unfold into an event.[45] If space has been the realm of the feminine, and time masculine, then affirming sexual difference means reconsidering the problematic of space and time.[46]

Addressing this problem would include problematizing the gendered nature of space and time and the dualism between interiority/time and exteriority/space. A way forward would be to complexify the simplified masculine/feminine dualism whereby the masculine time/transcendent/infinite has been valued over the feminine space/immanent/finite. Imagining a feminine third space bringing together these dualistic linked postulates would open into an "*expanse* of jouissance here and now right away."[47] Bridging transcendence with immanence through an ecofeminist materialist framework would be the intensification of the here and now, which includes the intensification of mundaneness. Encountering the Mother Tree is both the intensification of the sacred and mundane. The Mother Tree offers an encounter with Mother God since her existence resists conceptualization. Instead, it is a faceless, non-representational expanse of the here and now, at least right here and right now, but also opening to the possibility of the future.

Conclusion

For a mind trained to think in delineated concepts, categories, and frameworks, breathing life into ambiguity is awakening a muscle. For some, this chapter will raise the specter of the well-trodden debate between essentialism and social constructivism, whereby essentialism/non-essentialism is another dualism. I offer a post-deconstructive essence: an essence resistant to presence. If I am offering an essence of the feminine, it is not an essence that can be explicitly stated or known but precisely that which resists explanation or knowledge. It is an essence without a metaphysics of presence.[48] When words are used as a means to an end in addressing dualistic debates, they eventually create valued hierarchies of domination and control. Offering words to conjure new patterns is a more liberatory practice.

Poetry is a way to speak words as gifts, to welcome open a new space. If we can't represent Mother God through representational concepts, perhaps words can be offered words as gifts, to whisper prayerful sentiments, expressing an interest in Her. These words can act as pathways to expand her jouissance in the here and now. Pearson's "Running Cloud Speaks" does just that, through bridging thought with things, mind with matter:

> In the beginning was Thinking Woman
> who has always existed.
>
> Thinking Woman sends thoughts outward into space
> and whatever She thinks comes into being.
>
> She thought the rocks and the clouds
> and the snow and the juniper trees
> and the clear rivers and they appeared.[49]

As demonstrated in this poem, an ecofeminist relational ontology considers matter and spirit as radically intertwined. As above, so below. A thought is not something that merely hangs in the symbolic. It finds a way to bridge the concept in the mind with a star in the sky. If you can think it, perhaps there is a way to find who, what, or where one's thought meets the material world. To quote sociologist and philosopher Jean Baudrillard: "Animals have no unconscious, because they have a territory. Humans only have an unconscious because they lost their territory."[50] In nature, animals are constantly navigating their territory. Territorial behaviors are enacted in the here and now, through their bodies. They don't have a concept of territory as interiority because it is a process they are engaged with. There is no "away" in the mind. The mind *is* trees, fences, streams, lakes, hills, mountains . . .

Animals live out their desires in the moment and on the land. They don't repress desires into something intangible like the "unconscious" because those desires are played out in the material world in the here and now. Energy expenditure of animals in the wild is reserved for three things—sex, territory, and food. It takes calories to make calories, and because animals don't store things like humans do—food in refrigerators, crops in silos, memories in the unconscious, fetuses in test tubes, money in a bank account—energy and calories are precious. Sure, some animals store food for the wintertime, but not to the scale that humans do. Humans internalize the mind as they territorialize their space.

Building off Baudrillard's quote, I say that animals have no Mother God, but they do have a Mother Tree. Animals haven't lost a Mother God because they have the Mother Tree: an entity that gives them shelter and nourishment—materials that constitute home. Humans have lost Mother God because we don't have a Mother Tree. Once we lost connection to territory—land, ground, Earth—She was lost. She became neuter, repressed, faceless, space. The neutralized feminine spirit, Mother Nature—a non-material, non-representable figure in the symbolic order became, and her home is the unconscious.[51] Atop this faceless other—the repressed feminine, the "unconscious"—was the foundation of patriarchal metaphysics.

Emerging from the cage/home of the unconscious, women may embark on their own wilderness experiences. Others, both men and women, may demand we "lock her up."[52] We may even reinscribe our own logic of colonization upon ourselves—internalized forms of oppression—through force of habit, fear, and the confusion that comes with non-representational thinking. The cold air of sheer potentiality stings the surface of the skin as it brushes across one's face. The comfort of representation calls us back. There is comfort in knowing. There is calm in closing off. But remaining open is the work of the wild. Fluidity and flexibility in opening and closing is a practice. Knowing when to not know is an art. And knowing when to speak and when to listen is divine.

Some things on this Earth are unspeakable . . .

Some humans say trees are not sentient beings,
But they do not understand poetry . . .

Now I am a woman longing to be a tree . . .
What shall I do with all this heartache?[53]

Notes

1. Luce Irigaray, *In the Beginning She Was* (London: Bloomsbury, 2012), 4.
2. Val Plumwood, *Feminism and the Mastery of Nature* (New York: Routledge, 1993), 48. Backgrounding is the denial of dependency on a subordinated other. The individual or group in the superordinate position (on the valued top) relies on and uses the services of the subordinate while denying any sort of relationship or dependency on the subordinate's contributions. For example, humans rely on the natural world for our existence: we breathe oxygen, eat food, and drink water which comes from the Earth. However, humans deny any sort of dependence on the Earth and her systems. Many expect the Earth to give us

gifts (crops, water, air) without acknowledging our gratitude and dependence on these gifts.

3. Nietzsche, *Beyond Good and Evil*, trans. Helen Zimmern (North Carolina: Project Gutenberg, 2019), 1.

4. As stated by Jack London State Park Aide Michelle Dowdall on in person visit July 9, 2022.

5. Edmund Burke, *A Philosophical Enquiry into the Origin of Our Ideas of the Sublime and Beautiful* (South Bend: Notre Dame University Press, 1968.), 196.

6. Rudolf Otto, *The Idea of the Holy*, trans. John W. Harvey (London & New York: Oxford University Press, 1956), 13–24.

7. Susan St. Marie, email communication July 14, 2022.

8. Breck Parkman, retired Senior State Archaeologist for State Parks in the San Francisco Bay area, email communication, July 14, 2022. Arthur Dawson, local historian, email communication, July 17, 2022. Also thanks to Kristina Ellis, Tours and Education Manager Jack London State Park.

9. Damian Carrington, Niko Kommenda, Pablo Gutierrez, and Cath Levett, "One Football Pitch of Forest Lost Every Second in 2017 Data Reveals." *The Guardian*, June 27 (2018). www.theguardian.com/environment/ng-interactive/2018/jun/27/one-football-pitch-of-forest-lost-every-second-in-2017-data-reveals

10. Strategic essentialism is a term coined by Gayatri Spivak in a 1984 interview with Elizabeth Grosz. Strategic essentialism is a political tactic whereby minority groups, nationalities, and/or ethnicities mobilize on the basis of their shared culture, ethnicity, or gender. While one might be anti-essentialist, this might actually prevent political action. Elizabeth Grosz and Gayatri Chakravorty Spivak, "Criticism, Feminism, and the Institution," *Thesis Eleven*, 10–11.1 (1985): 175–87.

11. Catherine Malabou, *Changing Difference*, trans. Carolyn Shread (Cambridge: Polity Press, 2011), 4.

12. Luce Irigaray, *This Sex Which Is Not One*, trans. Catherine Porter (Ithaca, NY: Cornell University Press, 1985), p 122.

13. Irigaray, *This Sex Which Is Not One*, 122–123.

14. Irigaray, *This Sex Which Is Not One*, 124.

15. Mary Daly, *Beyond God the Father: Toward a Philosophy of Women's Liberation* (Boston: Beacon Press, 1993), 19.

16. Luce Irigaray and Michael Marder, *Through Vegetal Being: Two Philosophical Perspectives* (New York: Columbia University Press, 2016), 87.

17. Irigaray, *In the Beginning She Was*, 4.

18. Karen Warren, ed. *Ecological Feminist Philosophies* (Bloomington: University of Indiana Press, 1996).

19. Plumwood. *Feminism and the Mastery of Nature*, 41.

20. Plumwood, *Feminism and the Mastery of Nature*, 31.

21. For a full list of dualisms, see Plumwood. *Feminism and the Mastery of Nature*, 43. Plumwood does not claim this list as complete: "completeness is impossible, since any distinction can in principle be treated as a dualism."

22. Plumwood. *Feminism and the Mastery of Nature*, 45–46.
23. Plumwood. *Feminism and the Mastery of Nature*, 45.
24. For more on Plato's feminism and his attitude toward nature, see Plumwood, *Feminism and the Mastery of Nature*, 80–81.
25. Vandana Shiva, "Ecofeminism and the Decolonization of Women, Nature, and the Future," *YouTube*, March 25 (2020), 13:00–13:55. www.youtube.com/watch?v=hVbbov9Rfjg
26. Susan Griffin, "Timber: What Was There for Them," in *Woman and Nature: The Roaring Inside Her* (Berkeley: Counterpoint, 2016), 56–64.
27. The term "death of nature" comes from Carolyn Merchant's *The Death of Nature: Women, Ecology, and the Scientific Revolution* (New York: Harper Collins, 1989). The term "forgetting of her" comes from Irigaray. For Irigaray, the philosophical discourse of Presocratic philosophers Empedocles and Parmenides begins with the "forgetting of her" in a twofold manner. First, man encounters the feminine. After this encounter something remains which they cannot seem to express. They theorize about it, name it God, chase after it, but "only the memory of an experience lasts," this memory of her that will be effaced over time. Irigaray, *In the Beginning She Was*, 3.
28. Malabou, *Changing Difference*, 93.
29. Malabou, *Changing Difference*, 93.
30. Charlene Spretnak, *Relational Reality: New Discoveries of Interrelatedness that are Transforming the Modern World* (Topsham: Green Horizon Books, 2011).
31. Merchant, *Death of Nature*, xx.
32. Notable feminist philosophers of science include Sandra Harding, Evelyn Fox Keller, Donna Haraway, Nancy Tuana, and Carolyn Merchant.
33. Suzanne Simard, "How Trees Talk to Each Other," *TEDSummit*, July 31 (2017). www.ted.com/talks/suzanne_simard_how_trees_talk_to_each_other?language=en
34. Evelyn Fox Keller, *A Feeling for the Organism: The Life and Work of Barbara McClintock* (New York: Henry Holt, 1984), 198.
35. Stacy Morford, "Women Have Disrupted Research on Bird Song, and Their Findings Show How Diversity Can Improve All Fields of Science," *The Conversation* (September 11, 2020). https://theconversation.com/women-have-disrupted-research-on-bird-song-and-their-findings-show-how-diversity-can-improve-all-fields-of-science-142874
36. Belden Lane, *Backpacking with the Saints: Wilderness Hiking as Spiritual Practice* (New York: Oxford University Press, 2015), 170.
37. Lane, *Backpacking with the Saints*.
38. Jennifer Levine, "Why Redwoods are One of the Great Wonders of the World," *Cell Mentor*, September 7 (2016). https://crosstalk.cell.com/blog/why-redwoods-are-one-of-the-great-wonders-of-the-world
39. Online Etymology Dictionary, "Finding," *Etymonline* (2014). www.etymonline.com/word/finding

40. Carol Lynn Pearson, *Finding Mother God: Poems to Heal the World* (Layton: Gibbs Smith, 2020), xi.

41. Suzanne Simard, *Finding the Mother Tree: Discovering the Wisdom of the Forest* (New York: Knopf, 2021), 12.

42. Simard, *Finding the Mother Tree*, 14.

43. Robin Wall Kimmerer, *Braiding Sweetgrass: Indigenous Wisdom, Scientific Knowledge, and the Teachings of Plants* (Minneapolis: Milkweed Editions, 2013), 208–9. Species loneliness is a state of isolation and disconnection from the natural world. It is "a deep, unnamed sadness stemming from estrangement from the rest of Creation, from the loss of relationship."

44. Delores S. Williams, *Sisters in the Wilderness: The Challenge of Womanist God-Talk* (Maryknoll, NY: Orbis Books, 1993), 45, 96.

45. Jason Wirth agrees that "'the wild' is one of those great third terms." Jason Wirth, "Spotlights 2.42, Jason Wirth on Philosophy, Zen, and Ecology," *Yale Forum on Religion and Ecology Spotlights Podcast*, 2.42 (2022), 30: 12. www.youtube.com/watch?v=DwjM46rHl1s_For Irene Klaver, "the wild is to stand out *and* to disappear." Irene Klaver, "Silent Wolves: The Howl of the Implicit," in *Wild Ideas*, ed. David Rothenberg (Minneapolis: University of Minnesota Press, 1995), 117.

46. Through philosophy, and with the development of instrumental rationality by the logic of colonization, space becomes the servant of time. "In the beginning there was space and the creation of space . . . And time is there, more or less in the service of space." Luce Irigaray, *An Ethics of Sexual Difference*, trans. Carolyn Burke and Gillian C. Gill (Ithaca: Cornell University Press, 1993), p. 7.

47. Irigaray, *An Ethics of Sexual Difference*, 64.

48. Catherine Malabou offers an analysis of this in *Changing Difference: The Feminine and the Question of Philosophy*, trans. Carolyn Shread (Cambridge, UK: Polity Press, 2009), 90–112. Timothy Morton also discusses the move beyond essentialism/non-essentialism in "Treating Objects Like Women: Feminist Ontology and the Question of Essence," in *International Perspectives in Feminist Ecocriticism* ed. Greta Gaard, Simon C. Estok, and Serpil Oppermann (London: Routledge, 2013), 56–69. Malabou offers a "resistant essence" or a "stamp of impossibility," while Morton's terminology is "weird essentialism." For a comparison of Malabou's "resistant essence" in her post-deconstructive feminism and Morton's "weird essentialism" in his object-oriented feminist ecology, see Sam Mickey, *Coexistentialism and the Unbearable Intimacy of Ecological Emergency* (Lanham, MD: Lexington Books, 2016), 152–60.

49. Carol Lynn Pearson, *Finding Mother God*, 40 (shortened version).

50. Jean Baudrillard, *Simulacra and Simulation*, trans. Sheila Faria Glaser (Ann Arbor: University of Michigan Press, 1994), 139.

51. Irigaray, *This Sex Which Is Not One*, 124.

52. This phrase was chanted by Donald Trump and his followers to the

first female presidential candidate Hillary Clinton in 2016. I am astounded at how representative it is of the feminine/unconscious connection.

53. Joy Harjo, "Speaking Tree," in *Conflict Resolution for Holy Beings* (New York: W. W. Norton & Company, 2015), 118–19.

The Language of Trees

Figure I.2. Forest in winter, near Zürich, Switzerland. *Source*: Courtesy of Laura Pustarfi.

Interstice

The Forest

Go out in the woods, go out. If you don't go out in the woods, nothing will ever happen and your life will never begin.

—Clarissa Pinkola Estés, *Women Who Run with the Wolves*

You must go in quest of yourself, and you will find yourself again in the simple and forgotten things. Why not go into the forest for a time, literally? Sometimes a tree tells you more than can be read in books.

—C. G. Jung, *Letters of C. G. Jung, Vol. 1*

Trees are often viewed as discrete beings who rise from the soil and stretch toward the clouds, linking the earth below with the sky above. But it is important to remember that in the forest they are hitched together in a vast network. As Suzanne Simard has shown, trees are communicating with each other by transferring information, water, and nutrients with the help of fungal collaborators through the mycorrhizal networks. Trees also communicate via airborne compounds, warning each other of incoming insect predation, for example.

In human language, the word "forest," as opposed to the much earlier "wood," is a legal term deriving from the Latin *foresta*. The word may have originated from *foris*, meaning outside or to exclude, or alternatively from *forum*, a closed space, market, or jurisdiction. The Old French *forêt*, Old High German *forst*, and Middle English *foreste* among other related terms arose in the Middle Ages to designate woodland set aside by royalty for pleasure, recreation, and sanctuary for non-human creatures. Robert Pogue Harrison notes in *Forests: The Shadow of Civilization* that royal forests were designated only after top predators like wolves were eradicated from the area, and forests were enclosed with laws and penalties not applicable in other woodlands. Forests were, from the outset, entwined with privilege and exclusion. Contemporary forests are also sometimes set aside and protected with histories of exclusion of Indigenous and local peoples, though with intended public access. The United States has allotted parkland from its vast forests, beginning with Yellowstone National Park in 1872.

The forest speaks also in the imagination. Dante Alighieri's *selva oscura*, or shadowed forest, opens *The Divine Comedy* in a dark, pathless wood, invoking the terrifying landscape of the European mind combined with the Christian awareness of sinfulness as a separation from God. On a similar note, author and poet Sumana Roy takes inspiration from Pablo Neruda in exploring the wonders and fears of losing herself in the forest in her book *How I Became a Tree*. And photographer Anne Brigman evokes Ovid's *Metamorphoses* in her striking monochromatic images of trees intertwined with female nudes, often of herself or her sister. In these depictions, the integration of tree bodies and human bodies conjures connection and even a sense of communication.

In the following section, Luke Fischer examines the language of trees in conversation with European Romantic poets, finding in trees an expressive form of arboreal communication. Then, Dan Bradley explores the conifer forest of the Pacific northwest, relating the importance of silence and darkness to this realm.

—Laura Pustarfi

3

Speaking Trees

The Language of Nature and Arboreal Communication

LUKE FISCHER

> And that is the language of nature (*Natur-Sprache*) in which each thing speaks from its character and always reveals itself . . .
>
> —Jacob Böhme, *De signatura rerum*[1]

> *Being that can be understood is language* . . . Thus we speak not only of a language of art but also of a language of nature . . .
>
> —Hans-Georg Gadamer, *Truth and Method*[2]

We are all familiar with the idea of speaking trees from fairy tales and stories that we heard and read in our childhood. But is there any truthful sense in which we can talk of a language of trees, or is the notion of communicative trees no more than an enchanting fiction? In our age of literalism and reductive scientism, many people would likely respond to this question in the negative. In contrast, the present chapter explores ways in which we can genuinely think of trees as speaking, not in the literal sense of having an audible voice (with the requisite organs of mouth and larynx) but in that they express themselves in their manners of growing and interacting with their environments. In the context of a broadened concept of language and Logos,[3] I also argue for significant continuities between the wisdom and language of trees, on the one hand, and human intelligence and language, on the other.

In recent years the work of pioneering scientists has drawn attention to remarkable respects in which trees communicate with one another. The final section of this chapter aims to indicate the significance of integrating this new knowledge of tree communication into a conception of the language of nature and, specifically, a language of arboreal being.[4]

Historical Background to the Language of Nature

If we contemplate the history of Western consciousness as manifest in the development of philosophy, science, religion, and theology, it becomes clear that the view of nature as an inanimate realm devoid of wisdom is basically a modern development, which begins to cement itself around the time of the Scientific Revolution, although there are significant precursors to this eventuation.[5]

Correlative to the progressive *subtraction* of mind, soul, and wisdom from nature is the growing significance of human self-consciousness in modernity as the predominant or exclusive site of intelligence and language within the natural order. Cartesian dualism is the paradigmatic metaphysical form of an opposition between an inanimate, mechanistic nature and self-conscious human intelligence, but variants of this dualism come to expression in diverse aspects of modernity. The *experiential* (rather than metaphysical) sense of dualism reached its consummate expression in the period from the late nineteenth to the first half of the twentieth century in the existentialist philosophies from Nietzsche to Sartre and Camus. Here, the human being exists in an intrinsically meaningless universe, which can be granted significance only through the free, yet alienated, acts of the individual.

Conceptions of the Logos, Language, or the Word held an important place in earlier visions of the natural world as embodying and manifesting wisdom. In the Genesis of Judaism and Christianity, God creates the world through His acts of speech: "God said, Let there be light: and there was light."[6] The creative ground of existence, therefore, is the Divine Word or the Word of God. The beings that exist and cohere in the cosmos derive from Divine Speech and thus they can also be viewed as the language of God. Since beings *are* language or derived from divine speech acts, it follows that they are intrinsically meaningful and imbued with divine wisdom. In Christianity, of course, the embodiment of the Logos in the cosmos is taken further than in any other religion, as the Logos, who was one with God in the beginning (Prologue of John), is not only the creative ground of the whole cosmos that embraces the latter, but also incarnates within the cosmos as an individual human being. Despite the significant differences between pagan and Judeo-Christian cosmology, there is also a cosmic sense of the Logos in pre-Socratic thought. For Heraclitus, for example, everything is a manifestation of fire and the intelligible order of the Logos, which also underlies philosophical knowledge as articulated in language. We find further cosmic senses of the Logos in the Hellenistic period and later antiquity—in Stoicism, Neoplatonism, and Hermeticism (alongside and in connection with Judaic and Christian conceptions). While there are significant differences among these cosmo*logies*, a common thread is the vision of the universe as a language that embodies divine wisdom.

In the Middle Ages it was common to speak of (1) the Divine Logos, which is manifest in (2) "the book of nature," and finds its human analogue in (3) our various languages or tongues. The related idea of a "language of nature" (*Natursprache*) plays a central role in the thought of the Reformation theosophist Jacob Böhme and is taken up again in the Romantic period—especially in Novalis's poetic philosophy—which aimed imaginatively to reconnect humanity and nature.[7] Despite the efforts of various luminaries in the periods of romanticism (Schelling, Goethe, Coleridge, among others) and transcendentalism (Emerson and Thoreau), a reductive, materialistic view of nature as devoid of any inherent meaning or wisdom has largely prevailed in Western modernity (however, with the rise of the environmental movement, environmental humanities, and ecologically minded science this default position is again being seriously questioned). More specifically, "language" has contracted into a predominantly human possession (3, above), with ideas of a "language of nature" (2) and a divine, creative Logos (1) becoming marginal to the scientific, intellectual, and general culture.

While in earlier periods the primary incentive for learning to read the "book of nature" is parallel to that of reading the Bible, namely, to near God by understanding His word, the aspect of the book of nature—or language of nature—that especially concerns me here relates to the essences or quiddities ("whatness") of beings as such (the "plantness" of the plant, the "treeness" of the tree, the "fir-ness" of the fir tree). If nature itself is a language, then phenomena are "signs" that possess a hidden meaning, just as words possess a hidden meaning to someone who does not understand the language. The meaning of these phenomena is nothing less than the essences of different beings and their relations (a notion also central to the "language of nature" in both Böhme and Novalis).

My aim here is to consider the Logos insofar as it is immanently at work in nature and, especially, the language of trees, in the sense that the distinctive manifestations of diverse beings can be understood as these beings *saying themselves* (the question of whether there is a Divine Logos that entirely transcends the natural order will be left aside). Here it is important to underscore that while some views of the Logos could imply that the only active "speaker" is the creative ground of the whole of nature and thereby reduce natural beings to the passive status of "the spoken," insofar as organisms are involved in their self-manifestation I regard them as actively "speaking." While trees do not speak in any respect that directly resembles the human voice or human writing—nor in a respect that resembles the calls of birds, or the singing of whales—they express themselves in their manner of growing and distinctive ways of responding to their environment. This manner of arboreal speaking is not dissimilar to the way in which a person manifests their character in their body language, gait, gestures, and mannerisms—all the sublinguistic ways in which our human behavior *says who we are* or *manifests our character, mood or attitude in a situated context*.[8]

What is the philosophical benefit of considering natural beings, and more specifically plants and trees, as language—as the phenomenal manifestation of invisible essences, as "signs" that express a "meaning"? The problem with any form of dualism between nature and mind, the physical and the intelligent, is that it makes the appearance of the latter (in each of these binaries) unintelligible, even miraculous. If, for example, nature is a purely physical reality devoid of wisdom and consciousness, how and why do intelligence and consciousness suddenly emerge in the human being (and perhaps some animals)? If the rest of nature cannot speak, why do human beings possess languages? Forms of materialist monism also fail to give an adequate account; they tend either to conflate mind and matter ("mind is nothing more than a complex organisation of matter") or to regard mind as an epiphenomenon of merely material processes, which again makes the emergence of intelligence a kind of inexplicable miracle.[9] If we regard nature, in contrast, as always already imbued with meaning, intelligence, and language, then it becomes far more intelligible that humans should possess the capacities of speaking and thinking. While I do think that there is something distinctive, even elevated, about human linguistic capacities, intelligence, and consciousness, these capacities are also latently at work within other dimensions and realms of nature (including our own organisms).

Moreover, this conception of the language of nature opens a space for the recognition of the diversity of modes, forms and degrees in which intelligence, wisdom, and language appear in the cosmos. In that the site of intelligence in the last few centuries has been predominantly restricted to the human being, we no longer have an intuitive sense for other forms of mindedness, which was natural to earlier periods of Western consciousness (and remains natural to many other cultures around the world, especially Indigenous cultures that have maintained deep ties to the environment over millennia).[10] Modern rational consciousness has become the only readily available model for thinking about intelligence in general. For this reason, even the most well-intentioned environmental thinkers in their attempts to extend concepts of agency, animation, mindedness, and wisdom to other-than-human beings—animals, plants, rivers, and so on—often do so in the manner of a Cartesian anthropomorphism. Moreover, this model of the mind is not even entirely true of human beings. It is not uncommon for us to perform intelligent tasks on "auto-pilot." Furthermore, we experience meaningful—even coherent—narratives during our dreams at night that involve agency and decision-making on the part of a protagonist, yet which commonly lack our waking self-awareness. Consciousness and intelligence do not presuppose a self-possessed rational subject that apprehends itself as itself.

Human beings are not distinctive in that they are manifestations of intelligence and wisdom, but rather in that intelligence and language at the human level are greatly liberated into a *free capacity and possession of the individual*.[11] Trees *are* language or express *their being*, whereas human beings, in addition to *being* language, possess a highly developed capacity for second-order speech, for language *about* the language of being (though these orders are also implicated in one another). More specifically (as I elaborate below), the life of trees manifests an expressive, gestural language. This language of arboreal being has its closest human analogue in body language, but analogies with human speech can also be drawn—a tree's potent concealment in a seed can, for example, be likened to a pregnant silence in a conversation, while a mature tree can be likened to an articulated poem. Moreover, as Merleau-Ponty vividly elaborates, human speech also incorporates a fundamental *gestural* dimension, which communicates the "emotional sense" of words.[12] In these respects, there are essential continuities between body language and verbal language, arboreal language and human language.

While my conception of language and Logos also encompasses inorganic nature, for our current purposes I will limit the scope to organic nature. Here we can immediately discern at least three levels of intrinsically meaningful forms. There is (1) the intelligent form and language of living formation, transformation, and metamorphosis, (2) the language and meaning of intelligent behavior (what used to be called "instinct," but also includes associative learning) and (3) language and intelligence as autonomous, individual capacities. What is latent in (1) becomes more explicit in (2) and (3), and what is revealed in (3) is anticipated in (1) and (2). These various stages also overlap and interpenetrate one another in diverse ways.

Here are a few concrete examples. (1) A flower (for example, a snowdrop or a daffodil) expresses a radial symmetry while the human embryo is formed with a bilateral symmetry, but neither the plant nor the embryonic human being sit at a desk and draw up a plan of this geometry. The geometry is intrinsic to the unconscious formative processes, which latently mean respectively "flower" and "human being." (2) A spider constructs an intricate web in which flies and other insects will be caught, while a bowerbird constructs his bower out of twigs and collects bits of blue as part of a ritual to attract a mate, but neither the spider nor the bowerbird plan in advance their designs and their ends. A Japanese Pufferfish (*Torquigener albomaculosus*) does not have an *a priori* overview of the wondrous mandala that takes him a full week to carve with his body and fins into the sandy bottom of the sea—a pattern that we could imagine as a beautiful solar wheel or symbol carved into the wall of a temple. Nor does each sunflower in a field follow the apparent path of the sun having first deliberated about various possible courses of action. I do not decide in abstraction that I will walk with a bent, lethargic gait that expresses my melancholy; I may not even know that my mood is thus manifest to others. (3) Human thinking and language as free capacities (as well as to some degree, relatively liberated capacities in other creatures) are employed to describe and interpret the forms of the world, to elucidate the immanent language of living beings. Unsurprisingly (from our standpoint), human intelligence—the wisdom immanent in nature raised into a free, individual mental capacity—finds a reflection of its own intelligence in the world.

As examples of how these stages interpenetrate and resemble each other, think of how a caterpillar must behave in a certain way (2) in order to transform into a butterfly (1) or how a queen bee emerges with a distinctive form (1) and role (2) in the hive on the basis of being fed a special diet ("royal jelly") by worker bees in her larval period (2).[13] Consider how a hermit crab adopts a discarded shell (2) that, in a way, becomes a part of her body (1). Or reflect upon how tree roots (1) in their communication and interaction via mycorrhizal networks resemble and anticipate features of animal, and even human, communication (3).

Before turning to an elaboration of arboreal language, I would like to clarify my perspective on the language of nature by responding to a potential critic who objects that only human communication in words properly warrants the designation "language" and that the self-manifestation of other beings is fundamentally non-linguistic. To this objection, I have two responses. First, as I have outlined, this restrictive conception of language (Logos) is a relatively recent historical development and by no means self-evident. Second, it is important to know that a conception of "intensification" or *Steigerung*, which is indebted to the poet-scientist Goethe, underlies my broad conception of language. "Intensification" refers to the way in which something that only comes to a latent or rudimentary expression in one natural form achieves a higher development or fuller expression in another form. For example, Goethe regards the petal of a plant as an intensification of the leaf. In flexibly applying the notion of intensification to the whole of nature, one comes to discern continuities across and within natural kingdoms.[14] What matters in connection with the language of nature is not the precise choice of terminology, but the comprehension of such continuities. If a reader prefers to reserve the term "language" exclusively for the verbal communication of humans, this poses no problem in itself. In this case I would, however, insist that phenomena such as the growth and responsiveness of trees be regarded as "latent-language" or "pre-language." Only an approach that discerns continuities via intensification can avoid the dual deficiencies of unity without difference ("everything is language in the same sense"), on the one hand, and difference without unity ("humans are the exclusive site of language and thus excepted from the rest of nature"), on the other. Put otherwise: human language is the flower of the logos-structure of the world.[15]

The Expressive Language of Trees

The suggestion that trees are a self-expressive language immediately raises two important questions. First, what are the basic characteristics of arboreal language? Second, how can we come to understand, interpret, or read the language of trees?

Beginning with the second question, it can be said that if trees are indeed a language with inherent meaning, then most of us today are illiterate.[16] We are like young children who stare at the letters on a page and see only squiggles and curious yet unintelligible patterns. We point at the arboreal letters, perhaps compare their shapes with one another and note similarities and differences, for example, between the branches of multiple trees, but we certainly do not read the various forms of a particular tree, its stages of growth and decay, its responses to its environment, and so on, as the coherent expression of a meaningful utterance. We remain excluded from the inner or intensive dimension of meaning that grants an invisible coherence to the arboreal letters and words. Since we are thus shut out from comprehending the speaking of arboreal being, we seem to be also at an impasse with regard to the first question above. How can we understand the character of arboreal language when we seem to lack an entry point into this language?

We can, nevertheless, progress in our inquiry, by considering the different possible relations between the sensible "signs" of a language and their nonsensible "meaning." This relation can be arbitrary such as in many of the symbols of mathematics. The multiplication sign "x" and the minus sign "–," for example, possess their meanings as a matter of convention—their visible appearance is not an expressive clue to their meaning. However, in the domain of art we find signs with a non-arbitrary character that serve in the mediation of their meaning, which also cannot be reduced to convention. Beethoven's instrumental music can be appreciated by people all over the world as can Indian music, even if an understanding of a composer's cultural background sheds light on the meaning of the music. This is the case because music conveys an affective sense by way of an intrinsic (non-arbitrary) relation between its sensible form and its meaning, which transcends convention (even though the latter also plays some role in distinctive musical traditions). The same point holds for many other art forms, such as sculpture, dance, architecture, and painting. If the language of trees shows affinities to the non-arbitrary symbolism of art, then we may begin to learn arboreal language by approaching it as a realm of aesthetically expressive forms.

The language of trees can perhaps be most immediately compared to something like living sculpture or organic architecture—think of how a forest resembles a great cathedral (and vice versa), with its vaulted ceiling, column-like trunks, dome-like canopy, and sculptural expressiveness of branches. It also suggests something like a wild architecture in the home that it provides to so many creatures—mammals, birds, reptiles, insects, worms, and others.

Trees are commonly distinguished from other plants by virtue of the height, solid structure, and longevity of their mature forms. Whereas the life cycle of an annual plant is completed in the course of the seasons—the plant dying in the winter, and seeds germinating in the spring—their arboreal equivalents are the deciduous trees that lose their leaves, flowers, and fruit—partially die—but they maintain their structural forms and a less vigorous state of life during the winter (the vegetal equivalent of animal hibernation), holding the potential for the rebirth of leaves and blossoms in their closed buds. What the soil is to the seeds of annual plants, the trunk and branches are to the buds of trees. As a few thinkers and poets have remarked, trunks and branches suggest a soil-like formation that has been raised into the air, and the new growth of trees manifests, in a sense, airborne plants on plants.[17] The common brownness of trunks, older branches, and roots is also suggestive of their kinship with the soil. The process of lignification—the formation of woody tissue—that belongs to the maturation of trees also shows a certain kinship with the inorganic realm in its approximation of the hardness of stone. This wooden structure supports arboreal longevity and makes deciduous trees evocative of skeletons in winter. While crystals are forms of the mineral kingdom that somewhat approach the vegetal realm in their geometric growth, trees are forms in which vegetal life—in its hardened wood—nears the mineral kingdom (though there remains a crucial difference between the external, accretive "growth" of crystals and the internal, organic development of trees). The woodening tendency (*Verholzung*) is apparent not only in trunks, roots, and branches but also in the woody seed-bearing structures and fruits of numerous trees: cones of conifers, "gum nuts" of eucalypts, fruits of nut trees, seed pods of banksias. This tendency is an elementary sign of "treeness."

Some of the other elementary, non-arbitrary signs of different kinds of trees (which they may share with other plants) include the contrasting manners of branching, trunking, rooting, leafing, budding, blossoming, fruiting, environmental relations, and interacting with vegetal and non-vegetal neighbors. The far-spreading, at times horizontal, branches and sub-branches of a large common oak (*Quercus robur*), with their irregular twists and turns, differs from the gesture of the narrow branches of a fir tree, which are relatively straight, remain close to the linear axis of the trunk and taper as they rise. This apical dominance of the fir's trunk is reflected in the predominance of the axis of each main branch in relation to its sub-branches, which is further reflected in the sub-branches in their relation to the linear, needlelike leaves growing along them (this fractal-like, morphological repetition and its resulting geometry is suggestive of a vegetal intensification of the repeating pattern of crystals). The overall conical form of the fir, in turn, contrasts with the broad canopy of a free-standing oak tree.

Aiming to deepen an emergent sense of these distinctive arboreal expressions, we can compare the somewhat asymmetrical, wavy lobes of a common oak leaf with the ovate surface, serrated margin, pointed tip, and relative symmetry of a birch leaf (*Betula pendula*). The latter has a refined, delicate quality, while the former in its profusion of rather undifferentiated, rounded lobes (compare it to the highly distinct lobes of a Japanese maple leaf) has an inchoate potency that seems to echo the tree's irregular branching, and the elemental strength and massiveness of an old oak tree. In this manner we can begin to decipher the gestural language of trees.

However, we are still a fair way from grasping a particular kind of tree as a cohesive expression of arboreal agency. This comprehension requires, for example, that we manage to trace in diverse aspects of the oak tree—the morphology of its various parts and its relations to its environment—the variations and metamorphoses of a cohesive gesture. It requires that in the flower and fruit (acorn) we find a metamorphosis of related gestures and tendencies that we have identified in the leaves, the branches, and elsewhere. And, furthermore, as we apprehend them, all these features must become absorbed into a fluid continuum, such that they appear as unbroken moments in the expressive dance of its being.

How is such a comprehension possible? Our ordinary modern consciousness remains outside the whole and can conceive it only as an aggregate of parts that lacks an intensive unity of expression. Observing a tree, we apprehend an exterior spatial object—a merely "extensive whole" (which is a failure to grasp the true whole)—that is distinguishable into discrete parts. We see an exterior *Gestalt* that consists of mutually external components—branches, leaves, trunk, and others. There is one domain, however, in which we have widely cultivated an *intensive* mode of understanding and appreciation that apprehends a differentiated whole from within, namely art, but it remains generally unknown that this same mode of apprehension can be applied to nature, and is, in fact, a crucial key to a deeper understanding of and relationship to the natural environment.[18]

When we appreciate a melody, we grasp it as an intensively differentiated unity of expression. We do not start with separate notes and then add them to one another. The sequence of intervals and their rhythm reciprocally determine the sense of one another and the sense of the whole in a fluid, dynamic continuum. This dynamic whole of the melody expresses a character that has a distinctive mood—spritely, melancholic, heroic, and so on. The same is true of a more complex aesthetic whole. The second movement of a piano sonata affects my sense of the first and third movements and vice versa, all three movements serving to articulate a complex and extremely differentiated whole, and one that I grasp intensively or from within as the inaudible sense of the audible—the soul or spirit, so to speak, of the metamorphic organism of tones.[19]

Our usual perception of trees, by contrast, resembles a tone-deaf person, who, in place of the intensive expressiveness that is apparent to a musician, hears a disconnected and discontinuous succession of sounding notes that lack any expressive coherence. Nonetheless, it is possible to awaken to an intensive appreciation of arboreal language, in which a tree's performance of its being assumes a cohesive sense in a manner that is analogous to an aesthetic apprehension of music, dance, or sculpture.

The intensively differentiated whole of a tree can be apprehended in perceptual ("sensory") and imaginal ("reflective") modes of understanding, which also reinforce one another. The difference between our ordinary grasp of a tree as an "exterior whole" and appreciating a tree as an aesthetic, intensive whole, became especially apparent to me in a vivid experience of intensive perception. This event resembled Martin Buber's account of the difference between encountering a tree as a dialogical I–You relationship and our usual I–It experience. Buber describes the I–You encounter as follows: "There is nothing from which I would have to turn my eyes away in order to see, and no knowledge that I would have to forget. Rather, everything—including picture and movement, species and type, law and number—is indivisibly united in this event. Everything belonging to the tree is in this: its form and structure, its colours and chemical composition, its intercourse with the elements and with the stars, are all present in a single whole."[20]

My own experience of such a shift from an I–It consciousness, in which a tree's parts are disconnected from one another, to an I–You encounter, in which they appear as integrated in the seamless whole of the presencing tree, occurred some years ago when I took part in a course on Goethean science, devoted to the theme of wholeness.[21] It involved close observations, field studies, intellectual learning, and imaginative exercises focused on the living forms of plants and animals. One late afternoon following several days of these practices, I was conversing with friends at a table in a garden and my eye was caught by the contours of a nearby tree. I was suddenly drawn into a state that felt like a paradisiacal vision, in which I experienced the formative gesture that expresses itself in an unbroken manner in every part of the tree. I felt myself to be following the tree's trunking and branching and leafing in a wholly continuous manner. I did not see branches, leaves, or other apparent parts in distinct perceptions or as things, but as within a single, expressive movement.

While Buber may be right that grace is a factor in the shift from an I-It experience to an I-You encounter, the above anecdote illustrates that practices such as Goethean observation and imagination can facilitate this shift.[22] With this in mind, we can build on some of our earlier examples.

I look out again at a birch tree and silently ask its overall gesture to impress itself on me. I sense the lightness, the ethereal quality of the entire form, how it seems to float or hover above the earth. I look at the giant oak tree (*Quercus robur*) again, sense its powerful presence. I pick up an acorn and feel the weight of the single fruit/seed. I reach up to a low branch of a birch tree and pick a mature catkin, which holds numerous incredibly light winged-seeds along its cylinder; when separated (with ease), each seed looks a little like a tiny butterfly with a brown body and diaphanous wings.[23] The ethereal whole of the entire *Gestalt* of the birch tree, the delicate quality of the leaves, the almost weightless seeds come to appear as expressions of a single melody or dance, just as the *Gestalt* of the oak tree, its gnarled, stretching branches, its massive trunk, the solid, rounded acorns, the crumpled leaf-surfaces, asymmetric lobes, irregularly bunched leaves, and color (the particular intensity of green) express a contrary character of substantial strength.[24]

As one observes and reads more about a tree's parts, its life cycle, its relations to its environment, animals, and other plants, its preferred climate, and its place in vegetal evolution, one can aim to bring this information beyond the stage of an accumulation of separate facts and look for a related expressiveness in all these aspects. Thereby, comprehension of the expressive whole becomes ever richer and more differentiated. A Goethean understanding of metamorphosis is instructive.[25] Can a flower, for example, be seen as a metamorphosis of the leaf forms? Do the stamens and styles resemble contracted petals? In Horse Chestnut flowers

(*Aesculus hippocastanum*) I notice how the white of the filaments (as well as the white of the styles) and their orange-ish anthers resemble the white of the petals and their spots of yellow and pink. In an upright panicle with its numerous flowers, I come to see a concentrated intensification of the majesty of the entire tree (in line with Goethe's view of flowers as the highest expression of a plant).[26] The wide surface area of its compound, obovate leaves and the relatively large fruit capsule and woody "chestnut" also seem to fit with the emerging picture of the whole.

Regarding a fir tree I aim to deepen my previous sense of a related gesture in the contracted straight form of its leaves—its needles—(so different from the broad-leaved Horse Chestnut tree), the linear verticality of its trunk, and the closely held branches. The whole tree seems to emphasize a gesture of contraction, uprightness, linearity, geometric concision. I sense a related gesture in the woodiness of cones and in the slowness (relative to deciduous trees), yet endurance, of its growth. The predominance of the relatively dark green leaves of the conifer also expresses this quality (so different from the light green leaves—the youthful vitality and suppleness—of many deciduous trees in spring). These factors seem connected to its ability to persist through cold winters. The tree comes to encapsulate a picture of reflective interiority and quiet endurance.[27]

I soon find myself writing poems about conifers, and analogies with human, even moral, qualities naturally suggest themselves in the poetry. While this takes my consideration of trees well beyond the standard objective approach of science, in light of the earlier-discussed continuity of the Logos of nature, I view such metaphorical correspondences between the human and the arboreal as more than mere fictions. Here is a recent poem called "Invisible Service" (the conifer that sparked the poem was a Norfolk Pine and not a "true pine"):

> A pine tree on the medium strip
> stands upright as a saint
> in the bare winter light
> while turbid streams of cars
> roll past without pause—
> breathing in their fumes,
> returning pure air,
> the sky's sole witness—
> a green fletched arrow
> aimed at the sun.[28]

An earlier poem about a fir tree evokes a similar central figure of spiritual determination:

> Your branches
> like tiered roofs
> of a Chinese temple,
> cupped beneath the sky
> and sleeved with snow.
>
> An El Greco figure
> beside the oaks and birches,
> your single mission's
> apparent each night:
> the ascent of earth to star.
>
> Through the blizzards
> ever green, your ascetic fingers
> never part from prayer.[29]

How different do these pictures of the introverted, ascetic conifers appear, by comparison, to the flamboyant expressiveness of the Horse Chestnut tree? While these poetic evocations move beyond the normal attitude of scientific objectivity (as a philosopher and poet I am not constrained by scientific norms), perhaps they give expression to something of the creative potency (as the Goethean scientist Nigel Hoffmann calls it) and gestural character of these trees, one that could also be elaborated in a more detailed manner by an imaginative scientist.[30] Further, it is arguable that an overemphasis in modern science on a certain form of objectivity, which insists on a strict (and often naïve) separation between the subjectivity of the knower and the known object, has significantly contributed to our alienation from nature—the modern opposition between nature and human consciousness, which we touched on at the outset of this chapter. A more interconnected poetic vision can be an aid toward overcoming this alienation and reconciling nature and mind. The human qualities poetically imagined in these trees should not be regarded as mere anthropomorphic personification, but rather as at least to some degree revelatory of the ways in which trees latently anticipate qualities that appear in a more intensified and interior form in human beings, ways in which the metaphorical superimposition of arboreal qualities and human qualities can shed light on both.

I have long been fascinated with different species of Banksia trees—to offer a final sketch of an approach to the whole gesture of a tree—which are common in Sydney, where I have spent much of my life. Like conifers they show a strong tendency toward woodening, most evidently in their seed pods, which are also commonly called "cones." However, rather than the moist soils, mountainous regions, and cold climates in which conifers are often found, banksias frequently grow in warm climates with well-drained and quite sandy soil (such as the coastal areas of Sydney). Like conifers they are pictures of perennial endurance, but endurance through hot summers and periods of little rain, rather than icy winters. They tend not to grow very tall and their branches spread outward in a gnarled fashion (very different from the tall uprightness of a fir, spruce, or cypress tree)—an arboreal embodiment of the harsh, infertile conditions to which they have adapted. The Banksia flower spikes, however, often stand boldly upright. Each spike resembles a cylindrical brush, thick with at first closed flowers. Around its axis grow hundreds (if not thousands) of flowers consisting of a perianth that internally divides into four filaments and anthers, and of one long carpel (pistil)—gestures of contraction, elongation, and undifferentiated concentration (the flowers do not differentiate into separate parts such as sepals, petals, and stamens; the perianth consists of four united tepals).

Whereas conifers as gymnosperms do not produce flowers (members of the pine family [*Pinaceae*], for example, have male cones and female cones), the inflorescences of banksias (angiosperms) are the most intensified expression of the tree as a whole. Their bright yellow, red, or orange colors and uprightness make them suggestive of large, glowing candles, and express a sunlike radiance and intensity. In the *Banskia integrifolia* the whorls of leaves seem to rise up beneath its flower spikes (their cylindrical geometry is also a three-dimensional intensification of the circular formation already apparent in the whorls of leaves), as though bearing them upwards as the crowning achievement of the tree, offering them to the air, the light, the sun—as well as to pollinators including insects, birds, and marsupials.[31] The Banksia is a bold word of fire, a unity of earthly matter (wood), warmth and light. It shows a resilience to the apparent harshness of its environmental situation and asserts itself in upright, radiant flower spikes. In terms of the four classical elements, it is the union of earth and fire, the terrestrial and the solar.

If the banksia were a human person, it would express triumph in the midst of adversity. Think of Beethoven continuing to compose masterpieces even when deaf. Or imagine an elderly woman recounting her difficult biography to you. For a while your head is bowed, and your face assumes a pained grimace as you hear about the suffering she has undergone. But when you look up, you're surprised to notice an invincible radiance in her eyes, which shows that in spite of all the hardship she remains undefeated, no, more than this, that the radiance and the adversity belong together essentially, that the radiance has flourished from the soil of hardship.

Communication among Trees

While each particular tree is recognizable as an instance of a certain kind (a species, genus, family, etc.), it also expresses itself in a singular way in its dynamic, holistic response to its environmental situation. A mature oak tree standing alone in a field will have a broad crown, in contrast to an oak in a dense forest, where it forms a common canopy along with the surrounding trees.[32] The dynamic responsiveness of a tree to its shifting environmental situation can itself be regarded as an expressive language that embodies a latent form of interpretation—a wise interaction with the significant "signs" of light, temperature, moisture, wind, neighboring trees, animal activity, pollinators, and so on.[33] Moreover, the numerous symbiotic and intrinsically meaningful relationships among the flora and fauna of a forest exhibit something like a superorganism in which the diverse inhabitants depend on one another for survival and collaboratively form a larger whole, in a manner that resembles the reciprocal interdependence of the vital organs of an animal.

Drawing the boundaries of an organism always has a certain arbitrariness about it. For example, human beings require oxygen to breathe, and trees play a vital role in oxygenating the air. The arboreal release of oxygen results from the complex process of photosynthesis, which involves the intake of carbon dioxide (which we, among other creatures, exhale) and water and the capacity to draw energy from sunlight. In short, our breathing depends on trees, and trees depend on the sun. Where then does the human organism end? At the boundary of the individual's skin, at the boundary of the earth's atmosphere, at the sun . . . ?

Nevertheless, with respect to trees, drawing boundaries becomes especially problematic. Trees are not at all self-enclosed organisms with internal organs. Their organs or parts are always in dynamic relation to their surroundings: roots in relation to the soil and available water, leaves in relation to the air and light, branches and crowns in relation to those of other trees. Is the radiance of the sun inside or outside the organism of a tree? If I had to attribute a skin to trees, I would probably suggest the sky. In many respects, a particular tree resembles an organ of a greater organism (rather than an organism unto itself): the superorganism of the forest and even of the entire earth together with the solar system in its terrestrial significance—in the alternation of day and night, the cycle of seasons, and so on. There is an ecstatic openness in the form of existence which is a tree.[34]

The work of ecologists in recent decades has illustrated the extent to which organisms are mutually dependent on one another and their environments for their survival and thriving; it has also demonstrated how the intelligence and wisdom of trees (among other plants) includes their capacities to communicate with one another and other organisms. In short, linguistic or proto-linguistic capacities of coding, sharing, and interpreting information have become evident in trees.

The wide-ranging research on arboreal intercommunication includes diverse ways in which trees communicate by means of volatile organic compounds, electrical signals, and chemical signals (among other means).[35] This communication can take place above and below the ground. Acacia trees, for example, start producing toxic, bitter tannins when giraffes or antelopes browse on them, and they release ethylene gas from their leaves that, floating to other nearby acacias, prompts them likewise to produce these tannins.[36] Giraffes—broadly aware of this dynamic interconnection—tend to feed on downwind trees. Suzanne Simard's research on the ways in which trees in a forest share nutrients and resources (carbon, nitrogen, phosphorous, water, etc.) and communicate by way of mycorrhizal networks (networks of fungal threads or mycelium) that connect their roots is an especially vivid case of subterranean arboreal communication and symbiosis.[37]

Birch trees and Douglas Firs (which share the same mycelium), for example, send carbon, nitrogen, water, and other substances to one another, in response to which trees are in need. Furthermore, a tree already suffering from a particular pest or disease can send chemical signals through the fungal network and thereby warn other trees, such that they can instigate a defensive response. At certain points in her book *Finding the Mother Tree*, Simard likens this mycorrhizal interconnectedness to a neural network.[38] Especially important to a forest ecosystem are the most mature trees, which Simard calls "Mother Trees." These have the richest mycorrhizal networks, which can be connected to hundreds of other trees, and vitally assist seedlings and saplings in their vicinity.

While I am sympathetic to notions of arboreal subjectivity, agency, character, and language, it is also important to reflect on the differences between human and arboreal communication, which the notion of a "Mother Tree" could potentially obscure rather than clarify. A particular tree as a particular (for reasons indicated above) does not have the same ontological standing as an individual human being (or as a particular animal subject) and, in turn, the level of awareness with which a tree communicates must differ from that of humans. As previously discussed (section 1), intelligent action and communication do not presuppose self-conscious awareness.

If there is an equivalent of "individuality" in the world of trees, it does not coincide with the particular as such. Despite the evident agency and embodied wisdom in the dynamic and responsive life of each tree, it makes more sense, I think, to situate arboreal individuality in the particular *as its genus or family or clade* (understood as an evolving potency rather than as a rigid category) or *in the forest as a superorganism*—in some broader dimension of being or level of organization. In light of the interconnectedness and interdependence of trees in a forest, Simard also similarly speaks of the latter as a single organism.[39]

The metaphor of a Mother Tree is fitting insofar as it reflects the notion that an older tree nurtures younger trees in a manner that resembles the features of a human mother caring for her children. (Mother Trees also privilege their own seedlings and offspring in the sharing of resources.) However, as a particular—even an especially significant one—a Mother Tree does not possess the individuality of a particular human mother.[40] Thus, the expression could be misleading in over-individualizing a particular tree and in attributing to it the equivalent of an adult-human level of self-conscious communication—only in the language of chemical signals transmitted via mycorrhizal threads (rather than in that of spoken, written, typed, or encrypted words). In addition, this tends to be implicitly reductive of our concepts of communication and language in their common application to human linguistic capacities (as most of us have an intuitive sense that trees do not communicate with the self-consciousness of a human adult). In contrast, by conceiving the language of nature (section 1 above) in such a manner that earlier evolutionary forms of life (e.g., trees) anticipate and prefigure later ones (e.g., humans) without them being collapsible into one another—and with a continuity of the Logos that runs through the whole of nature, yet attains its most liberated, individualized, and self-conscious realization in human beings (where it is most emancipated from organic formation and unconscious or semi-conscious forms of intelligent behavior)—it is possible to come to a non-reductive yet inclusive conception of language and communication in fungi, plants, animals, and humans.

Of course, the expression "Mother Tree" can, if it is treated with hermeneutic vigilance, be interpreted as a metaphor in this sense of a language of nature—as an arboreal prefiguration of parental care. Moreover, the expression "Mother Tree" is employed in a memoir aimed at a general audience; in her scientific publications Simard uses the uncontroversial term "hub trees." Nevertheless, the notion of a "Mother Tree" provides a good opportunity for reflection on the relations and differences between human subjectivity and arboreal subjectivity. Another possible expression that sits midway between the drier scientific notion of "hub trees" and the overtly anthropomorphic "Mother Trees" would be something like "Beneficent Trees"—understood as generous, vital organs of the forest. Furthermore, we could liken (following Simard's suggestion) an entire mycorrhizal network, which subterraneously connects numerous trees, to a single neural network—something like the brain of a forest.[41] These considerations are also relevant to any attempt to explicate the epistemic significance of my own poetic evocations of arboreal persons (such as the ascetic fir tree above); though it is pertinent that these poems tend to treat the particular *as an exemplar of its kind*.

The findings of pioneering ecologists and plant scientists concerning the intelligence, wisdom, and communication of trees can, I think, be interpreted in a meaningful way in the context of what I have outlined as the language of nature and the language of trees. Arboreal communication can be understood as part of the way in which trees *speak themselves* in their manner of growing, relating to their environments, and interacting with fungi, plants, animals, and other neighbors. The communication of trees—in an irreducibly arboreal fashion that corresponds to their way of being in the cosmos—anticipates and prefigures modes of language and interpretation that emerge in a self-conscious form among human beings. The advancing scientific research on plant communication at the same time extends our understanding of the extent and capacities of arboreal language and communication beyond earlier conceptions and thus expands our understanding of the language of nature.

Notes

1. Jacob Böhme, *Sämtliche Schriften*, vol. 6 (Stuttgart: Frommann-Holzboog, [1622] 1730), 7.

2. Hans-Georg Gadamer, *Truth and Method*, trans. Donald G. Marshall and Joel Weinsheimer (New York: Bloomsbury, 2013), 490.

3. The sense of "Logos" that I have in mind is delineated in the course of this chapter, but, as a preliminary indication of this sense, it can be said that being as a whole has the structure and significance of language.

4. In the interests of space, I have had to omit consideration of a further relevant sense of the language of nature, namely, the manner in which trees have already spoken themselves in human language, the manner in which the language *of trees* is also *the language* of trees. For some suggestions along these lines, see Luke Fischer, "Horse Chestnut," *The Mind of Plants*, ed. John Charles Ryan, Monica Gagliano, Patricia Vieira (Santa Fe, NM: Synergetic Press, 2021), 360–78.

5. See Owen Barfield, *Saving the Appearances: A Study in Idolatry* (Middletown, CT: Wesleyan University Press, 1988).

6. "Genesis 1:3," *The Bible: Authorized King James Version* (London: Oxford University Press, 2008), 1.

7. For a more detailed historical overview of the idea of a "language of nature," see Axel Goodbody, *Natursprache: Ein Dichtungstheoretisches Konzept der Romantik und seine Wiederaufnahme in der modernen Naturlyrik (Novalis—Eichendorff—Lehmann—Eich)* (Neumünster: Karl Wachholtz Verlag: 1984), 22–46. On the significance of a "language of nature" in Novalis (Friedrich von Hardenberg), see Goodbody, *Natursprache*, 49–103; Kristin Pfefferkorn, *Novalis: A Romantic's Theory of Language and Poetry* (New Haven, CT: Yale University Press, 1988). Böhme's concept of a *Natursprache* also bears a connection to the notion of "signatures" in Paracelsus.

8. This point bears a connection to ideas in biosemiotics about the continuities of semiotic or interpretative processes from the level of the interaction of cells, to plant and animal communication, to sublinguistic and linguistic forms of human communication. On the relevance of biosemiotics or "phytosemiosis" to plant communication, see Kate Rigby, "Art, Nature, and the Poesie of Plants in the Goethezeit: A Biosemiotic Perspective," *Goethe Yearbook* 22 (2015): 23–44. See also Wendy Wheeler, "'Tongues I'll Hang on Every Tree': Biosemiotics and the Book of Nature," *The Cambridge Companion to Literature and the Environment*, ed. Louise Westling (Cambridge: Cambridge University Press, 2014), 121–35.

9. For a phenomenological argument against metaphysical dualism and materialist monism see Luke Fischer, *The Poet as Phenomenologist: Rilke and the "New Poems"* (New York: Bloomsbury, 2015), 15–68.

10. The clear sense for the agency and wisdom of more-than-human nature in certain Indigenous cultures has also been a significant force in the movement in various countries to extend legal rights and personhood to the environment

(Mother Earth, rivers, etc.). See Alessandro Pelizzon, "Earth laws, rights of nature and legal pluralism," in *Wild Law—In Practice* (New York: Routledge, 2014), 176–90.

11. Variations of this idea can be found in Novalis, Rudolf Steiner, and Henri Bergson. Novalis articulates this idea with great concision in the following philosophical fragment: "*Thinking*, like the *blossom*, is surely nothing else but the finest *evolution* of the plastic forces—it is simply the general force of nature raised to the nth dignity." Novalis, *Notes for a Romantic Encyclopaedia: Das Allgemeine Brouillon*, trans. David W. Wood (Albany NY: SUNY Press, 2012), 189. Steiner, among other things, relates the maturation of the capacity for abstract thinking in the individual human being to the liberation of the forces of organic growth in the grown-up. Steiner writes, for example: "At the beginning of human life on earth—most clearly so during the embryonic period—the forces of the etheric body [i.e., life forces] act as powers of configuration and growth. As life progresses, a part of these forces becomes emancipated from activity in configuration and growth and is transformed into powers of thought . . . It is of the greatest importance to know that ordinary human powers of thought are refined powers of configuration and growth. A spiritual principle reveals itself in the configuration and growth of the human organism." Rudolf Steiner and Ita Wegman, *Extending Practical Medicine*, trans. A. R. Meuss (London: Rudolf Steiner Press, 1996), 6. Bergson regards the human intellect as an emancipation of consciousness from instinct and life, which he also connects to the human alienation from nature. Henri Bergson, *Creative Evolution*, trans. Arthur Mitchell (Mineola, NY: Dover Publications, 1998).

12. Maurice Merleau-Ponty, *Phenomenology of Perception*, trans. Donald A. Landes (New York: Routledge, 2012), 193.

13. The examples of butterflies and bees are partly indebted to Henri Bergson. Bergson, *Creative Evolution*, 140–41. The continuities between organic formation and animal behavior are also a key theme of Merleau-Ponty's lecture course on nature. Maurice Merleau-Ponty, *Nature: Course Notes from the Collège de France*, trans. Robert Vallier (Evanston, IL: Northwestern University Press: 2003).

14. See, for example, Luke Fischer, "A Poetic Phenomenology of the Seasons," *The Seasons: Philosophical, Literary, and Environmental Perspectives* (Albany, NY: SUNY Press, 2021), ed. Luke Fischer and David Macauley (Albany, NY: SUNY Press, 2021), 69–92.

15. The phrase "the logos-structure of the world" is indebted to the title of the following book: George Kühlewind, *The Logos-Structure of the World*, trans. Friedemann-Eckart Schwarzkopf (Great Barrington, MA: Lindisfarne Books, 1992).

16. This not only has to do with "plant blindness" (our tendency to overlook plants) but also with our lack of a conception of a language of trees. On "plant blindness" see J. H. Wandersee and E. E. Schussler, "Preventing Plant Blindness," *The American Biology Teacher* 61 (1999): 82–86.

17. Novalis writes in a fragment: "Trees seem the most noble among all plants, because their countless individuals only so indirectly still depend on the soil and are, as it were, already plants on plants." Novalis, *Novalis Schriften,* part 2/vol. 2, ed. Ernst Heilborn (Berlin: De Gruyter, 2018, 649), 649; my translation. In his agricultural lecture course, Rudolf Steiner presents a picture of the trunk as raised up earth and as an expression of the soil's living qualities. Rudolf Steiner, *Agriculture Course: The Birth of the Biodynamic Method,* trans. George Adams (Forest Row: Rudolf Steiner Press, 2004), Lecture 4 (June 12, 1924), 65–86. This notion has been explored in detail by various Goethean scientists.

18. What I call "intensive" understanding in this chapter is closely connected to what Goethe calls "intuitive judgment" (*anschauende Urteilskraft*). See Luke Fischer, "Goethe contra Hegel: The Question of the End of Art," *Goethe Yearbook* 18 (2011): 130–31; Eckart Förster, "Goethe and the 'Auge des Geistes,' " *Deutsche Vierteljahrsschrift für Literaturwissenschaft und Geistesgeschichte* 75, no. 1 (2001): 87–101. On the significance of artistic modes of understanding for scientific inquiry, see Dalia Nassar, *Romantic Empiricism: Nature, Art, and Ecology from Herder to Humboldt* (New York: Oxford University Press, 2022); Nigel Hoffmann, *Goethe's Science of Living Form* (Ghent, NY: Adonis Press, 2013).

19. Elsewhere—drawing on the works of Goethe and Merleau-Ponty—I have referred to such a comprehension of music, art, and other phenomena, in which sensible appearances mediate and become transparent to a non-sensible, differentiated unity of meaning, as "sensible ideas." See Fischer, "A Poetic Phenomenology of the Seasons." On the connection between music and biological form, see Frederick Amrine, "The Music of the Organism: Uexküll, Merleau-Ponty, Zuckerkandl, and Deleuze as Goethean Ecologists in Search of a New Paradigm," *Goethe Yearbook* 22 (2015): 45–72.

20. Martin Buber, *I and Thou,* trans. Ronald Gregor Smith (London: Bloomsbury, 2013), 6; translation altered.

21. Goethean science is a rich tradition of holistic, phenomenological scientific inquiry (deserving of far wider attention), which is inspired by the example of the scientific studies (on comparative morphology and optics) of the great German poet J. W. von Goethe as well as by the late nineteenth- and early twentieth-century writings of Rudolf Steiner, which build on Goethe's approach. A good entry point for readers unfamiliar with Goethean science is the volume of essays, *Goethe's Way of Science: A Phenomenology of Nature,* ed. David Seamon and Arthur Zajonc (Albany, NY: SUNY Press, 1998). On Goethe's broad significance for contemporary environmental thought, see Luke Fischer and Dalia Nassar, "Introduction: Goethe and Environmentalism," *Goethe Yearbook* 22 (2015): 3–22. The above-mentioned course in Goethean science took place at the Nature Institute in Ghent, New York, and was led by Craig Holdrege.

22. Martin Buber, *I and Thou,* 6. By "imagination," I am here referring to the research methodology of Goethean science, which involves precisely

imagining, for example, the development of a tree from seed, to seedling, to sapling, to mature tree, and so on. This leads to a more intimate understanding of the subject of research.

23. The image of a butterfly is also used in my poem "Five Glances," *A Personal History of Vision* (Crawley, WA: UWAP, 2017), 14.

24. On the gestural relations between the leaf surfaces and morphology, on the one hand, and the irregularly spaced bunching of oak leaves, on the other—though with specific regard to *Quercus alba*—see Craig Holdrege, "Phenomenon Illuminates Phenomenon: White Oak and Sugar Maple," *In Context 26* (Fall 2011): 14–18. On *Quercus robur* (common oak), see Jan Albert Rispens, *Bäume sprechen lassen: Eine Exkursion in die vielfältigen Erscheinungsformen der mitteleuropäischen Baumwelt* (Stuttgart: SchneiderEditionen, 2019), 42–73.

25. See Johann Wolfgang von Goethe, *The Metamorphosis of Plants*, trans. Douglas Miller (Cambridge, MA: The MIT Press, 2009).

26. See Luke Fischer, "Horse Chestnut," *The Mind of Plants: Narratives of Vegetal Intelligence*.

27. On the difference between the "youthful" mood of a broad-leafed forest and the "reflective," serious, primeval mood of a coniferous forest, see Gerbert Grohmann, *Die Pflanze*, vol. 1 (Stuttgart: Verlag Freies Geistesleben, 1959), 119. The book is also available in English translation.

28. This poem appears in the anthology *Canto Planetario* (Mexico: Ayame Editorial).

29. Luke Fischer, "Fir," *A Personal History of Vision*, 52.

30. Nigel Hoffmann, "The Unity of Science and Art: Goethean Phenomenology as a New Ecological Discipline," *Goethe's Way of Science*, 165.

31. For a rich and detailed Goethean study of *Banksia integrifolia*, see Hoffmann, "The Unity of Science and Art: Goethean Phenomenology as a New Ecological Discipline," 147–67.

32. In his book *Thinking Like a Plant*, Craig Holdrege gives various examples of how trees dynamically respond as a whole (cohesively and in all their parts) to their environmental situation. Craig Holdrege, *Thinking Like a Plant: A Living Science for Life* (Great Barrington, MA: Lindisfarne Books, 2013), chapter 4.

33. See, for example, Monica Gagliano's discussion of the significant continuities between the language of human gestures and the gestures of plants in "Breaking the Silence: Green Mudras and the Faculty of Language in Plants," *The Language of Plants: Science, Philosophy, Literature*, ed. Monica Gagliano, John C. Ryan, Patricia Vieira (Minneapolis: University of Minnesota Press, 2017), 84–100. See also Kate Rigby, "Art, Nature, and the Poesie of Plants in the Goethezeit: A Biosemiotic Perspective."

34. In a relevant discussion, Marder celebrates the openness of the plant to the other in contrast to Hegel's assessment of the absence of animal self-sufficiency in plants as a relative deficiency. Marder, *Plant-Thinking*, 67–74. However, while I

find Marder's book original and illuminating, I disagree with his specific denial of wholeness or unity to plants in his discussion of Goethe's theory of plant metamorphosis (*Plant-Thinking*, 81–90). Like other postmodern thinkers, Marder tends to emphasize difference at the expense of any unity and only manages to conceive the latter as an oppressive totality that subordinates its parts or particulars. In contrast, the intensive unity, of which Goethe speaks, overcomes all opposition between unity and difference, the one and the many, such that the unity is found by way of the differentiations, the one is found by way of the many, the theme is its variations, and the part, in a synecdochic logic, is the whole. For an in-depth discussion of Goethean wholeness, see Henri Bortoft, *The Wholeness of Nature: Goethe's Way Toward a Science of Conscious Participation in Nature* (Great Barrington, MA: Lindisfarne Books, 1996).

35. For an multidisciplinary overview of diverse research on the communication of plants, see the volume of essays *The Language of Plants*.

36. This phenomenon has caused the death of antelopes. Wouter van Hoven, "*Mortalities in Kudu (Tragelaphus Strepsiceros) Populations Related to Chemical Defence in Trees*," *Journal of African Zoology* 105, no. 2 (1991): 141–45.

37. See Suzanne Simard, *Finding the Mother Tree: Discovering the Wisdom of the Forest* (New York: Vintage Books, 2022).

38. Simard, *Finding the Mother Tree*, 5, 228–29.

39. See Suzanne Simard's talk "How Trees Talk to Each Other," TED Summit (2016). Accessed November 3, 2002: https://mothertreeproject.org/about-mother-trees/resources

40. In *Finding the Mother Tree*, Simard draws strong ties between her relationship as a mother to her children and the role of "Mother Trees" in the forest.

41. Various contemporary scientists have likened aspects of trees to a human or animal brain and there is a new field of plant physiology known as "plant neurobiology." For an overview, see Monica Gagliano, John C. Ryan, Patricia Vieira, "Introduction," *The Language of Plants*, vii–xxxiv. Charles Darwin already likened the sensitivity and movement of root tips to a brain (see Matthew Hall, *Plants as Persons: A Philosophical Botany* [Albany, NY: SUNY Press, 2011], 138–41). A more general association of plant roots with the head or brain has a long history. Plato, in the *Timaeus*, describes the human being as an upside down plant whose head is rooted in the heavens, with the implicit, but undeveloped, analogue of the roots of plants being their head (cf. Marder, *Plant-Thinking*, 56–57). In the early twentieth century Steiner elaborated detailed ontological analogies between plants and humans (including their significance for farming, nutrition and medicine), with the latter represented as the inversion of the former. See, for example, Rudolf Steiner, *The Foundations of Esotericism*, trans. Vera and Judith Compton-Burnett (London: Rudolf Steiner Press, 2019), Lecture 3 (28 September, 1905), 16–23.

4

The Silence of Primeval Forests

DANIEL O'DEA BRADLEY

Silence is one of the most striking and characteristic experiences of many northern conifer forests. This is particularly true of forests dominated by Coast Redwood, Western Hemlock, and Western Red Cedar. These forests grow in conditions with enough moisture for the trees to create a thick canopy through which little light can penetrate. This creates an open, park-like understory dotted with ferns and mosses that is among the most beautiful and inviting of all places on Earth. There is a paradoxical nature to this inviting character, however, for the quietness and shade of these rich, dark green spaces and the luxuriousness of their vegetal excesses is predicated on a type of plant life starkly lacking in edible foodstuffs. These trees present us with a very quiet world without the busyness or noisy recreation that is natural to us as social, rational animals. We thereby encounter in these woods a great welcome but also a deep foreignness.

In this chapter, I draw on our understanding of conifer ecology and the philosophy of Luce Irigaray to examine the ways that the beauty of these quiet, dark forests can be an encounter with vegetal-being in its own right and as such can teach us important truths that have often been neglected by Modern philosophy and the contemporary culture more widely. It is true that we have begun to overcome the Enlightenment's excessive regard for light and its concomitant disregard for the nonvisual. Thus, over the last fifty years, we have paid explicit attention to truths that emerge from experiences such as that of listening in the dark to the voice of the other. However, postmodern attention to the aural has often only reinforced a hostility to silence and thereby remains mired in some of the limitations of the modern project. This is unfortunate, for in other traditions, silence is regarded as crucial for opening contemplation of the deepest philosophical and spiritual truths. The redwood/hemlock/cedar forests I describe here are deeply appealing in their own right and also help us reintegrate something of these more positive approaches to silence into our modern sensibility.

The chapter is divided into three sections, each of which can be read independently: (1) a cultural hermeneutic that critiques the modern prejudice against darkness and silence from which postmodernity has not been able to escape fully. (2) an introduction to Luce Irigaray as a potential entry into a more positive appraisal of the quiet and opaque aspects of materiality. (3) an eco-phenomenological investigation of the redwood and hemlock-cedar forests of the American Northwest. For readers most interested in trees, it may seem an excessively long preparation for our entry into the woods. But I am claiming that a thoughtful experience of the forest will yield rich truths that remain inaccessible to the dominant strands of modern and postmodern culture. This is a strong claim requiring that we see the deficiencies of our contemporary intellectual period in at least some depth in order to appreciate what is so special about the truth of the forest. However, for those uninterested in this dialectical preparation, please jump directly to section 3.

Modernity's Refusal of Silence and Darkness

Very little about trees as trees can be got into a play.[1]

—J. R. R. Tolkien

"Silence" can be experienced in a myriad of ways, but for human beings perhaps its primary meaning is constituted by the lack—one could even say the foreclosure—of speech. The quietness of silence is thus most fundamentally the quieting of human speech. This explains why there can be something akin to silence in the roaring of a mountain stream or the crash of ocean waves. While they are certainly audible, noises such as the repetitive movements of water carry low levels of intelligibility in most contexts,² which is why people can fall asleep to them. The great noisiness of human existence is that of words. In fact, reading text messages and emails may technically be silent but they are some of the noisiest of all our activities.

As such (as the absence of speech), silence is an ambiguous way of being oriented towards reality. Certainly, silence can be the descent into duplicity, treachery, disloyalty, and a kind of inhuman animality of which only a rational animal—a being with speech that fails to use it—is capable. On the other hand, silence has been a crucial part of some of my most significant and beautiful experiences, including that of walking in a northwestern coniferous forest. This is not some quirk of my personality, and a quick look at the great spiritual traditions of human history reveals that they almost uniformly praise silence as a necessary aspect of the search for truth. And yet the contemporary culture of Western philosophy seems able to recognize only the negative and dangerous possibilities in silence.

This remains true even as our critiques of the excesses of modernity have opened us to a re-evaluation of the potential goodness that lies beyond the circle of light. It is now commonly accepted that over-privileging ocular metaphors in our search for truth is a natural temptation for beings for whom sight is such a dominant sense. We know the technical role that "form" (Gr. *Eidos*: shape, that which is seen at a glance) plays for Plato. Further, we know that this tendency became even more unbalanced and unfettered in the period of high-modernity, an epoch self-consciously dedicated to the banishment of darkness. This *Enlightenment* is tied intellectually to the repudiation of metaphysics, culturally to a prejudice against premodern modes of thought, and sociologically to a valorization of autonomy as the highest good. Even in his "pre-critical" period, Kant notes that metaphysics is "a dark ocean without shore or lighthouse."³ As the high priest of Modernity, he will later tie that darkness to the childishness and backwardness of premodern peoples.⁴ He begins his essay "What is Enlightenment?" by chiding the mass of humanity for a "laziness and cowardice" that has kept them mired throughout history in "self-caused immaturity," and left them as "dumb" and "placid" as domestic cattle. From the quiet and the dark of the past, the courage and work ethic of his Germanic contemporaries will soon allow humanity to emerge into the untainted light of rational discourse.

Now, of course, over the last number of decades we have become highly aware of the ways that this equation of truth with the pure brilliance of enlightenment carries its own characteristic tendencies toward illusion, violence, and injustice. And we now find it chilling that Kant ends his essay by justifying the use of violence by an Enlightened despot against the benighted masses; "But only the man, who is himself enlightened, *who is not afraid of shadows*, and who commands at the same time a well-disciplined and numerous army as guarantor of public peace—only he can say what [the sovereign of] a free state cannot dare to say: 'Argue as much as you like, and about what you like, but obey!' "[5] For Kant, we may yap in the dark until the cows come home, as long as that does not interfere with the power of a political order imperturbably grounded in Enlightenment principles.[6]

In the process of challenging this Enlightenment hubris, however, our metaphors have often merely switched from critiquing that which remains in the dark to critiquing that which remains underground—the subterranean forces at work buried within the structures that unconsciously shape our world in the service of certain interests and distorted desires. In other words, our contemporary culture is marked by an attunement to the violence of the gaze and the remedy of listening to the word of the other. We may sometimes exaggerate the difference between Greek specularity and Hebraic aurality, but there is a deep truth that must be recalled to philosophy from outside of its own tradition. This is the truth that while the desire for comprehension is beautiful and good, it carries a characteristic temptation, which is possession through knowing; as etymology reminds us, *comprehendere* originally meant "lay hold of, capture, seize, accost."

For this reason, Levinas will always remain within the canon. Even if he lacks the subtlety or virtuosic skill of Derrida, he remains the more fundamental thinker of the two. In a remarkable few pages at the beginning of *Totality and Infinity*, Levinas provides a compelling critique of the Enlightenment link between luminosity, knowledge, and autonomy precisely on the basis of a hermeneutics of suspicion that has its progenitors in Freud and particularly in Marx. As Levinas writes, "theory designates comprehension—the *logos* of being—that is, a way of approaching the known being such that its alterity with regard to the knowing being vanishes. The process of cognition is at this stage identified with the freedom of the knowing being encountering nothing which, other with respect to it, could limit it."[7]

Levinas's thought, however, goes beyond the critique of ideology and the cultivation of critical consciousness and rises to the level of philosophy proper. We see this in the way that he is not satisfied by the attempt of phenomenology to overcome alienation. Levinas shares with phenomenology a deep hunger for intimacy with something outside the self, but he is able to see the kinship of phenomenology with high Modernity precisely on the technical philosophical question of horizon. He is attuned to this kinship by way of a cultural hermeneutic that focuses on the shared use of the language of light. Levinas is correct to say that "since Husserl the whole of phenomenology is the promotion of the idea of *horizon*, which for it plays a role equivalent to that of the *concept* in classical idealism." He is, of course, aware that the whole impulse of phenomenology is to reject the modern imperialism of the concept by returning to the 'things themselves' and the ways that things always exceed the immanence of abstract intelligibility. But Levinas's great insight is to recognize the continuity of "horizon" and "concept"—a continuity revealed by his unrelenting hermeneutic of light:

> that which guarantees the independence and the extraneity of the existent [in phenomenology]—is a *phosphorescence*, a *luminosity*, a generous *effulgence*. The existing of an existent is converted into intelligibility; its independence is a surrender in *radiation*. To broach an existent from Being is simultaneously to let it be and to comprehend it. Reason seizes upon an existent through the void and nothingness of existing—wholly *light* and *phosphorescence*. Approached from Being, from the *luminous horizon* where it has a *silhouette*, but has lost its face . . .[8]

Levinas's answer to the conspiratorial pact between imperialism and enlightenment/phenomenology is to listen to the voice of the other: "Existents [as opposed to beings] are both involved in being and personal, called upon to answer at their trial and consequently already adult—but, for that very reason, existents that can speak rather than lending their appearance to an anonymous utterance of history. Peace is produced as this aptitude for speech. The eschatological vision breaks with the totality of wars and empires in which one does not speak."[9] Later he will say, "the relation between the same and the other . . . is language" or again "the relation between same and other . . . is primordially enacted as conversation."[10]

There is much that is true in Levinas's claim here. Only through attention to speech are we able to develop a personalism in philosophy that yields otherwise unavailable understanding of reality and ourselves. Further, I think there is something true about the claim that this insight is not native to Greek philosophy but comes from Judaism and the Afro-Asiatic linguistic traditions from which the Semitic world springs. Nonetheless, this cannot be the end of our cultural-historical hermeneutic. Levinas's philosophy—and our intellectual culture more widely—is deeply marred by a continuing intellectual progressivism he inherits from the Enlightenment, which sees history, in a very prejudicial way, as a one-directional march from superstition and slavery to modernity, civilization, and peace. Levinas accepts that we move from the darkness of savagery to the Enlightenment of science and technology, which sets us free from idolatry and the paganism of local gods. But he sees this as an insufficient and merely preparatory development. Finally, for Levinas, we are to progress beyond the Enlightenment to a new stage in which the solipsistic brilliance of modernity is salved by the call of the other, modernity's adolescent valorization of autonomy thereby being superseded by the maturity of justice.

This fundamental and underlying framework of his thinking sets the stage for those who follow him, such as Derrida, to continue to move away from phenomenology (and back to Kant) in favor of an increasingly abstract transcendentalism and rigid formalism, by which *philosophically* truth is severed from the concrete embodied world, thereby foreclosing an epistemology oriented toward sensuous experience, and *religiously* we re-establish the modern disregard for materiality, thereby foreclosing the possibility for the sacramental and liturgical.[11] What is it that we actually encounter in dialogue with the other? Levinas tells us: "its formal characteristic, *to be other*, makes up its *content*."[12]

At its worst Platonic idealism sets us apart from the world in the pursuit of a purely theoretical vision, so that there is nothing to feel or to smell. But after Levinas there remains nothing even to see. Thus, Marion can write:

> What do we look at in the face of the other person? Not his or her mouth, nevertheless more expressive of the intentions than other parts of the body, but their eyes—or more exactly the empty pupils of the person's eyes, their black holes open on the somber ocular hollow. In other words, in the face we fix on the sole place where precisely nothing can be seen. Thus, in the face of the other person we see precisely the point at which all visible spectacle happens to be impossible, where *there is nothing to see, where intuition can give nothing [of the] visible*.[13]

The epitome of this pure formalism in which there is nothing to see or to feel is *The Erotic Phenomenon*, which is one of the most mistitled books of all time, for in it we are presented with little of the erotic and no phenomena at all. The result is an axiology which requires human intervention to achieve the first glimmer of goodness. As Marion explains in *The Crossing of the Visible*, the painter goes down to hell to come back with a monster, "*monstrum*, the presentable par excellence, the brute unseen, the miracle."[14]

Over the last number of decades, other traditions of philosophy less directly indebted to Levinas have also challenged the excesses of our Enlightenment heritage by incorporating aurality and a more positive role for experiences of the dark. In "Night and Shadows: The Space and Place of Darkness,"[15] David Macauley gives a rich summary of many of the most important critiques of ocular-centrism that mark our postmodern sensibility, and he notes that already one hundred years ago Bachelard had called for a "metaphysics of night."[16] But we have not yet incorporated a similarly renewed appreciation for that which does not rise to speech. We have no metaphysics of silence.

For the most part, our critique of the ocular has still given us no more than an attunement to the voice that calls in the dark. Certainly for Levinas, but in the dominant culture more widely, silence is still irrevocably and absolutely tied to the brutish and the violent—to the animal, the pagan, and the savage. These are pejorative terms, and they indicate a Modern Western bigotry that we would do well to overcome. Our motivation to do this should include reasons of impersonal and abstract justice. But the problem goes beyond the violation of a legalistic moralism, for it produces not only a justification for the mistreatment of the nonmodern "other," it also generates a deep alienation within the lived experience of those who adopt this intellectual prejudice. It is not a coincidence that our word *pagan* comes from the Latin *paganus*, an adjective to describe anything "rural or from the countryside." Similarly, our word *savage* comes from the Latin *silva*: "a woods, forest, or orchard." In much of contemporary society and philosophy, we see a deep disconnect between the urban elites and those disregarded people and places in the rural hinterland. Through the pioneering work of Ulrich Grober and its development by Cristina Bonfiglioli and others,[17] we now know that changes in the axiological status of the forest played a significant role in the rise of the entire Modern project. Timber shortages in sixteenth- and seventeenth-century Europe led bureaucrats and other urban thinkers to see trees merely as resources to be managed as efficiently as possible, and this contributed as much as Galilean physics to a mechanistic/resource view of the natural world. City trees and urban parks and gardens are among the most wonderful things in the world. But leaving the city to spend time among the trees in the *sylvan-savage* silence of a mountain forest and in the quiet towns of rural people who love them, the *pagani*, will open vast new areas for philosophers to explore.[18]

The current tagline for the *Washington Post* is "Democracy dies in Darkness," and we often hear that transparency in politics and social life is always a good thing, that "sunshine is the best disinfectant." Thus, outside the Academy, our wider culture has not yet fully integrated the postmodern rehabilitation of darkness, but it clearly shares the valorization of noisiness in the presumption that the rupture of silence by the spoken word is *always* a good thing. We are so immersed in the idea that for healthy relationships and personal growth *everything* should incessantly and without reserve be voiced that it seems obvious to many people. Recently we have become bombarded with the slogan, "If you see something, say something."[19] In the arts, this is manifest in our preference for drama as the exemplary genre. Plays are the ideal form for exploring human dialogue, but as Tolkien pointedly notes, "very little about trees as trees can be got into a play."[20]

The result is a noisy, yappy culture increasingly cut off from the body and the natural world, which are seen as nothing more than raw resources for pleasure or the projects of the will. This culture is not only aesthetically unappealing, it also has drastically reduced the considerations available for our moral decision making. As just one example, consider the tools at our disposal for evaluating a sexual encounter. What criteria can we use? The only ones available are purely formal and include no consideration of the nature of the act or its concrete context. Even more shockingly, we have no moral resources to include any consideration of the consequences. As long as our partner said "yes" loud enough for a witness to hear, there are no more questions to ask. A person's life can be ruined by the result of the encounter, but we have no way of taking that into account in our moral evaluation.

In other words, it is increasingly obvious that we must move beyond our modern formalism and reestablish an ethics of the body. To be clear, I have no interest in flipping the modern axiological binary of culture-nature. I do not advocate any form of irrationalism, and I am as happy to put "nature" in scare quotes as anyone else. I value critiques that bring to light the violence and illusion that infect the dark and subterranean aspects of our lives, and I agree that consent must remain a central category in social ethics. Thus, hermeneutics, critical consciousness, and a focus on methodology must continue to play an important role in any compelling philosophy. But how can we incorporate these insights into a philosophical project that makes a central place for silence, for touch, for smell, and ultimately for the sacredness of material things? This is particularly important for our reflection on trees, for they have often been privileged examples of sacred material beings in so many premodern societies.

Luce Irigaray

> From my early infancy, the vegetal world has been my favorite dwelling.[21]
>
> —Luce Irigaray and Michael Marder, *Through Vegetal Being*

Luce Irigaray offers us a critical but hopeful way into the quiet, opaque richness of the material world in which trees play such a prominent role on Earth. Irigaray is certainly not unaware of the fact that silence can be deadly. Being silenced can be a grave injustice, and it is a characteristic part of the patriarchal oppression of women. In fact, for Irigaray silence is part of the definition of patriarchy, which she calls "a new logical order that censures women's speech, gradually making it inaudible."[22] As such, a central aspect of feminism includes cultivating ways for women to "emerge from silence and subjugation."[23] Further, being silenced is not only a sociological or political injustice. It is an ontological problem that opens the most fundamental question of what it means to be a human being. This is partly for the reasons that concern Levinas and other postmodern and postcolonial thinking. In a patriarchal order women can make sounds and use words, but that only masks a deadening silence that exists on the ontological order. As Irigaray explains, under the conditions of modernity: "discourse designates men as subjects . . . [while] the world as inanimate object belongs to the universe of the other. Women thus maintain a relationship to the real environment, but they don't subjectivize it as their own. They remain the locus for the experience of concrete reality, but they leave the matter of its structuration to the other."[24] Persons to which this happens lose their subjectivity and fall not into an animal existence, but far below into the deadening silence of the inorganic. "They are deprived of a subjective order by which they can unify their corporeal vitality. A body can be sound only if it has a personal or spiritual objective, keeping it together or bringing it to life."[25]

Yet, while Irigaray recognizes the dangers of silence, she is also one of the most forceful critics of the modern polemic against silence, for she sees that tendency as a part of an epochal drive to devalue anything that does not fit within the dominant forms of subjectivity. For this reason, despite its explicit promise as a way to overcome alienation and cultivate relation, the postmodern sensitivity to language remains stuck within modern solipsism. As Irigaray argues, "to say that the heart of proximity belongs to speech comes down to having already removed it from its carnal touching." By way of this over-emphasis on speech that denies a silent intimacy, "each is thus separated from oneself, and from the other."[26] The result is our inability to escape the ongoing alienation that had motivated our turn to language in the first place. Thus, after the postmodern turn, our solipsism is twofold. Not only is our time marked by an upswell of feelings of isolation from the non-human world, but we also continue to find ourselves cut off from other human beings as well. But even worse, our newfound attempts to heal our relation with the other creatures often seems only to exacerbate the divisions within humanity itself.

Irigaray's alternative solution requires a new (and culturally radical) cultivation of silence. This silence does not eradicate the difference between speaking and nonspeaking beings, so the distinctiveness of humanity remains a real one. For human beings, silence will be a task rather than an initial condition, and it will always contain a preparatory element as an opening onto new forms of spoken relationships. Nonetheless, silence has its own unique role as a path to truth that cannot be ignored without truncating our solidarity with each other and with non-human beings:

> Silence safeguards things and the other in their withdrawal—their integrity, their virginity. It lets them be before any monstration, any appearing: left to their will, their growth. The veil of mystery, which then shields them, shelters them in their innocence. It is different from that veil which re-covers them because of their submission, as a thing and as an other, to a language that has always already veiled them. In the first case, the veil is woven of the air in which every living being is born, lives, grows. In the second case, the veil is already an

artifice that submits every living being to the same—dwelling and being—preventing it from unfolding in accordance with its roots. . . . If some permanence exists, it is in part, fluid: it safeguards, and even gives, silence.[27]

To be clear, this is neither quietism nor irrationalism. Rather Irigaray wants us to be attentive to the ways that silent materiality and yappy consciousness are not totally foreign to each other, but rather interweave. She tells us that women's struggles and a flourishing human culture more widely "must be rooted in respect for life and culture and with the continuous passage of the natural into the cultural, the spiritual into the natural."[28] And she says we thrive when language is not purely abstract, fiduciary, and fungible, but remains partly figurative, "concrete, close, related to what is natural, to perceptible forms."[29]

It is not that the material substrate of our experience *determines* our sensibility and culture. She is not an essentialist. But she is not a constructivist either, as if matter is purely passive and inert just waiting to be imprinted upon by our will, such that prior to human consciousness and language the material world is marked merely by disorder and lack of differentiation—the monstrous, brute unseen. What she sees that is missed in most recent philosophy and late-modern culture is that we do not need spoken or written language in order to establish alterity or relationship. A privileged example that she notes is the way that the differentiation between the mother's self and the other of the child is in place well before this difference is given meaning in and by language.[30] Materiality already has a quiet *logos* that allows for differentiation, order, and being without the noisiness of abstract, symbolic speech acts. Thus, the forms this takes in childbirth, she says, "don't necessarily accord only with those our cultural imaginary relays: loss of paradise, traumatizing expulsion, etc."[31]

To cultivate silence is not merely to enter the irrational but to open an encounter with the deep material wellsprings both of oneself and the other. This is why silence can yield such intimacy. In regard to one's self, one's own culture, and one's own community, this involves a kind of genetic phenomenology by which we re-traverse the emergence of spirit and forms of thought out of materiality. Irigaray recognizes that we cannot bring to consciousness the entire process by which the intelligibility of things comes to be experienced in this or that particular way. Thus, she accepts that our truths are marked by a certain opaqueness and contingency;

nonetheless, she also argues that a great deal of contemporary alienation can be overcome by doing the work to show how present meanings are not merely arbitrary, but rather emerge temporally out of a long cultural and personal intimacy with the non-human world. As Irigaray writes: "It is impossible for each individual to re-create the whole of History. But I do think that any individual, a woman or a man, can and must recreate her or his personal and collective history. For this to be accomplished everyone's body and opinions must be respected. Everyone should be able to be aware of her or his obligations. No one ought to believe."[32] The polemic against belief, here, is directed against the alienating rationalism that is the product of the enlightened despotism of Kant and the high modernity he represents. Kant's target was the ungrounded but earthly authority of human tradition. Irigaray's target is the grounded, but unearthly forms of bureaucratic rationalism that govern our lives in ways that are justified by the efficiencies produced by rigorous methods but that remain indifferent to the organic and cultural histories of our lived experience.[33]

Because of the fundamental place that Irigaray gives to silence, it is natural that there should be a substantial body of research in the secondary literature on this topic. Irigaray herself puts reflection on silence to use in many more places than I could ever explicate here,[34] but I want to touch briefly on two applications she mentions as a final preparation before we enter the woods. The first is a brief and rather humorous response she writes in the 1980s to a young PhD student interested in the way AIDS could change male sexuality. In her reply, she suggests that men could progress intellectually more from learning to be quiet than from any disease. Most men, she says, "are only finally satisfied when they can play about with a noisy machine in front of others . . . its sonorous performance conveying the proof of their sexual power." But this is only a dissipation of sexual energy in ways that diminish rather than cultivate strong sexual relationships: "Today, sophisticated sexual practice ought to be distinguishable from the use of a weapon, from noisy exhibitionism, from speaking arrogantly, claiming to be right, using theory in a bellicose way, etc. Our sexual liberations should imperceptibly change our sociocultural environment. Machines handled by men ought not to make more noise than those tolerated in a woman's hands."[35] Her appeal to male quietness is perhaps nowhere more applicable than to the forests of the American West, where snowmobiles, side-by-sides, RVs with generators, hikers with battery-powered speakers and other machines make an increasingly pervasive din.

The second short application of silence in Irigaray's work has to do with contemporary art. For her, painting should be a natural place to look for an encounter with the quietness of the material world. But as Irigaray explains, when she examines the work of women artists, she finds something that fails to live up to the promise of the medium. "Having wanted to contemplate beauty created by women, I found myself faced instead with distress, suffering, irritation, sometimes ugliness." She goes on to explain that contemporary art functions in this way as a manner of breaking an imposed and oppressive silence. She says that for too long women "have been obliged to keep quiet about what they experience and have often converted these unarticulated sufferings into physical symptoms: mutism, paralysis, etc. Daring to manifest individual and collective pain publicly has a therapeutic effect, bringing relief to the body."[36]

While important, the value of this loud, wordy painting is merely therapeutic, and we can hope that it will help to prepare for what art can do best, which is creating a quiet, material beauty. Irigaray continues, "in breaking out of our formal prisons we may discover what flesh we have left. I think *color is what is left of life without forms*, beyond truths or beliefs."[37] Our worry about snowmobiles and jet skis reminds us that even in the heart of the forest, we are never free from sociopolitical tensions and questions of justice and that the ways we enter the forest are already shaped by the formation of our character. Irigaray's discussion of loud and quiet painting reminds us that philosophical reflection must be oriented toward the ethico-political but also that it must not allow this to become an exclusive focus that prohibits deeper ontological questions from being raised as well. It should be self-evident that forest ecology raises sociopolitical questions, but it should be equally obvious to those who have experienced them that they open ontological questions as well. As we enter the redwood or cedar-hemlock forest, we easily and naturally enter the ontological world as described by Irigaray, a world not dominated by form, but saturated in green.

Redwood/Cedar-Hemlock Forests

The clearest way into the universe is through a forest.[38]

—John Muir, *John of the Mountains*

Trees are among the most extraordinary beings in the cosmos, and they have radically transformed our planet by giving life great new extension both temporally and spatially. The simplest and most evolutionarily ancient plants are algae that live only for a few days or weeks. By contrast, many species of trees have evolved to live for over a thousand years. Even more dramatically, while life can thrive in the three dimensions of an environment constituted by water, space is a much greater problem on land where life remains mostly bound to a two-dimensional surface. Some birds and insects and a few mammals can fly through the air, but a gaseous atmosphere provides only temporary passage for life—and even the best flyers must eventually "land." Bacterial and algal films clinging to soil and rock can extend only a few millionths of a meter above the surface of the earth. Trees open radically new dimensions by extending an enduring dwelling for life hundreds of feet above the surface of the earth and pushing roots deep into the soil to form great mycorrhizal networks that link forests together below the surface.

If all trees provoke wonder and delight and contribute so importantly to the ontology of life on earth, I want to speak about an association of trees that create a particular kind of reality: the lush temperate forests of western North America, constituted by redwood, cedar, and hemlock trees. These trees sustain a special and remarkably beautiful type of forest that runs in a narrow and almost unbroken band along the Pacific Ocean from the Alexander Archipelago of Southeast Alaska to the Santa Lucia Mountains of California. Further inland (east of the Cascade Mountains), these forests are not nearly as dominant, but they do occupy favorable places in the valleys and north or east facing slopes of the Selkirk Mountains and northwestern Rockies. Unlike many other types of conifer, redwoods, cedars, and hemlock trees form a dense forest canopy that blocks much of the sunlight from reaching the forest floor, and this creates a humid understory in which every inch of ground and much of the tree trunks are covered in delicate herbs, mosses, ferns, and lichens. The dark-green filtered light and emerald-green surfaces make these forests some of the most beautiful places on earth, and the open understory, quiet stillness, and soft moss underfoot make them some of the most inviting. Thus, we are drawn to these forests with an irresistible pull, and yet there is very little that is edible here—for humans or any other animals—and that makes them dauntingly forbidding as well. I want to argue that these characteristics provide a unique opportunity for human beings to experience a form of vegetal life that is deeply foreign to our own and yet that is also, in its beauty and majesty, an invitation to a relationship that opens an understanding of truth quite different from that of the Moderns, for whom truth is based exclusively on relationships with other conscious beings (i.e., those with faces).

I have been drawn to these forests since I was a child and love them more than almost anything else. But they are hard to describe. They are certainly still and silent, and this is the way people often speak about them.[39] In some sense, though, these words are very inadequate descriptors, for they merely tell us that the forest is *not* noisy or busy—in other words they reveal more about us than about them. But this is a part of arboreal reality. It is an experience of an alterity much more radical than any face—and neither trees nor forests have faces. Walking in these woods, however, is much more than merely a rupture of the categories of our understanding. Much of it has to do with color, and thus with sight. But it is an unusual kind of seeing. It is the opposite of a mountaintop vista from which one surveys the landscape. There is no horizon in these woods, so the unity of beings is greatly diminished. You see trunks of trees, but even the lowest branches often soar out of view. Ferns, mosses, and lichen cover the surfaces of the soil, tree trunks, and branches alike, blurring any hard boundaries. Thus, Deleuze's distinction between the rhizome and the singular tree is not very revealing, nor is Heidegger's image of the forest clearing. We need new philosophical reflections on the way our immersion in the deep dark green light under these trees invites us to belong to the forest and share in its vitality while remaining so deeply foreign to us. This interweaving of invitation and difference is a characteristic of all forests, but the ones I am speaking about here manifest it to an extreme degree.

The trees that elicit this response are exceptional among life forms, both in terms of biomass and lifespan, but they are not closely related genetically. In fact, *Sequoia sempervirens* (Coast Redwood), *Thuja plicata* (Western Red-Cedar), and *Tsuga heterophylla* (Western Hemlock) have an evolutionary history in which their lineages have been separated by astonishingly vast reaches of time. The Western Red Cedar is not a true cedar at all but, like the Sequoia, it is a cypress (Cupressaceae) and thus in an entirely different family than *Tsuga heterophylla*[40] and the rest of the pines of Pinaceae. Cupressaceae diverged from Pinaceae in the Carboniferous period over 300 million years ago (early in the history of life on land and well before the *rise* of dinosaurs)! The sequoia themselves branched from the *Thuja* 180 mya.[41] To put this in perspective, the clade *Caniformia* split apart only 40 mya, and that was enough time for creatures as radically different as skunks, grizzly bears, and walruses to develop from a common ancestor. The ancient evolutionary divergence among the trees means that the similarity in the forest-spaces created by redwoods, cedars, and hemlock, are not the result of some unique evolutionary breakthrough; rather, they are called forth by the interweaving of special environmental conditions and the deepest history of seed-bearing plants.

These trees are conifer gymnosperms, all of which are wind pollinated. In this they are unlike the flower-bearing angiosperm trees, such as oak, maple, and beech, that dominate the same latitudes in much of the rest of the world (eastern North America, Europe, and eastern Asia). Conifers are unusual at these hospitable latitudes not only geographically but historically as well. For much of the Miocene epoch (23–5 mya), the Northwest of North America was dominated by broad-leafed (angiosperm) trees, and conifers were limited to small areas high in the mountains. As the climate became cooler, drier, and more seasonal in the Pliocene, these conifer patches began to expand into massive forests in upland areas, but it was not until the early Pleistocene (c. 1.5 mya) that conifers had displaced flowering trees all the way from the prairies of the Interior Plains to the Pacific Ocean. The climates on the western slopes of the Cascade Mountains have enough rain to create the lush-canopied forests we are describing, but due to the seasonal variability of the Pleistocene (and up to the present), summers remain dry enough that broad-leafed trees cannot replace their conifer competitors, whose tough waxy needles are less efficient but able to retain more water.

Western North America also has significantly less high-wind events than land facing the Atlantic or Eastern Pacific, which are prone to hurricanes. These conditions (seasonally dry climate with low winds) allow conifers to achieve extreme characteristics, including very slow growth, long life-spans, great heights, and high levels of biomass. The broad-leaf oak-maple forests of the Northeast can achieve maximum leaf area in as little as four years, while it may take half a century for conifer forests in the drier conditions of the West to achieve the same result. But this slower growth and lack of high winds mean that they can stand for much longer. The oaks of Europe and eastern N. America, such as the Northern Red Oak, and other hardwoods, such as beech, maple, and hickory, are considered ancient at 250 years and rarely reach their upper limit of 500 years. Conifers growing in the West face less chance of being toppled by high-wind events, and because they are so slow growing, they face less damage from fungal pathogens. Thus, Ponderosa Pine and Douglas Fir often live longer than deciduous trees, even though their life-span is limited by periodic stand-replacing fires. In the wetter conditions of our dense-canopy conifer forests, fires are much less of a problem, and conifers can live even longer. Western Red Cedars can survive 1,500 years or more and Coast Redwoods more than 2,000 years. Similarly, while hardwood trees reach a maximum of 150 feet tall, a Western Hemlock or Red Cedar can grow taller than 200 feet, and the tallest Douglas-Fir and Redwoods reach heights of well over 300 feet. Thus, these forests contain unusually old trees, and they are unmatched anywhere else on Earth in height or forest biomass, including tropical rainforests.

We might not all be aware of these statistics, but nevertheless, one has a feeling of vegetal exuberance and great antiquity on entering these forests. We know instinctively that these trees not only predate our own existence, but that of our parents, grandparents, and great-grandparents, and thus the limit of internal time-consciousness. Related to our experience of these trees as belonging to mythological time (from time immemorial), is the fact that they are also very little affected by the temporal rhythm of the seasons. They are evergreen conifers, so there is no great re-birth in early spring as leaves return, or the flush of flowers in late spring, or the fruiting of late summer and autumn. Thus, they are not only very, very long-lived but also unperturbed by cyclical variations and therefore have a less ambiguous relation to time than animals do.

Certainly, Husserl and Heidegger are right that only time allows for consciousness. In fact we can say that consciousness is a gift of time. But this time that "gives" is the time of the lived-body (*Leib*) inhabiting a realm of meanings, not the material-body (*Körper*) navigating a world of forces. The time of forces is hard on us as animals. Many people reach their physical peak in their late twenties and thus live more than two-thirds of their time on Earth in decline. This wear and tear of temporality is not only physical but includes emotional scarring, ethical weakening, and psychological narrowing.[42] This is true not only for human beings but seems to be a part of our deep animal heritage. Most mammals are playful, curious, and deeply relational—when they are young. Maturation, on the other hand, brings knowledge though experience but also a real restriction of the vitality of animal life. Irigaray recognizes this aspect of our human existence but points out that external time can also bring a slow accumulation of wisdom that goes beyond conscious thought. This wisdom is not like the cycling of the seasons or the cycling of fashions, but is closely analogous to the accumulation of vegetal life over many years in an ancient forest. We can encounter and learn from the green stillness of the forest to see time in a much more enduring and imperturbable kind of way that draws us into truths that are not ontologically grounded in consciousness.

The timescale of these trees is vastly foreign to human experience, but the forests are not sublime in the romantic sense evoked by the intrepid explorer standing before a vast chasm or mountain glacier. Looking up at the rugged peak of Early Winter Spire from Washington Pass, we are awed by the intimidating grandeur and ruggedness of the mountain. We may be called to climb it, but the whole affair is about overcoming great challenges and attaining seldom-seen views. This type of majestic mountain is as beautiful as a forest, but it calls forth a quite different relation.

Unlike a mountain, forests welcome us into their midst to share in their way of being. This is true of hemlock-cedar woods in a special way. Forests in adjacent areas constituted by other conifers, such as Western Larch, Douglas-Fir, Subalpine Fir, Engelmann Spruce, Ponderosa Pine, and Lodgepole Pine, are also inviting but not in such a direct way. These latter trees do not form canopies that block the same amount of light, so their understory tends to be choked with impenetrable brush and marked underfoot by dry soils that cannot sustain the moss and ferns of the thick-canopied forests. The brushy understory means that these woods are often most easily accessed during the winter on skis, and slaloming through Larch and Lodgepole Pine provides some of the best recreation in the West. The rest of the year getting to these trees requires making trails, often through rugged terrain. This is difficult work, but there are many reasons that make it worthwhile. While Redwood and Cedar make poor firewood, Douglas Fir and Larch are prized for winter warmth. Pine and fir woods are also much more likely to experience small forest fires than those on the rainy side of the Cascades. The patchy distribution that results from fire opens forest edges and glades that are ideal for collecting morel mushrooms and huckleberries, and it maintains open hillsides where biscuitroot and balsamroot thrive. Larger and more regular fires in the fir and pine forests also create prairies where camas can grow in large fields providing food security for many people. Further, the slopes on which these forests grow often have great topographical variation, and trails that were originally designed to access the forest soon become valuable in their own right as avenues for mountain biking and hiking.

While providing fewer opportunities for gathering resources or outdoor recreation than pine and fir forests, the redwood/cedar/hemlock forests are even more *directly* inviting. Standing at their edge, the dark-green light and pillar-like trunks open a space that is a transition to a world as quiet, dark, and solemnly beautiful as the most sacred human architecture. Unlike a cathedral, however, the soft moss on the forest floor mean that our feet are as engaged with the beauty of this world as our eyes and noses, and on a dry day you immediately feel that you could sit or lie down almost anywhere. The open understory means you are not limited to a trail and can walk in any direction. A cathedral or mosque also invites exploration, but even the largest have a self-contained nature. This adds to our feeling that they are sacred in the sense of being set apart from the ordinary and everyday. In the forest, however, this same feeling of the sacred is accompanied by an invitation to unlimited possibilities for exploration, far beyond the scale of a lifetime.

These forests are indescribably inviting and lovely, and the fact that we can walk or lie anywhere means that they provide a limitless welcome that in my experience is matched only by certain alpine turfs and sandy beaches. But the invitation is to a quiet, still, even solemn encounter. This is because there is not much to *do*. These forests do not usually grow on steep slopes, so there is little topographical variation to provide for the excitement of mountain biking, rock climbing, or whitewater kayaking. These lush trees cannot handle heavy snow or their branches break, so they do not grow in areas that are good for skiing. Unlike a forest with a more open canopy, the lowest branches grow high above the ground, so we usually cannot even engage in that most elemental form of arboreal recreation: climbing a tree.

There are few recreational opportunities in these forests, but even more importantly there is almost nothing to eat. This is true not just for humans but for all animals. Most of the riotously abundant life in these forests is locked up in wood and tough resinous needles. Partly, this has to do with the nature of these trees as gymnosperms. Most gymnosperms, and all conifers, rely on obligate wind-pollination. This means that their reproduction is a very unspectacular affair conducted without flowers. They do not produce any of the nectar that flowering trees use to draw bird and insect pollinators into their forest world. Angiosperms also produce fruits that aid in offspring survival. These fruits naturally facilitate the development of mutualistic relationships with animals who disperse and fertilize their seeds, in the process producing vast amounts of edible nutrients. Even without fruits, some conifers do create mutualistic relations with animals who cache seeds. For example, Lodgepole Pines have developed an association with Crossbills and grow large seeds (90 mg) to make them attractive to the birds. The even larger seeds (180 mg) of the Whitebark Pine are distributed by Clarks Nutcracker. In contrast cedar, hemlock, and redwood seeds are so tiny (only 3 mg) it takes well over 100,000 to make a pound. They are designed not to be found and to provide only a very small meal if they are. The trees that bear these inconspicuous seeds are not colonizers but late-succession species that rely on slow growth and the slow replacement of competitors that they can eventually out-shade. Thus, they do not need to get their seeds quickly to disturbed areas, and with low insect, bird, and mammal densities in these late-succession forests, they are not facing high levels of foraging pressure. Thus they just do not need relations with dispersers or pollinators and are able to keep all forms of predation low.

Without soft leaves, the nectar from flowers, fruits, or mutualistic seed relations, herbivores have a very hard time living in these forests, and without those as the basis for a food chain, carnivores cannot live at high densities either. This is why these woods are so alien to us and why they are so quiet—which is to say the same thing. The first great communicative acts on earth, and therefore the first great relationships, are chemical: communication using hormones and pheromones. New levels of relationality and beauty later became available through the sense of sight: flowers letting pollinators know they have nectar and pollen, fruits letting their dispersers know they are ripe, and—most beautifully of all—animals courting their potential partners. Aurality again raises new possibility for relationship. Sound is called upon for courtship in beautiful ways, but at an even higher level it facilitates emotionally rich communication between mother and child. In some birds and higher mammals, this oral communication eventually develops to include the relationship between father and child. In turn, this shared parenting gives rise to the emotional depth embodied in communication between males and females long after courtship is finished for the season. Finally, think of the noisy communication between fully social species: monkeys, apes, wolves, elephants, whales, porpoises, and human beings.

The cedar, hemlock, redwood forests do not invite this chatter. This is why the silence we encounter there has a deep alterity. It also has a positive quality, however. It is a chance to enter a vibrant encounter with a riot of vegetal life so very different from us—a place where we are guests but cannot live and where even our animal cousins are only visitors. And yet, this place is so clearly good. That goodness is manifest most powerfully in the beauty of the green. This link between green and goodness is so pronounced that Hildegard of Bingen famously talked about *viriditas*. In her work, the color green, divine creation, and the vitality of the earth all interweave in a poetic resonance that cannot be clearly and distinctly articulated in propositional language. The silence of the forest is related negatively to the lack of sentient life, but positively to the greenness of vegetal life. Similarly, the stillness is related negatively to a lack of the busyness of animal existence and positively to a very different kind of temporality.

This is possible because the trees are quite different from us but not absolutely indifferent to us. Plants are able to turn carbon dioxide and sunlight into the substance of their own body while producing oxygen as a waste product. If O_2 levels get too high, however, catastrophic wildfires result in great devastation to plant life,[43] and if CO_2 levels get too low, planetary temperatures plunge making plant life difficult or impossible. There are geological mechanisms that outgas CO_2 and bind O_2 into solid oxides, but these are long and slow. The processes of respiration by which animals and fungi absorb O_2 and release CO_2 are much nimbler and more responsive, thereby helping to keep temperatures and oxygen levels within a range in which both plants and animals can thrive. I think Irigaray is right that sexual difference is one of the great ontological questions, for in the interweaving of sameness and difference at that nexus life emerges in such rich ways. The relation between autotroph (creatures that produce their own energy) and heterotroph (creatures that consume other creatures for their energy) has a similar kind of ontological depth. In our age of fossil fuels, greenhouse gases, and climate change, perhaps the photosynthesis/respiration[44] difference is as important as sexual difference.

Significantly, this heterotroph/autotroph difference is more primordial than the rise of consciousness. We can encounter it in these forests, but the experience contains a great deal of dialectical negativity. We learn to think without busyness and noise, but what we encounter is not merely rupture and alterity. In fact in this experience, otherness and lack of resistance go hand in hand. We learn to encounter a truth that is outside the organizing structures of consciousness that the Moderns link so closely to "Enlightenment" and the sight of an object against a horizon. But we also learn to think outside the negotiations between subjects that the Postmoderns (or late Moderns) link so closely to discussion and oral consent. Forest-thinking points to truths that are not derived from our categories of language or our negotiations and contracts. It does not deny those domains of truth, but points to a goodness and reality that precedes and exceeds them. This means that the material world contains a truth and therefore a moral salience that is not derived only from our consciousness. So do our own bodies.

This opens entire areas of metaphysical and ethical reflection that have remained closed to modern and postmodern philosophy. However, we must keep in mind Irigaray's insistence that the result will not merely be an inversion of modern binaries—as if culture could ever be determined by nature or mind determined by body. This has practical consequences for our relation to the forest. In particular, while this way of being will nurture a quiet stillness in us, it will not be the kind of quietism and pure passivity that European romanticism sometimes ascribes to Indigenous peoples.[45] For example, the Coast Salish nations have profound respect for cedar trees and collect cedar bark moderately and in ways that protect the tree from infection so that it does not die as a result of the harvest. For some purposes such as the construction of a canoe, however, a large old tree is needed, and in that case, with ceremonial practices and prayers of gratitude, the tree is killed. Even more importantly, where cedars thrive, they can create unbroken forests that stretch for dozens of miles. Prior to colonization, it was widespread practice for Indigenous peoples in this range to cut down trees to clear openings into these vast forests to make room for crabapples, hawthorn trees, fruiting bushes, and berry patches, creating forests gardens that still manifest much greater plant species diversity today than the surrounding forest, even though they have been abandoned for 150 years.[46]

Instead of merely inverting modern binaries, the experience of the forest is conducive to thinking of truth, and in particular the truths of axiology, in a genuinely different way. These truths and these values are not grounded in consciousness—neither the autonomously chosen ends of deontological ethics nor the experiences of pleasure that provide the ground for utilitarians. Of course for any truth to enter philosophical discourse, it must rise to consciousness in some way. The ways that this might occur remain underdetermined by the phenomena and therefore require human creativity to develop. But already we have reasons to trust in a type of philosophy that begins in silent contemplation of the verdant exuberance of the forest and confidence that this rich, green silence will be a constant source of renewal.

I believe we already see hints that this work starting from the quiet of the forest will open new ways of thinking about some of the deepest philosophical questions and will address some of the thorniest contemporary problems. I think it will help to defend Edith Stein's attempt to integrate phenomenology and metaphysics—against the protestations of both the phenomenologists and the metaphysicians. Relatedly, I think it will also support those who argue that we cannot let the question of being collapse into the question of the meaning of being. While these are fabulously interesting conversations to which it is well worth dedicating one's life, they are clearly *long* conversations. From the depths of the forest they even seem a bit long-winded, so I am happy to linger in this dark-green light a little longer and put them on hold for now. Already, and even without leaving our wooded refuge we have encountered some of the deepest truths. We know that the indifference and even monstrosity of Levinas's *il y a* and Derrida's *Chora* are deeply inadequate as characterizations of the reality of the non-human world. The phosphorescence of phenomenology is not necessarily violent (although of course it can be), for it has neither the first nor the last word. The first faint dawning of Plato's sun rises on a world that is quiet and dark but already beautiful and good.

Notes

1. Tolkien, *The Monsters and the Critics and Other* Essays (New York: Harper Collins: 1983), 142.

2. On the other hand, there are some contexts, such as whitewater canoeing and commercial fishing in an approaching storm, in which the sound of water is intensely noisy.

3. Kant, *The Only Possible Ground for a Demonstration of the Existence of God*, trans. David Walford (Cambridge, MA: Cambridge University Press, 1993), 2:66.1–6.

4. As always, Kant remains ambiguous about that which lies beyond reason. Darkness marks the pre-critical prison of superstition and backwardness, but it can also be the rupture of the categories in an encounter with transcendence. See *Observations on the Feeling of the Beautiful and Sublime*, trans. Frierson and Guyer (Cambridge, MA: Cambridge University Press, 2011).

5. Kant, "What Is Enlightenment?," trans. Mary C. Smith (Columbia University). My emphasis. www.columbia.edu/acis/ets/CCREAD/etscc/kant.html

6. See also his comparison between Critical Philosophy and the power of the police to stop criminal behavior in the "Preface" to the *Critique of Pure Reason*, although border patrol provide an even more apt metaphor for his thinking there and telling indication of the problematic nature of his philosophy. Kant, *Critique of Pure Reason*, trans. Paul Guyer and Allen W. Wood (Cambridge, MA: Cambridge University Press, 1999), xxvi.

7. Levinas, *Totality and Infinity*, trans. Alphonso Lingis (Pittsburgh: Duquesne University Press, 1969), 42.

8. Levinas, *Totality and Infinity*, 45. My emphasis.

9. Levinas, *Totality and Infinity*, 21.

10. Levinas, *Totality and Infinity*, 39.

11. This is not the place to defend the claim that Derrida's work inevitably pushes us toward formalism, but we could start with his own understanding of his work as "quasi-transcendental." For me the most telling place that this becomes manifest is in *Acts of Religion* where he argues that he will use his "quasi-transcendental privilege . . . to grant the distinction between, on the one hand, the experience of belief . . . and, on the other, the experience of sacredness," 72. He sees that these remain interwoven, but he privileges the ethical encounter with the other in faith over the experience of the material world in liturgy and ritual. In the end, as for Kant, the liturgical must become fully subordinate to the ethical—a formal ethics in which the otherness of the other becomes the final arbiter of goodness. For a more complete defense of this claim, please see my article: Daniel Bradley, "Desert Ethics: Conviction, Self-renunciation, and Passion in Teresa and Derrida," in *Conviction: Finitude, Freedom, and the Hermeneutics of Selfhood*, ed. Andrzej Wiercinski (New York: Brill/Fink Press, 2023).

12. *Totality and Infinity*, 35. My emphasis.

13. Marion, *In Excess*, trans. Robyn Horner and Vincent Berraud (New York: Fordham University Press, 2004), 115. My emphasis.

14. Marion, *The Crossing of the Visible*, trans. James K. A. Smith (Stanford, CA: Stanford University Press, 2004), 29.

15. David Macauley, "Night and Shadows," *Environment, Space, Place*, no. 1 (Fall–Winter, 2009–10).

16. Macauley, "Night and Shadows," 1.

17. Grober, "Deep Roots: A Conceptual History of "Sustainable Development" (Nachhaltigkeit)," *Research Gate* (2007); Cristina Bonfiglioli. "Sustainability: A Single Word and a World of Meanings." In *Sustainability and the Anthropocene*, ed. Róisín Lally (Lanham, MD: Lexington Books, 2019).

18. Please be clear, my critique of a modern moralism that still exhibits great prejudice towards what it sees as "savage" and "pagan" is not an attempt to eradicate moral judgment or to encourage the expression of whatever "natural" impulses we feel. Similarly, what we learn from Indigenous traditions is not that we should be more morally permissive. For an early and powerful articulation of the opposite point of view, see Ella Deloria's *Waterlily*, in which she shows how regulated and therefore civilized the Sioux culture is and how terribly things go wrong when people leave the moral regulations of society to live alone in an uncivilized way. To celebrate the non-modern and the non-urban is not to celebrate the uncivilized.

19. Interestingly the public relations employee who came up with this phrase said he wanted to help after 9/11 and was inspired by the WWII era slogan "loose lips sink ships." That WWII slogan, however, actually evinces a premodern sensibility counseling restraint and silence, while the War on Terror slogan is marked by the late modern tendency to say everything that comes to mind without critical reflection on what should be left in silence.

20. Tolkien, *The Monsters and the Critics and Other Essays*, 142.

21. Luce Irigaray and Michael Marder, *Through Vegetal Being* (New York: Columbia University Press, 2016), 9.

22. Irigaray, *Je, Tous, Nous*, trans. Alison Martin (New York: Routledge Press, 1993), 17.

23. Irigaray, *The Irigaray Reader*, ed. Margaret Whitford (New York: Oxford: Blackwell, 1991), 43. She continues, "let us not be the guardians of silence, of a deadly silence," 44.

24. Irigaray, *Je, Tous, Nous*, 35.

25. Irigaray, *Je, Tous, Nous*, 105.

26. Irigaray, *The Way of Love*, trans. Heidi Bostic and Stephen Pluhacek (New York: Continuum Books, 2002), 33.

27. Irigaray, *The Way of Love*, 32–33.

28. Irigaray, *Je, Tous, Nous*, 13.

29. Irigaray, *Je, Tous, Nous*, 110.

30. Irigaray, *Je, Tous, Nous*, 42.

31. Irigaray, *Je, Tous, Nous*, 42.

32. Irigaray, *Je, Tous, Nous*, 28.

33. This claim would have to be worked out at the level of a critique of transcendentalism. It would compare the "sensible transcendental" of Irigaray (*An Ethics of Sexual Difference*. trans. Carolyn Burke and Gillian Gill [Ithaca,

NY: Cornell Press, 1993], 129) to the "a priori transcendental" of Kant's abstract method. It would have to show that Modernity's goal, from Descartes through Kant and beyond, is the development of the transcendental grounds of the intellect in order to set the will free from the earthly conditions to which it finds itself bound. While for Irigaray, the goal is to re-root the intellect in its material conditions in order to fulfill our desire for intimacy with the beauty of our bodies and other parts of the material world.

34. See, for example, "In Almost Absolute Silence," ch. 11 of Irigaray, *I Love to You*, trans. Alison Martin (New York: Routledge, 1995) and "The Silence of Mary" in her most recent book, Irigaray, *A New Culture of Energy: From East to West*, trans. Stephen Seely (Columbia: Columbia University Press, 2021).

35. Irigaray, *Je, Tous, Nous*, 64.

36. Irigaray, *Je, Tous, Nous*, 108.

37. Irigaray, *Je, Tous, Nous*, 108. My emphasis.

38. Muir, *John of the Mountains: The Unpublished Journals of John Muir*, ed. Linnie Wolfe (Madison: University of Wisconsin Press, 1979 [1938]), 313.

39. Journalist Gordon Hempton has famously "discovered" "the quietest place in the United States." This is a bit of a journalistic gimmick, but it is not a coincidence that he located it in the Hoh Rainforest, in Olympic National Park—a cedar-hemlock forest. https://onesquareinch.org

40. Just to confuse things, the *Tsuga* are not really hemlocks either but cousins to firs and true cedars in the Subfamily Abietoideae.

41. Mao et al., "Distribution of living Cupressaceae reflects the breakup of Pangea," *PNAS* 109n20 (2012): 7793–98.

42. Clearly these aspects of our lives involve consciousness, but it is beyond the scope of this paper to show that there is a type of habituation at work in them that is as much akin to the effect of water on stone over time as to the self-transparency of the *ego cogito*.

43. This mechanism may not be quite as determinative as we once thought, but it still plays an important role in plant survival. See R. Vitali, C. M. Belcher, J. O. Kaplan, et al., "Increased Fire Activity under High Atmospheric Oxygen Concentrations," *Nature Communications* 13 (2022): 7285.

44. Plants respire as well, but because their tissues contain more energy when they die than the seed from which they came, the totality of their energy budget always tips toward the photosynthesizing side. In the case of a redwood tree, the caloric difference between seed and dead tree is staggering.

45. For example, see Alexander Pope's "An Essay on Man" (1734). The problem persists to this today. *Avatar* became the highest-grossing film by calling on our deep sense of alienation and portraying a stunningly beautiful natural world that makes a central place in the spiritual life for trees. No matter how adulatory its reference to indigeneity, however, it did a deep disservice in portraying these

alternatives to western modernity as purely passively receiving the bounty of nature.

46. Chelsey Geralda Armstrong, Jacob Earnshaw, Alex C. McAlvay, "Coupled Archaeological and Ecological Analyses Reveal Ancient Cultivation and Land Use in Nuchatlaht (Nuu-chah-nulth) Territories, Pacific Northwest," *Journal of Archaeological Science* 143 (July 2022).

Thinking (Like) Trees

Figure I.3. Rooted at home, St. Petersburg, Florida. *Source*: Courtesy of David Macauley.

Interstice

Arborescence

It occurs to [him] where the word radical came from. Radix. Wrad. Root. The plant's, the planet's, brain.
 The greatest delight which the fields and woods minister is the suggestion of an occult relation between man and the vegetable. I am not alone and unacknowledged. They nod to me, and I to them. The waving of the boughs in the storm, is new to me and old. It takes me by surprise, and yet is not unknown. Its effect is like that of a higher thought or a better emotion coming over me, when I deemed I was thinking justly or doing right.
 Here's a little outsider information, and you can wait for it to be confirmed. A forest knows things. They wire themselves up underground. There are brains down there, ones our own brains aren't shaped to see. Root plasticity, solving problems and making decisions. Fungal synapses. What else do you want to call it? Link enough trees together, and a forest grows aware.

—Richard Powers, *The Overstory*

In his influential *Sand County Almanac*, Aldo Leopold advises us to "think like a mountain" as a possible avenue to appreciate profound interconnections within ecological communities. If this suggestion proves intelligible or at least poetically persuasive, it stands to reason that thinking like—or perhaps with—a tree might be an enticing option as well for those seeking to commune with the capacious wild world.
 Trees have quietly entered human language and thought in remarkable ways. We now speak of decision trees, evolutionary trees, and logic trees. We refer to the roots of a problem, to branches of knowledge, and to leaves of a book. Trees have been adopted in the sciences, in philosophy, and in literature as potent images, guiding templates, and governing tropes that assist us in deliberating upon complex problems, narratives, and theories.

It is likely that we think *with* and *through* things in our environments—tools, writing devices, musical instruments, cooking and sewing equipment, art supplies, utensils—as much as we think *about* them. Increasingly, entities in the world also become extensions of our own minds and often prosthetic supplements tethered to or entwined with our porous and vulnerable bodies. In this regard, what causes us to think is typically a sensual or affective *encounter* with something else and not merely an object of cognition or recognition. We may come to understand and think with, or even think like, trees and other plants through gardening, carpentry, cooking, planting, climbing, and cultivation; in other words, by collaborating with their varied shapes, textures, material forms, and kinds rather than only through disinterested contemplation of them.

Arborescence evokes and involves sundry resemblances with trees in terms of their qualities of growth, form, appearance, and structure. Descartes, in fact, once characterized all of philosophy as being "like a tree whose roots are metaphysics, whose trunk is physics, and whose branches, emerging from the trunk, are all the other sciences." Darwin later proposed a model for the development of life whereby "[t]he affinities of all the beings of the same class have sometimes been represented by a great tree." More recently, arboreal similes have been contested by writers like Deleuze and Guattari who view tree metaphors as hierarchical or limiting descriptions that do not accurately depict memory or thought, even as they acknowledge their wide influence.

In any event, it is imperative not to dissolve individual living trees into abstractions and supersensible ideas, to reduce them to assemblages of research data points, or to impoverish them solely as economic resources, including even carbon sinks. The roots, branches, trunk, leaves, and fruit of a tree are allied with one another and often belong to a much vaster underground and above ground network—or internetwork—that may begin to exhibit a form of awareness or a kind of intelligence through learning and archiving of memory (of drought, heat, radiation, blight as well as resilience) in tree rings, DNA, and seeds as it matures and grows more complex and connected. Arborescence implies a constant becoming and animated, life-sustaining movement, as when woody-fingered roots and fungi filaments shunt themselves along the forest floor in search of water and minerals, or when tree limbs and leaves stretch gracefully toward apertures of light.

Questions related to intelligence have emerged recently within critical plant studies as books like *The Mind of Plants*, *Plant-thinking*, *Plant*

Theory, and *The Imagination of Plants* are being discussed and debated. In the next section, Matthew Segall takes up some of the challenges involved with thinking about notions of mind in the vegetal world, a subject that joins us to arboreal communication, ontology, and ethics, as well. As we consider these subjects, it is helpful to remember that "thinking" and "thanking" are cognate terms, and thus it is prudent for us to be grateful for what trees and forests offer the planet as we wait patiently for the wisdom that flows from the wooded world.

—David Macauley

5

Vegetal Imagination

Schelling and Whitehead as Exemplars of Marder's Plant-Thinking

MATTHEW DAVID SEGALL

Michael Marder's "vegetal metaphysics" turns to the power of plant-thinking in an attempt to bring modern philosophy to its senses. Marder's critical account of the history of Western metaphysics chronicles the way philosophy's theoretical incoherencies and practical inadequacies stem in part from its disregard for vegetal reality. For example, he criticizes Aristotle for the "violence" his formal logic of identity and non-contradiction "unleashed against plants,"[1] diagnoses Hegel's negative dialectic as a symptom of his "[allergy] to vegetal existence,"[2] and regrets Husserl's essentializing "failure to think the tree" itself.[3]

In Marder's terms, philosophy must learn to think like a plant: "The plant sets free the entire realm of petrified nature, including mineral elements, if not the earth itself."[4] In this chapter, I attempt to answer Marder's call for a vegetal revitalization of philosophy. Guided by the *Naturphilosophie* of Friedrich Schelling (1775–1854) and the *Philosophy of Organism* of Alfred North Whitehead (1861–1947), I aim to resurrect several potent root images from the history of Western philosophy. Unlike the idealist tradition, which retreated from the world of the senses and so failed to consider an ontology intrinsic to life, Schelling and Whitehead's process-relational nature philosophy encourages cultivation of root images connecting our human minds to the soil out of which they grow.

Marder, like Schelling and Whitehead, conceives of Nature "as suffused with subjectivity."[5] He likens the life of the plant (*phytos*) to the whole of Nature (*physis*), arguing that plant-life "replicates the activity of *physis* itself."[6] "*Physis*," continues Marder, "with its pendular movement of dis-closure, revelation and concealment, is yet another . . . name for being."[7]

Heraclitus is usually claimed by process philosophers as the first of their kind. Relevant fragments to this effect include: "The sun is new every day" (fragment 32); "Into the same river you could not step twice" (fragment 41); and "Everything flows" (quoted by Plato in *Cratylus*, 401d). Another oft-cited fragment (123)—"nature loves to hide" (*physis kryptesthai philei*)—should not be understood as a negation of the generous growth of the plant realm described by Marder.[8] As with the plant world, there is more to Heraclitus's elliptical statements than first meets the eye. The earliest recorded use of *physis* in ancient Greek literature is in Homer's *Odyssey*, where it refers specifically to the "magic" and "holy force" of the *molü* plant given by Hermes to Odysseus to keep his "mind and senses clear" when faced with Circe's sorcery. The *molü* plant grows duplicitously into "black root and milky flower" and can be safely uprooted only by the gods.[9] As Marder notes above, *physis* suggests not only a tendency toward concealment in the darkness of the Earth, but also a complementary tendency toward revelation in the light of the Sun. As is typical both of plant-life and of the semantic polarity of his sentences, there is an underlying duplicity in Heraclitus's thought. Understanding the poetic meaning of his occult philosophy, or of a plant's process of growth, is aided by the cultivation of an organic or process-relational logic of vegetal imagination. The logics of techno-scientific manipulation and abstract conceptual analysis, in attempting to expose the roots of mind and nature to total illumination, succeed only in desiccating them, leaving behind but a lifeless husk.[10] Instead of objectifying nature's plantlike life, vegetal imagination approaches it hermeneutically, not by "[shying] away from darkness and obscurity," but by letting plants "appear in their own light . . . emanating from their own kind of being."[11] Marder's plant-thinking approaches a logic of imagination in that he aims to begin his vegetal philosophizing not from the putatively purified perspective of disembodied rationality but *in media res*, always in the middle of things: "To live and to think in and from the middle, like a plant partaking of light and of darkness . . . is to . . . refashion oneself—one's thought and one's existence—into a bridge between divergent elements: to become a place where the sky communes with the earth and light encounters but does not dispel darkness."[12] In the Western philosophical tradition[13] speculations about humanity's relation to the plant world date back at least to Plato, who wrote in *Timaeus* that the philosopher is a "heavenly plant" or "heavenly flower." "We declare," Plato has Timaeus say,

> that God has given to each of us, as his daemon, that kind of soul which is housed in the top of our body and which raises us—seeing that we are not an earthly but a heavenly plant—up from earth towards our kindred in the heaven. And herein we speak most truly; for it is by suspending our head and root from that region whence the substance of our soul first came that the divine power keeps upright our whole body.[14]

In arguing that "plants are resistant to idealization,"[15] Marder dwells upon "the vegetable vein" of Plato's philosophy in an attempt to re-envision the latter's oft-characterized two-world metaphysical theory as a transformative "pedagogic endeavor."[16] The real import of Plato's dialogues, in this sense, is not the theoretical content defended by Socrates or his various dialogue partners, but the practical transformations that the intellectual dramas aim to inspire in the reader. The *Republic*'s Myth of the Cave, for example, is often read as Plato's most extravagant metaphor for the otherworldly role of the philosopher, who "descends to the gloomy underworld to initiate a prison break by delivering those living in the shackles of the senses to the heights of intellection."[17] But Marder challenges any straightforward metaphysical interpretation of Plato's metaphor as a call to detach our souls from the appearances of this world by reminding us that Socrates, our constant companion throughout all Plato's dialogues, hardly fits the model of the ivy tower intellectual. Socrates, an eager participant in the aristocratic *sympósia* and the democratic *agorá* alike, "came back to the cave of appearances to give those imprisoned there a chance to emerge into the broad and luminous expanses of Ideas."[18] Marder reads the Myth of the Cave as "a story of . . . seed germination" describing "how heavenly plants sprouted from the dark soil of appearances to the light of Ideas."[19] In Plato's *Theaetetus*, Socrates describes himself as a midwife of ideas who helps guide the growth of concepts out of the soil of his interlocutors' souls and into the light of the Good.[20] In the *Timaeus*, Plato describes perhaps the most mysterious of his dialogue characters, the Receptacle, in a similar way as "the wet-nurse of becoming."[21] It is as though Socrates is Plato's human personification of the cosmic matrix or Receptacle of divine Ideas. By providing resistance to and suffering with the elemental powers of ingressing Ideas, a process of growth is allowed to unfold as Ideas learn through the trials of experience what in eternity they did not know: the idea of Fire sees light, shadow, and color; the idea of Water flows and feels wet; Air blows and feels dry; and Earth rests heavy.[22] Plant-life is resistant to idealization because it displays the same ambiguous process-relational character as Socrates and the Receptacle. All three are expressions of the loamy matrix that, in the course of evolutionary history, allows unconscious *physis* to metamorphose into consciousness of itself as Spirit.

The repression of vegetal existence, according to Marder, began as early as Aristotle, who was willing to grant of plants, due to their lack of both locomotion and perception, only that they "*seem* to live."[23] The "seeming" life of plants presents a taxonomic problem for Aristotle, whose formal logic forces a clear distinction: either plants are ensouled, or they are not. But for the polar logic of vegetal imagination (no longer subject to the principle of non-contradiction or the law of the excluded middle, as we'll see), the "seeming" life of plants reveals precisely what has been repressed by so much of Western metaphysics: that it is towards the ambiguous ontology of plant-life that philosophy must return if it hopes to reconcile with the uncertain ground of sensory experience. Aristotle does finally grant a kind of life to plants by pointing to their nutritive capacity (*to threptikon*), which in animal life is homologous to the haptic sense (i.e., touch).[24] Touch is the basis of all *aesthesis*, only subsequently becoming differentiated into the other specialized senses.[25] In light of the vegetal origins of sensation, Marder is led to wonder

> whether the sensory and cognitive capacities of the psyche, which in human beings have been superadded to the vegetal soul, are anything but an outgrowth, an excrescence, or a variation of the latter. The sensitivity of the roots seeking moisture in the dark of the soil [or leaves seeking light in the brightness of the sky] . . . and human ideas or representations we project, casting them in front of ourselves, are not as dissimilar from one another as we tend to think.[26]

The next to carry forward Plato's plant-thinking was Plotinus, into whose philosophy Marder writes that "there is no better point of entry . . . than the allegory of the world—permeated by what he calls "the Soul of All"—as a single plant, one gigantic tree, on which we alongside all other living beings (and even inorganic entities such as stones) are offshoots, branches, twigs, and leaves."[27] Plotinus's World-Tree grows from a single inverted root. The inverted root of the World-Tree is an image of the ever-living One that, though it "gives to the plant its whole life in its multiplicity"[28] itself remains forever unaffected by the dispersion of the living. While Marder, Whitehead, and Schelling reject the doctrine of emanational monism often attributed to Plotinus, there are indications of a subtler view in the *Enneads*. Plotinus explicitly rejects the idea of some preplanned or destined direction of growth for the World-Tree's many limbs and leaves. As the Tree's branches proliferate, they grow further from the radical unity of their origin, becoming mixed with and dispersed into matter, mistaking themselves for independent "little trees."[29] Such chaotic proliferation might be irksome to standard idealists, but not Plotinus, who as Marder points out insists on keeping being open to a form of freedom rooted in the divergent proliferation of the World-Tree itself.[30] Plotinus's radical claim that all things, including plants, "aspire to contemplation"[31] serves to relativize human mentality by "dehumanizing and deanimalizing the intellect."[32] Each mode of existence, whether mineral, plant, animal, or human, engages in its own form of thinking, with plants partaking in "growth-thought [*phutikē noesis*]."[33] In this phytotypical mode of thought, contemplation imitates the divine as thinking acquires extension: like God, "[plants] have a power of thinking that is immediately creative and produces the object they think." In other words, "the plant not only *expresses* a truth but also *makes* a truth by . . . becoming what it thinks."[34] Even the quietest seed, like the World-Soul, expresses its silent logos by thinking itself into time in the form of a growing tree. Marder: "Our speaking breaks this silence, heavy with meaning and full of life. In purporting to express it more authentically, we disrupt the quietness inherent to *logos* and forget about the existence of that reason which is not straightforwardly human."[35] Despite his resonances with Plotinus's plant-thinking, Marder is weary of becoming "awash with the acute nostalgia for the lost unity of the seed,"[36] calling instead for an "anarchic radical pluralism,"[37] a title which could just as well describe Schelling and Whitehead's process ontology. Nonetheless, though they reject monistic eternity in favor of pluralistic process, all three carry forward Plotinus's root image of an archetypally informed vegetal cosmos. Marder, striving to be more Plotinian than Plotinus, revises the ancient plant thinker's last words (substituting "plant" for "god"): "Try to bring back the plant in you to the Plant in the All!"[38]

Fifteen hundred years later, David Hume had his own bout of vegetal thinking in the midst of composing his *Dialogues on Natural Religion*, dialogues in which Cleanthes at one point is made to deploy an ontophytological critique of Philo's over-determined analogization of the universe to an animal. Unlike an animal, argues Cleanthes, the universe we experience has "no organs of sense; no seat of thought or reason; no one precise origin of motion and action." "In short," Cleanthes jests, "[the universe] seems to bear a stronger resemblance to a vegetable than to an animal."[39] Cleanthes does not really believe the universe is a self-generating plant but only suggests as much in order to undermine the credibility of Philo's animal analogy.[40] Philo responds by accepting the critique of the animal analogy, but then opportunistically turns the relative credibility of the vegetable analogy against Cleanthes' own argument for design: "The world plainly resembles more . . . a vegetable, than it does a watch or a knitting-loom," says Philo. "Its cause, therefore, it is more probable, resembles . . . generation or vegetation. . . . In like manner as a tree sheds its seed into the neighboring fields, and produces other trees; so the great vegetable, the world, or this planetary system, produces within itself certain seeds, which, being scattered into the surrounding chaos, vegetate into new worlds."[41] Philo, of course, is no more sincere in his vegetal speculations than Cleanthes was in his. He doubts whether philosophy will ever have enough data to determine the true nature and cause of the universe. In the intervening two centuries since Hume published his *Dialogues*, mathematical and technological advances have allowed scientific cosmology to drastically expand and complexify the range of data available to assist the natural philosopher's speculative imagination. Modern scientific cosmology and astrobiology—especially when interpreted in light of Marder's "plant-nature synecdoche," which posits that plants are "the miniature mirror of *physis*"[42]—has only made Hume's vegetal conjecture more scientifically plausible. Despite the breadth of his "ontophytological" deconstruction of Western metaphysics, Marder makes no mention of Hume's imaginatively generative double gesturing toward plants.

Hume had Philo argue against the plausibility of divining the nature of the whole based on an acquaintance with its parts,[43] but in daring to ontologize the vegetal life of the whole of nature (making its "life" more than a mere metaphor), Marder displays his allegiance to the ancient hermetic principle of correspondence,[44] shifting its verticality into a mereological register, as Whitehead himself does:[45] as it is without, so it is within; as it is within, so it is without.

The hermetic principle of polar correspondence between the one above and the many below is not simply an abstract mental concept. It is a magical symbol whose power is enacted not only in the ideal meanings of the mind, but in the living movements of *physis*. These movements are made most obviously apparent by the mysterious seasonal life cycle of the plant realm. Though Hume clearly recognized that plant-life presented a definite limit to traditional metaphysical speculation, he remained uninitiated into the death/rebirth mystery esoterically encrypted in this vegetal threshold. Whitehead also invoked the hermetic principle of polarity by balancing Plato and Plotinus's preferential treatment of the One with his own more Heraclitan "Category of the Ultimate": *Creativity*. Whitehead's ultimate category dissolves the classical metaphysical dichotomy separating the single supreme Creator from Its many subsidiary creatures. "Creativity," writes Whitehead, "is the universal of universals characterizing ultimate matter of fact. It is that ultimate principle by which the many, which are the universe disjunctively, become the one actual occasion, which is the universe conjunctively."[46] Through this process of creative advance from disjunction to conjunction, a novel entity is created that was not present in the prior dispersion. "The novel entity," continues Whitehead, "is at once the togetherness of the "many" which it finds, and also it is one among the disjunctive "many" which it leaves; it is a novel entity, disjunctively among the many entities which it synthesizes. The many become one, and are increased by one."[47] The many down below thereby enter into and pass through the one up above, just as the one up above enters into and passes through the many down below. "The way up and the way down is one and the same," as Heraclitus put it.[48] Schelling also creatively inherits the hermetic principle of correspondence by analogizing the metaphysical polarity of the many below and the one above to the physical pulsation—the systole and diastole rhythm—of living nature. "The antithesis eternally produces itself," writes Schelling, "in order always again to be consumed by the unity, and the antithesis is eternally consumed by the unity in order always to revive itself anew. This is the sanctuary, the hearth of the life that continually incinerates itself and again rejuvenates itself from the ash. This is the tireless fire through whose quenching, as

Heraclitus claimed, the cosmos was created."⁴⁹ Schelling offers the telling example of a tree to show how this cosmogenetic rhythm resonates through the whole to the parts and back again:

> Visible nature, in particular and as a whole, is an allegory of this perpetually advancing and retreating movement. The tree, for example, constantly drives from the root to the fruit, and when it has arrived at the pinnacle, it again sheds everything and retreats to the state of fruitlessness, and makes itself back into a root, only in order again to ascend. The entire activity of plants concerns the production of seed, only in order again to start over from the beginning and through a new developmental process to produce again only seed and to begin again. Yet all of visible nature appears unable to attain settledness and seems to transmute tirelessly in a similar circle.⁵⁰

Marder's "post-metaphysical task of de-idealization" makes him especially attentive to the association between the aesthetic power of plant-life (particularly flowers) and the pathos of death: flowers—"the free beauties of nature,"⁵¹ as Kant called them—have since the beginning of history been customarily "discarded along the path of Spirit's glorious march through the world," "abandoned" and thereby "freed from dialectical totality."⁵² "In contrast to the death borne by *Geist*," continues Marder, plant-life can become "neither mediated nor internalized."⁵³ Idealist philosophy is therefore always in a rush to "[unchain] the flower from its organic connection to the soil and [put] it on the edge of culture as a symbol of love, religious devotion, mourning, friendship, or whatever else might motivate the culling."⁵⁴ The result of modern rationality's "thorough cultivation" and "biotechnological transformation" of plant-life is "a field of ruins."⁵⁵

The "economic-teleological" principle guiding modern instrumental ratiocination—whereby, for example, "trees in and of themselves have no worth save when turned into furniture"⁵⁶—is related to Kant's failure to grasp the life of *physis* as anything more than a merely regulative principle guiding our judgment. While he found it acceptable for human subjects to *think* the internal possibility of a living nature, he refused to grant that living organization could be understood as constitutive of nature itself such that humans might come to truly *know* the life of nature (much less come to know our own knowing as an expression of this very life). "It is absurd," Kant writes, "to hope that another Newton will arise in the future who would explain to us how even a mere blade of grass is produced."[57] It followed that the only avenue open to reason in its untamable desire to know *physis* was by way of the economic-teleological principle, whereby the natural philosopher, in order to know his object, "must first manufacture it."[58] Modern rationality, in its techno-capitalist phase, has succeeded in reducing the entire planet to an externality of the human economy: Earth is raw material on one end of the chain of consumption, and on the other, a garbage disposal for toxic waste. In order to avoid the deleterious ecological effects of such an economic system, it is necessary to heal the vegetal repression and sensorial alienation from which it stems.[59]

Schelling rejects the anthropocentric Kantian program that justifies treating nature as the raw material awaiting human capitalization. Instead, he inverts transcendental idealism by transforming it into transcendental physics, such that nature is intuited as more than a mere a collection of finished products. Nature is also and primarily a creative productivity that "is as active in geology as in [human] ideation," as Schellingian philosopher Iain Hamilton Grant puts it.[60] It is therefore not only human beings who act to shape a passive nature, since "nature is its own lawgiver."[61] The human imagination is understood by Schelling to be a potentization of nature's original creativity.

Whereas Kant argued that "real metaphysics" must be "devoid of all mixture with the sensual,"[62] Marder suggests that the idealist reduction of plant-life to dead linear crystals "[survives] in human thought in the shape of Kantian immutable categories and forms of intuition to which all novel experiences must in one way or another conform."[63] Instead of forcing living experience to obey the crystalline categories of thought, Marder's plant-thinking, like the process-relational imagination, "destroys the Procrustean bed of formal logic and transcendental *a priori* structures—those ideal standards to which no living being can measure up fully."[64]

Vegetal imagination is the esemplastic power[65] through which concepts incarnate in the concrescing occasions of the world, like seeds taking root in the Earth, growing skyward through branch, leaf, flower, and fruit, only to fall again into the soil to be born again, and again . . . Plant-thinking breaks through the crystalline molds of "dead thought"—what Bergson called "the logic of solids"[66]—to bring forth instead a *fluid* or *plastic* logic, a way of *thinking-with* the creative life of *physis*, rather than attempting either to flee from or control it.[67] Whereas in a crystalline logic of solids, thought "has only to follow its natural [intrinsic] movement, after the lightest possible contact with experience, in order to go from discovery to discovery, sure that experience is following behind it and will justify it invariably,"[68] in a fluid logic of plastics, thought roots itself in the life-process, overflowing the sense-bound understanding's *a priori* categorical antinomies and pre-determined forms of intuition to participate directly in the creativity of cosmogenesis. "A theory of life that is not accompanied by a criticism of knowledge," according to Bergson, "is obliged to accept, as they stand, the concepts which the understanding puts at its disposal: it can but enclose the facts, willing or not, in preexisting frames which it regards as ultimate."[69] The plasticity of vegetal imagination, on the other hand, preserves the unprethinkability of a plantlike nature, remaining "faithful to the obscurity of vegetal life" by protecting it from the searing clarity of crystallized rationality.[70] Still, the vegetal imagination grants us a sensitive intimation of the very root of its own image-producing force: as Bachelard suggests, there, "in the heart of matter[,] grows an obscure vegetation,"[71] just as, in "the life of our hearts," we are "enable[d] to understand the life of the universe."[72]

Schelling is not only one of a handful of philosophers to escape deconstruction by Marder's vegetal re-invention of metaphysics, he even earns Marder's praise for defending the continuity between life and thought.[73] Schelling suggests that "every plant is a symbol of the intelligence,"[74] and that this symbolic intelligence finds expression precisely in the plant's power of "sensibility," which—even when the pendulum of organic nature has swung toward its opposite but complimentary pole of "irritability"—remains the "*universal* cause of life."[75]

According to Elaine Miller, another plant-thinker, while Hegel approaches plant-life and *physis* more generally as appearances to be taken up and sublated by human reason, Schelling's *Naturphilosophie* approaches Nature as possessed of its own kind of intelligence: "Schelling does not claim that the human intellect works in the way that a plant grows, but rather that the growth of a plant exhibits the kind of intelligence that nature is. Nature itself is a visible manifestation of the ideal, a manifestation of a power of reason that is not limited to human consciousness."[76] Miller argues that Schelling's main problem with Hegel's dialectical understanding of nature stemmed from the latter's "[reduction of] nature to a passing moment of spirit." "Human subjectivity," she continues, "insofar as it believes it can overcome its plantlike fragility, loses sight of its connection to the life-and-death rhythms of nature."[77]

Schelling offers the polar connection between Earth and Sun as an illustration of the life-producing relationship between gravity and light that is responsible for calling forth intelligent plant-life out of the planet.⁷⁸ Occult philosopher Rudolf Steiner similarly remarks that any attempt to understand the inorganic, mineral dimension of Earth independently of the plant-life it supports will remain hopelessly abstract: "Just as our skeleton first separates itself out of the organism," says Steiner, "so we have to look at Earth's rock formations as the great skeleton of the Earth organism."⁷⁹ Steiner further argues that the cultivation of vegetal imagination will allow the philosopher to come to see "the plant covering of our Earth [as] the sense organ through which Earth spirit and Sun spirit behold each other."⁸⁰ The mineral and plant realms are to Earth what the skeleton and sensory organs are to the human body. As Plotinus wrote, "Earth is ensouled, as our flesh is, and any generative power possessed by the plant world is of its bestowing."⁸¹ Plant-life has all too often been relegated to the margins of natural philosophy, attended to only to insult it rather than to be inspired by it. And so the natural philosophical imagination has withered and desiccated into a mind/matter dualism. Rejuvenating *Naturphilosophie* would mean making plant-life the matrix from which all philosophical thinking emerges. Plants are transitional organisms, not quite mineral and not quite mental. They invite the intellect to loosen the seals separating their categories, allowing them to perceive the vegetal life actively mediating every phase of nature's metamorphosis.

A process philosophy rooted in the power of vegetal imagination requires an inversion of our ordinary experience of the universe. It is as if the world were turned inside out and we found ourselves walking upside down upon the Earth, with our head rooted in the ethereal soil of formative forces streaming in from the cosmos, our limbs yearning for the living ground, and our heart circulating between the two in rhythmic harmony. Rather than stretching for the abstract heights of the intelligible as if to steal a glimpse of heaven, the force of vegetal imagination returns philosophy's attention to the Earth beneath its feet, and to the roots, branches, leaves, flowers, fruits, and seeds of *plants*, Earth's most generous life forms, and indeed the co-generative source (with the Sun) of life itself. Thinking with vegetal imagination is thinking with a plant-soul. Plant-souls, according to Marder, partake of a "kind of primordial generosity that gives itself to all other creatures, animates them with this gift, . . . allows them to surge into being, to be what they are."⁸²

Only by finding its vegetal roots can philosophy become *planetary*, true to the Earth and to the plant-power of imagination. But because the imagination is not a static unity but in fact abyssal/ungrounded, its plant-like growth must be inverted: it has "underground stems" and "aerial roots," as Deleuze and Guattari put it.[83] Or, as Gaston Bachelard suggests (echoing Plato's *Timaeus*), the properly rooted philosopher is like "a tree growing upside down, whose roots, like a delicate foliage, tremble in the subterranean winds while its branches take root firmly in the blue sky."[84] For Bachelard, the plant is the *root image* of all life: "The imagination [must take] possession of all the powers of plant life," he writes. "It lives between earth and sky . . . [it] becomes imperceptibly the cosmological tree, the tree which epitomizes a universe, which makes a universe."[85] For Bachelard, the inverted philosopher's tree functions to integrate the virtues of growth, depth, uprightness, truth, soil and sky. Simply put, "the imagination is a tree."[86] Bachelard warns that without the integrative virtues of the tree, the philosopher may become a "sickly soul." He offers an example by way of a "botanical diagnosis" of Sartre, who in *Nausea* describes his experience of being frightened by the absurd perception of a chestnut tree's roots as a meaningless knotty mass of boiled leather: "a root which has lost its tree," as Bachelard puts it.[87] Bachelard counsels us to go beyond the absurdity of the disembodied intellect by reconnecting with the root source of our consciousness in the plantlike imagination.[88]

It is important to reiterate that Marder's plant-thinking, like Schelling and Whitehead's process-relational logic of imagination, "rejects the principle of non-contradiction in its content and its form,"[89] at least for the purposes of speculative metaphysics.[90] It also rejects the corollary law of identity. A plantlike, polar logic of imagination allows concepts to grow together with percepts and identities to become infused with difference. According to Bachelard, "Philosophers, when confronted with outside and inside, think in terms of being and non-being."[91] Indeed, both Schelling and Whitehead affirm Plato's argument in *Sophist* that "not-being" is a kind of being.[92] "Every kind," Plato writes, "has a plurality of Being and an infinity of Not-being."[93] This is to say that every actuality, every concrete reality, includes within it both what it *is* and what it *is not*. Actualities are composed of being *and* nothing, a polarity that throws them into *becoming*. Each actual entity, though it at first appears to be merely a finite particular act appearing here and now, encloses within itself a deep history of evolutionary memories and opens out toward an erotic lure of future possibilities. Actual entities are thus nonlocal *occasions* that are both "here-now" in the present and "there-then" in the past and the future (and each in different ways). "Thus a profound metaphysics is rooted in an implicit geometry," Bachelard continues," which—whether we will or no—confers spatiality upon thought; if a metaphysician could not draw, what would he think?"[94]

On paper, strict adherence to the logical principles of identity and non-contradiction may prevent the mind from making simple errors. But if reality is an ecology of living processes rather than a pile of dead things,—if, as Plato has Timaeus say, cosmogenesis is such that "living creatures keep passing into one another . . . as they undergo transformation"[95]—then adhering to these principles too strictly ends up blinding the mind to the creative advance of nature. Thinking nature otherwise requires reimagining the disincarnate logos driving so much Western philosophy. An *incarnate logos* attuned to the vegetal imagination not only thinks nature, but it also becomes *nature thinking*. "The human who thinks like a plant," Marder continues, "literally becomes a plant, since the destruction of classical *logos* annihilates the thing that distinguishes us from other living beings."[96] Unlike modern rationality, which is said to be self-grounding, plant-life is open to otherness, dependent on something other than itself (i.e., earth, water, air, and light). In the same way, vegetal imagination receives its power from the elemental life of *physis*. It is no longer "I" who thinks nature; rather, "*it thinks in me*."[97] As Frederick Beiser wrote of Schelling's intellectual intuition, through it "I do not see myself acting but all of nature acting through me."[98] Thus, in Bachelard's words, "the [philosophical] tree is everywhere at once."[99] Or as Schelling himself put it, the philosopher who is vegetally attuned to the rhythms of *physis* becomes "nature itself philosophizing (*autophusis philosophia*)."[100]

Notes

1. Michael Marder, *Plant-Thinking a Philosophy of Vegetal Life* (New York: Columbia University Press, 2013), 21.
2. Marder, *Plant-Thinking*, 126.
3. Marder, *Plant-Thinking*, 75–78.
4. Marder, *Plant-Thinking*, 127.
5. Marder, *Plant-Thinking*, 35.
6. Marder, *Plant-Thinking*, 28; both "plant" and "nature" derive from the same Greek prefix (*phuo-*) and verb (*phuein*), meaning "to generate," or "to bring forth."
7. Marder, *Plant-Thinking*, 28–29.
8. Marder, *Plant-Thinking*, 28.
9. Homer, *The Odyssey*. Translated by Robert Fitzgerald (New York: Farrar, Straus, and Giroux, 1998), book 10, lines 328–42.

10. Marder, *Plant-Thinking*, 30.
11. Marder, *Plant-Thinking*, 30.
12. Marder, *Plant-Thinking*, 178.
13. Even earlier than Plato, the Indian *Bhagavad Gita* used the image of an inverted Ashwattha tree to describe the cosmos. While some Hindu historians suggest the *Gita* was conceived (if not written down) in the third or fourth millennium BCE, most scholars place its origins around the sixth century BCE (see *A Sourcebook in Indian Philosophy*. Eds. Sarvepalli Radhakrishnan and Charles A. Moore [Princeton, NJ: Princeton University Press, 1957], 99). "The branches of this cosmic tree extend both below and above (below in the material, above in the supraphysical planes)" (see Sri Aurobindo, *Bhagavad Gita and Its Message*, edited by Anibaran Roy [Pondicherry, India: Sri Aurobindo Ashram Trust, 1995], 15.2).
14. Plato, *Timaeus*, 90a–b. In *Complete Works*. Edited by John M. Cooper (Cambridge, MA: Hackett, 1997).
15. Marder, *Plant-Thinking*, 13.
16. Michael Marder, *The Philosopher's Plant: An Intellectual Herbarium* (New York: Columbia University Press, 2014), 16–17.
17. Marder, *The Philosopher's Plant*, 16.
18. Marder, *The Philosopher's Plant*, 18.
19. Marder, *The Philosopher's Plant*, 17.
20. Plato, *Theaetetus*, 149a. In *Complete Works*. Edited by John M. Cooper (Cambridge, MA: Hackett, 1997).
21. Plato, *Timaeus*, 52d.
22. Plato, *Timaeus*, 52e.
23. Italics added. Aristotle, *De anima*, 410b23. Translated by J. A. Smith. 2009. Retrieved from http://classics.mit.edu/Aristotle/soul.html
24. Aristotle, *De anima*, 413b1–10.
25. Marder, *Plant-Thinking*, 38.
26. Marder, *Plant-Thinking*, 27.
27. Marder, *The Philosopher's Plant*, 39.
28. Plotinus, *Enneads* 3.8.10, 5–15. In *The Six Enneads*. Translated by Stephen Mackenna and B. S. Page, 2009. Retrieved from http://classics.mit.edu/Plotinus/enneads.html
29. Plotinus, *Enneads*, 3.3.7, 25.
30. Marder, *The Philosopher's Plant*, 44.
31. Plotinus, *Enneads* 3.8.30, 2–3.
32. Marder, *The Philosopher's Plant*, 47.
33. Plotinus, *Enneads* 3.8.8, 10–20.
34. Marder, *The Philosopher's Plant*, 50.
35. Marder, *The Philosopher's Plant*, 48.
36. Marder, *The Philosopher's Plant*, 49.

37. Marder, *Plant-Thinking*, 58.
38. Marder, *The Philosopher's Plant*, 56.
39. Hume, *A Treatise on Human Nature: Being an Attempt to Introduce the Experimental Method of Reasoning into Moral Subjects and Dialogues on Natural Religion*. Edited by T. H. Green and T. H. Grose (London: Longmans, Green, and Co., 1874), 417.
40. Cleanthes truly believes the universe to be a law-abiding machine designed, built, and maintained by a perfect God.
41. Hume, David. *Natural Religion*, 421.
42. Marder, *Plant-Thinking*, 120.
43. Hume, *Natural Religion*, 416.
44. Hermes, *The Emerald Tablet*, line 2. Various Translations. www.sacredtexts.com/alc/emerald.htm. Accessed January 27, 2016.
45. Whitehead, *Process and Reality: An Essay in Cosmology* (New York: The Free Press, 1929/1978), part IV.
46. Whitehead, *Process and Reality*, 21.
47. Whitehead, *Process and Reality*, 21.
48. Fragment 123; translated by Panikkar, Raimon. *The Rhythm of Being* (Maryknoll, NY: Orbis, 2010), 266.
49. Friedrich Wilhelm Joseph Schelling, *The Ages of the World*. Translated by Jason Wirth (Albany, NY: SUNY Press, 1815/2000), 20–21.
50. Schelling, *Ages*, 21.
51. Immanuel Kant, *Critique of Judgment*. Translated by J. H. Bernard. Mineola (NY: Dover, 1790/2005), 59.
52. Marder, *Plant-Thinking*, 126.
53. Marder, *Plant-Thinking*, 126.
54. Marder, *Plant-Thinking*, 123.
55. Marder, *Plant-Thinking*, 128.
56. Schelling, *Werke*, 1/7, 18; excerpted and translated by Bruce Matthews, *Schelling's Organic Form of Philosophy: Life as the Schema of Freedom* (Albany, NY: SUNY Press, 2011), 4.
57. Kant, *Critique of Judgment*, Section 75.
58. Immanuel Kant, *Opus Postumum*. Edited and translated by Eckart Förster. Translated by Michael Rosen (Cambridge, UK: Cambridge University Press, 1804/1993), 240.
59. Marder, *Plant-Thinking*, 22.
60. Iain Hamilton Grant, *Philosophies of Nature After Schelling* (New York: Continuum, 2008), 53.
61. Schelling, *SW* IV, 96 (translation by Grant, *After Schelling*, 25).
62. Kant, *De mundi sensibilis*. Translated by Matthews, *Schelling's Organic Form*, 4.

63. Marder, *Plant-Thinking*, 163; Hegel also considered plant growth to be linear, like crystals, whereas proper animals are elliptical in their movements (Marder, *Plant-Thinking*, 119).

64. Marder, *Plant-Thinking*, 164.

65. A term coined by Samuel Taylor Coleridge and modeled on Schelling's own neologism *Ineinsbildung* (see *Biographia Literaria* [New York: Leavitt, Lord, and Co., 1834], Ch. 10).

66. Bergson, *Creative Evolution*. Translation by Arthur Mitchell (New York: Barnes & Noble, 2005), xvii.

67. Marder, *Plant-Thinking*, 166.

68. Bergson, *Creative Evolution*, xviii.

69. Bergson, *Creative Evolution*, xx.

70. Marder, *Plant-Thinking*, 173.

71. Gaston Bachelard, *On Poetic Imagination and Reverie*. Translated by Colette Gaudin (Putnam, CT: Spring Publications, 2005), 11.

72. Bachelard, *Poetic Imagination*, 36.

73. Marder, *Plant-Thinking*, 157.

74. Friedrich Schelling, *System of Transcendental Idealism* (Charlottesville: University Press of Virginia, 1800/1978), 122.

75. Schelling, *Philosophy of Nature*, 146.

76. Elaine Miller, *The Vegetative Soul: From Philosophy of Nature to Subjectivity in the Feminine* (Albany, NY: SUNY Press, 2002), 124.

77. Miller, *The Vegetative Soul*, 147.

78. Schelling, *Ideas for a Philosophy of Nature* (Cambridge, UK: Cambridge University Press, 1797/1988), 185–86.

79. Steiner, *The Spirit in the Realm of Plants*. Translated by G. F. Karnow (Spring Valley, NY: Mercury Press, 1984).

80. Steiner, *The Spirit in the Realm of Plants*.

81. Plotinus, *Enneads* 4.2.27.

82. Marder, *Plant-Thinking*, 46.

83. Gilles Deleuze and Felix Guattari, *A Thousand Plateaus: Capitalism and Schizophrenia*. Translated by Brian Massumi (Minneapolis: University of Minnesota Press, 1987), 15.

84. Bachelard, *Poetic Imagination*, 85.

85. Bachelard, *Poetic Imagination*, 85. The inverted tree is a common motif in hermetic literature.

86. Bachelard, *Poetic Imagination*, 85.

87. Bachelard, *Poetic Imagination*, 85.

88. Bachelard, *Poetic Imagination*, 85–86.

89. Marder, *Plant-Thinking*, 164.

90. To be clear, Whitehead's rejection is qualified, as the principle of non-contradiction still applies to analysis of the physical pole of concrescence.

The conceptual pole, however, in that it feels a variety of contradictory potentials, is not subject to such a logic (*Process and Reality*, 348).

91. Gaston Bachelard, *The Poetics of Space*. Translated by Maria Jolas (Boston: Beacon Press, 1994), 212.

92. Whitehead, *Adventures of Ideas* (New York: The Free Press, 1933/1967), 222, 228; Schelling, *Ages*, 14–15.

93. Plato, *Sophist*, 256d–e. Excerpted and translated by Grant, *After Schelling*, 44.

94. Bachelard, *The Poetics of Space*, 212.

95. Plato, *Timaeus*, 92b–c. Excerpted and translated by Grant, *After Schelling*, 53.

96. Marder, *Plant-Thinking*, 164.

97. Schelling, *On the History of Modern Philosophy*. Translated by Andrew Bowie (Cambridge: Cambridge University Press, 1827/1994), 48.

98. Beiser, Frederick. *German Idealism: The Struggle Against Subjectivism, 1781–1801* (Cambridge: Harvard University Press, 2002), 583.

99. Bachelard, *Poetic Imagination*, 85.

100. Quoted in Grant, *After Schelling*, 188.

Trees and Time

Figure I.4. Redwood cross-section, Big Sur, California. *Source*: Courtesy of Laura Pustarfi.

Interstice

Rings

> Then it came to me, my life. I remembered my life / the way an ax handle, mid-swing, remembers the tree. / & I was free.
>
> —Ocean Vuong, *Time Is a Mother*

> When a tree is cut down and reveals its naked death-wound to the sun, one can read its whole history in the luminous, inscribed disk of its trunk: in the rings of its years, its scars, all the struggle, all the suffering, all the sickness, all the happiness and prosperity stand truly written, the narrow years and the luxurious years, the attacks withstood, the storms endured.
>
> —Hermann Hesse, *Trees*

> But people have no idea what time is. They think it's a line, spinning out from three seconds behind them, then vanishing just as fast into the three seconds of fog just ahead. They can't see that time is one spreading ring wrapped around another, outward and outward until the thinnest skin of Now depends for its being on the enormous mass of everything that has already died.
>
> —Richard Powers, *The Overstory*

The rings of trees retain history, a memory of the passage of time within their arboreal bodies. Trees grow from the cambium layer under the bark by adding cells to both their exterior and interior wood, which in many species becomes the expanding circles visible in a cross-section of the trunk. Often the light layer of wood shows growth during the spring and early summer, while the darker layer reveals slower development in the fall and winter. These rings, while not always annually regular, are distinct enough to display not only age and growth rates but also information about the surrounding ecology and climate. While many trees possess rings, tropical species frequently do not.

Famously, one of the oldest trees ever found, Prometheus, a bristlecone pine (*Pinus longaeva*) in California's Inyo National Forest, was felled in 1964 by a young dendrochronological researcher, discovering only too late that his study subject boasted 4,844 rings. An older Great Basin bristlecone pine was found still living in 2012 at 5,062 years old. The tree was cored in the 1950s but only recently examined and dated in 2010. The Nevada Museum of Art hosts a clock developed by artist and philosopher Jonathon Keats that measures time in centuries based on five bristlecone pines living on Mount Washington. These long-lived trees can be considered what historian Jared Farmer terms "elderflora." Farmer also suggests the importance of "chronodiversity," or the variation of ages of trees in a forest or among a species, along with biodiversity, which highlights the importance of arboreal spans of time.

Cross-sections of elder trees in public parks boast pinpoint markings when historical events may have taken place during the life of the tree. One cross-section on display in Muir Woods, California, includes events such as Columbus's 1492 journey and the signing of the Declaration of Independence in 1776. Artist and filmmaker Tiffany Shlain's *Dendrofemonology* reinterprets the tree cross-section on deodar cedar (*Cedrus deodara*) with a feminist focus. Shlain includes goddess worship as of 50,000 BCE, Wu Zetian's rule of China starting in 690 CE, first wave feminism in the late nineteenth century, along with contemporary events such as Tarana Burke's #metoo movement and Oregon's inclusion of a nonbinary gender category on IDs as of 2017. In both cases, the body of the tree as cross-section makes visible the passage of human time.

In Big Sur, California, one of the editors (Laura) happened upon the trunk of a redwood (*Sequoia sempervirens*) in a mundane spot and stopped to reflect on the scene. Running her fingertips along the exposed face of cut wood, she traced decades of completed life as a chiasm formed between her own body and the body of this particular redwood. Touching the rough surface, she noticed the rings were smooth in relation to one another rather than each being pronouncedly separated from the next. The jagged edges in the plane of the wood were caused by the mechanical blade tearing through the entirety of the tree. A drop of sap near the bark lingered on her palm—a remnant of the life of the tree. The once-hidden annual memories of this individual tree were seemingly made visible and accessible to her. The tree's exposed internal body evoked distant recollections and the slow passage of time, each expressed on successive rings in the deep wood.

In the following section, John Ryan speaks of the memory of trees through the poetics of Aboriginal Australian writers. Alphonso Lingis addresses the lifespan of trees and burial practices that honor the arboreal world. Both authors consider ways that trees preserve a historical record for a community. The rings of living, growing trees also record ecologically destructive practices. Future generations of humans as well as the vast diversity of plants and animals clearly depend on the choices we now make.

—Laura Pustarfi

6

"Old Trees Hold Memory"

Aboriginal Australian Perspectives on Memory, Trauma, and Witnessing in the Arboreal World

JOHN CHARLES RYAN

For more than sixty thousand years, Aboriginal Australian cultures have recognized trees as sacred agents of sustenance, healing, identity, and memory.[1] An outlook on trees as sentient non-human kin is especially evident in Aboriginal Dreaming stories "born from our Mother the land."[2] In her memoir *Under the Wintamarra Tree* (2002), for instance, Australian novelist Doris Pilkington Garimara recounts her birth in the 1930s beneath a mulga (*Acacia aneura*) in the Pilbara region of Western Australia. In the old tree's shade, her mother and aunt "spread out their bedding on the ground, preparing a birthing place well away from the camps, as was the tradition of all the Mardu women before them."[3] Exiled as a child from her birthplace due to the assimilationist policies of the Australian government, Garimara returns five decades years later with her mother, Molly, to search for "that actual wintamarra tree under which I was born."[4] Although the original mulga is long dead, she observes, "its roots are still there down in the earth, and four new trees have grown up."[5] Garimara's arboreal memories highlight the interwoven material-spiritual significance of mulga to Aboriginal societies across Australia. Mulga seed is ground to make bread, mulga wood is crafted for spear throwers, and the saccharine exudate left on leaves by insect larvae is eaten as a bush food.[6] Mulga seed, moreover, is implicated in ancestral creation narratives, as depicted in Papunya artist Clifford Possum Tjapaltjarri's "Mulga Seed Dreaming" (1983).[7] Centered on the large canopy of a tree under which people gather, Tjapaltjarri's painting echoes Garimara's lifelong affective identification with mulga (figure 6.1).

Focusing on Aboriginal Australian narratives of tree wisdom, this chapter explores dendro-mnemonic entanglements toward a conception of *arboreal memory* as an ecology of human–non-human remembrance. As Garimara intimates, trees are *subjects of memory* insofar as humans often have positive recollections of them as vibrant loci of pleasure, imagination, conviviality, and, indeed, consanguinity. The mulga marking Garimara's birthplace also represents the complex manner in which trees

Figure 6.1. Mulga (*Acacia aneura*) in Central Australia. *Source*: Wikimedia Commons. Photo by Mark Marathon. CC BY-SA 4.0.

memorialize—through their embodied presences in landscapes—heterogeneous personal, community, and national events of significance. (Consider, for contrastive purposes, the Bodhi Tree's galvanization of the Buddha's enlightenment in 500 BCE and Splittereiche oak's embodiment of the destruction of Dresden, Germany in 1945.) In the context of memorialization, trees become *agents of memory* through their mediation, modulation, and amplification of recollective processes. Yet, beyond a construction of memory as an exclusively human attribute, research in vegetal cognition affirms that trees are *bearers of memory*. As memoried beings, trees exert their cognitive capacities selectively in adaptive response to unstable ecological conditions.[8] To understand the wisdom of trees as a function of memory, then, is to embrace the mnemonic modes endemic to arboreal life. Bearing these distinctions in mind, this chapter begins with an overview of plant memory as a scientific precept before turning to Aboriginal Australian narratives of memory *of/in* the arboreal world. For Lisa Bellear, Ali Cobby Eckermann, Charmaine Papertalk Green, Peter Minter, and other poets, arboreal memory is a transcorporeal phenomenon that underlies trees' capacity to witness ecocidal trauma while enlivening possibilities for biocultural recuperation and healing.

Wisdom in the Absence of a Brain: Scientific Perspectives on Arboreal Memory

Developments in the field of plant cognition highlight the conjunction between the wisdom of trees and their powers of memory. Notwithstanding burgeoning scientific interest in the premise, elaborations of vegetal memory date back at least to the work of Charles and Francis Darwin in the late nineteenth and early twentieth centuries. The concluding paragraphs of *The Power of Movement in Plants* speculate that the tip of the radicle, with its "diverse kinds of sensitiveness," mediates sensory processing in plants and, consequently, is analogous to the animal brain.[9] Later, the younger Darwin propounded an inclusive view of mnemonic agency as a feature of plants that "like all other living things, have a kind of memory."[10] In his wide-ranging disquisition *Rustic Sounds* (1917), Francis Darwin postulated the existence of a "percipient region" located at the tip of embryonic grass that coordinates stimuli transmission.[11] Francis regarded plant mentation—including consciousness, memory, and desire—as a salient concern that botanists should investigate. For Darwin, unresolved scientific questions surround "the faint beginnings of consciousness, whether plants have the rudiments of desire or of memory, or other qualities generally described as mental."[12] Emphasizing vegetal alterity, furthermore, he advised that the "germ of consciousness" in botanical life be approached without presuming "a psychological resemblance between plants and human beings, lest we go astray into anthropomorphism or sentimentality."[13]

Extending Charles and Francis Darwin's provocations, recent analyses of vegetal memory propose an aneural model of cognition independent of the presence of a brain, spinal cord, and nerves. Research in non-human memory asserts the capacities of trees and other organisms proscribed historically from the domain of intellection and, consequently, denied consciousness, behavior, learning, and other sentient qualities.[14] Conceptualized broadly as "a process by which organisms acquire, encode, store, and retrieve information," memory supplies the latticework for experiential knowledge acquisition whereby organisms enhance fitness by modifying behaviors.[15] Decoupled from the cerebrocentric construction of cognition, the notion of arboreal memory signifies trees' ability "to store and recall information from previous events and then change their responses to future stressful conditions."[16] Memorizing alterations in light, temperature, pressure, stress, and other variables, trees assess and anticipate environmental changes.[17] As a non-centralized, non-cerebral process with both long- and short-term expressions, arboreal memory facilitates the ecological acclimation of tree life.[18] As a case in point, young silver birches subjected experimentally to shifts in solar exposure regulate their growth by comparing the light–dark ratio of lab conditions to ratios recalled from previous days.[19] As such, memory-driven learning underlies decision-making, self-defense, kin recognition, and related arboreal behaviors.[20]

As both scientific and Indigenous knowledge systems demonstrate, wise trees—described, for instance, as "sentinels"[21] and "mother trees"[22]—recall experiences of ecological events and pass these memories to subsequent generations to enhance their progeny's fitness. Rather than an individualized process restricted to "memory banks"—growth rings, branches, roots, seeds, and other anatomical parts—that somatically inscribe habitat conditions over time,[23] arboreal memory also functions in a complex manner between trees and across generations. In this sense, researchers distinguish between, on the one hand, a plant's somatic memory within its lifespan and, on the other, memories passed from the plant to neighbors and offspring.[24] Epigenetic—or inherited—memory primes trees to respond more efficiently to stress.[25] Studies have shown that sentinel plants communicate threats to younger individuals, allowing them to evade or minimize adverse impacts.[26] Conveyed from sentinels to seeds, transgenerational memories of temperature, light, salinity, dormancy, pathogens, and herbivores influence the maturation of offspring by suppressing genes associated with germination until conditions turn favorable.[27] This exchange of environmental experience enables seeds to avoid sprouting at the same time and place. Indeed, the imparting of wisdom from older to younger trees via mnemonic mechanisms underscores the importance of age and diversity to long-term ecosystem resilience.[28] What's more, while trees remember, they also forget. Applied selectively, memory dissipation boosts the fitness of ensuing generations for, as ecologist Peter Crisp and colleagues claim, "in some circumstances, it may be advantageous for plants to learn to forget."[29] This point evokes Nietzsche's notion of active forgetting as the process of banishing trauma, a capacity required for humans to flourish.

In many cases, however, the strict demarcation between somatic (individual) and transgenerational (epigenetic) memory blurs. This is acutely so with respect to ubiquitous underground fungal systems known as mycorrhizal networks that mediate arboreal memory through the rhizosphere, or root-soil interface. Symbiotic partnerships with mycorrhizae supply trees with the energetic matrix required for memory and underlie "the diverse intelligence present among humans and forests."[30] According to ecologist Suzanne Simard, "the topology of mycorrhizal networks is similar to neural networks."[31] Simard's *Finding the Mother Tree* (2021) offers a narrative account of the sophisticated memory-based networks predicated on interactions between trees, fungi, fish, bears, and people in the Pacific Northwest. Roots scavenge decaying salmon nutrients transported by bears from rivers to trees. Via the rhizosphere, mother trees—ancient firs, spruces, and cedars—sequester salmon-derived nitrogen in their rings, furnishing millennia-long histories of fish runs and changing environmental conditions traced in arboreal bodies and embedded in forest systems.[32] Vital to coordinating these collective memory interchanges, mother trees send carbon and other organic compounds to bolster their symbionts, a process that also augments the health of neighboring trees and promotes biodiversity.[33] Elder trees, or sentinels, that have witnessed fluctuating climatic conditions over thousands of years convey genetically-encoded memories via seeds to kin, neighbors, and, even, other species. As a result, subsequent generations of trees—made ready, by inherited wisdom, to cope with ecological instabilities—"ought to be the most successful in rebounding from whatever tumult lies ahead."[34]

Simard's research into mycorrhizal-mediated memory in forests calls attention to the role of Indigenous environmental knowledge and practices in eco-mnemonic assemblages. Vastly predating the scientific recognition of plants' cognitive potentialities, Indigenous conceptions of arboreal life position trees as bearers of memory, keepers of stories, and wellsprings of conviviality. In reflecting on the white pine (*Pinus strobus*), for instance, Potawatomi ecologist Robin Wall Kimmerer identifies a fluid interplay between individualized, somatic memory and collective, transgenerational modes:

> Far from being just a fixed expression of genetic inheritance, individual pines record their journey through life in the form of their body, sketching their autobiography. Gazing out at the pines around my reading nook I see what their childhoods must have been like, in the stature and density of the stand. I see the age and health of their children and grandchildren; I see the way their neighborhoods changed with immigration, their annoyance with balsam, and their camaraderie with blueberries.[35]

Coded genetically, arboreal memory is also expressed corporeally through a tree's somatic relationships to kin (children and grandchildren) and co-inhabitants (balsam and blueberries). Reading white pine rings under a stereomicroscope, Kimmerer declaims, "the tree has written its story in the life of its own body."[36] Understanding arboreal memory as a multidimensional process, therefore, requires appreciating how arboreal bodies express ecological wisdom while memory itself moves like an energetic current between trees, humans, and other beings. To this effect, the next section explores conceptions of arboreal memory in Aboriginal Australian cultures.

Trees of Birth and Naming:
Arboreal Memory in Aboriginal Australian Culture

Evoked as sentinels and mothers, large primeval trees inscribe memories of past environmental conditions in their bodies.[37] Enacting dendrochronological agency, trees keep "unerring time. In their rings, trees record many climate melodies, played in different places and different eras."[38] In contrast to the corporealized memories of an individual tree within its lifespan, transgenerational memory entails the dissemination of experiences from mother trees to seeds, progeny, and community. What's more, recognizing the propinquity of trees, humans, and other life forms, biocultural memory entails an interspecies mnemonics arising from "the stored experiences and information (e.g., evolutionary, ecological, historical) shared by living beings with one another and with their territories."[39] Shaping and reshaping tree-people conjunctions, forests thus become biocultural "repositories of memory."[40] Arboreal memory as biocultural—a concept integral to Simard's studies of mycorrhizal interchanges—also resonates in Aboriginal Australian narratives of trees. For instance, Wiradjuri author and activist Kevin Gilbert's poem "Tree," published in 1988, discloses an arboreal perspective on humanness in which a tree imparts existential wisdom to its addressee: "I am you and / you are nothing / but through me the tree."[41] For Gaagudju Elder Bill Neidjie, as well, ancient trees are percipient fellow-beings who listen, feel, desire, dream, remember, and thrive within the biocultural groundwork of the Dreaming: "That tree e listen to you, what you! / E got no finger, e can't speak / but that leaf e pumping his."[42]

Vital to locating arboreal memory within an Aboriginal framework are Law, Dreaming, and Country as signifiers of deep ancestral interconnectedness. In the view of Kombumerri-Wakka Wakka philosopher Mary Graham, biocultural memory emerges from a "relationist ethos" predicated on a "sacred web of connections" between self, kin, culture, and land.[43] Reflecting the behavior of trees and other non-human entities, Law signifies "a permanent, standing obligation to look after Land, society and social relations."[44] Dreaming, moreover, refers to the multitudinous creation narratives underlying "Aboriginal ontogenesis."[45] Dreaming stories emphasize the activities of Creator Beings—trees, plants, vines, herbs, seeds—who contoured the landscape through their interactions with other entities.[46] For Graham, flora, fauna, landforms, and waterbodies are "all our ancestors, because they all came before us."[47] Additionally, Country—a forest, desert, wetland, marine habitat, or other biocultural complex—is "a matrix of relations, narratives, obligations [with a] soft, inclusive structure, spirit, agency and memory."[48] In an Aboriginal sense, arboreal memory integrates the deep-time mnemonics of the Dreaming, guiding community commitments to Country in the present, as set out by Law. As a case in point, the boab tree (*Adansonia gregorii*) is central to the traditional cultural stories of Northern Australian people. Among the Yarralin of the Northern Territory, for instance, the Dreaming entity Walujapi (a female black-headed python) disseminated the seeds of large trees, such as boabs, as she traversed the land.[49] Local residents today observe traditional obligations to old boabs regarded as sacred trees marking the path Walujapi walked during the Dreaming.[50]

Viewed in the light of consilience, scientific and Indigenous conceptions of arboreal memory concur that knowledgeable older trees—endowed with extensive mnemonic networks—safeguard, nurture, and educate younger ones.[51] Gladys Idjirrimoonya Milroy and Jill Milroy of the Palyku cultural group of Western Australia acknowledge the indispensable function of trees as memory agents fortifying biocultural systems. Their assertions align with those of plant researchers who similarly underscore the importance of mother trees to continuing ecosystem health.[52] For Milroy and Milroy, "trees anchor the earth; they provide the eternal maternal bloodline that nourishes us all."[53] The wisdom of arboreal life becomes palpable through lifelong experiences with trees as family members who "give birth and nurture and care for their babies, just like humans."[54] Reminiscent of Doris Pilkington Garimara's filiation with the mulga, Milroy and Milroy explain that "trees are the midwives when children are birthed on the banks of dry riverbeds where the tall gums grow, and where each child has a birth tree."[55] Sharing in the corporeal exigencies of being, trees accompany us through the courses of our lives and "in our passing, we are held once more in the loving embrace of trees, held aloft, wrapped in paperbark, hollow logs, a resting place."[56] Similarly, narrating the funerary significance of trees, Oodgeroo Noonuccal's poem "Tree Grave" (1966) concerns the swamp oak (*Casuarina glauca*) whose material presence is announced in the opening lines, "When our lost one left us / For the Shadow Land, / In bark we bound him."[57]

Throughout Aboriginal Australia, sheoaks in the genera *Casuarina* and *Allocasuarina* are understood to have an exceptional capacity for long-term memory. Noonuccal's poem "Tree Grave," in particular, illuminates the acoustic phenomenon known as "sheoak whispers"—the distinctive enunciation of the species in relation to its Dreaming and Country. In the Noongar language of the Southwest region of Western Australia, sheoak (*Allocasuarina fraseriana*) is known as *kwela* where *kwel* denotes "name." Noongar cultural custodians recognize the sheoak as the tree of naming—a percipient arboreal persona who remembers the names of everything and everyone, alive and deceased, animate and inanimate, and vocalizes those names through its whispers.[58] As expounded by Noongar

Elder Noel Nannup in conversation with botanist Steven Hooper, "Kwel is the tree of names. It knows every person who's ever lived and inhabited this area through the DNA of their skin and hair."[59] Evocative of Kevin Gilbert's poetic narration of dendro-anthro-entanglement,[60] for Nannup, trees and other plants are "what connects you to Country. They're part of the totemic system. They're part of you, you're part of them."[61] Nannup further elaborates the sacred junction of people, trees, fungi, soil, memory, embodiment, and wisdom:

> As we live in a place, walk through it, follow the songlines, we shed our skin. The skin falls into the soil because [Southwest Australia has] the most nutrient-deficient soil on the planet. [The soil] replaces that nutrient deficiency through fungi favored by several of our trees, particularly sheoaks. Because we shed our skin, the mycorrhizae underneath them take it up. Our DNA is in those trees. That's the connection. That means it's the tree of names. In the wind, if you tune in, you'll hear the voice of every person who's ever lived.[62]

Within the context of Noongar Dreaming, Nannup poetically narrates the complex diffusion of intergenerational memory between people, fungi, and sheoaks. Set in motion by the act of walking on Country, the shedding of skin and the uptake of DNA through the rhizosphere evoke Simard's narrative of arboreal memory mediation through mycorrhizal pathways.

"Of Memory Deep Inside":
Arboreal Memory and Embodiment in Aboriginal Poetry

With their roots, rhizomes, heartwood, piths, trunks, branches, fruits, and flowers, trees are somatic agents—enfleshed beings with sensing bodies markedly different yet uncannily kindred to our own. One interpretation of arboreal memory is as somatic recollection, exemplified by the materializing of temporal passage and the archiving of climatic fluctuations in tree rings. Characterizing nonconscious memory as a "constituent of the vibrant and multidimensional intelligence of plants," Michael Marder emphasizes that, "whereas humans remember whatever has phenomenally appeared in the light, plants keep the memory of light itself."[63] Yet, plants perceive a broad spectrum of stimuli including light, as Marder notes, but also chemicals, temperature, electricity, vibration, and sound.[64] Emitted from roots, leaves, and flowers, volatile organic compounds drive plant communication, constituting "an ancient chemical language shared with bacteria, fungi, and animals."[65] As geneticist Daniel Chamovitz elaborates, plants exhibit a suite of visual, auditory, olfactory, gustatory, tactile, kinesthetic, and mnemonic abilities.[66] A dialogical conception of arboreal memory, then, signifies both how humans remember trees through bodies and, conversely, how trees enact their own somatic mnemonics via sensory interchanges with beings, elements, and habitats. Aboriginal Australian poetry, indeed, inflects a view of arboreal memory as a function of trees' corporeal agencies.[67] On the ghost gum (*Corymbia apparerinja*)—a species integral to the Dreaming of Central Australia and featuring extensively in Albert Namatjira's paintings—Bundjalung poet Evelyn Araluen evokes how tree "skins soak the light" in a dance of radiance and remembering.[68]

Intimated by Araluen, a somatics of arboreal memory likewise figures into Ali Cobby Eckermann's "Leaves" and "Today,"[69] Charmaine Papertalk Green's "Honey to Lips Bottlebrush,"[70] and Peter Minter's "The Tree, The Tree."[71] Eckermann is a Yankunytjatjara-Kokatha poet whose writing interbraids human and non-human modes of memory. "Leaves" stands out in particular for its unsettling of Western ontological demarcations between trees and people. The poem opens probingly with, "that lone tree on the ridge / is that my father? / it stands like him."[72] Elicited through sensorial imagining, familial remembrance weaves rhizomatically into arboreal memories. Sensuous contact with trees in their dwelling places dispels the pretense of estrangement between "tree," on the one hand, and "father," on the other, as discrete, irreconcilable kinship categories. Rather than the inert backdrop against which recollection plays out, the tree is a responsive, altruistic, and consoling presence: "I crawled there once and sat / in his shade he did not know me / yet gave me leaves."[73] Acts of corporeal co-engendering—of climbing, lying, watching, waiting—enable the memories that trees inscribe in their flesh to perfuse the memories embodied in human beings. All corridors of remembrance return to the tree, as heralded by the question, "if I climb to him now / and lie in his limbs / will our story unite?"[74]

Evocative of Garimara's mother mulga, the Milroys' birthing trees, and Nannup's tree of names, "Today" begins with an unembellished revelation, "today I found the tree under / which my mother was born,"[75] and which, the speaker clarifies, holds her mother's placenta and ashes. Here, Eckermann alludes to the tradition among Aboriginal women of burying a child's placenta at the birthplace. After laying a newborn in an earthen depression, Cape York women would inter the afterbirth, connecting the infant indelibly to the land.[76] In this spirit, "Today" traces the balletic movement of memory between beings and bodies—across generations of mothers, fathers, children, and plants—as "today I became a weeping tree / a vision of memory deep inside."[77] Comparably somatic in emphasis, Wadjari-Bardimaia poet Charmaine Papertalk Green's "Honey to Lips Bottlebrush" enunciates the varied sensory and temporal registers of arboreal memory.[78] The poem recounts synesthetic memories of bottlebrushes (*Callistemon* spp.), wattles (*Acacia* spp.), and other trees characteristic of the Southwest Australian flora:

> Sucking nectar bottlebrush sweet
> Wattle seeds eating tasting time ago
> Visions of firesticks ancestors' walking
> Tracks etched into land across land.[79]

Narrated by Papertalk Green, sensuous encounters between trees and people entail the interlacing of tactility (sucking), gustation (sweetness), kinesthesia and topaesthesia (walking), ocularity (visions of firesticks ancestors), and transgenerational somatic recollection (tasting time ago). The interpenetration of sensory modalities engenders bodily consciousness in the reader of the deep-time conjunctions between trees and humankind in Aboriginal culture. The poem, moreover, places emphasis on the gustatory consummation of "honey to lips bottlebrush"—a refrain repeated throughout—summoning ancestral memories of *red fire dotted campsites* as "still wind still ancestors come to visit."[80]

For cultural groups such as the Wajarri and Bardimaia of Western Australia, wattles, bottlebrushes, boabs, ghost gums, and other trees are memory-keepers and memory-bearers whose felt experiences take shape within the lineaments of Country and Dreaming. In this context, Koori poet Peter Minter's ode "The Tree, The Tree" extends the tradition within Aboriginal poetry of lyricizing trees as fellow-beings with distinctive subjectivities. Accordingly, the poem asserts the longstanding human-arboreal interdependencies that are mediated by transgenerational memory networks. "The Tree, The Tree" announces its literary inheritance through epigraphs from Oodgeroo Noonuccal and Kevin Gilbert. Consisting of more questions than statements, the dialogic structure of Minter's narrative, at the same time, recalls Noongar poet Jack Davis's "The Red Gum and I" (1970), a poem addressing the marri tree (*Corymbia calophylla*) as a percipient subject with the ability to assuage colonial trauma.[81] In Davis's poem, the speaker implores the tree, "Take me through the bark / Into the sap stream."[82] Like Davis's red gum, Minter's tree is a subject commanding poetic attention as "my addressee," a phrase populating the ode. Incorporating the near-homonymic resonance between "tree" and "thee," the melodious narrative opens with:

> What am I, the tree
> who stands before thee
> just as thee are tree for me,
> Or I am thee.[83]

Further along, Minter asserts the somatic presence of the tree in lines such as "How do I plea / before the solid trunk before me?"[84] What's more, the poem attends to the tree's temporal calculus in the phrases "time's payee" and "time's one durée, that final key" as well as the questions "Who are you, tree? / Who has the time of living's key?"[85] Contrasting images of incarceration and liberation in the final line, Minter's framing of the tree as "my detainee, my devotee" generates an unresolved friction elucidating the co-implication of human and arboreal lives particularly from an Aboriginal perspective on colonial history.

"It Is Still There: Our Story": Arboreal Memory and Transgenerational Trauma

Through their cognitive-corporeal exertions, trees resist the essentialization of their lives as icons, symbols, motifs, memes, and memorabilia in service to the imperial memory of settler society. Minter's "The Tree, The Tree" illuminates the interrelation between trees, memory, trauma, and colonialism in Australia. As witnesses to biocultural disintegration, native Australian trees "keep the memory of light itself," in Marder's terms,[86] yet also narrativize the pernicious residues of colonization directly through their bodies. Research indicates that plants retain long-term memories of trauma.[87] In a study by plant physiologist Michel Thellier and colleagues from 1982, for instance, Spanish needle (*Bidens pilosa*) remembered the puncturing of its cotyledon (embryonic leaf), triggering adjacent buds to grow faster in response.[88] If plants communicate memories of physical harm *within* and *among* themselves, then it stands to reason that they also sequester memories of the biocultural suffering inflicted on land and people. Aboriginal narratives, such as Oodgeroo Noonuccal's "Municipal Gum" (1966)[89] and Jack Davis's "Forest Giant" (1992),[90] offer poetic groundwork for appraising such an assertion. Like many other dendro-poems in Aboriginal literature, "Forest Giant" employs direct address to engender dialogue with the tree: "You have stood there for centuries / arms gaunt reaching for the sky."[91] The image of emaciated limbs stretching overhead signals the position of Australian trees within a mnemonic continuum—from the deep, nourishing memoryscapes of the Dreaming to the relatively recent yet intensely traumatic experiences of settler colonialism. Bearing witness to ecocide, the tree-addressee speaks—wordlessly, through somatic signification—of shared human-arboreal suffering as, "Now you and I / bleed in sorrow and in silence."[92]

Echoing Davis's poem, Noonuccal's "Municipal Gum" elegizes the erosion of a tree's vitality in a denatured urban plantscape in lines such as, "Gumtree in the city street, / Hard bitumen around your feet."[93] Like the dendro-narratives of Davis and Noonuccal, Lisa Bellear's "Beautiful Yuroke Red River Gum" (1996),[94] Jared Thomas's "The Healing Tree" (2008),[95] and Ali Cobby Eckermann and Joy Harjo's "Story Tree" (2021)[96] focus on the biocultural impacts of settler colonialism alongside the potential for healing through the recuperation of ethical human-tree relations based in Law. Bellear was a Goernpil poet of the Noonuccal people, much of whose writing concerns urban cultures and ecologies. The few extant trees in the postcolonial plantscape of Yuroke, a locality within Greater Melbourne, are "survivors of genocide" who, like urban Aboriginal dwellers, "watch / and camp out, live, breathe in various / parks 'round Fitzroy."[97] In Australia, red river gums (*Eucalyptus camaldulensis*) and other native trees continue to be cleared, at a startling rate, for urban, suburban, and rural expansion.[98] Bellear's image of the isolated gum in Yuroke draws attention to the ecocide—or, more precisely, *dendrocide*, the broadscale eradication of trees—that began with colonization in the late-eighteenth century and continues in the present. Within the painful recollection of dendrocide, however, inheres the embodied memory of "a scarred tree which overlooks the / Melbourne Cricket Ground."[99] While in one sense connoting ecovandalism, Bellear's reference also brings to mind the extensive tradition of dendroglyphs. For Aboriginal societies, the ceremonial carving of trees has constituted a form of cultural expression for thousands of years. Often inscribed in old, contorted individuals, dendroglyphs are mnemonic media imparting vital information to future generations through the vibrant materiality of arboreal life. In Northern Australia, for example, Aboriginal people carved images into boab trunks to create dendroglyphs that remain vital to biocultural heritage.[100]

Evocative of Bellear's "Beautiful Yuroke Red River Gum," Nukunu poet Jared Thomas's "The Healing Tree" concerns ancestral tree-people filiations in urban environments. Beginning and ending with allusions to the medicinal virtues of Australian trees, the short story traces the recovery of the protagonist, fifty-five-year-old Alf, from addiction, incarceration, and dislocation. Although most Aboriginal people now live in urban areas, the problem of "Indigenous invisibility" persists, contributing to a lack of awareness of health issues reflecting derogatory assumptions about what defines an Indigenous person or community.[101] For Alf, embodied interactions with trees—chewing stems, digging roots, drinking medicines—constitute a substratum for resolving physical and psychological malaise: "Yep, this yirta here's a real good medicine tree, cure almost anything, even a broken heart."[102] Memories of native gums and pines catalyze the recuperation of traditional arboreal knowledge and, thus, inspirit Alf's process of recovery: "He remembered the trees, the gums and native pines sitting by the soft edges of the creek bed or contorting through the rocks and slate of the hills. Alf especially remembered his father's uses for the trees. He closed his eyes and concentrated on the aroma of lemon-scented gum, wafting from the nearby South Terrace Park Lands."[103] Olfactory recollection—"the aroma of lemon-scented gum"—presents an especially potent agent of healing, connecting Alf to ancestral trees even in their absence from the urban plantscape. By the story's end, "he dreams only of the yirtas, the trees. All he wants to do is chew on their leaves hungrily, hoping they'll fix his broken heart."[104]

Thomas's narrative of Alf's recovery points to the *storiedness* of trees—their embodiment of memory and potential for healing. Comparably, in "Story Tree," an epistolary poem co-written by Eckermann and Mvskoke poet Joy Harjo, trees intervene in the "concrete and / sorrow of this poem."[105] Harjo alludes to the Council Oak Tree, the founding site of Tulsa, Oklahoma, chosen in 1836 by the Lochapoka Creek people as their council ground: "It is still there: our story and / The tree *who* holds it in place, and the memory of the fire."[106] In this instance, Harjo's use of "who" rather than "that" signifies the personhood of the memory-bearing oak. Trauma disrupts the lives of people and trees alike, as the speaker alludes to her son who labors on the railroads rather than following "the path of plant and animal knowledge."[107] Eckermann replies, "There are no trains here. The railway lines have been removed, the station house vacant in disrepair."[108] Familial reflection evolves into ecological imperative as, "Millions of trees are demolished to build the railroad. Now barely a tree survives. You and I know old trees hold memories. It is tragic these trees have been destroyed."[109] Notwithstanding the logic of ecological regeneration, the legacy of interspecies trauma persists: "Miles of empty railway corridors are re-sown with native seeds, the regeneration of saplings an offering to the native animals and birds, a haven built by those who have destroyed what was. Of course I am excluded. I am no longer fauna and flora. There is no returning. There is no re-turn. Truth is a lonely weight to carry."[110] Dialogic in structure, Eckermann and Harjo's epistolary narrative imbricates personal, cultural, and arboreal memory within the history of dendrocide in Australia, a "truth" underlain by dendrophobia, the fear of unknown trees and forests.

Conclusion: From Dendrophobia to Dendrophilia, Embracing New Memoryscapes

Aboriginal literature reminds us that the wisdom of trees lies in their dual capacity to witness trauma and cleanse its lingering residues. In the work of Bellear, Eckermann, Papertalk Green, Minter, Thomas, and other Aboriginal writers, trees are mnemonic agents—both memoried and remembered. Bringing Indigenous and scientific epistemologies into dialogue promotes an integrative view of arboreal memory as a somatic and transgenerational phenomenon consolidating relations between trees, people, and other beings. In an era of pervasive plant loss, the challenge ahead is to (re)imagine new memoryscapes based on modes of being-with the arboreal that integrate trees' mnemonic agencies. At the same time, forging memoryscapes requires countering dendrophobia, the fear of what forests might contain or conceal.[111] In Australia, this transformation of arboreal values entails shifting away from entrenched notions of native trees as ominous, unsightly, or inferior. Indeed, there are implications not only for literature, art, and philosophy but also for forest conservation and management. If older trees have a larger reserve of memory, they should be preserved as sentinels who protect the community.[112] And as Simard's work makes clear, forest memory networks draw attention to the urgent need to protect mother trees who ensure communication and health in forests.[113] Acknowledging Aboriginal people's wisdom of trees—disseminated, seed-like, through poetry and other narratives—engenders new arboreal cultures in Australia. Countering dendrophobia, we might embrace dendrophilia, a love for trees as wise fellow-beings in all their forms.

Notes

1. Philip A. Clarke, *Aboriginal People and Their Plants*, 2nd ed. (Dural Delivery Centre, NSW: Rosenberg Publishing, 2011); Chris Clarkson et al., "Human Occupation of Northern Australia by 65,000 Years Ago," *Nature* 547 (2017): 306–10; Bill Neidjie, *Story about Feeling*, ed. Keith Taylor (Broome, WA: Magabala Books, 1989).

2. Gladys Idjirrimoonya Milroy and Jill Milroy, "Different Ways of Knowing: Trees Are Our Families Too," in *Heartsick for Country: Stories of Love, Spirit and Creation*, eds. Sally Morgan, Tjalaminu Mia, and Blaze Kwaymullina (Fremantle, WA: Fremantle Press, 2008), 22–42, on 24.

3. Doris Pilkington Garimara, *Under the Wintamarra Tree* (St. Lucia, Qld: University of Queensland Press, 2002), 23.

4. Garamara, *Under the Wintamarra Tree*, 203.

5. Garamara, *Under the Wintamarra Tree*, 208.

6. Clarke, *Aboriginal People*, 125, 160, 208.

7. Clifford Possum Tjapaltjarri, "Mulga Seed Dreaming, 1983," Araluen Arts Centre, https://araluenartscentre.nt.gov.au/exhibitions/lineage-legacy/mulga-seed-dreaming. Accessed May 20, 2022.

8. Yutcelia C. F. Galviz, Rafael V. Ribeiro, and Gustavo M. Souza, "Yes, Plants Do Have Memory," *Theoretical and Experimental Plant Physiology* 32, no. 3 (2020): 195–202, https://doi.org/10.1007/s40626-020-00181-y; Suzanne W. Simard, "Mycorrhizal Networks Facilitate Tree Communication, Learning, and Memory," in *Memory and Learning in Plants*, eds. František Baluška, Monica Gagliano, and Guenther Witzany (Cham, Switzerland: Springer International Publishing, 2018), 191–213.

9. Charles Darwin and Francis Darwin, *The Works of Charles Darwin: The Power of Movement in Plants*, eds. Paul Barrett and R. B. Freeman (London: Routledge, 2016), 419, original publication 1880.

10. Francis Darwin, *Rustic Sounds and Other Studies in Literature and Natural History* (London: John Murray, 1917), 51.

11. Darwin, *Rustic Sounds*, 50.

12. Darwin, *Rustic Sounds*, 51.

13. Darwin, *Rustic Sounds*, 52.

14. Guenther Witzany, "Memory and Learning as Key Competences of Living Organisms," in *Memory and Learning in Plants*, eds. František Baluška, Monica

Gagliano, and Guenther Witzany (Cham, Switzerland: Springer International Publishing, 2018), 1–16, on 9–10.

15. Simard, "Mycorrhizal," 206.

16. Galviz, Ribeiro, and Souza, "Yes, Plants," 195.

17. Ralf Müller-Xing, Qian Xing, and Justin Goodrich, "Footprints of the Sun: Memory of UV and Light Stress in Plants," *Frontiers in Plant Science* 5 (2014): 1–12. https://doi.org/10.3389/fpls.2014.00474

18. Peter Crisp et al., "Reconsidering Plant Memory: Intersections between Stress Recovery, RNA Turnover, and Epigenetics," *Science Advances* 2, no. 2 (2016): 1–14, on 5. https://doi.org/10.1126/sciadv.1501340

19. Richard Karban, *Plant Sensing and Communication* (Chicago: University of Chicago Press, 2015), 33.

20. Simard, "Mycorrhizal."

21. Rafael V. Ribeiro and Ricardo da Silva Torres, "Sentinel Plants as Programmable Processing Units: Insights From a Multidisciplinary Perspective About Stress Memory and Plant Signaling and Their Relevance at Community Level," *Plant Signaling & Behavior* 13, no. 10 (2018): 1–3. https://doi.org/10.108 0/15592324.2018.1526001

22. Suzanne Simard, *Finding the Mother Tree: Discovering the Wisdom of the Forest* (New York: Alfred A. Knopf, 2021).

23. Simard, "Mycorrhizal," 202.

24. Yuehui He and Zicong Li, "Epigenetic Environmental Memories in Plants: Establishment, Maintenance, and Reprogramming," *Trends in Genetics* 34, no. 11 (2018): 856–66, on 857. https://doi.org/10.1016/j.tig.2018.07.006

25. He and Li, "Epigenetic," 856; Ribeiro and da Silva Torres, "Sentinel."

26. Ribeiro and da Silva Torres, "Sentinel," 1.

27. Mayumi Iwasaki, Lena Hyvarinen, Urszula Piskurewicz, and Luis Lopez-Molina, "Non-Canonical RNA-Directed DNA Methylation Participates in Maternal and Environmental Control of Seed Dormancy," *eLife* 8, no. e37434 (2019): 1–17. https://doi.org/10.7554/eLife.37434

28. Galviz, Ribeiro, and Souza, "Yes, Plants," 200.

29. Crisp et al., "Reconsidering," 1.

30. Simard, "Mycorrhizal," 197.

31. Simard, "Mycorrhizal," 191.

32. Simard, *Finding*, 281.

33. Simard, *Finding*, 275.

34. Simard, *Finding*, 277.

35. Robin Wall Kimmerer, "White Pine," in *The Mind of Plants: Narratives of Vegetal Intelligence*, eds. John C. Ryan, Patrícia Vieira, and Monica Gagliano (Santa Fe, NM: Synergetic Press, 2021), 423–31, on 427–28.

36. Kimmerer, "White Pine," 428.

37. Ribeiro and da Silva Torres, "Sentinel;" Simard, "Mycorrhizal;" *Finding*.

38. Keith R. Briffa, "Annual Climate Variability in the Holocene: Interpreting the Message of Ancient Trees," *Quaternary Science Reviews* 19, nos. 1–5 (2000): 87–105, on 87. https://doi.org/10.1016/S0277-3791(99)00056-6

39. José Tomás Ibarra et al., "Becoming Tree, Becoming Memory: Social-Ecological Fabrics in Pewen (*Araucaria araucana*) Landscapes of the Southern Andes," in *The Cultural Value of Trees: Folk Value and Biocultural Conservation*, ed. Jeffrey Wall (New York: Routledge, 2022), 15–31, on 16.

40. Ibarra et al., "Becoming," 16.

41. Kevin Gilbert, "Tree," in *Anthology of Australian Aboriginal Literature*, eds. Anita Heiss and Peter Minter (Montreal: McGill-Queen's University Press, 2008), 84–85, ll. 9–11, original publication 1988.

42. Neidjie, *Story*, 23, ll. 4–7.

43. Mary Graham, "A Relationist Ethos: Aboriginal Law and Ethics," *Earth Ethics Australia* 1 (2019): 1–6, on 6.

44. Mary Graham, "Aboriginal Notions of Relationality and Positionalism: A Reply to Weber," *Global Discourse* 4, no. 1 (2014): 17–22, on 18. https://doi.org/10.1080/23269995.2014.895931

45. Morgan Brigg and Mary Graham, "Human Futures and the Incomplete Dreaming Story of COVID-19," *ABC News*, accessed May 25, 2022, para. 4. www.abc.net.au/religion/dreaming-story-of-covid-19-morgan-brigg-and-mary-graham/13899068

46. Mary Graham, "Some Thoughts about the Philosophical Underpinnings of Aboriginal Worldviews," *Australian Humanities Review* 45 (2008). http://australianhumanitiesreview.org/2008/11/01/some-thoughts-about-the-philosophical-underpinnings-of-aboriginal-worldviews

47. Graham, "A Relationist Ethos," 6.

48. Graham, "Aboriginal Notions," 19.

49. Deborah Bird Rose, *Dingo Makes Us Human: Life and Land in an Australian Aboriginal Culture* (Cambridge, UK: Cambridge University Press, 2000), 42.

50. Gerald E. Wickens and Pat Lowe, *The Baobabs: Pachycauls of Africa, Madagascar and Australia* (Berlin: Springer, 2008), 65.

51. Milroy and Milroy, "Different Ways;" Noel Nannup and Steven Hopper, "Synergies: Walking Together—Belonging to Country," YouTube, May 9, 2016. www.youtube.com/watch?v=aeGqTpLDYjQ

52. He and Li, "Epigenetic;" Ribeiro and da Silva Torres, "Sentinel;" Simard, "Mycorrhizal;" *Finding*.

53. Milroy and Milroy, "Different Ways," 37.

54. Milroy and Milroy, "Different Ways," 27–28.

55. Milroy and Milroy, "Different Ways," 35.

56. Milroy and Milroy, "Different Ways," 36.

57. Oodgeroo Noonuccal, *My People*, 4th ed. (Milton, Qld: John Wiley & Sons, 2008), 6, ll. 1–8, original publication 1970.

58. John C. Ryan, "The Virtual and the Vegetal: Creating a 'Living' Biocultural Heritage Archive through Digital Storytelling Approaches," *Global Media Journal* 9, no. 1 (2015): 1–10, on 6–7.

59. Nannup and Hopper, "Synergies," mins. 24:49–25:03.

60. Gilbert, "Tree."

61. Nannup and Hopper, "Synergies," mins. 10:37–10:46.

62. Noel Nannup, "Noel Nannup: Point Walter," YouTube, June 30, 2016, mins. 4:56–5:35. www.youtube.com/watch?v=Gy2kUbrTJTk

63. Michael Marder, *Plant-Thinking: A Philosophy of Vegetal Life* (New York: Columbia University Press, 2013), 156.

64. Richard Karban, "The Language of Plant Communication (and How It Compares to Animal Communication)," in *The Language of Plants: Science, Philosophy, Literature*, eds. Monica Gagliano, John C. Ryan, and Patrícia Vieira (Minneapolis: University of Minnesota Press, 2017), 3–26, on 4–10.

65. Robert A. Raguso and André Kessler, "Speaking in Chemical Tongues: Decoding the Language of Plant Volatiles," in *The Language of Plants: Science, Philosophy, Literature*, eds. Monica Gagliano, John C. Ryan, and Patrícia Vieira (Minneapolis: University of Minnesota Press, 2017), 27–61, on 28.

66. Daniel Chamovitz, *What a Plant Knows: A Field Guide to the Senses* (London: Scribe Publications, 2012).

67. John C. Ryan, "Literary Ethnobotany and Human-Plant Intercorporeality in Aboriginal Australian Poetry: 'Into the Sap Stream,'" in *The Bloomsbury Handbook to the Medical-Environmental Humanities*, eds. Scott Slovic, Swarnalatha Rangarajan, and Vidya Sarveswaran (London: Bloomsbury, 2022), 345–59.

68. Evelyn Araluen, *Dropbear* (St. Lucia, Qld: University of Queensland Press, 2021), 4, para. 1.

69. Ali Cobby Eckermann, *Inside My Mother* (Sydney: Giramondo Publishing Company, 2015).

70. Charmaine Papertalk Green and John Kinsella, *False Claims of Colonial Thieves* (Broome, WA: Magabala Books, 2018).

71. Peter Minter, "The Tree, The Tree," Red Room Poetry, 2021. https://redroompoetry.org/poets/peter-minter/thetree

72. Eckermann, *Inside*, 61, ll. 1–3.

73. Eckermann, *Inside*, 61, ll. 10–12.

74. Eckermann, *Inside*, 61, ll. 16–18.

75. Eckermann, *Inside*, 88, ll. 1–4.

76. Nicole Ramsamy, "Indigenous Birthing in Remote Locations: Grandmothers' Law and Government Medicine," in *Yatdjuligin: Aboriginal and Torres Strait Islander Nursing and Midwifery Care*, eds. Odette Best and Bronwyn Fredericks (Cambridge, UK: Cambridge University Press, 2021), 169–86, on 172.

77. Eckermann, *Inside*, 88, ll. 13–14.

78. Papertalk Green and Kinsella, *False Claims*, 53–54.

79. Papertalk Green and Kinsella, *False Claims*, 53, ll. 16–19.
80. Papertalk Green and Kinsella, *False Claims*, 53, ll. 21, 26, italics original.
81. Jack Davis, *The First-Born and Other Poems* (Sydney: Angus and Robertson, 1970).
82. Davis, *The First-Born*, 38, ll. 3–4.
83. Minter, "The Tree, The Tree," ll. 1–4.
84. Minter, "The Tree, The Tree," ll. 21–22.
85. Minter, "The Tree, The Tree," ll. 12, 40, 49–50.
86. Marder, *Plant-Thinking*, 156.
87. Chamovitz, *What a Plant Knows*; Crisp et al., "Reconsidering;" He and Li, "Epigenetic."
88. M. Thellier, M. O. Desbiez, P. Champagnat, and Y. Kergosien, "Do Memory Processes Occur Also in Plants," *Physiologia Plantarum* 56, no. 3 (1982): 281–84. https://doi.org/10.1111/j.1399-3054.1982.tb00339.x
89. Noonuccal, *My People*, 45, original publication 1966.
90. Jack Davis, "Forest Giant," in *Little Books of Trees*, ed. Joanna Karmel (Canberra: National Library of Australia, 2010), 4, original publication 1992.
91. Davis, "Forest Giant," 4, ll. 1–2.
92. Davis, "Forest Giant," 4, ll. 10–11.
93. Noonuccal, *My People*, 45, ll. 1–5.
94. Lisa Bellear, "Beautiful Yuroke Red River Gum," in *Fire Front: First Nations Poetry and Power Today*, ed. Alison Whittaker (St. Lucia, Qld: University of Queensland Press, 2020), 15–16, original publication 1996.
95. Jared Thomas, "The Healing Tree," in *Anthology of Australian Aboriginal Literature*, eds. Anita Heiss and Peter Minter (Montreal: McGill-Queen's University Press, 2008), 236–40.
96. Ali Cobby Eckermann and Joy Harjo, "Story Tree," Red Room Poetry, 2021. https://redroompoetry.org/poets/ali-cobby-eckermann/story-tree
97. Bellear, "Beautiful," 15, ll. 18–20.
98. Anne Davies, "Clearing of Native Vegetation in NSW Jumps 800% in Three Years," *The Guardian*, August 3, 2018. www.theguardian.com/australia-news/2018/aug/04/clearing-of-native-vegetation-in-nsw-jumps-800-in-three-years
99. Bellear, "Beautiful," 15, ll. 16–17.
100. Department of Natural Resources, Environment, the Arts and Sport, *Judbarra / Gregory National Park and Gregory's Tree Historical Reserve Joint Management Plan* (Katherine, NT: Department of Natural Resources, Environment, the Arts and Sport, 2011).
101. Warren Jennings et al., "Rapid Review of Five Years of Aboriginal and Torres Strait Islander Health Research in Australia—Persisting Under-Representation of Urban Populations," *Australian and New Zealand Journal of Public Health* 45, no. 1 (2021): 53–58.
102. Thomas, "The Healing Tree," 236.

103. Thomas, "The Healing Tree," 236-37.
104. Thomas, "The Healing Tree," 240.
105. Eckermann and Harjo, "Story Tree," sect. "Ali, Sister," ll. 4-5.
106. Eckermann and Harjo, "Story Tree," sect. "Ali, Sister," ll. 14-15.
107. Eckermann and Harjo, "Story Tree," sect. "Ali, Sister," l. 43.
108. Eckermann and Harjo, "Story Tree," sect. "Dear Sister," ll. 1-2.
109. Eckermann and Harjo, "Story Tree," sect. "Dear Sister," ll. 4-5.
110. Eckermann and Harjo, "Story Tree," sect. "Dear Sister," ll. 8-11.
111. Owain Jones and Paul Cloke, *Tree Cultures: The Place of Trees and Trees in Their Place* (Oxford, UK: Berg, 2002), 28.
112. Ribeiro and da Silva Torres, "Sentinel."
113. Simard, "Mycorrhizal;" *Finding*.

7

Birth and Death in Trees

Alphonso Lingis

Figure 7.1. Woman in a white dress lying on the ground in the forest. *Source*: Pexels.com. Photo by Carolina Basi. CC0.

After we die, trees accompany us. Evergreen and long-lived yews, cypresses, and Eastern red cedars are the trees most seen in cemeteries. Their stately, compact, somber forms attend the grief and endurance of those who visit the graves of the dead.

Natural or green burials often involve biodegradable clothing, no embalming, a shroud and burial container, locally grown flowers, a small memorial gathering in a natural setting, and burial in a shallow grave in a protected forest or meadow. The decomposing body releases nutrients for the trees, shrubs, and pastures. This strikes many people not only as natural—the destination of dead bodies in nature—but as a positive transformation of our bodily tissue that lives on in trees.

The more we learn through empirical research about humans and about trees, the more new questions arise: What is an individual? What is life? What is an individual life? What is our life? What is the life of a tree? What relationship is indicated when we use the same concept to designate both life in us and in trees?

Anthropologist Marilyn Strathern emphasizes the local origin and range of the cardinal terms that we regularly use as though they were of universal validity: individual, society, gender, alienation, property, commodity, exchange, power. If we formulate an understanding of what life and trees are in another society through the terms and concepts of Western sciences, it will likely just appear as incoherent and irrational "beliefs." To understand the discourse of another culture, we must construct a new concept of and perspective on what a tree is. And indeed what a human is. What birth is. What death is. What it is to be born in the forest and into the forest. What it is to die in the forest and into the forest.

Individual Life

We speak of "life on earth" and other planets as though life were a medium or substance in which living things form and subside. Though we apply the same word *life* for a tree and ourselves, we recognize that life in us is individual. My life is mine and it comes to an end when I do. Life is also individual in trees; the life in a tree extends its whole height and depth, one process maintaining and organizing its material mass, its growth and reproduction; one process making it separate from other trees and other species. One process subsisting across years or centuries.

The biggest dinosaur yet discovered, *Argentinosaurs yuinculensis*, is 131 feet long, weighing some 110 tons; blue whales grow to 110 feet long, weighing 220 tons. The sequoia named General Sherman stands 274 feet high, its trunk is 102.6 feet in circumference at the base, and it weighs 6,100 tons. A bristlecone pine, whose location is kept secret for its protection, is 5,076 years old. In 2020, Alerce Milenario, also called Gran Abuelo, a Patagonian cypress in the Alerce Costero National Park in central Chile, was determined to be 5,484 years old.

An Individual is Multitudes

Living beings reproduce themselves. A living being also comprises the lives of different species, exterior to it and within it.

Eukaryotes are organisms whose cells have a nucleus and are enclosed by a plasma membrane. They contain mitochondria to create Adenosine triphosphate molecules from glucose and, in algae and plants, chloroplasts to generate glucose from sunlight, providing energy to drive many processes in cells. Evolutionary biologist Lynn Margulis argues that mitochondria and chloroplasts were once free-living microorganisms that were absorbed within eukaryotes. Such eukaryotes are thought to have evolved between 1.7 billion and 1.9 billion years ago. Multicelled organisms have similarly absorbed microorganisms and other species of eukaryotes within themselves.

The giant tubeworms *Riftia pachyptila* live in craters of deep-sea volcanoes in the eastern Pacific Ocean in depths up to 2,500 meters and in temperatures up to 54°C. They grow to two meters in length. They have no digestive systems. As larva, they ingest from the environment sulfur-oxidizing chemoautotrophic bacteria, *Candidatus Endoriftia persephone,* that henceforth exist within them and provide them with nutrients they assimilate. They grow up to eighty-five centimeters per year. These tubeworms form huge aggregations of up to several thousand animals per square meter, among which some sixty other animal species live. Giant tubeworms, *Lamellibrachia luymesi,* found in seeps in the depths of the Gulf of Mexico, develop slowly to over three meters and can live up to three hundred years. They grow in masses of hundreds to thousands, forming habitats for over a hundred species of brachiopods, mollusks, sponges, arthropoda, and chordates.

Humans harbor microbiota—bacteria, fungi, protists, archaea, and viruses—on their surfaces, inside their bodies, and inside their cells. They live on the skin, mammary glands, uterus, and ovarian follicles; in the lungs, gastrointestinal tract, biliary tract, pancreas, and liver; in saliva, oral mucosa, conjunctiva, and seminal fluid. Enormous numbers of them exist. According to the latest research, human bodies have on average thirty trillion human cells and thirty-nine trillion microbiota, including thousands of different species therein

Microbes in the gastrointestinal tract break down many of the proteins, lipids, and carbohydrates in our diet into nutrients that our bodies can then absorb. They produce folic acid, niacin, and vitamins B^6 and B^{12}. They produce anti-inflammatories that regulate some of the immune system's response to disease. They break down toxins.

In the late nineteenth century, infectious diseases such as cholera, puerperal fever, typhoid fever, malaria, and polio were discovered to be caused by microorganisms—"germs." This led to public health campaigns to inculcate us, encourage cleaning of hands and utensils, and promote civic works to provide sanitary drinking water and dispose of human waste and wastes of all kinds. The public has come to consider all germs as noxious. But only some hundred species of bacteria of the thousands that our bodies harbor are responsible for infectious diseases. The goal of an utterly antiseptic environment is counterproductive: lack of exposure to microbial species that have co-evolved with us can lead to weak immune systems and outbreaks of asthma and allergies.

We have come to marvel over our immune system, which independently of our personal will and decisions—indeed of our consciousness—so warily and so nimbly protects our bodies. To the same measure that electron microscopy captivates us with the forms and beauty of microorganisms, and research brings us to marvel over their dynamic relationships with one another and with our bodies, should we not gradually free ourselves of the disquiet and disgust that we are occupied inside and out by "germs" and instead embrace the multitudes upon multitudes of these wondrous lives within us?

How many microorganisms and macro-organisms flourish in the life of a tree! Fungi, bacteria, and archaea inhabit the roots, wood, bark surface, and foliage. The fixed carbon produced in trees and spread by their roots are nutrients for microbes. Mycorrhizal fungi surround and encase tree roots; they decompose organic material and provide nutrients and moisture to the tree. Rhizobium bacteria perform nitrogen fixation. Archaea promote plant growth and development, provide stress tolerance, improve nutrient accumulation, and protect against pathogens.

There are five to six hundred species of oak trees in Asia, Europe, Africa, and North America. The Jurupa or Hurungna Oak, in the Jurupa Mountains in California, is more than thirteen thousand years old. Seven hundred and fifteen lichens species grow on oaks supplying food, shelter, and nesting material for both invertebrates and vertebrates. One hundred and eight species of fungi thrive on oaks, fifty-seven of them only on oaks. Mycorrhizal fungi coat the root systems, gathering and distributing nutrients and messages to the tree and among other trees.

Many fungi live on the decaying wood of oak trees. Numerous species of beetles feed, breed, and hide in this matter. Five hundred thirty-two species of caterpillars feed on the leaves of oaks. Oak flowers are eaten by red and grey squirrels and many insects. The pollen is gathered by bees. Deer, raccoons, flying squirrels, gray squirrels, red squirrels, chipmunks, opossums, and rabbits eat the acorns of oak trees, as do wild turkeys, crows, woodpeckers, blue jays, quail, and wood ducks. Birds and bats feed on the beetles, butterflies, moths, and ants that live in these trees.

Born in Trees

In North America, eighty-five species of birds—13 percent of the bird species on the continent—nest in cavities of trees. Woodpeckers, flickers, and sapsuckers excavate cavities, usually new ones each year, in live trees. Red-cockaded woodpeckers can take two or three years to hollow out a cavity in living pines. Chickadees and nuthatches shape their nesting holes in the decayed wood of old trees. Pied flycatchers, marsh tits, and treecreepers nest in crevices in oak bark.

Bluebirds, starlings, wood ducks, owls, kestrels, purple martins, and house wrens do not excavate their own cavities but use those fashioned by woodpeckers or located naturally decayed cavities. Tree squirrels, mink, raccoons, opossums, bats, red squirrels, chipmunks, weasels, dormice, and deer mice also nest in vacated woodpecker nests and cavities started by fungal decay in trees.

Crowned hornbills (*Lophoceros alboterminatus*) live in forests of southern and northeastern Africa. They are black with white bellies and white tips on their long tails. Their eyes are yellow, their beaks, with casque on top, are red. They are fifty to fifty-four centimeters (20–21 in.) in length. They search for a cavity in a large tree trunk, high and even above the canopy. They shape the interior, plastering crevice walls and arrange nesting material. Then the female walls up the entrance of the cavity with excreta and mud brought by the male, leaving only a vertical slit a half inch wide. The male will bring her varied food and succulent fruits that obviate the need for water. Four or five white eggs are laid. The female undergoes a complete molt, discarding her feathers through the slit. She also puts her rear end to the slit and shoots out her feces, as will the chicks when they are born. The eggs hatch in twenty-five to thirty days. The male brings the female and the chicks fruits, berries, seeds, and also geckos, frogs, slugs, and snakes. If the male is killed during the nesting period, other male hornbills in the vicinity come to take over feeding. After two months, the female breaks out, and the chicks rebuild the wall with its slit. She now has full new plumage and aids the male in feeding the chicks. After three or four more weeks, the chicks break out and fly in the winds.

Katherine and I went to Tana Toraja, a region of high mountains on the island of Sulawesi in Indonesia. Over centuries, the Toraja people have carved the flanks of mountains into terraces for wet rice cultivation. Houses stand high on wooden piles, built without nails or screws, solely by tongue-and-groove construction. The massive roofs are made of multilayered split bamboo and shaped in soaring arcs like harps whose invisible strings are fingered by the winds.

Although today most of the inhabitants have adopted Christianity, the ancient rituals still govern their civil organization, agricultural and economic practices, and ceremonies. The *Aluk To Dolo* (Way of the Ancestors) prescribed complex rituals for birth and life—*rambu tuka* (smoke rising), the ascending smoke ceremonies, and for death *rambu solo* (smoke descending). The most important and most elaborate rituals are funerals for adults.

Pak Tandi arranged for us to attend two such funerals. He explained that a funeral is often held weeks, months, or even years after the death so that the deceased's family can raise the necessary funds. The funeral ceremonies usually last four days, sometimes ten days. People from every community with which this community has ancestral, marital, economic, or political relations come to the funeral, some from other islands and other countries. We watched them arriving at the ceremonial arena in procession, clad in their finest clothing. With them are groups trained to perform chants and dances. They bring pigs and water buffalo to be sacrificed. Pak Tandi took us to cliffs where graves had been cut into the rock, some at great heights. In wooden balconies set on the cliffs, the carved wooden statues of the dead watch and protect the living.

One day Pak Tandi led us through the forest. The late afternoon sun sent low shafts of light guiding us between the tree trunks and the canes of giant bamboo. We stopped before a huge tree whose trunk had a dozen patches of black palm fibers. Inside, Pak Tandi said, are the bodies of babies—of stillborn babies, and babies who die before their first milk tooth emerges. A baby without teeth cannot speak, cannot spread falsehood. The baby that dies is brought here immediately. The family bores a hole in the trunk of the tree and places the baby upright inside. The opening is closed with palm fibers; eventually the tree will grow over the opening and seal the baby inside itself. The tree that is chosen, a Tarra tree, has white milk sap, which flows when the hole is cut in it and surrounds the baby with its vital milk that the mother is unable to give it. And the tree draws the baby into its life.

The love of the parents continues in the tree. The tree continues its ascent to the skies. When it is time for the mother tree to let them go, the babies, unable to crawl or walk, are wafted by the wind, ascend to *papua*—the separated, sacred dimension.

Figure 7.2. Tree burial, Kambira Village, Tana Toraja. *Source*: Wikimedia Commons. Photo by mattjlc. CC BY 2.0.

The Place and Ecology of Trees

Figure I.5. Banyan with child, St. Petersburg, Florida. *Source*: Photo by David Macauley.

Interstice

Banyan

Places remember what people forget.
There are seeds that need fire. Seeds that need freezing. Seeds that need to be swallowed, etched in digestive acid, expelled as waste. Seeds that must be smashed open before they'll germinate. A thing can travel everywhere, just by holding still.
Buddha's words: A tree is a wondrous thing that shelters, feeds, and protects all living things. It even offers shade to the axmen who destroy it.
There are no individuals in a forest, no separable events. The bird and the branch it sits on are a joint thing.

—Richard Powers, *The Overstory*

By at once rooting themselves downward, spreading their branches laterally, and ascending into the sky, trees actively generate, shape, and maintain a robust sense of place in the landscape as well as being reciprocally altered by their immediate surroundings. In so doing, they are often interlaced thoroughly with the local ecology, providing sanctuary, sustenance, and shelter for a vast selection of interdependent organisms, anchoring and fostering a biological community that typically flourishes for many generations.

The banyan is emblematic in this regard because it drops signature aerial roots to the earth, extends a broad canopy, and develops thick secondary trunks, thereby building an ever-widening circumference that can cover more than an acre of land. Banyan trees are native to the Indian subcontinent and possess a unique method of pollination by providing a home and food for fig wasps that then enables the plants to produce fruit for birds, who disperse the seeds. After it dies and decays, the tree, also known as the strangler fig, can create a hollowed-out cavity or "columnar tree" where it once stood and that in turn offers a dwelling place for other plants and animals. The banyan further possesses a wealth of medicinal properties, and its leaves, bark, juice, and roots have been employed by ayurvedic practitioners to treat an array of illnesses, including diarrhea, gum disease, inflammation, and diabetes. In this manner, the tree reaches its influence into and enhances the human domicile.

Banyans have been designated the national tree of India, where they are linked historically with animist sensibilities. The trees are venerated within Hinduism, and are associated with immortality, along with the triumvirate of gods: Brahma (roots), Vishnu (bark), and Shiva (branches). In the *Bhagavad Gita*, we hear Krishna speak of the Tree of Life: "There is a fig tree / In ancient story, / the Giant Aswattha, / The everlasting, / Rooted in heaven, / Its branches earthward: / Each of its leaves / Is a song of the Vedas, / And he who knows it / Knows all the Vedas." It is widely believed, too, that Siddhartha Gautama, the historical Buddha, obtained enlightenment under a fig species (*ficus religiosa*), closely related to the banyan, one referred to as the Bodhi Tree. And so the tree is regularly coupled with mindfulness and meditation practices.

In the forthcoming section, Michael Marder and Edward Casey explore the places and prolific edges of trees. Dalia Nassar investigates Alexander von Humboldt's insights into the dynamic relationships between organisms and their environments, focusing on the collaborative roles of trees. These subjects are tied as well to arboreal communication, ontology, and temporality, topics taken up earlier in this volume.

—David Macauley

8

The Place of Trees
Taking Trees over the Edge

MICHAEL MARDER AND EDWARD S. CASEY

We tend to think of trees as quintessentially non-human—as radically other than we are—standing solitary and stalwart, leading a life of their own, existing in ways we can barely understand. Trees go their own way, we go another. Or so we imagine . . .

Places are something else. They present themselves as prototypically human, being where we *reside*: they are there where we are. Many of them are made for us, and some are made by us—made to be occupied. And if certain places are not directly habitable, we adapt to them or else modify them to fit our needs and interests. In this respect, places are, or can become human—sometimes all too human.

In this chapter—jointly authored on a conjoint theme—we bring trees and places together by concentrating on the places of trees themselves. We imagine, at the limits of philosophical imagination, the places of trees within a nascent phenomenological framework suited to them—and human places, as they are experienced in interaction with those of trees. Our guiding set of questions is: how do trees, or plants more generally, construe, shape, and get shaped by the places where they grow? In what ways might sessile beings, whether plants or animals, relate to and cognitively map their habitats? What are the positive implications of the impossibility of getting out of such places, the immanence of their "here" unopposed to a "not-here"?

Our intention is to *give place back to trees*: to examine what kind of places they create and occupy, regardless of whether these places fit human dimensions or not and irrespective of whether we fit (into) them. In short, we aim at doing at least preliminary justice to the *mysterium coniunctionis* of trees and places. We shall discover several major ways in which this conjunction occurs, one of which is found in the way that the edges of places and trees interlace with each other. And it is from such considerations that we shall find trees and human beings converging in unexpected ways. By uncovering certain tacit affinities, we shall come to regard trees as our quiet companions on earth—just as we, at our best, are theirs, as well.

Site, Space, and Place

It is one thing to think of place as metrically determinable—measurable in repetitive units. Such is a site, which is not only measurable in this determinate way but part of a stretch of space that is suitable for some particular activity: that is, quite literally, *useful*. Hence the common phrase: "site *for* . . ." We take "site" in Whitehead's sense of space regarded as something measurable and functional in certain definite ways. It is what happens when place is construed as a matter of *space* regarded as a homogeneous medium. What is qualitative about a given place—its accessibility, its changing coloration, its very history—is rendered indifferent or nugatory when the place is construed as a site. Site is the fate of place when it is taken up in certain pragmatic or scientific contexts. Even if in these contexts it is basic and elemental, it is secondary to place as lived—as inhabited, mobilized, animated.

The placedness of trees cannot be reduced to their site specificity. Only for certain determinate purposes, such as the estimation of real estate with an eye to its commercial value, is it so construable. But our interest in this chapter lies in determining the active placement of trees—the way they occupy the air that surrounds them as well as how they grow out of, and into, the earth, dynamically interacting with the soil in which they are rooted. Rather than a fixed entity, the place of trees is of a piece with their vegetal inhabitants, which means that, above and below ground, such places grow, decay, and metamorphose along with the plants themselves.

Indeed, the sense of what is above and below (gravitropism) from the perspective of a plant relies on physiological cellular-level mechanisms available already to a germinating seed. It is vital to the proper development (more precisely, the placement: placing as a living activity) of organs, such as the shoots stretching up and the roots extending down, on the body of a plant.

The place of trees is, therefore, always *places*, at least two in one—a literal *topos ouranios* and a *topos géinos*, atmospheric and chthonic—and an exuberant, proliferating multiplicity between the two. In twentieth-century French thought, trees have been taken as the living figures of *verticality*, from Paul Claudel's suggestion that "in nature, the tree alone is vertical, along with man"[1] to Gilles Deleuze and Felix Guattari's juxtaposition of tree structures and rhizomes. The alleged verticality of trees implies the verticality of their places. How can we think through the logic of verticality in the case of the arboreal bi-axial or bi-polar existence? And how can we valorize such verticality rather than holding it up to critique and derision, as happens in the Introduction to *A Thousand Plateaus*?

One early indication is the Heraclitus fragment 60: "the way up and the way down are one and the same [*hodos anō katō mia kai ōutē*]." But, when it comes to trees, they are not altogether the same: the upward movement thrusts toward an entire *region*—for example, the sky—while the way down leads into the nether region of the earth, which, for another pre-Socratic, Xenophanes, strives toward infinity (*apeiron*) beneath the upper limit (*peiras anō*) we tread with our feet (fragment 12, cf. Arist. de Coelo ii. 13; 294a 21). A lived verticality is, therefore, never simple; its coordinates and trajectories embedded in and between elemental milieus do not follow the rules of formal logic or mathematics. There is here the paradox that while trees are for the most part well anchored, they *give way*, or, more precisely, they *give ways* and can be said to *gesture toward* whole areas of the natural world, areas that extend down and up, and in both cases *out*. The multiple extensions out from the tree itself—the extensions that, in an important sense, *are* the tree itself—merge with those out from its local or specific place, the *place of* the tree, where it is located, where it is to be found, and where it locates *itself*.

In light of the relatively uncomplicated linear form of a section of the trunk between the roots and the branches, the lateral dimension of vegetal growth recedes to perceptual and ideational backgrounds. Nonetheless, the places of trees (both their habitats, such as forests, and the places that the trees themselves dynamically *are*) do not, as we've just seen, limit themselves to the vertical axis alone. Due to the modular pattern of plant growth, the branching character of arboreality provides an image of *branching places*, of the place itself as a vertical, horizontal, and lateral branching out, opening unto other places by way of fresh interaction with the elemental realm. (We return to these "directionalities" in the last part of the chapter.)

The phenomenology of trees includes all the various ways in which aerial and earthen vegetal placing occurs: directionally, as vertical or horizontal or something in between, or in terms of mode of engagement: with the air surrounding them and with the earth beneath them, and other ways. In these two very basic ways, and others, we can say that a given tree finds or makes its place. *Its place*: this cannot be reduced to its pinpointable position, nor can it be adequately construed in terms of what Deleuze and Guattari call "striated space," that is, the occupation of space regarded as a universal medium that can be unitized in certain determinate ways. The place of trees is closer to "smooth space" in the nomenclature of *A Thousand Plateaus*: space that is configured by the way in which movement or other interaction occurs. But smooth space is conceived by the French thinkers largely in terms of nomadic dispersions of human beings, whereas our concern is with the *local* facticity of trees—where "local" signifies *placial*.

The key to understanding the locality of place is its uniqueness. Such placement is always unique, *uni-local*, just here rather than there, yet expansive within the single locus to which a given tree or plant is confined. It is expansive within the limits of growth of a given arboreal or plant organism, while offering a *place-within-a-set-of-places*, whose outer limits are the terrestrial and the aerial *regions*. Nevertheless, it is the place of *just this tree, only that plant*. How this place compares with other places is a matter of comparative indifference: "comparative" because it is of concern mainly to the scientist, the grower, the owner—who characteristically think of tree-placement in terms of site, where the just-here is what it is mainly with regard to a larger tract of land or earth, that is, to *all that space*.

Our aim is to understand the *singularity of tree placedness and placing*: what makes it unique in each and every case, just *this place* and not its position in a generic (much less universal) space. And yet such placement also has certain features that obtain for other trees as well, both as individuals and as members of species.

Every tree not only *occupies* a unique place but in effect *creates* that place—creates it by its very being-there and its becoming or constant metamorphosis. Such placement entails a decisive and unique arboreal ontology of place that is not the same as that which obtains for ourselves or for other animal species—or for that matter, for rocks and other nonliving natural phenomena. We enter here into something quite remarkable: the singular *placeology* of trees. Other natural entities have their own peculiar placement, but that with which we are concerned in this chapter is quite special.

We realize this specialness when we consider the case of a tree farm—where trees are planted in perfectly straight rows. Here there is an effort to impose a site-specific positionality upon the planting and growth of trees, sometimes for perfectly admirable purposes (such as reestablishing a forest that has been lost to logging). Yet, even if the seeds or saplings of the planted trees are at a determinate and repeated metric distance from each other—say, five feet—the architectures of the branches and root systems of each developing tree will be unique: unique in their exact physical configuration, unique in their exposure to sun or contiguity with the soil, the precise ways by which they draw nutrients from the soil (i.e., in the case of a given tree and not just the *type of tree*, say a birch or an elm wherein there will be a certain convergence), and unique in the way the root system of a given tree interacts with that of another tree and the entire biome around it. The sitedness that determines the layout of the planted forest in its original format quickly gives way to a singularity of placement in the case of any given member of the growing forest.

One soon suspects that there is an intrinsic link between the growth pattern of a given tree and its unique placedness. The further along its growth—the more "mature" the tree is—the more its placiality takes on increasingly unique configurations. It is one thing to grow *as a type of tree*—here not only the metricality of positioning but also the speciated kind of tree do obtain—and quite another to grow as *this tree*: this member of this species. To be *this very tree* is tantamount to inhabiting *this very place*: setting forth its own way of becoming placiated.

Such a place is not merely *a place in space*—as if space were a larger whole that contains particular places as so many determinate contents. The uniqueness of arboreal placedness is such that each tree *is* its own place, whatever its relation to a larger containment space (such as may be determined by a predesignated limit or border of a planted forest). Each growing tree not only *has a place*—as if it were to occupy a predesignated site—but, more radically, *it is a place*, the place that is indefeasibly its own and not that of any other. We are talking about a radical singularity here—where we recall that the word "radical" has for its etymon *radix*, i.e., "root." No wonder it is tempting to draw examples of placial singularity from the root-life of trees—even if the upper parts of trees are also unique in each and every case. The growth of any given tree is *from the ground up*, and it is in the ground that its roots reside even as its branches reach out and beyond the ground. The roots reside therein for the most part, even if certain root systems—for example, that of the banyan tree—may also flourish above ground. But the exact positionality of roots considered as a matter of their exact spatial distribution is not what matters the most when it comes to placement.

What matters most is *arborescence*. By this term we refer to the animation, the ongoing growing life, of trees, their becoming in time rather than their positionality in space. Mattering most is that the placedness of trees is a *becoming in time* that is not reducible to a positionality in space—where "time" refers to the temporality of living process, that is, time as *undergone*, while "space" designates what is reducible to site and is subject to striation. In effect, time undergone is expressed in the very corporeity of trees—for instance, in the tree rings that register, in the annular fashion, patterns of the annual growth, all the way down to the nutrients a particular plant received in any given year. We must come to see that the sense of place that characterizes the life of trees does not belong to space so conceived, but is allied with time construed as ongoing process. Place can be said to manifest the *unhidden life of trees*—there where they show themselves becoming, or leave material traces of such becoming. This is not just a becoming *in place* but a *becoming of place itself*: a placialization-in-time.

For place is not ever-the-same. It is always becoming, just as much if differently from that which becomes in it—or rather, as we've been arguing, *as it*. For place is not something constant but is continually evolving, ever different in ways that we can see as well as assess—and manipulate in ways that suit the human species all too readily. Just so a tree-in-place is ever altering, evolving within its own speciation, indeed *as* its speciation: where "speciation" refers not to the exemplification of a preestablished species but to the unique configuration of a member of that species, its *individuation*.

Philosophical readers will recognize that we are here headed toward the worldview of Bergson—except that he never took up place in any serious way, confining himself to the two exclusive categories of space and time. Yet, place is a third way of becoming—completing the *triton genos*—which we must not overlook, especially when it comes to living, organic phenomena such as trees and plants.

Taking Places, Giving Places (With Trees)

Places and their occupation tend to be associated with either generosity or extreme egoism. Inherently generous, a place is an opening, within determinate limits, welcoming whomever or whatever is in it. It *provides space*—living space—for occupants. Only by overwriting or overriding the welcome of the place itself do I claim it for myself or cede it to others.

In his *Pensées*, Pascal hears in the words "my place in the sun" a primordial and still ongoing possessive appropriation of the earth: *Mine thine*. "This is my dog," said these poor children. "That is my place in the sun." There is the origin and image of the usurpation of the whole earth [*l'image de usurpation de toute la terre*]."[2] The expression "my place in the sun" sounds particularly pertinent to plants, which receive a significant portion of their nourishment from solar energy in the process of photosynthesis. But, while ever since Plato and, still before him, since pre-Socratic thinkers and their ancient Egyptian sources, the sun has been seen as a universal, generative, and generous excess, the claim one lays to one's place "in" it carves out an exclusive, private, and privative niche, into which no other is to be admitted or, if so, with a price to pay. Do plants take their places in the sun *à la* Pascal? Do they first usurp the whole earth, as the fraught evolutionary and biological term "plant colonization of land" implies?

The remarkable thing is that by *taking* their places plants *give* place to other things. In their consumption or decay, they make room for and are succeeded by many other forms of life, indeed by the entire livable world. Covering the whole *earth*, they bring the *world* into existence: the world as we and other living creatures come to know it. This is the basis of a widespread sociality among plants and trees alike, and a concrete basis for human social life as well.

The cryptic formula taking = giving violates all the rules of capitalist economy and of binary formal logic. It does not fit the framework of "zero-sum" games, where the recipients of advantages and benefits obtain these goods at the expense of those to whom they are denied. Nor does it correspond to a physicalistic model of occupation, according to which no two bodies may be found in the same place at the same time. How do plants overstep or outgrow such rules, frameworks, and models: all based on a metaphysics of determinate presence? In a nutshell, as they take their places, plants do not do so to the exclusion of others but, magnet-like, draw insects, birds, and other animals, fungi, bacteria, and other plants toward themselves, that is to say, toward the places they inhabit in a non-exclusive, non-exclusionary manner.

The place of this date palm I am looking at now is this one and no other, just as the tree itself is unmistakably this one, its leafy crown towering over the grass and shrubs underneath and standing out between the bare branches of plane trees it is surrounded by. Unique, the date palm is uniquely welcoming, its hospitality being of a piece with the place where it grows: the tree gathers around and on itself the birds and the fruit flies who feed on its succulent fruit, the mosses and the lichens spreading over the lower part of its trunk, children running with happy shrieks around it, and myself as quietly admiring it. One way to think about such green hospitality is through the prism of the distinction between places, sites, and space as discussed earlier. Although it provides nourishment for birds and insects, the date palm is much more than a useful or usable site, inasmuch as it is a living expression of its species and of the dynamic interaction of this particular vegetal being with its environment. And although it takes up space—in the sense that no other palm tree, plane tree or shrub grows where it does—it convokes into being a place that was not there before. In effect, this might be one of the keys to the seemingly contradictory formula taking = giving: the *vegetal taking up of space is giving place*. This is place for growth and interaction but also for fading and dying: place both animated and animating, de-animated and de-animating.

The line of thinking we are pursuing here goes well beyond the question of literal occupation. To "take place" is not just to occupy a locale; it also means to happen, to occur. There is no event, there is no time, without something taking place. A tree takes place. A tree happens. It is a tree-ing. The event of *this* date palm tree unfolds (grows, flourishes, blossoms, rots . . .). And it happens in this very place, right here, where it grows, the place it cannot abandon without losing its being and identity. (A curious exception is yet another palm tree, the so-called stilt palm, *Verschaffeltia splendida*, which while moving imperceptibly nevertheless moves in the sense of locomotion; by growing new stilt-like roots, using them as support structures for the trunk, and abandoning old roots, it gets the chance to forage for light and resources in areas quite distant from the original site of its growth.) Just as much, the place of the tree cannot abandon this tree so long as the tree is in that place. If the tree withers away or is cut, the place will no longer be *of* this tree and its growth; it will no longer be that place at all; the logic of substitution applicable to abstract space simply does not apply in this case. The places of trees are temporally finite, even as they render possible the time, the *evental* aspect, of what is taking place in and as them.

The Edges of Trees in Place

Trees often occupy the edges of our experience: as when we view a setting sun through a row of trees that serve as the outer edges of our visual field, providing its framing as it were. Similarly, if less dramatically, the trees that ring the yard of the house I inhabit constitute its de-lineation: "my property ends over there," we say, gesturing toward the trees that are situated at the edge of the plot on which we live. But even when trees are not on the outer edges of a landscape on which the sun is setting or at the limits of our own home property, they tend to be relegated to the outer edges of everyday experience, literally "marginalized" there and taken for granted. On closer inspection, however, we realize that trees actively populate many parts of our lives and precisely in their status as edges. Among these everyday situations are the following (and the reader can easily supply others):

- the intimate internal edges in a garden we have cultivated, variegating its contents and providing a characteristic configuration of the vegetal presence of the garden;

- the dense edges of a thick forest through which we are slowly making our way: edges that tell us much about the character and extent of that forest, even as it forecloses views of what lies beyond it;

- the tops of tall trees reaching into the sky, thereby marking the most elevated point of our visual field; no wonder Avicenna could consider such upward positionality as demonstrating the existence of a vegetal soul that moves against nature within nature.

In these various ways and countless others, trees act to *give edge* to our ongoing experience: to give to it a characteristic contour, to delimit its extent, to suggest, to foreshadow, and at the same time to foreclose what lies beyond it, and to populate it with edges integral to the space where we are now standing or walking or otherwise moving about in our ongoing life-worlds. Trees are edge-donative, lending their edges so as to give shape and specificity to wherever we or other non-human living beings may happen to be, whether high up or low down or somewhere in the middle. We appreciate the presence of trees all the more when we are in circumstances where there are no trees at all: such as when we are at sea or in a desert wholly devoid of trees. Then, the horizon comes to the fore—the very thing that is precluded in the thick of a forest.

Speaking of a horizon, a place arguably entails irreducible broadness, the spread or the spreading out, which—not necessarily of a geometrical or geographical order—is capacious enough for existence, notably for a settled form of existence. Greek (*plateia, platys*) and Roman (*platea*) etymologies point in this direction. At the same time, there is the category *plant*, in which differences between flowers and mosses, annual and perennial varieties, trees and grasses, are flattened. And, besides this epistemic flattening, *plant* also involves an ontic (if not an ontological) and practical flattening, the leveling of the earth in an attempt to create the places of crop cultivation that are at the root of humanly habitable places. While trees, particularly the fructiferous varieties and those used as timber, are also subject to cultivation, they undermine the different modes of flattening inherent in planthood. The verticality of trees, like that of high mountains, implicitly forbids human habitation, while welcoming plenty of birds, insects, and other animals. And this is not to mention how the dense and tall arboreal community of the forest hides the horizon from view, rendering the phenomenological notion of experience itself unworkable, and, perhaps, in so doing, inviting fresh elaborations of a *horizonless* experience that takes its bearings from the places of the trees themselves. Although Heidegger has already pointed in this direction with his notion of *Lichtung*, or the clearing, there remains much to do with respect to a phenomenology of trees and their places.

But trees not only provide edges to what we experience around us. They have *their own edges*: edges of the branches that spread out from the trunk of a given tree; of the trunk itself; and in the roots of trees, however invisible these may be if fully buried. Such edges are not just outer, as are those of the examples we have just discussed. They may also be inner—located within the trees themselves: in the bark, in the pulp of the trunk, inside roots and tubers. These internal edges are everywhere in trees even if we overlook them when we are taken by the more conspicuous edges of the tree as a whole (as very early in the morning when the sun illuminates a certain tree, bringing it into the light).

Every tree possesses a congeries of edges—themselves of multiple kinds and sizes even in the case of a single tree, ranging from the enormity of a redwood tree we confront to the tiny tips of the bristles on a low-lying conifer. All such edges configurate in unique patterns—unique to the species of a given tree but also accruing to a given tree as it makes its way to full growth, which is never quite complete in the teleological sense of the term. Trees are intensely edge-bearing: *bearing edges out* in unique patterns that catch our eye and *holding them in* by way of patterns that we can sometimes touch more easily than we can see as such. Many of these patterns are in accordance with "modular growth"—growth that reiterates a basic "module" and reconfigures it in ever-new combinations. The edges of the same module positioned differently are never quite the same. This is the vegetal version of what Husserl called "free variation in imagination." But we are talking about a free variation in perception that occurs when we find ourselves in the presence of trees, and the variation is not in the presentation of an *eidos* as it is for Husserl; we have to do with the variation of a given module, itself interacting with the environmental conditions and the rest of the place it is found in.

Tree edges can serve both as *borders* and as *boundaries*. They are the former when they are situated at certain precise locations in a formal garden, as when a straight row of carefully cultivated trees is planted to delimit a given avenue, as in Le Nôtre's garden at Versailles; taken together, such trees constitute a definite chartable space. In other cases, such as British gardens (and most casually constructed home gardens), the edges furnished by trees are irregular and easily traversable: taken together as a single cluster, such edges amount to boundaries taken as permeable edges. Borders and boundaries are usually associated with the mapping of national or state territories, but both forms of edging can create configurational limits in many other contexts, as with the forests that figure into certain Shakespeare's plays and that furnish imagined perimeters to human interactions.

Not only do trees have inherent and highly diverse edges, but so do the *places* of trees: all such places have characteristic edges of which we are at least dimly aware as we stand on the ground these places occupy. Such places are composed of porous edges that can be permeated by various fluids or traversed by mobile animals (including ourselves), thereby replicating the osmotic mechanisms by which a plant draws water and other nutrients from the soil. A tree cannot move itself over the already existing edge of its own place, but the edges of trees themselves move, expanding or contracting in keeping with the seasons, the phase of growth, and other such factors. A tree also sends essentially detachable parts of itself well beyond its own literal edge and stable place in the shape of seeds or pollen—not to mention leaves that are equally fecund since they decay into the soil and replenish it. The edges of trees are themselves mobile, with their movements occurring as growth, decay, or metamorphosis (these being the three types of motion, in addition to locomotion, recognized by Aristotle)—all this happening within its own given place.

In short, the edges of a tree extend *all over its own place*. This place, which we are approaching from several perspectives in this chapter, is itself comparatively stationary. For this is the place of a given tree—or a cluster of trees—and to count as *that* place, *the* place of *this* tree or group of trees, it must be edged in certain perceptible ways. These ways create a unique pattern for that of which they together constitute the place: no two arboreal places are ever just the same but differ significantly from tree to tree, each tree not only calling for its own place but *creating* that place, *being* its place. Moreover, no one tree is ever the same as itself if we consider various time scales that obtain for seasonal changes, as well as for the growth and decay of that tree in a given place.

Such complex singularity of placement distinguishes the situation of trees from that of built or constructed ways of being-in-place: ways that vary from city blocks to the foundations of houses, to country roads and highways, bookcases to kitchen cabinets. Each of these diverse things brings with it its own characteristic and largely predetermined place, usually created in keeping with a definable use or purpose that calls for a particular mode of placement that is comparatively easy to replicate: a standing bookcase with its inset rows, a road that can support heavy vehicles, and so on. But trees cannot be said to have any such definite, replicable pattern of implacement. If there are patterns at all, they are not replicated in the delimited forms assumed by the places of what is ready-to-hand for human utilization. Each tree, as well as each type of tree, has its own way of being-in-place.

We are arguing that trees, indeed each and every tree, has a place of its own. How are we to understand such a place? To begin with, it will be located on the earth and in the earth:

- *on the earth* considered as a material basis from which a given tree arises: this is what we conventionally call "the ground," and it is composed of soil with all that this contains by way of ancillary forms of life: worms, fungi, etc.; as well as non-living things such as rocks;

- *in the earth*: trees are not stationed on the surface of the earth like Christmas trees propped up in living rooms, they go down into it, thanks to their root systems; this is not only a matter of descent but of active engagement with the earth itself: with and in its soil and whatever it contains, living or not; it is a matter of an active immersion in that very place.

From what we have said, one major claim emerges. This is that the placement of trees always occurs in an *edge-to-edge pattern*, a pattern that is as pervasive as it is multiple. Trees are not isolated entities that live autonomous, self-sufficient lives but rather beings—events as much as entities—that subsist only by living from edge to edge. These edges proliferate even as they diminish periodically.[3] The most elaborate such inter-edged existence is found underground, where trees communicate with each other and across species and biological kingdoms through entire networks of connective forces: forces that include bacteria and other microorganisms that convey a variety of tacit messages from one tree to another. Trees live edge-to-edge underground. But they communicate at their upper edges as well, given that the leaves of trees are now known to pass on information from one tree to others near it via airborne biochemicals. What is transmitted is not only information in the usual sense of the term as referring to something quantified and coded: we are speaking of qualitative sensory messages that animate an entire world of "e-co-affectivity" in Marjolein Oele's apt term, a world that consists in a myriad of "interfaces" that constitute entire eco-worlds, whether above or below the ground.[4] It can also be characterized as a world in which "ecoproprioception" (in George Quasha's suggestive word) is the animating force: whereby an organism reaches out to an entire environment and comes to know it by way of diverse sensory systems.[5]

The proliferation of edges plays a very important role in a plant's survival. Like all sessile beings, plants are literally tethered to the places where they grow, which means that in a situation of danger (an attack by herbivorous animals or insects), they cannot flee from that place. It is, therefore, of utmost importance for a plant, whether it is a tree or not, to continuously monitor the fluid situation in its vicinity in order to pick up the slightest signals of impending threats, which would allow it to activate various physiological defense mechanisms. This is quite established in plant science, but what purpose do the edges of plants serve? Our response is that the more multifaceted the living edges of plants (leaves, branches, but also brachiated roots), the more sensitive they can be to whatever is going on in the places of their growth. Trees, indeed, present some of the most multifaceted living edges among all other plants, such as grasses or flowers. A slightly different angle and placement of apparently replicated, redundant structures (modules) afford them such increased sensitivity. It is like an incredibly complex construction of a 3-D model of the place, a model that is not "ideal" (it is neither a blueprint nor anything like *eidos*) but is of a piece with the place itself.

In sum, in exploring the place(s) of trees in particular, we are talking about how trees link up at their edges—how they interface with the soil and the atmosphere as well as with other trees and certain plants as well. It is a matter of existing edge-to-edge. With trees we are into an edge world—a world altogether, and in countless ways, on edge.[6]

Arboreal Directionalities:
A Living Infrastructure of the Place of Trees

The variegated directionalities of growth in trees are vivid instantiations of phenomenological intentionality in the vegetal world, a directedness-toward that, according to Husserl, constitutes the basic dynamic structure of human consciousness. The place of a tree is a knot, into which these arboreal directionalities are tied. Here, we attempt not so much to disentangle this knot as to follow some of its many twists and turns, complications, and co-implications.

Branches of trees have a way of reaching out in a quasi-protentional manner, exceeding themselves as it were. It is tempting to regard them as intentionally arrayed: seeking sunlight, proffering leaves for the absorption of water, *there for a purpose*. Vegetal *branching out* bears, in effect, on a middle region between earth and sky in a tentacular manner. One of us cherishes a very early memory of being drawn to depict tree branches as a challenging and exhilarating task for a fledgling artist of eight years old. This memory is preserved in an early painting that is a study of the arboreal branching of a very large tree on a local college campus. "I was quite aware of the massive trunk that anchored the tree, but I was much more struck by the exfoliation of the branches. Taken together, trunk and branches—and the roots beneath—established a unique place on that campus in Topeka that I could still locate today after seventy years of absence."

The other co-author often reminisces about a tall birch tree that grew in front of the apartment complex in Moscow, Russia, where he lived together with his parents as a child. "Whether bare in wintertime or covered with earing-like catkins and leaves in spring and summer, gently swaying birch branches that invariably greeted me whenever I glanced out the window. It was as though the branches led a life of their own, independent of the trunk and the roots, their elegant, pliable yet sturdy, extensions faithfully facing me whenever I turned their way." Could it be that children are more attuned to the very middle region of branching-out that trees, among other kinds of plants, call forth into being? If so, are children (not forgetting the child within each adult, too) more in tune with the intensities of existence that wells up in and as the middle—a middle expressly valorized by Deleuze and Guattari?

Many trees are inherently *tentacular*, as if equipped with arms of their own, extending into the sunlight and the open air, sometimes seeming to exude an expressivity proper to themselves. Their brachiated being contrasts starkly with certain types of roots, such as bulbs and other tuberous roots, which tend to turn in upon themselves, as if seeking obscurity. Instead of turning *out* as with branches, they turn *in*. And they accomplish this in-volution characteristically *in the earth*. The up-here-above of branches stands in stark contrast with the down-there-below of tuberous roots.

Based on this difference, we can discern two basic kinds of place that trees occupy and/or create: two expressions of the process of arboreal placialization. One is open-ended and outward-going, mitotic as it were—self-differentiating at every phase. This yields place as *ramified*. The other is closed-down and inward-tending, coalescing rather than exfoliating, consolidating rather than thinning-out. This is place as *amalgamating*. Trees offer both kinds of places; more than this, they *are* both—and both at once.

Each kind of place is essential; together, they are co-essential. There is no tree that does not have elements of both; indeed, that *is both*. How is this so? It is by a process of self-differentiation whereby trees not only grow upward and downward, that they placialize themselves in these two primary avatars—each of which carries with it characteristic kinds of growth and, depending on the species of a given tree, peculiar modes of place. Two primary *kinds* of place result from the exfoliation of trees: arboreal and terraceous, each with its own modes of variation. On the one hand, trees placialize themselves in a primarily *outwardizing* direction; on the other hand, as terraceous they become placial in a mainly *inwardizing* tendency.

To these two primary placializations of trees must be added a third: *lateralizing*. For trees grow not only up but *out*—out to the side. The result is a peculiar kind of sidewise place that realizes a third directionality: a way *around*: around a central trunk or, in the case of trees with multiple trunks, circling them as if in a loosely fitting girdle or garland of placiality. In this respect, one of us cannot help but think of a three-hundred-year-old prickly juniper tree, growing in the Principe Real Garden in Lisbon, Portugal. While the tree itself is seven meters tall, its sprawling branches, supported by a meshwork of columns and horizontal bars reach the length of fifteen meters in all directions. A welcome refuge from the scorching sun in the summer, the extended place of this tree is the square that emerged around and under it—thanks, precisely, to its lateralizing growth. Such arboreal mid-regions are often less conspicuous than the upper parts (i.e., the "crown") or, by inference, the lower parts (the "anchor"), but they are no less vital to the overall placiality of trees. For trees invite circumnavigation—if not by our moving body, then by our circulating look, which often follows the midriff placiality with as much interest as the upward moving branches or the downward-tending roots.

In plant science, too, the middle gains significance. Think of a seed, for instance. On the verge of germinating, it is the middle that stretches in two or more directions at once; otherwise, it would not have been a middle. In the course of stretching out, elongating, exiting the enclosure of a point, which is far from fixed, it calls into being the extremes it spans and many other midpoints (in fact, an infinite number of them) between these extremes. Beyond any objective measures, the distance between is vital space, the field of existence, the place of plants. The spans of the middle are the times of life. In the middle, all referents are too dynamic to warrant any certainty, expanding and contracting, growing and decaying, uncoiling, recoiling, metamorphosing. The end and the beginning, at which these vegetal activities are arbitrarily cut short, give off the appearance of a polar opposition. But they, too, are variations on the middle. Polarity is the residue of a middle that has undergone oppositional growth and that, in its sway, has assigned their respective meanings and places to antipodean positions.

The directionality of trees is thus threefold: up and out, around and about, and downward going. These are not three strictly separate vectors of a tree but three modes of its placial animation in which the placialities overlap and sometimes merge at their edges: so much so that we rarely bother to distinguish them as separate parts but take them in as one continuous flow of being-in-place. To regard them as discrete parts would be to spatialize them unduly—whereas we are arguing that place occurs as a process, as something ongoing and ever-changing, something happening not just in time but *as time*.

To regard the disposition of these three parts as "triaxial"—however tempting this may be—is to overly objectify them. We must resist this temptation. Even to talk, as we have ourselves, of three "regions" or "directionalities" of arboreal placement is to invoke terms that are spatial rather than properly placial in character. It is to come from the outside of arboreal placement rather than doing justice to the way that trees configure themselves from within: in place rather than in space. The challenge is to do justice to the intrinsic and quite unique placedness of trees themselves. How are we to find the language for how they exist placially, and how may we resist the very strong impulse to convert this *how* of placialization into the *what* of settled spatial terms such as "axial" or "dimensional" or any of a number of other such spatially overdetermined terms?

It is a matter of doing justice to the flowing of place rather than its stabilization, much less its quantification: a flowing that is a *becoming*: becoming a variant of itself through placial proliferation. This is not to deny that there are certain basic discernible tendencies in the life of a given tree—tendencies that allow us to apprehend them in place and as place. When one writes about place in the dynamic sense we endorse, the very language one is drawn to use is overdetermined and predetermined by a spatial sensibility that has virtues of economy and elegance but that fails to capture the uniquely configured, frequently very dense, and always complex placiality of trees themselves.

∼

In this chapter we have explored the placedness of trees—what it means for trees to have a place, and what that place is like. This is only a preliminary sketch, but precisely as such it opens up avenues for future exploration. We hope to investigate these avenues in future work, but we offer this as a first step in that direction.[7]

Notes

1. "In nature, the plant alone . . . is vertical, along with man [*L'arbre seul, dans la nature . . . est vertical, avec l'homme*]" [Paul Claudel, *La connaissance de l'Est* (Paris: Gallimard, 2000), 148].

2. Blaise Pascal, *Pensées*, translated & edited by Roger Ariew (Indianapolis: Hackett, 2004), 21.

3. We are reminded here of Leibniz's definition of matter as a garden within a garden within a garden, resulting in an infinity within something finite.

4. See Marjolein Oele, *E-Co-Affectivity* (Albany, NY: SUNY Press, 2021).

5. See George Quasha's discussion of "ecoproprioception" in his *Poetry in Principle* (New York: Spuyten Duyvil, 2019), 546, 72–73, 78.

6. For further on this sense of world in its sheer variety and certain philosophical consequences, see Edward S. Casey, *The World on Edge* (Bloomington: Indiana University Press, 2017).

7. See Edward S. Casey and Michael Marder, *Plants in Place: A Phenomenology of the Vegetal* (New York: Columbia University Press, 2024).

9

Organisms and Environments
What Alexander von Humboldt Learned from Trees

DALIA NASSAR

Often[1] described as the "father of American environmentalism" and the founder of modern ecology, Alexander von Humboldt[2] is perhaps the first European thinker to develop a comprehensive, empirically grounded vision of nature as a dynamic, organized, and developing unity.[3] Although it was Ernst Haeckel who coined the term "ecology [*Oecologie*]" some seven years after Humboldt's death in his 1866 *General Morphology* [*Generelle Morphologie*], it was Humboldt's way of thinking and his understanding of the natural world that made Haeckel's coinage of the term possible. In fact, Haeckel appeared to have had Humboldt in mind when he wrote that "by ecology, we understand the whole science of the relationships between organisms and their surrounding external world, which we could count as their 'conditions of existence' in a wider sense."[4] Thus, while Haeckel gave us the term *ecology*, it was Humboldt who elaborated the idea of nature as a dynamic "household (*oikos*)" in which living beings mutually influence and support one another.[5] As Humboldt put it in one of the first statements of his five-volume *Kosmos* (1845–1856), "nature is, for thinking observation [*denkende Betrachtung*], unity in multiplicity, the connection of the many in form [*Form*] and mixture, of natural objects and natural forces, as one living whole [*als ein lebendiges Ganzes*]" (*Kosmos* 1, 10, 5–6).[6]

But it was well before the publication of *Kosmos* that Humboldt began to conceive of nature as a living unity, composed of mutually influencing and supporting members. His first concrete ecological observations go back to his time in South America. In March 1800, Humboldt and his scientific companion Aimé Bonpland arrived in Lake Valencia or Lake Tacarigua in present-day Venezuela. In contrast to their expectations, they encountered a region suffering from drought. Through conversations with Indigenous locals, Creole farmers, and his own investigations, Humboldt came to a surprising conclusion: the felling of trees and the replacement of forests by farms had fundamentally transformed the climate and the soil. What was once a verdant area, with regular rain, had become a desert. This is how he puts it:

> When forests are destroyed . . . as they are everywhere in America by the European colonists, the springs . . . dry up, or become less abundant. The beds of the rivers, remaining dry during a part of the year, become torrents whenever heavy rain falls on the heights. With the disappearance of sward and moss from the sides of the mountains, the waters falling in rain are no longer impeded in their course: and, during heavy showers, instead of slowly augmenting the level of the rivers by progressive filtrations, they furrow the sides of the hills, bear down the loosened soil, and form those sudden inundations that devastate the country. And so it results that the destruction of the forests, the want of permanent springs, and the existence of torrents are three phenomena closely connected to one another. (*PN* 4, 143–44; translation altered)

In this statement, which had a profound impact on environmental policy across the world—from the United States to India—Humboldt points to two crucial, but hardly recognized, facts: the influence of trees (forests) on the environment and the influence of human beings on the environment.[7] While Humboldt's predecessors (including Buffon, Kant, Herder, and Goethe) had recognized that living beings are affected by their environments, they had not considered how living beings themselves affect their environments: that is, how living beings, including humans, fundamentally transform the climate, soil, plants and animals of a region.

If the relationship between living being and context (organism and environment) is not unilateral but bilateral, it follows that living beings are inextricably linked to their context. The one (context, nature, environment) cannot exist without the other (the living beings, organisms, that inhabit it). The climate of Lake Valencia cannot exist without the trees—and vice versa: the trees cannot exist without this climate. What this means is that nature (the environment) is not a static backdrop that pre-exists living beings but rather a dynamic relationship *between* living beings and their surroundings over long periods of time.

Humboldt's insight was radical for his time. What is surprising is that his insight remains radical today. Although it might appear to us as entirely straightforward, we continue to find it difficult to conceptualize the dynamic relationship between living beings and their environments. As biologist Sonia Sultan puts it in her 2015 book, *Organism and Environment*, while "conceptualizing the relationship between organisms and their environments is pivotal for both ecological and evolutionary investigations," it remains the case that "[i]n both disciplines, this relationship is generally seen as an interaction between separate entities, in the sense that an individual whose traits are *internally* (i.e., genetically) determined confronts an *externally* defined and measurable environment."[8]

In other words, some two hundred years after Humboldt, we remain bound to a notion of the "environment" that fails to take into account his ecological insight. For what he saw is that the "environment" is not a stable backdrop for animal (and plant) activity but instead an ongoing dynamic collaboration between living beings and their surroundings. This means that the two—organism and environment—are absolutely interdependent. The one cannot exist without the other: the climate and soil of Lake Valencia cannot exist without the trees—and vice versa: the trees cannot exist without regular rain and nutrient-rich soil. To conceive of them as *originally* separate entities that *then* somehow come together is to misunderstand them and their relation.

This leads us to several questions: How did Humboldt come to see organisms and their environments as a dynamic collaboration? How did he come to recognize that a particular environment does not pre-exist its inhabitants, and that the inhabitants do not pre-exist the environment? What were Humboldt's methods and tools, and what concepts, frameworks, and approaches did he develop to discern and communicate the dynamic relation between living beings and their surroundings? Finally, what are the implications of Humboldt's ecological insight: for our understanding of the world, and for our understanding of ourselves in the world?

My aim in this chapter is to answer these questions by exploring the specific role that plants, and in particular trees, played in Humboldt's ecological insight. For it was in observing the activity of trees that Humboldt concluded that living beings are not only influenced by their environments but that they also influence (and indeed transform) their environments. This nonlinear relationship between organism and environment is, as I hope to demonstrate, most evident in trees, which are at once more plastic and open to their world than animals *and* actively transform their world on both the smallest and the largest scales. Consider the influence of trees on the hydrological cycle of the Amazon forests: transpiration during the late dry season brings the dry-to-wet transition forward by two to three months. Thus, the loss of trees will not only result in drought, as Humboldt recognized, but may also lead to rainforest collapse and the emergence of savannah.[9] My claim, then, is that trees—and their distinctive relation to their environments—provided Humboldt with his first ecological insight and led to the founding of ecology as a distinct discipline.

The Physiognomy of Plants

In January 1806 after returning from South America, Humboldt delivered his first lecture at the Prussian Academy of the Sciences in Berlin. The lecture, which was published two years later in Humboldt's "favorite work," *Ansichten der Natur* [*Views of Nature*], provides insights into Humboldt's methodology and the knowledge he gained during his travels.[10] Titled "Ideas for a Physiognomy of Plants," the lecture introduces Humboldt's audience to a new way of looking at the natural world: a way that he calls "physiognomy."

Just as we discern a person's character through their gestures, body language, and expressions, so the physiognomist of nature—the new scientist that Humboldt wants to establish—discerns the character of a landscape through the expressions and gestures of plant and animal life. Accordingly, the physiognomist of *plants* is interested in what Humboldt calls the *form* of the plant—those aspects of a plant that make the greatest impression on the viewer: whether it attains to great heights (like palms) or twists and turns (like lianas), whether its leaves are broad like those of the banana tree or narrow like conifer needles. But this is not all. In addition, Humboldt contends that it is through the physiognomy of plants that we can go on to develop a physiognomy of *nature*—that is, an understanding of the contexts, regions, or environments in which the plants grow.

What exactly does Humboldt mean by plant form? And how are we supposed to discern this form? In turn, how is the "science of plant forms" that Humboldt aims to develop different from botany? And how does studying the form of plants lead to the study of the "environment" in which the plants grow?

Humboldt gives a first response to these questions in an early passage in "Ideas for a Physiognomy of Plants"—a passage as complex as it is insightful. He writes:

> whoever can grasp [*umfassen*] nature with *one* look [*mit einem Blick*] and knows to abstract localized phenomena will see how, with the increase in invigorating heat from the poles to the equator, there is also a gradual increase in organic power and abundance of life. But with this increase, certain beautiful aspects are reserved to each different section of the earth: to the tropics, the diversity and immensity of plant forms; to the north the aspect of meadows and the periodic reawakening of nature upon the first breaths of the spring airs. Besides its particular advantages, each zone has its own character [*Charakter*]. The old and profound power of organization [*die urtiefe Kraft der Organisation*], despite a certain liberty in the abnormal development of specific cases, binds all animals and vegetable life forms to firm, perpetually returning types [*alle tierische und vegetablishce Gestaltungen an feste, ewig widerkehrende Typen*]. In the same way that one discerns a certain physiognomy in individual organic beings, just as descriptive botany and zoology, in the strict sense of the word, are the analysis of animal and plant forms, so too there is a *physiognomy of nature that applies, without exception, to each aspect of the earth.* (DA 5, 181; VN 160; final emphasis added)

We are told, first, that the "physiognomy of plants" aims to grasp nature with "one look." Reiterating the aim articulated by many before him—from Buffon to Herder and Goethe—Humboldt emphasizes vision and the ability to see the many *in* one, or *at once*. This seeing with "one look" is not a compilation of random facts. Rather, the goal is to see the various parts *in their relations* to one another, to discern how they influence and transform one another, and how *together* they contribute to an integrated and dynamic unity.

Seeing nature with one look, Humboldt elaborates, involves grasping the "character" of a particular landscape. And this requires discerning the "perpetually returning types" of animals and plants. The science that Humboldt aims to develop is a science of appearances and, more specifically, of *reappearing forms*. By studying these reappearing forms, Humboldt claims, we will also be able to study a region or a landscape. In other words, to grasp the distinctive character of a natural environment, it is necessary to discern the forms that emerge within it and understand their relations to one another and to the environment.

From this we can surmise the following: Humboldt's idea of plant geography involves discerning the appearance of certain *Urformen* [fundamental forms] across regions. Once we have determined which basic forms reappear across the earth, and in which relations and contexts, we can move to consider whether there is a relationship between *form* and *context*, that is, whether certain plant forms grow next to certain other plant forms; which climate, altitude, latitude, and what kind of soil, lend themselves to which forms; and, whether certain forms reappear across vastly different geographic contexts and in what conditions they reappear. By posing and responding to these questions, we begin to develop a picture of the relation between forms and their contexts, and thereby distinguish contexts not only in terms of climate or soil but also on the basis of the plants (and animals) that inhabit them. These insights will, eventually, lead us to pose the more complex, and crucial, question: how might a particular context exert influence on a particular form, and vice versa, how might a particular form exert influence on its context?

To respond to these questions, we must consider Humboldt's notion of form more carefully, and its relation to the physiognomy of nature. As noted, physiognomy involves discerning character through gesture, body language, and expression. In other words, physiognomy implies visibility and expressiveness. This means that the aims of the physiognomist of nature are to focus on what is most expressive, most striking, what has the greatest "mass [*Masse*]"—and to locate *therein* the character of the region. As Humboldt puts it, "physiognomy bases its division, its choice of its types, upon everything that has mass: upon the stem, the branches and appendicular organs (leaf form, leaf position, leaf size, composition and the luster of the parenchyma), that is, upon the now so suitably named 'vegetation organs,' the organs upon which the preservation (nourishment, development) of the individual depends" (DA 5, 295; VN, 239). This emphasis on immensity, on what is most visible and striking, strongly contrasts with the interests of the botanist, who generally focuses on small, almost hidden parts of the plant—the sexual organs, or at times, the fruit. Thus, while the botanist homes in on what is not impressive, it is precisely "impression" that guides the work of the physiognomist.

This gives us a first insight into what form and physiognomy imply. But it also leaves us with questions. After all, the methodology of the physiognomy of plants is working with the assumption that the external characteristics of a plant, its overall structure and gesture, say something *about* the plant. The question is: how does Humboldt justify this assumption?

As the subtitle of *Kosmos* indicates, Humboldt's goal is to offer a "physical *description* of the world [*physische Weltbeschreibung*]." A physical *description*, he emphasizes, differs from a *history*, in that its concern is not with determining the "obscure beginnings of the history of organisms [*den dunkeln Anfängen einer Geschichte der Organismen*]."[11] In other words, a physical description aims to remain with what is visible, expressive, and not move to explain the phenomenon through something invisible, or through obscure and intractable origins. Accordingly, Humboldt's choice of words in speaking about his methodology are worth noting. Distinguishing his methodology from "abstraction [*Abstraction*]," he writes that the goal of physical geography is to "depict [*schildern*]" and "observe [*betrachten*]" (*Kosmos* 1, 28–29).

For Humboldt this means focusing on form. This enables and supports remaining with the visible. Rather than replacing phenomena with something other than themselves (whether a conjectured history, or an external cause), the focus on form demands working with what is before us—the phenomena and their relations—and discerning fundamental laws *therein*. In other words, through forms we arrive at the most important insights *without* losing sight of the visible phenomenon: insights into the ways in which a form expresses itself differently at different stages of development, transforms over time and through its various relations, as well as insights into these relations and what they tell us about the form, including relations between forms (i.e., between living beings) and between forms and their habitats (living beings and their environments).

But how exactly is the new scientist supposed to discern forms *and* gain insight into the distinctive character of the landscape *through* these forms? Specifically, how is this new scientist to grasp the relationship between living being and its environment *without* reducing the one to the other or regarding them as originally separate entities that come together only after they have independently developed? In other words, how can the physiognomist see the two as members of an ongoing collaboration—where the one cannot exist without the other? Humboldt's answer to these methodological questions is art, and more specifically, landscape painting. He contends that the distinctive view of the natural world offered by landscape painting is one that the physiognomist of nature must seek to cultivate. What then is this distinctive view or perspective?

For one, the landscape painter is interested in the overall impression that a landscape makes. This means that she is interested in those expressive aspects, which give the landscape its unique character. In contrast to a botanist, who aims to categorize, distinguish, and separate plants, the landscape painter, Humboldt remarks, binds them together. Thus, even when the landscape painter portrays different species of, for instance, palm and fern within a landscape, she portrays them in their relation to one another, as members of the same context. In turn, when presenting plants of the same species, or plants that strikingly resemble one another, the painter does not depict separate trees, but allows them, as Humboldt puts it, to "run one into the other," and thereby portrays them as *members of a forest* (DA 5, 184; VN, 162).

To give his audience a concrete sense of what he means, Humboldt considers the diverging ways that a painter and a botanist treat leafy hardwoods. While the botanist distinguishes different hardwoods (oak, beech, walnut), the landscape painter allows them "to run one into the other." This is because the painter is interested in the overall impression that hardwoods make on the viewer—an impression that has to do with their distinctive form *and* with the way in which this form is *informed* by the hardwoods' context. By homing in on form, and seeing form in its larger context, then, the landscape painter reveals something that would otherwise be missed: namely, that form is inextricably linked to context. *How* a plant appears—the size of its leaves and trunk, the shape of its crown, its growth pattern—has to do with *where* it appears, and vice versa—and how a context appears (the kind of impression it makes on us) has to do with which plants inhabit it.

When a landscape painter captures trees *in* the forest, and captures the forest *through* the trees, she is working with precisely this insight: that the form of the trees *expresses* the forest environment, and the forest environment is an *expression* of its trees. By working with forms, expressions, and gestures, and discerning relations through these forms, then, the landscape painter presents trees and forest (living being and environment) as interdependent realities—as members of an ongoing collaboration, in which the one can only emerge with and through the other. In this way, landscape painting showcases and highlights precisely that which is so difficult for us to conceptualize. And it is precisely this ability to depict the one in and through the other, and to see them in one glance, that the new scientist must, Humboldt contends, develop and emulate. The question then is: what kind of science emerges from this way of regarding nature?

Plant Forms and Contexts

The two works most relevant to answering this question are the 1806 lecture, which eventually became an essay, "Ideen zu einer Physiognomie der Gewächse [Ideas for a Physiognomy of Plants]," and the 1807 essay, "Ideen zu einer Geographie der Pflanzen [Ideas for a Geography of Plants]." In both, Humboldt enumerates different plant forms and considers them in relation to their contexts. These forms are based on "impressions," that is, the gesture of a plant and its most striking external characteristics. Accordingly, they do not generally align with taxonomic categories. Following the example of landscape painting, Humboldt's contention is that plant forms will not only teach us about distinct plants but also about the landscape in which they grow. How does Humboldt justify these claims? Or better: what are the insights that we gain by looking at nature in this way? And how do these insights lead to a richer understanding of the natural world?

In the essay on plant physiognomy, Humboldt enumerates sixteen plant forms. In the French edition of *Géographie des Plantes*, he distinguishes fifteen forms, while in the German edition, *Geographie der Pflanzen*, he offers seventeen forms.[12] Humboldt is clear that his list is incomplete given that new plants will be discovered, and perhaps also new forms. Further, he emphasizes that the forms he distinguishes are based on *his* knowledge—whether gained through personal experience or through reading other's descriptions. This means there is always the possibility of adding more forms.

When he distinguishes a form, Humboldt describes both its individual characteristics—detailing, for instance, the shape of the tree's leaves, its usual size (height and width), its overall gesture—and its growth patterns—where and when it grows, under which conditions, next to which other plants, and so on. His aims are, he explains, "to dare to come to a recognition of the laws that determine the physiognomy of nature, the scenic vegetational character of the entire surface of the earth, and the vital impression evoked by the aggregation of contrasting forms in various zones of latitude and elevation" (DA 5, 295; VN 239). While the latter two goals might seem to be non-scientific—concerned with understanding the "scenic character" of the earth and the "vital impression" that emerges through careful observation—Humboldt insists that all three go together, such that the first (most scientific sounding) of the goals is achievable only through the latter two.

What does the first goal consist in? What are the "laws that determine the physiognomy of nature"? And why does studying the sixteen or seventeen plant forms give us insight into these laws?

To answer these questions, it is helpful to consider a form that Humboldt distinguishes. This will allow us, on the one hand, to gain a concrete sense of how his notion of form differs from taxonomic categorization, and on the other, to understand the connection between the form of *plants* and the physiognomy of *nature*. In other words, it will allow us to see how discerning the "character" of individual plants makes it possible for us to develop a "total impression" of the landscape. And this, ultimately, will lead us to the "laws" of nature that Humboldt wants to distil.

I will focus on the conifer form (*Nadelholz*), which is one of the most well-known tree forms, especially in the Northern Hemisphere.[13] Pines, for instance, appear only in the Northern Hemisphere, although other conifers are found in the Southern Hemisphere, and Humboldt saw them in the high mountains of Peru and Mexico. Conifers have, as Humboldt puts it, a "singular appearance." This has to do with their unusual height (think of the California redwoods), the width of their girth, and "the almost umbrellalike spread of the horizontal or uplifted branches" (DA 5, 273; VN 224). But it also has to do with their needle-like leaves, which he describes as expressions of the "greatest contraction [*größte Zusammenziehung*]" (DA 5, 276; VN 226). In addition, he classifies conifers as a "social plant," insofar as they grow together. We have entire forests composed of just one or two conifer species—a phenomenon, Humboldt notes, that is rare in South America.

In Mexico and Peru, conifers can be found only in the highest and coolest regions. This corresponds to conifer growth in Europe, whether on the Pyrenees, the Alps, or in Saamiland, which suggests a relationship between conifers and altitude, and allows Humboldt to take "a broad view" of the plant form—a view from which he is able to consider the relationship between the conifer and mountains more generally (DA 5, 265; VN 219).

First, he observes the relationship between conifers and the snow line. While in the Pyrenees and Alps, conifers are the trees that reach the highest point before the snow line, in Saamiland the birch (a hardwood) reaches further up. Thus, as we climb the mountain, we encounter conifers, and then birches. However, upon descending the mountain, we note uniformity in growth. For what *comes after* conifers as we go down is *always* the same. In the Swiss and Italian Alps, and in the Pyrenees, conifers are followed by alpine roses and a number of species of rhododendra.[14] In Saamiland, the same pattern is found but with a different species of rhododendra. The same, strikingly, applies in Mexico and Peru. In these regions, too, we find that blossoming shrubs begin to appear immediately after conifers as we descend the mountains. In this instance, however, these blossoming shrubs do not belong to the genus *Rhododendra* or even the family *Ericeae* but to an entirely different taxonomic family. Humboldt writes:

> Should we wish to pursue this last zone of vegetation before the line of perpetual snow all the way to the tropics, by our own observations we would name in the Mexican tropics, *Cnicus nivalis* and *Chelone genitanoides*; in the cold mountains regions of New Granada, the woolly *Espletia grandiflora, E. Corymbosa,* and *E. argentea*; in the Andes of Quito, *Culcitium rufescens, C. ledifolium*, and *C. nivale*—yellow-blossomed Compositae, which here take the place of the somewhat more northerly hairy-leaved shrubs of New Granada that are so physiognomically similar to them, the *Espeletia*. (DA 5, 266; VN 219)

Cnicus nivalis and *Espletia grandiflora*, which grow in Mexico and Peru, belong to the daisy family, while the flowers in the north largely belong to the *Ericeae* family. Nonetheless, they bear a clear physiognomic resemblance to one another—even if their sexual organs differ. They are all shrubs with blossoms. Furthermore, they all make for a striking contrast with the blossom-less conifers that come before them. Thus, Humboldt concludes, "Such replacement and repetition of similar, almost identical forms in regions separated by oceans or broad expanses of land is a wondrous law of nature. It holds sway even over the most peculiar types of flora" (DA 5, 266; VN 219). By focusing on form rather than taxonomic categories, Humboldt recognizes a pattern across the various regions: in Mexico and Peru, just as in the Swiss and Italian Alps, the Pyrenees, and Saamiland, conifers are followed by bushy shrubs with striking blossoms.

This should give us some pause. For not only do we find plants of different species and families bearing a strong physiognomic resemblance to one another, we *also* find that these physiognomic resemblances have some relation to *where* the plants grow (i.e., on a mountain, at a certain altitude) and *next to whom*. Conifers on mountains are followed by *the same form*: that of bushy shrubs with striking blossoms. What Humboldt is pointing to is a *physiognomic pattern* that reveals relationships *between* different plants and *between* plants and their regions. By focusing on form, Humboldt discerns a "reiteration" of forms across regions. The daisies in the Southern Hemisphere *replace* and *repeat* the rhododendrons in the Northern Hemisphere.

By focusing on form, we are surprised to find variations of the same forms repeated across vastly distant regions. While numerous species and families are native to only one part of the world, forms *are not* native, but are found in many different parts of the world. One can thus draw the conclusion that there are certain fundamental forms (*Urformen*), which, as Humboldt puts it, "morphologically replace one another in the different parts of the world" (DA 5, 281; VN 230).

The question then is: what does this tell us? What do we learn by focusing on plant forms in relation to their region and geographical distributions? What, in other words, is the significance of the "wondrous law of nature," of the fact that certain forms reappear across distant zones, at times in different contexts?[15]

When considering the conifer form, a certain pattern becomes apparent, which we would have otherwise missed. If we did not think in terms of forms but rather in terms of species or genus, we would not have noticed that blossoming shrubs on mountains always come after conifers. Accordingly, by focusing on form, we begin to see that *certain forms* occupy *certain regions* in *certain ways*. And this allows us to discern a relationship between form and context. We see that the form, conifer, and the form, shrub, often appear together, and they appear in cool, mountainous regions. If we did not focus on form but on species or genus, we would fail to recognize this pattern and thus miss the connections among conifers, shrubs, and mountains.

Humboldt is careful, however, not to overlook forms that do not appear to exhibit a similar connection between form and context—that is, cases where we find the same form appearing in vastly different geographic regions, such that one might reach the opposite conclusion, namely, that form is *independent* of context. Indeed, some of Humboldt's statements might be read to imply precisely that.

Speaking of the willow form, for instance, Humboldt writes that "among willows of the most contrasting climates, the similarity of the foliage, the branching, and the whole physiognomic formation is exceedingly great, perhaps greater even than that of the conifers" (DA 5, 287; VN 234). Further, Humboldt insists that while we can explain the increase or decrease in *populations* through environmental factors, we cannot explain *form* through environmental factors. This is how he puts it:

> The composition of the soil and the conditions of temperature and humidity, upon all of which the nourishment of plants depends, certainly promote the thriving and increase in the number of individuals that make up a species; the tremendous height, however, to which the trunks of only a few ascend while in the midst of many closely related species of the same genus is not determined by soil and climate, but rather, in the plant and animal kingdoms, by a *specific organization, by innate natural qualities* [*spezifische Organisation, durch innere Naturanlagen bedingt*]. (DA 5, 273; VN 224; emphasis added)

In other words, although geographic and climatic conditions play a role in determining whether a population thrives, they do not "explain" the specific organization or innate natural qualities of living beings. While we can draw on these conditions to explain demographics—why there are so many conifers in a particular region and so few in another—we cannot draw on them to explain the distinctive form of the conifer.

Immediately after this passage, Humboldt offers an example to illuminate what he means by "specific organization" and "innate natural qualities." He distinguishes two very short trees: a two-inch willow that has been "stunted by cold or the mountain altitude," and a small phanerogam, native to the southern tropics, which "reaches a height of barely three French lines [a quarter of an inch]." The two plants are very short, but their shortness is accounted for differently. The two-inch willow is not short *by its specific organization*. Rather, its shortness is clearly due to geographic and climatic influences. The phanerogam's height, by contrast, has to do with its specific organization.

It is striking that Humboldt turns to the willow to make this point—that is, the form which he also describes as the "most persistent." The willow's growth is significantly stunted by certain climatic influences, and it does not achieve its usual heights. Even the most persistent form is affected by its geographic and climatic conditions. The implication is that form—as persistent as it might be—is *also* sensitive and plastic, growing in dialogue with its context.

What exactly is the nature of this dialogue? If we observe the two-inch willow, we see that every one of its parts is affected by its conditions: not only its branches and leaves are extremely small but also its trunk and roots. This shows that its parts are not acting separately but in unison. Thus, although the roots are not as affected by the strong winds and high altitude as the other parts of the tree, they do not grow large but rather achieve a size commensurate with the rest of the plant. Accordingly, the willow's parts are *integrated*—they are parts *of* a whole—and emerge and grow in dialogue with one another. Put differently, the willow *as a whole* responds to its environment, and for this reason, *each* of the willow's parts is an expression of both the willow form *and* the willow's context. Each of the parts is a part of a whole, and thus tells the story of the willow as it responds to its context.

This gives us a better understanding of Humboldt's conception of form. Form does not imply an isolated being that is morphologically distinguished from its environment. Rather, form points to both the distinctive internal organization of a living being *and* the ways in which this internal organization responds to its environment. In the case of the two-inch willow, we see in the willow itself—inscribed in its very structure—not only the distinctive willow shape but also the environment in which the willow has developed.

That form is an expression of both a living being and its context is also evident in leafy hardwoods—to return to Humboldt's example when he invokes the landscape painter. Consider the oak. A solitary oak growing on a hill looks decisively different from an oak growing in a forest. The crown of a solitary oak spreads out in all directions, eventually achieving a dome shape. By contrast, the forest oak develops a small crown, and its growth is patterned on the growth of the other trees in the forest. An oak in a hardwood forest is an expression not only of the individual tree or the species oak but also of the forest itself. The forest is not "outside" the individual oak tree but literally inscribed in it its very form—in the same way that the mountain and the wind are inscribed on the two-inch willow. Ultimately, then, form tells us the story of the plant *and* its world.

Furthermore, the example of the willow highlights the fact that we (as knowers) are able to discern climatic influence *only because* we know the form (i.e., the willow form). If we were not familiar with the willow form, we would be unable to discern the influence of the environment on this two-inch willow—and would erroneously assume that the willow is by its "specific organization" and "innate natural qualities" short.

This has significant implications for understanding the relationship between living beings and their environment. For one, it reveals that the relation between them is not an either-or relation (i.e., *either* the organism is self-organizing and self-enclosed *or* it is determined by external factors and has no internal integrity). These are, in fact, the options that Kant provides in his 1790 *Critique of the Power of Judgment*, where he contends that organized beings must be understood *either* as "cause and effect" of themselves, as self-causing, *or* as externally caused, that is, caused by environmental conditions which—for Kant—amount to mechanical relations.

The disjunction in Kant's argument has to do with his conceptualization of internal purposiveness, which means, first, that organisms are not mechanically explicable, and second, that they are not passive but actively self-organizing. Environmental external purposiveness, however, implies both: mechanical explicability *and* passivity. Accordingly, from Kant's perspective, only the disjunctive either-or is coherent. *Either* organisms are self-organizing, *or* they are caused by something external to themselves.

Importantly, Kant's perspective remains alive today in theories of the organism which—like Kant's—contend that the organism must be, as Daniel Nicholson puts it, both "explanans *and* explanandum." In other words, understanding the organism requires *studying the organism*—and not something *other than or external to it*. Indeed, to continue with Nicholson, the crucial characteristic of the organism is that its "existence depends on its own activity." This means that the organism cannot be determined by activities that are not its own. That would amount to death. Or, as Nicholson puts it, "If the organism stops following these norms, it ceases to exist."[16] Kant recognized that this either-or was untenable: clearly organisms are *both* self-organizing *and* influenced by their environment. There must, therefore, be some way by which to conceive of them as self-causing and active *and also* caused and passive. Or, to put it in Nicholson's language, there must be a way by which to think of the organism as dependent on its own activity *and also* dependent on the activities outside of it. Neither Kant nor Nicholson, however, is able to offer this alternative.[17]

Humboldt's focus on forms provides a way out of this dilemma. On the one hand, it allows us to see how forms *reappear* across the earth. This shows that forms persist. The implication is that they are not mere outcomes of their surroundings but that they, as Humboldt puts it, possess "specific organization" and "innate natural qualities." On the other hand, the reappearance of forms across the earth happens *differently*. Either the form is affected by its context (e.g., the willow or the oak) or it appears in relation to other forms and in specific geographic locations (e.g., the conifer and shrub). Living beings, in other words, are sensitive to their surroundings: they are changed by climate, soil, altitude, geography, and human activity.

In the place of a logical argument, Humboldt offers us a perspective—mirroring the perspective of the landscape painter—from which we are able to see that living beings express *both* themselves *and* the world in which they live. By taking up this perspective, we do not commit the two usual mistakes: of either regarding the living being in opposition to its context (as an autonomous, enclosed entity, or as somehow existing prior to its context) or seeing it as a mere outcome of its context. Rather, the focus on form allows us to see living beings *in relation* to their context. Thus, in the place of the logical disjunctive, *either-or*, Humboldt's perspective offers a *both-and*: living beings are *both* self-organized *and* formed by their context.

Through the both-and perspective, logical oppositions are reconciled. The idea of a self-organizing being or a persisting form no longer appears to contradict the notion of a living being that responds to and transforms in relation to its context. Rather, from this perspective, the two *go hand in hand*. And they go hand in hand both epistemologically (i.e., for us knowers) and ontologically (for the forms). Epistemologically, we cannot separate the two because it is only by recognizing the persistence of form that we are able to discern how forms adapt or modify in varying contexts. Ontologically, the persistence of form is precisely what *enables* the form's plasticity, that is, its ability to respond and modify in relation to its context. For it is only if the form is persistent—if the living being is a unity composed of necessary and integrated parts—that it can *respond* to its context. After all, the willow *form* does not fundamentally alter—we can still see that it is a willow. Furthermore, the willow responds to its context as a whole—such that *all* of its parts express both the willow and the willow's context.

By turning our attention to form, we begin to recognize something that we would otherwise miss: living beings are neither passive in relation to their environments—the mere outcome of their environments—nor are they self-enclosed entities that are separate from their environments.

Rather, they are *both* possessive of innate qualities *and* sensitive to their contexts. By taking up the *both-and* perspective that the notion of form affords us, by beholding the two *at once*, we begin to see that it is *precisely because* living beings are integrated unities that they can *also* respond to their environments. In other words, through this double-focus we are able to overcome the conceptual problem that Kant had elaborated—a problem that may perhaps be impossible to overcome if we remained on the level of definition or argument. In the place of conceptual distinctions, Humboldt offers a perspective, a point of view, from which living beings are revealed as *transforming forms*, as *both* self-organizing *and* open, integrated, *and* porous. Or, as Humboldt puts it, "In all living organisms . . . are paired the fixed and the fluid" (DA 5, 116; VN 107).

The Clues of Trees

Humboldt's claim is that the physiognomy of *plants* will naturally lead us to the physiognomy of *nature*. Accordingly, the question arises as to how plants differ from animals such that their study will (more directly) result in a study of their environment. Perhaps the most obvious difference involves place and movement. Although as seeds, plants can travel vast distances, once in the soil, they are largely sessile.[18] This means, as Humboldt puts it in *Kosmos*, that after plants "have taken root, they become dependent on the soil and on the strata of air surrounding them. Animals, on the contrary, can at pleasure migrate from the equator toward the poles" (*Kosmos* 1, 183). Although not *all* animals can easily migrate—and many can only travel short distances in their brief lifetimes—it is certainly the case that animals are not rooted in a particular location in the way that plants are. This greater independence from any one location is evident in the fact that animals maintain a metabolic system that is largely detached from their surroundings. While this is most clear in warm-blooded animals, even cold-blooded animals, Humboldt contends, exert some control over their body temperature—through movement. By going into the sun, they can regulate their body temperatures. In this way, animals express a form of self-sovereignty and self-regulation that plants do not.

In contrast to animals, Humboldt elaborates, plants "live primarily in and through their outer surface," that is, through leaves and somata. In other words, plants' most important organs—their vital organs—are not hidden or invisible but turned outward, facing their environment.

This morphological fact reveals plants' distinctive dependence "upon their surrounding medium" (DA 5, 246; VN 206). In fact, the deep connection between plants and their contexts makes it extremely difficult to draw a hard-and-fast distinction between the individual plant and its environment.[19] And it is also the reason why plants are not only expressions of their species but also their specific contexts—the two-inch willow does not only tell us the story of the willow but also the story of its environment (and environmental change). And this context is not expressed in only one of its parts (e.g., its crown or roots), but in *every part*: the roots of the plant as well as its crown and branches manifest its context.[20]

While animals also express their contexts, they do not express their *specific* context, nor is their expressiveness as visible as plants. A fish's form clearly expresses its element. However, the specific context that the fish inhabits—this particular part of the ocean, for instance—is not explicit in the fish's overall structure. This makes sense in light of animals' migratory nature. Accordingly, while there are parts of animals that tell us something about their history—bones and tooth enamel, for instance—these parts do not tell the story of a specific context (region, environment), but the animal's *own story*, that is, its overall health, its nutrition, its stress levels, and so on.[21] These parts are, furthermore, far less visible than the outwardly turned parts of the plants, and thus do not make a strong impression on the viewer. In the plant, *every part* is an expression of the plant's history *and* context. From roots to branches, to rings, foliage and canopy, the plant as a whole expresses the *particular place* it inhabits.

Plants are, however, not only receptive in relation to their surroundings; they are also active within it. The *kind* of forest that we encounter—whether it is cool and humid, or temperate and dry, whether its soil is nutrient rich or poor, how much carbon it stores, and how much rain it receives—depends on the plants that compose it. The forest environment, in other words, is realized in and maintained through the activities of its trees. A region *remains* what it is (cool and humid, for instance) because of the kinds of plants within it (bearing large leaves which provide shading and evaporation, for example). Or, alternately, a region changes because of the disappearance of plants. As Humboldt notes, "if a region has lost all of its plants, if the sand is shifting and lacks all sources of water, then the hot, vertically rising air hinders the precipitation in clouds, and millennia must pass before the organic life presses into the interior of the waste from its green shores" (DA 5, 181; VN 159). Similarly, plants are not only influenced by the quality of the soil—they also influence the soil: either by transforming it in ways that prohibit other plants to grow in the same soil, or by making it fertile, thereby making way for future plants. Heaths, for instance, make the soil sterile, and for this reason, Humboldt notes, heaths "have dominated these regions completely . . ." (DA 1, 51; EGP 66). By contrast, cryptogams in the Northern Hemisphere, and mosses and lichens in the tropics "prepare the soil for the growth of grasses and herbs," thereby playing a determining role in the region's future (DA 5, 104; VN 99).

What does this deep connection between plants and their contexts tell us?[22] First, it challenges the view that environments are "causing" plants, which implies that environments precede the plants that make them up. The truth is the opposite: what we mean by "environment" is inextricably tied to the living beings, and in particular the plants, that make it up. Accordingly, an environment is *not* independent of its vegetation. It is not simply a backdrop for animal and plant activity. Nor is vegetation (and animal life) independent of the environment. Thus, we can say that the living beings and their environments are *conditions* in and through which the other flourishes—or not. Perhaps even more aptly, we can say that living beings and their environments are *collaborators*, insofar as the one can only be what it is through the other. Neither is the cause of the other, nor precedes the other; rather, each is influenced by and influences the other, and the two can only exist *together*. The forest does not pre-exist the trees, nor do the trees pre-exist the forest. This was the ecological insight at the heart of Humboldt's investigations at Lake Valencia.

This also tells us why the study of plant *forms* is integral to—and a necessary first step towards—the study of nature more generally, that is, the physiognomy of nature. For plants are deeply connected to their contexts. And this connection, which involves dependence on and sensitivity toward context *and* the ability to bring about major transformation in that context, is expressed *morphologically* in the very structure of the plant—both in the general fact that plants are turned outward and their vital organs are visible and thus expressive, and in the more specific ways in which individual plant form shifts in relation to its context. In other words, there is nothing strange or arbitrary about studying forms in order to study regions. The form of the plant is *informed* by where the plant grows, and vice versa: the form of the region is *informed* by the kinds of plants that inhabit it. Accordingly, the physiognomy of plants directly leads to the physiognomy of nature. By studying form, we achieve a higher perspective, through which we can see how the living being is an expression of its context, and how the context is an expression of its living beings.

Conclusion: Humboldt's Ecological Insight

Humboldt's emphasis on plants was, in many ways, novel. For although many thinkers before him had examined the relationship between animals and climate or soil—Buffon, Herder, Kant, and Eberhard Zimmerman—few had focused on the relationship between plants and geography.[23] In turn, while European and Creole botanists such as Carl Friedrich Willdenow and Francisco José Caldas emphasized context, they did not see the relationship between plants and their environments as reciprocal.[24] This insight, however, is precisely what Humboldt sought to articulate.

By coupling the notion of form with the perspective of landscape painting, Humboldt developed what we might describe as an "expanded conception of form," that is, an understanding of form as an expression of the manifold and multidirectional relations between a living being and its context. Specifically, through the double-focus that the expanded notion of form enables, Humboldt overcame the difficulties that our usual cognitive procedures encounter—of seeing objects as originally separate, and regarding their relations in terms of external causality, that is, in linear or one-sided terms. By focusing on form, Humboldt was able to see plants as both active and passive in their contexts, see how they are both creators and receivers—and in this way challenge both reductive accounts of living beings *and* static conceptions of their relations. Accordingly, by working with the idea of form, which at first appears to stand in opposition to a modern ecological interest, Humboldt was able to home in on and better understand the distinctive relationship that plants have to their context, and thereby provided crucial clues for understanding the relationship between living beings and environments more generally.

Through his study of trees, Humboldt came to the realization that living beings are not caused by their environments. Rather, it is most accurate to speak of environments as "conditions" in which they develop and to regard living beings as *also* the conditions in which environments develop. There is no relation of external causality here, between two originally separate entities. Rather, what he discerned was a productive relating over time that resembles the causal nexus that Kant had reserved for organized beings.

What Humboldt saw, then, and what he tells the reader in *Kosmos*, is that integrated unities are not only to be found in living beings but also in the relations between living beings and nonliving beings, in the relations among trees, water, soil, altitude, latitude, human activity, and other elements. To understand life, Humboldt concluded, it is not adequate to conceive of life as something separate, inwardly turned and independent from what is not-life. Rather, to understand life requires recognizing that life and not-life engage in ongoing, life-like processes or relations that we call nature. This was, and remains, Humboldt's most important ecological insight.

Notes

1. This chapter draws significantly on my book and furnishes, in a more abbreviated form, some of the insights developed in it while also expanding upon them. See Dalia Nassar, *Romantic Empiricism: Nature, Art, and Ecology from Herder to Humboldt* (New York: Oxford University Press, 2022).

2. Humboldt wrote primarily in French, although two major outputs were composed in his native German: *Ansichten der Natur* (*Views of Nature*) and *Kosmos* (*Cosmos*). Another significant work, *Ideen zu einer Geographie der Pflanzen* (*Essay on the Geography of Plants*), was originally composed in French (*Géographie des Plantes*), but Humboldt translated it into German, and in the process made substantial changes. Humboldt also played a role in the English translations of his work, often adding new passages or introductions. Thus, to avoid confusion, I will use the German titles and refer to the English titles only if I am citing a passage that appears only in the English translations. For Humboldt's contributions to the English translations of his writings, see Alison Martin, *Nature Translated* (Edinburgh: Edinburgh University Press, 2018).

References to Humboldt's works will be made in the body and will be as follows:

DA: Humboldt, Alexander von. *Darmstädter Ausgabe*, edited with commentary by Hanno Beck. 7 volumes (Darmstadt: Wissenschaftliche Buchgesellschaft, 2018).

EGP: Humboldt, Alexander von and Aimé Bonpland, *Essay on the Geography of Plants*, edited with an introduction by Stephen T. Jackson; translated (from the French) by Sylvie Romanowski (Chicago: University of Chicago Press, 2009).

Kosmos: Humboldt, Alexander von. *Kosmos. Entwurf einer physischen Weltbeschreibung*, edited by Ottmar Ette and Oliver Lubrich (Frankfurt am Main: Eichhorn Verlag, 2004).

PN: Humboldt, Alexander von and Aimé Bonpland, *Personal Narrative of Travels to the Equionoctial Regions of America, During the Years 1799–1804*, edited and translated by Helen Maria Williams. 7 volumes (London: Longman, Hurst, Rees, Orme, and Brown, 1814–1829).

VN: Humboldt, Alexander von. *Views of Nature*, translated by Mark W. Person; edited by Stephen T. Jackson and Laura Dassow Walls (Chicago: University of Chicago Press, 2014).

3. Several studies in English have attributed to Humboldt the status of the founder of both environmentalism and ecology. See, for instance, Aaron Sachs, *The Humboldt Current: Nineteenth-Century Exploration and the Roots of American Environmentalism* (New York: Viking, 2006), which offers a nuanced account of Humboldt's influence on key figures in the American environmental movement; Andrea Wulf, *The Invention of Nature: Alexander von Humboldt's New World* (New York: Knopf, 2015), which traces Humboldt's influence on lesser known but equally significant figures in the environmental movement (in particular George Perkins Marsh); and Laura Dassow Walls, *The Passage to Cosmos: Alexander von Humboldt and the Shaping of America* (Chicago: University of Chicago Press, 2012), which investigates Humboldt's impact on American writers, especially Henry David Thoreau.

4. Ernst Haeckel, *Generelle Morphologie der Organismen* (Berlin: Georg Reimer, 1866), vol. 2, 286. As ecologists Juli Pausas and William Bond put it, "Ernst Haeckel was thinking of Humboldt's work when he coined the term 'ecology.'" Pausas and Bond, "Humboldt and the Reinvention of Nature," *Journal of Ecology* 107 (2019):1031–37, on 1031.

5. In a footnote in which he elaborates on the meaning of the term "*Kosmos*," Humboldt directly connects it to the Greek οἰκονομία, citing the work of the historian of Ancient Greece, August Böckh. Humboldt writes that two inscriptions in Ancient Greece identify *Kosmos* with οἰκονομία (*Kosmos* 1, 33n27). References to *Kosmos* will include volume number, although the edition I am citing includes *all* five volumes in one book.

6. Or as he puts it some pages later in the Introduction, "nature is not a dead aggregate," and goes on to quote Schelling's statement that nature is "to the enthusiastic researcher . . . the holy, eternally creative power [*Urkraft*] of the world, which brings forth all things from itself" (*Kosmos* 1, 25; see also *Kosmos* 1, 38).

7. The national parks' movement in the United States and Britain were strongly supported by Humboldt's explication of the relationship between trees and rain. In an 1847 speech to the U.S. Congress, Congressman George Perkins Marsh—an avid reader of Humboldt's works—described the negative impact of human activity on the environment, focusing on deforestation, and three years later, in 1850, the U.S. Commissioner of Patents Thomas Ewbank cited Humboldt's observations at Lake Valencia in support of the campaign for national

parks. Yellowstone National Park was established in 1872—the first in the world—though the campaign for designating it a national park had begun in the 1860s. See Matthew Lindstrom, ed. *Encyclopedia of the U.S. Government and the Environment: History, Policy, and Politics* (Santa Barbara, CA: ABC-CLIO, 2011), 836. In 1890, Yosemite became a national park, through the work of John Muir, who was also deeply influenced by Humboldt—however, as Aaron Sachs notes, by the later stage of his life, Muir had moved away from his Humboldtian origins in that he came to prioritize nature over the human cultures that inhabited it. See Sachs, *The Humboldt Current*, 28. See also Wulf, *The Invention of Nature*. For Humboldt's influence on India, see Richard Grove, "Conservation, Ecological Hegemony and Popular Resistance: Towards a Global Synthesis," in *Imperialism and the Natural Word*, ed. John MacKenzie (Manchester: Manchester University Press, 1990), 15–50, on 22.

    8. Sultan, *Organism and Environment* (Oxford: Oxford University Press, 2015), 31.

    9. This means that without trees, the wet season would start when the Atlantic intertropical convergence zone arrives during its annual southward migration. Fu et al., "Increased dry-season length over Amazonia," *Proceedings of the National Academy of Sciences* 110, no. 45 (Nov. 2013): 18110–115.

    10. See Humboldt's letter to Varnhangen von Ense (October 15, 1849). *Briefe von Alexander von Humboldt an Varnhagen von Ense*, ed. Ludmilla Assing (Leipzig: Brockhaus, 1870), 244.

    11. This is how he puts the distinction between description and history in *Kosmos*: "A physical description remains tied clearly [*nüchtern*] to reality, not from modesty, but according to the nature of its content and its limits, and it is alien to the obscure commencement of a history of organisms [*den dunkeln Anfängen einer Geschichte der Organismen fremd*], if the word 'history' is accepted here in its most useful sense. But world description may thereby remind us that in the inorganic layer of the earth [*Erdrinde*] are encountered the same basic elements [*Grundstoffe*] which form the framework of animal and plant organs. It teaches us that in these [forms], as in those [of nature], the same forces [*Kräfte*] govern, which combine and separate matter, and shape and liquify it in organic tissues . . . The nature-contemplating tendency of our minds is thus a necessity, which is to be followed from the physical appearances from the earth to its highest summit, to the development [*Erzeugung*] of the forms of plants, and from its self-determined motions into animals. So is the geography of organic life (the geography of plants and animals) connected to the description [*Schilderung*] of inorganic natural appearances" (*Kosmos* 1, 367).

    12. In the German edition of *Geographie der Pflanzen* Humboldt adds the aloe, the lily, and the fungus forms, and takes out the orchid form (See DA 1, 62–64). In the essay on plant physiognomy (1808), he brings back orchids, adds willow, myrtle, and laurel, but takes out mosses, lichens, and fungus. This is in

line with his attempt to focus on those plants with the greatest mass and that make the greatest impression.

13. Humboldt's conifer form seems to align with the taxonomic category, *Coniferae*; however, in his discussion Humboldt limits himself to trees that bear needle-like leaves, and thus leaves out shrubs that are taxonomically classified as conifers. Furthermore, Humboldt closely connects conifers to other trees bearing needle-like leaves, including the Australian casuarina (commonly known as the "Australian Pine"), which taxonomically belongs to an entirely different clade, given that the casuarina—unlike conifers—flowers (is an angiosperm). See for instance his statement that the leaves and branches of both trees (the conifer and the casuarina) express the "greatest contraction" (DA 5, 188; VN 165–66).

14. These species all belong to the Ericeae family, which is taxonomically classified as a member of the Heaths. Humboldt, however, resists this identification, instead identifying the *form* of the heath with "the very consistent and characteristic form of the Erica species, including Calluna" (DA 5, 259; VN 214). The rhodondedra and other plants from the Ericeae family are instead placed under the *myrtle* form. This has significant consequences, as we will consider below.

15. As Hanno Beck notes, in pointing to this "wondrous law of nature," in which the same forms (but not the same taxonomic categories) repeat or reiterate themselves, Humboldt paved the path for what the influential twentieth-century geographer Carl Troll (1899–1975) came to describe as "convergent life forms." Troll was deeply influenced by Humboldt, and it was in the Andes that he developed his notion of convergent life forms. See Hanno Beck, "Kommentar," in DA 5, 266–67. For Troll, see "Die tropischen Gebirge," *Bonner Geographische Abhandlungen* 25 (Bonn: Ferd. Immlers Verlag, 1959). Before Troll coined the phrase, the Swiss Botanist, Augustin de Candolle (1778–1841)—who was also very interested in Humboldt's idea of reiterating plant forms—articulated the view that species with no evident common evolutionary ancestor strongly resemble one another. On Condolle's interest in Humboldt, see Anne Marie Clara Godlewska, "From Enlightenment Vision to Modern Science? Humboldt's Visual Thinking," in *Geography and Enlightenment*, ed. David N. Livingstone and Charles W. J. Withers (Chicago: University of Chicago Press, 1999), 236–75.

16. Daniel Nicholson, "Reconceptualizing the Organism: From Complex Machine to Flowing Stream," in *Everything Flows: Towards a Processual Philosophy of Biology*, ed. Daniel Nicholson and John Dupre (Oxford: Oxford University Press, 2018), 154.

17. For the reasons that Kant was not able to do so, see my *Romantic Empiricism*, chapter 1. Ultimately, the issue that both Kant and Nicholson are contending with concerns the ways in which an organism is an "open system." Although it is widely agreed that organisms *are* open systems, insofar as they continually exchange energy and matter with their environments (they are thermodynamically

open), thermodynamic openness, as Nicholson elsewhere argues, is a necessary but not sufficient condition for understanding the organism. More is needed to grasp its distinctive character as a system, including an explication of how the organism "depends on the effects of its own activity," and as such follows "intrinsic norms" that clearly determine its relation to its environment and allow us to assess whether its environment is "good" or "bad" for it. Nicholson, "The Return of the Organism as a Fundamental Explanatory Concept in Biology," *Philosophy Compass* 9, no. 5 (2014): 347–59, on 354. However, as I will discuss below, trees challenge a straightforward distinction between the organism from its environment such that it is harder to assess whether an environment is good or bad for it. Humboldt's emphasis on trees reveals that trees are especially open beings—open to their environments in ways that other living beings may not be or may not be as explicitly. For this reason, it is very difficult to determine where the tree organism ends and the environment begins. Or in the words of botanist, Alexander Braun, "individuality in plants is as obscure and ambiguous as in animals it appears clear and simple." Thus while trees differ from animals in this respect, they also point to something that a focus on animals can easily overlook, namely that we are deeply connected to our environments in ways that cannot be conceptualized linearly, as Sultan contends. See Braun, "The Vegetable Individual in Its relation to Species," *American Journal of Science and Arts* 19 (1885): 297–318, on 300. See also note 19 below.

18. I want to emphasize that plants are *largely* but not exclusively sessile, because they do move—in relation to the sun or in relation to other plants (and also as species over time). However, as Humboldt notes, their movement is invisible to us. This is because the pace of their movement is extremely slow—in contrast to that of animals—and so we fail to see it. Thus he writes in *Kosmos*: "if nature had endowed us with microscopic powers of vision, and the integuments of plants had been rendered perfectly transparent to our eyes, the vegetable kingdom would present a very different picture from the apparent immobility and repose in which it appears to our senses. The interior portion of the cellular structure of their organs is incessantly animated by the most varied currents, either rotating, ascending and descending, ramifying, and ever changing their direction, as manifested in the motion of the granular mucus of marine plants . . . and in the hairs of phanerogamic land plants" (*Kosmos* 1, 179).

19. As Ellen Clarke has noted in her work on plant biological individuality, it is extremely difficult to distinguish plants from their larger contexts. For instance, a forest of aspens appears on the surface to be composed of individual aspen trees. However, the trees are not at all separated from one another, but are connected underground by multicellular runners. Through these runners, the "individual" trees share nutrients and other resources with one another, making what appears to be a super-organism. See Ellen Clarke, "The Problem of Biological Individuality," *Biological Theory* 5, no. 4 (2010): 312–25, on 321.

20. See Craig Holdrege, *Thinking Like a Plant* (Great Barrington, MA: Lindisfarne Press, 2013).

21. Through analysis of human teeth, for instance, researchers have been able to trace the Irish potato famine. See Beaumont and Montgomery, "The Great Irish Famine: Identifying Starvation in the Tissues of Victims Using Stable Isotope Analysis of Bone and Incremental Dentine Collagen," *PLOS ONE* 11, no. 8. https://doi.org/10.1371/journal.pone.0160065

22. With Margaret Barbour, I developed the notion of the "embodied history of trees" in order to articulate the distinctive relationship between trees and their environments, which is present in all living beings, but is most explicit in trees. Accordingly, trees grant us access to grasping this relationship in ways that animals do not. See Dalia Nassar and Margaret Barbour, "Tree Stories: The Embodied History of Trees and Environmental Ethics," *Cultural Politics* 19, no. 1 (2023): 128–47.

23. Humboldt sought to emulate Zimmerman's work on animal (bio-)geography but for plants. As Humboldt puts it in *Essay on the Geography of Plants*: "Zimmermann's classic work presents animals according to the differences in their geographic location on the earth," adding that his own goal is to do the same in relation to plants. The classic work to which Humboldt refers is *Geographische Geschichte des Menschen, und der allgemeinen verbreiteten vierfüßigen Thiere* (1780). In addition to Zimmermann, Treviranus is regarded as a founder of the field of biogeography. See Zammito, *Gestation of Biology: From Stahl to Schelling* (Chicago: University of Chicago Press, 2017), 243–44.

24. Willdenow's 1787 study of Berlin flora (*Flora Berloinensis*) introduced Humboldt to botany and inspired him to focus on plants, while his 1792 *Grundriss der Kräuterkunde* included a significant account of plant geography. See Frank N. Egerton, *Roots of Ecology*, 121. There has been a debate concerning Humboldt's relationship to the Colombian scientist Francisco José de Caldas (1768–1816), whom Humboldt met in 1801 and who joined Humboldt's party for several weeks. The question concerns the extent to which Humboldt was "original." Without going into too much detail, the debate around Humboldt's originality concerns his bio-geographical maps, and the extent to which he learned about them from Caldas. While Humboldt may have learned about them from Caldas—and followed Caldas's own maps—this does not touch on his understanding of the reciprocally formative relationship of living beings and environments, something that Caldas does not recognise. Furthermore, and as Jorge Cañizares-Esguerra has shown, these maps were widely used in late eighteenth-century South America, where the Andes were regarded as a "microcosm" of the universe, and the assumption was that studying their vegetation in relation to latitude would yield knowledge about other similar environments. Thus a more accurate picture would be that Humboldt learned not specifically from Caldas, but from the wider South American intellectual tradition. Jorge Cañizares-Esguerra, "How Derivative was Humboldt?" in *Nature, Empire, and Nation: Explorations of the History of Science in the Iberian World* (Stanford, CA: Stanford University Press, 2006), 96–111.

Trees and Aesthetics

Figure I.6. Cypress, Barcelona, Spain. *Source*: Photo by David Macauley.

Interstice

Cypress

> I am a forest, and a night of dark trees: but he who is not afraid of my darkness, will find banks full of roses under my cypresses.
>
> —Friedrich Nietzsche, *Thus Spoke Zarathustra*

> Under ancient cypress trees, weeping dreams are harvested from sleep.
>
> —George Trakl

> Flowers shape bees as much as bees shape flowers. Berries may compete to be eaten more than animals compete for the berries. A thorn acacia makes sugary protein treats to feed and enslave the ants who guard it. Fruit-bearing plants trick us into distributing their seeds, and ripening fruit led to color vision. In teaching us how to find their bait, trees taught us to see that the sky is blue. Our brains evolved to solve the forest. We've shaped and been shaped by forests for longer than we've been Homo sapiens.
>
> —Richard Powers, *The Overstory*

Beauty assumes a great manifold of forms. With trees, we might admire the sensuous qualities of color, smell, texture, or taste expressed through their bark, leaves, trunk, and fruit. We may delight in their radial symmetry, varied shapes, or striving heavenward. We routinely come to appreciate the multiple services they provide to us and to their surrounding habitat. And we often enjoy both their individual splendor and their cooperative citizenship in forests because of our emotional, seasonal, and imaginative connections to them.

The cypress is a coniferous, elegant, and generally pyramidal tree usually found in warm climates. Cypress trees possess a flamelike profile, an evergreen foliage, and an aromatic smell, and they are commonly associated with mourning, sadness, and death and so come to be planted frequently in cemeteries. Their fellowship with grief arose in classical mythology when Apollo gave Cyparissus (ancient Greek for "Cypress") a magnificent, tamed stag, whom the latter accidentally killed with his javelin. Cyparissus was so stricken with sorrow from this loss that he asked Apollo to permit him to mourn for all eternity. In a display of empathy, Apollo transformed Cyparissus into a cypress, and the sap that regularly drips down the tree's trunk can be interpreted as flowing tears. In this way, the scope of arboreal beauty has been enlarged to embrace an appreciation of more melancholic aspects of life.

Among other trees such as the mulberry, poplar, olive, and almond, Vincent van Gogh painted cypresses. As an artist who struggled with depression, these trees seemed to offer him consolation, especially after his mental collapse in 1889 when he entered an asylum in the south of France that included a cypress in its garden. There, he painted "Wheat Field with Cypresses," among many other depictions of these trees. Van Gogh, however, divested the cypress of funereal associations and instead invested it with vibrant color, swirling movement, and deep emotion. His visionary "Starry Night" also features a pair of cypresses typically overlooked by viewers due to the focus on the painting's hallucinatory crescent moon, celestial imagery, and agitated sky.

In the next section, David Macauley explores the wide-ranging and complex ways that we might look at—listen to, touch, and even smell—trees and better appreciate their beauty. David Rothenberg focuses on arboreal sounds and asks the provocative question, "Do trees sing?" Such aesthetic questions and controversies are often tethered closely with other issues related to what we value, especially in the field ecological ethics. What, for example, do we believe to be of defensible worth in the environment? How are valuations of trees and other living entities justified, ranked, and adjudicated when they conflict? And do we have a duty to protect or preserve natural beauty?

—David Macauley

10

Thirteen Ways of Looking at a Tree
Appreciating the Beauty of the Arboreal World

David Macauley

> I am warned by the ill fate of many philosophers not to attempt a definition of Beauty. I will rather enumerate a few of its qualities.
>
> —Ralph Waldo Emerson

> I was of three minds, / Like a tree / In which there are three blackbirds . . . I do not know which to prefer, / the beauty of inflections / Or the beauty of innuendos.
>
> —Wallace Stevens

In an anecdote within his remarkable novel *The Overstory*, Richard Powers depicts the children in a large family arguing about the beauty of five trees to which they have been individually connected. Each tree possesses its own aesthetic virtues: "the ash's diamond-shaped bark, the walnut's long compound leaves, the maple's shower of helicopter, the vase-like spread of the elm, the ironwood's fluted muscle."[1] In the end, the disagreement is resolved by a vote through which each child at first stands up staunchly for their own tree until a runoff election is decided in favor of the Ironwood, as votes are traded for candy or sibling love, and campaigning turns to creative plagiarizing of poetry. Solving or even addressing such a debate outside the realm of fiction would, of course, prove challenging, especially if one clings to a subjective view of judgment, as the children in the novel appear to do. The story does, however, poignantly raise issues about how to aesthetically evaluate the arboreal world.

By its very nature, such an undertaking is freighted with complexities. Trees exist in sundry shapes, sizes, colors, and kinds. There is little in terms of their outward features that all of them share. Some trees are tall and lean, others are short and bushy; some bear fruit, others generate cones; some possess flowers, others do not; many are green, others are white, brown, red, yellow, or a combination thereof. In fact, there is not even a consensus about what constitutes a tree as a biological organism, and frequently even less accord regarding what makes vast numbers of them attractive, pleasing, interesting, or beautiful.

It is natural to wonder whether there are pronounced commonalities between the Joshua Tree, the Ginkgo, the Sassafras, the Mango, the Sequoia, or the Lebanon Cypress, not to mention sixty to seventy thousand other species. Many trees exhibit exquisite order and proportionality through the allure of their branches, leaf shapes, and deeper essences, including radial symmetry and concentric rings. But there are also aesthetic divergences from apparent norms: bedraggled trees that cling heroically to windswept cliffs; silky bamboo that lacks growth rings, stem girth, and traditional wood; and specimens with eye-catching lightning strikes, beguiling fire scars, or unusual knots that tattoo their twisted trunks or gnarled bodies.[2] And yet most trees are viewed widely as displaying significant—and often unique—aesthetic qualities that incline us to speak of them as possessing a type of reliable and even intoxicating beauty.

In this chapter, I examine the aesthetic dimensions of trees and, to a lesser extent, the forests to which great numbers of them belong. I identify and assess different approaches to and models for arboreal appreciation, including those that emphasize form, function, sensuous qualities, use value, seasonal changes, holistic aspects, emotional responses, storytelling, sacredness, and our evolutionary relationship with these plants. I follow a syncretic framework to the appreciation of trees and forests, one that incorporates elements of both scientific and participatory models of environmental aesthetics. In doing so, I discuss features such as the verticality of trees, the ambient air, the sublime, and the comparison of forests with temples and museums. Finally, I show how the imaginative representation of trees by artists helps us to better know and defend living forests.

Environmental Aesthetics

Within environmental aesthetics, two broad perspectives exist. There is, first, a *cognitivist*—more "objective," conceptual, and scientific—model that stresses the need for knowledge of natural history and science to appreciate fully and rationally forests, mountains, deserts, seas, or skies. In this view, aesthetic perception both demands and is enhanced by an understanding of biology, zoology, geology, and chemistry or, in the case of trees, botany, ecology, and soil science. Second, there is an *engagement*—more "subjective," sensual, and emotive—model that emphasizes the necessity of active, somatic participation and immersion in the environment. By this account, we must walk the woods, swim in the waters, dig in the garden earth or, in the instance of the forest, explore it through camping, hiking, and climbing to cultivate a meaningful sense of beauty.[3] While each of these frameworks has multiple merits, a middle *syncretic* path that critically embraces the best of these two ostensibly polar views is possible and ultimately preferable, one that accepts and advances the value of interrelated and dialectical roles in aesthetic experience, including evaluations made by both the body and mind, both emotions and reason, and both art and science.

Challenges naturally exist for the two opposing perspectives. A cognitive model tends to assume the natural world is always accessible to science and its categories. There are often blurred edges to these realms and objects that do not fit natural kinds, however. Intellectual appreciation can also interfere with sensual enjoyment.[4] Thus, the Indian philosopher Krishnamurti writes, "Do you know that even when you look at a tree and say, 'That is an oak tree,' or 'that is a banyan tree,' the naming of the tree, which is botanical knowledge, has so conditioned your mind that the word comes between you and actually seeing the tree? To come in contact with the tree you have to put your hand on it and the word will not help you to touch it."[5] There are potential problems with an engagement view as well, including the apparent lack of restraint in imaginative "seeing as" and the concern that the natural world can get divorced from accepted realities and become overly mysterious, mystical, or unintelligible.

Because, on the one hand, imagination is neither limitless nor flawless and, on the other hand, science is not always the way we encounter the natural world, we might seek to make these competing views more compatible. We can notice the striking verticality of a tree or the delightful margins of a leaf through associations in art but appreciate these features as well by knowing the empirical truths at work behind their expressions. A syncretic view attempts to combine and blend the best aspects of both schools of thought. Moreover, it is consistent potentially with a range of conceptions of beauty. The leaves, wood, fruit, color, and shape of a particular tree, as well as the grove of trees in which they live, may exhibit beauty for very different reasons. Further, a syncretic approach tends to accord with our everyday experiences and judgments while acknowledging that sharp distinctions between the "natural" (biological) and "artificial" (technological) worlds often collapse when we seed, cultivate, graft, or prune trees and maintain, manage, or harvest forests.

Appreciating trees thus requires both an active, open, and embodied engagement with them as well as an awareness of the fields of botany, biology, and ecology. Holmes Rolston, an influential environmental philosopher, characterizes forests as among the most archetypal and elemental forces on earth and suggests that we first need to disenchant the woods so they can be enjoyed as living museums while permitting them to re-enchant themselves spontaneously on their own. In other words, we need to understand photosynthesis, oxidation, nitrogen cycles, and carbon bonding. "Science takes away the colors," Rolston admits, because "apart from beholders, there is no autumn splendor or spring green." However, it also reveals trees "solidly there," thriving without us, contributing to vast communities of life.[6]

Appreciating Trees

"Beauty is the form under which the intellect prefers to study the world," Emerson boldly avows. "All privilege is that of beauty; for there are many beauties; as, of general nature, of the human face and form, of manners, of brain, or method, moral beauty, or beauty of the soul." He adds, "We ascribe beauty to that which is simple; which has no superfluous parts; which exactly answers its end; which stands related to all things; which is the mean of many extremes. It is the most enduring quality, and the most ascending quality."[7]

In what follows, I embrace Emerson's advice and develop a broad range of perspectives for appreciating trees. I offer a pluralistic account of beauty and aesthetics, one that contains both subjective and more objective aspects. It is a syncretic outlook and middle synthesis that incorporates aspects of other frameworks. An implicit goal is to multiply angles and vantage points rather than to privilege a single vision. Stated in other language, it involves an effort to layer and thicken our perceptions of trees over time, an incremental approach that the cognate German words "verdichten" (to condense) and "Dichtung" (poetry) together suggest. As Nietzsche eloquently puts it, "There is *only* a perspective seeing, *only* a perspective 'knowing'; and the *more* affects we allow to speak about one thing, the *more* eyes, different eyes, we can use to observe one thing, the more complete will our 'concept' of this thing, our 'objectivity,' be."[8]

In addition to Emerson, I build on general insights provided by philosopher of art Ronald Moore, who maintains that an account of natural beauty can engage every level of sensory appreciation and be compatible with a broad range of theories. Moore further argues that scale is a not an insurmountable problem: "A grove of trees might be beautiful. For different reasons, a tree within that grove might be beautiful. For yet other reasons, a leaf on that tree might be beautiful. And for yet other reasons, the pattern of colors on that leaf might be beautiful. Put before a microscope . . . the leaf might yield additional, independent forms of beauty."[9]

Nevertheless, one persistent challenge to making informed aesthetic judgments about trees relates to plant blindness, which is the widespread tendency to ignore, neglect, or fail to notice and appreciate plant species. Plant blindness is likely due to a combination of factors, including the belief that plants matter less than humans and other animals; the fact that plants are stationary and hence do not catch our eyes as easily as moving organisms; and the truth that many plants are colored similarly. One possible response to this problem is to bring forth and foreground what was formerly a more homogeneous or unseen background by actively framing a tree through a camera lens, fence post, or building. Conscious and deliberate "looking" is often necessary to appreciate fully any phenomenon, and trees are no different in this regard.[10] Richard Powers characterizes the matter more bluntly: "No one sees trees. We see fruit, we see nuts, we see wood, we see shade. We see ornaments or pretty fall foliage. Obstacles blocking the road or wrecking the ski slope. Dark, threatening places that must be cleared. We see branches about to crush our roof. We see a cash crop. But trees—trees are invisible."[11]

What ensues, then, are thirteen ways of looking at and appreciating trees, a light-hearted reference and nod to Wallace Stevens's poem, "Thirteen Ways of Looking at a Blackbird."[12] These aesthetic approaches are interrelated and often overlapping rather than distinct and exclusive. Thus, a functional perspective shares features with a utilitarian view. An arboreal perspective based upon stories and narrative elements is allied to imaginative and artistic representations. Emotional affiliations with trees often involve an appreciation of their sensual and seasonal qualities. An ambient framework dovetails agreeably with a holistic view, and sacred outlooks on trees regularly identify with their formal traits, perceived virtues, or more immediate "suchness."[13]

1. Form

One appealing way to appreciate trees is through their form. Form can be construed in a variety of complex manners, but in the case of trees we might consider it to mean roughly the order or arrangement of parts, including the boundaries, shape, lines, and contours of a tall woody, perennial plant.[14] Classical notions of aesthetics tend to emphasize integrity, harmony, balance, and proportionality, and these ideas and ideals are frequently associated with form. Closely related are the geometric qualities and mathematical properties of an object. There is a long history within western philosophy of celebrating the formal aspects of aesthetic appreciation, particularly within the ancient Greek tradition. *To kalon* (το καλόν) expresses several related meanings of this sense of beauty, including both outward physical appearance and more internal ethical attributes that connote nobility, honor, or virtue.

Among the Greeks, the Pythagoreans looked to order and proportion to explain beauty, and they believed these qualities arise through number—that is, quantity. Plato agreed: the beautiful invariably involves "the qualities of measure and proportion."[15] By contrast, "deformity," which is "unsightly" involves a lack of measure.[16] Aristotle viewed beauty in similar terms, through "definite magnitude" and "order in its arrangement of parts."[17] Any living organism or whole composed of parts must be pleasing to the eye and perceptible in a single view. For Aristotle, small and vast organisms cannot be beautiful because our vision is unable to take them in all at once, a drawback that has arguably been surmounted with the aid of photography and film.

As noted, many trees exhibit a marked type of order and proportionality through their silhouettes and profiles, limb configurations, leaf shapes, and internal rings. Plants that are anchored to a single spot tend to display a radial symmetry. Their weight is balanced around a center axis, which extends down the trunk into woody taproots. Branches in effect help create the "architecture" of trees and by extension the "infrastructure" of forests—the holds, holes, and homes for a vast network of birds, squirrels, insects, and other creatures. Shooting straight up into the clouds, thrown out like the arms of Vishnu into the wind, or forking wildly like fireworks from a nodal point, primary and secondary branches channel water, create food-producing leaves, and expand the crown into the sky. Collectively, the boughs, limbs, sprigs, and spray of a tree also appear as sculpture to the human eye. We search for recognizable patterns and try to make sense of those that do not fit our expectations or experiences. Part of their visual appeal is assuredly related to the mathematical properties they often exhibit through fractal patterns, which appear similar at a variety of scales.

Tree shapes run the gamut from pyramidal (blue spruce, American beech), oval (sugar maple, white ash), and conical (bald cypress, gingko) to vase (elm, hawthorn), open (ash, hickory), and weeping (crabapple, hemlock). Again, geometry serves to govern a sense of their relative beauty and how we respond to them.[18] It also provides clues to how they can accentuate the aesthetics of a park, garden, city street, or yard. Round-shaped trees such as dogwood and black maple work well in formal landscapes, and they can be placed in a row to craft a linear appearance. Vase tree forms such as boxelder and striped maple fit comfortably near roads and paths given that they tend not to block our vision. Weeping trees visually soften a setting. Conical tree shapes function to define boundaries, serve as windbreaks, and help screen out noise and undesirable scenes.

The fact that trees grow upward and unite the earth with the sky, the below with the above, in a living column no doubt contributes toward their beauty and our aesthetic fascination with them. They inspire us as they aspire and strive heavenward toward the light. "I took a walk in the woods and came out taller than the trees," Thoreau remarks with panache.[19] Trees reach a maximum height of 430 feet, though the tallest known specimen on Earth is likely a coastal redwood in California that stands 380 feet tall. Our preference for verticality, uprightness, and erectness may relate to our own posture and bipedalism, into which we evolved. We tend to moralize physiology, one might say. Roots and branches, of course, move laterally as well as vertically, but this feature is less appreciated. Trees also "migrate" slowly over time with climate change even if they are more basically and definitionally sessile.[20]

A tree typically requires roughly the same length of time for it to return to the soil through decay once it has fallen as it did for it to rise to a final height. Until that happens, trees may stick around for a while to relish "dead verticality." "How curious it would be to die and then remain standing for another century or two," ruminates the poet, Gary Snyder. "If humans could do it we would hear news like, 'Henry David Thoreau finally toppled over.' "[21] Historian Jared Farmer calls attention to the under-appreciated importance of what he variously identifies as *chrono-diversity, elderflora,* and *perdurables* in emphasizing the ecological and social value of recognizing and protecting species of trees that have survived for many centuries and even thousands of years.[22] Trees possess the capacity to record passing time through growth rings and, like wise elders, to "witness" and quietly affect a deeper current of ecological events, often being among the oldest organisms in a biotic community.

In tree leaves, we discover formal beauty in widely varying shapes and sizes, especially in their lines, symmetry, and geometry. Leaves can be characterized through their margins—their blade-like edges—as palmate, digitate, lobate, scalloped, serrated, undulate, sinuate, bipartite, tripartite, and so on. In addition to a division between simple (single, undivided) and compound (multiple leaflets), leaves are identified by shape as linear, oblong, elliptical, deltoid, orbicular, ovate, and cordate, among many related terms. Part of the appeal of looking at and beholding leaves may lie in their rough resemblance to human hearts and hands, especially since we learn to "read" the contours, lines, and venation of these usually palm-sized objects to classify, categorize, and understand a larger living being—and the surrounding landscape—to which they belong.

Despite their great variation in appearance, Goethe speculated there may be an *Urpflanze* or primal and archetypal plant that takes the form of a protean leaf. This idea of the plant as a transformation of a leaf was developed on his journey through Italy between 1786 and 1788: "From top to bottom a plant is all leaf, united so inseparably with the future bud that one cannot be imagined without the other."[23] Goethe's enthusiasm for the leaf was shared by Thoreau who also saw it as a key organic form and ur-phenomenon endowed with creative vitality. The entire Earth, he thought, expresses itself externally through leaves given that it labors with the idea internally. It is not, however, "stratum upon stratum like the leaves of a book" but "living poetry like the leaves of a tree." Thoreau thus viewed the wings and feathers of birds as thin, dry leaves; he noted that ice starts out as delicate crystalline leaves; and he declared that the whole tree is but a single leaf, while rivers are much "vaster leaves whose pulp is intervening earth." "The Maker of this earth but patented a leaf," he proclaimed with exuberance in *Walden*.[24]

2. Function and Evolution

The close relationship between form and geometric shape finds a parallel in the connections with a further way to look at trees: through their functions and evolutionary dimensions. This perspective includes aspects endemic to their own individual lives and survival, the contributions they make to a more capacious forest community, and their roles relative to human society.

Trees provide a host of ecological functions and "environmental services," including sequestering carbon, creating shade, reducing noise, generating oxygen (two trees produce enough for one person), providing food, shelter, and habitat for many organisms, and holding soil in place. Beauty is often associated with these functions.[25] There is splendor in excellent performance and activities well accomplished, and the more one learns about the capacity of trees to sustain a diversity of life or to prevent erosion, for example, the more easily one grows to appreciate this beauty. These functions are commonly expressed by and fit their very form or shape: leaves evolved to synthesize light; roots fashioned to seek out water and secure soil; seeds grown to be dispersed by wind; branches perfect for generating shade and homes for birds and many other critters.

Naturalist and writer Annie Dillard is rhapsodic in her celebration of the force and functions of the arboreal world:

> It is amazing that trees can turn gravel and bitter salts into these soft-lipped lobes [leaves], as if I were to bite down on a granite slab and start to swell, bud and flower. Every year a given tree creates absolutely from scratch ninety-nine percent of its living parts. Water lifting up tree trunks can climb one hundred and fifty feet an hour; in full summer a tree can, and does, heave a ton of water every day. A big elm in a single season might make as many as six million leaves, wholly intricate, without budging an inch; I couldn't make one. A tree stands there, accumulating deadwood, mute and rigid as an obelisk, but secretly it seethes, it splits, sucks and stretches; it heaves up tons and hurls them out in a green, fringed fling. No person taps this free power; the dynamo in the tulip tree pumps out even more tulip tree, and it runs on rain and air.[26]

The value of trees to humans is enormous given that they also remove pollutants from the atmosphere—about ten pounds per tree each year on average—mitigate stormwater damage, increase the value of homes, and cool buildings up to twenty degrees in the summer. In effect, trees collectively act as a vital organ of the planet, like lungs on the animal body.

Trees, too, can serve as models, mentors, and measures for the human community. If, as conservatist Aldo Leopold recommends, it is possible to "think like a mountain," it might even be more plausible to conduct a business like a redwood forest. Such forests are instances of mature ecosystems that tend to be energy efficient, reuse their own waste, rely on diversity, avoid fouling their own territory, and optimize resources in ways that other less developed systems and, by extension, most human companies fail to do. We might conceivably "gather energy like a leaf," for example, in developing solar power that mimics photosynthesis in trees, as one advocate of biomimicry suggests.[27]

We evolved with and descended from trees, and without them we would not have come into existence as a species. In fact, part of the reason we possess "dexterous hands and whirling arms," opposable thumbs and binocular vision, as well as an aesthetic affinity for trees, stems from the fact that our distant ancestors spent millions of years in their midst, jumping between branches.[28] Trees serve as connections and compacts between human generations. Planting a tree binds us to the biotic community and living landscape but also ties one through time to future persons or, genealogically, to one's own family tree, especially when a young elm or maple, for instance, is established as a "green headstone" above the grave of a departed relative. Philosopher Jeremy Bentham even proposed that we embalm our ancestors and line them up along country roads in alternation with trees after protecting the faces of our relatives from the elements with a special coating of resin.

Studies have shown that there is a general public preference for certain tree shapes and that their relative attractiveness is related closely to function, including their provision for shelter, food, shade, safe sleeping, eating places, and vantage points. Trunk height, canopy layering, and canopy width relative to tree height all influence their perceived beauty. Briefly, trees with lower trunks are generally seen to be more appealing than trees with high trunks; trees with a high degree of canopy layering are perceived to be more attractive than those with lower degrees of layering; and flowering trees are considered more beautiful than non-flowering trees—likely because they are food sources and resource signals.[29]

Biologist Joan Maloof has attempted audaciously to measure the beauty of forests.[30] Acting on an awareness that aesthetic factors are often considered in environmental policy decisions about forest management, she devised a study in Wicomico County, Maryland, involving 338 university students to test whether mature forests are perceived as more beautiful than younger ones. The findings bore out this aesthetic viewpoint—83 percent preferred the mature forest—after students labeled trees as "unattractive," "neutral," or "beautiful" within two stands of pine, sweet gum, southern red oak, and American holly.[31] After being shown an educational presentation on forest ecology that focused on the ecological functions and services of trees without reference to their age or aesthetics, one group of test subjects also rated forest beauty higher than before viewing the presentation, though the difference was not statistically significant. Other forest studies have notably shown that the size of trees is the most significant predictor of perceived scenic beauty, with larger trees associated with greater estimates of beauty.[32] Maloof acknowledges that there are no standardized ways of measuring beauty, but her work represents an exploratory attempt to reveal how aesthetic preferences are biologically grounded rather than simply knowledge-based and to locate a shared quasi-objective foundation to the quality of beauty in forests.

Survival and fitness are clearly important evolutionary factors, both for trees and for us. For many organisms, there is a close correlation between beauty and health. The healthiest flowers, for example "can afford the most extravagant display and sweetest nectar, thereby ensuring the most visits from bees—and therefore the most sex and most offspring."[33] In a sense, flowers choose their mates based on health, using bees as proxies. In his influential work, *The Art Instinct*, Denis Dutton develops a powerful Darwinian theory of beauty, pointing to landscape preferences, including the place of trees, as they relate to human evolution.[34] In words that might sum up this way of looking at trees, Emerson writes: "Tis a law of botany, that in plants, the same virtues follow the same forms. It is a rule of largest application, true in a plant, true in a loaf of bread, that in the construction of any fabric or organism, any real increase of fitness to its end, is an increase of beauty."[35]

3. Holism

Despite initial appearances, trees are bound intimately with their surroundings and local environments, and they are customarily tethered to other trees and plants—epiphytes, for example—in their vicinity both under the soil's surface and above ground, including in the canopy. Trees share water, soil nutrients, light, and air space. Their roots and branches are often entangled. They are inhabited by creatures—birds, squirrels, monkeys, or insects—who move across and between their limbs and live in their trunks or on their branches. Even a single tree might reasonably be regarded less as a discrete material shape or thing that stands forth on the earth and more as a phenomenal field, an unfolding process, a site of exchange, or a configuration of forces that draws up water, dissolves minerals, converts carbon, and exchanges gases. In other words, trees are not simply separate, distinct, or detached individuals in a landscape but usually active members of an energetic biotic and abiotic community.

In this regard, beauty arises in a more systemic manner. It is not merely either an intrinsic value—the beauty of a single organism *in itself*—or the instrumental value of that being *for us*. As Emerson puts it, "The standard of beauty is the entire circuit of natural forms." "Nothing is quite beautiful alone; nothing but is beautiful in the whole," he surmises.[36] What matters less is the individual tree and more the greater whole—a network, an ensemble, a community, a material matrix or gestalt one might even say. From this standpoint, beauty is part of a "relation-scape" and hence context dependent.

As American naturalist John Muir notes, "When we try to pick out anything by itself, we find it hitched to everything else."[37] With trees, that "everything else" includes roots, soil, rain, sunlight, clouds, worms, ants, birds, moss, and so much more. This "so much more" is evident with tree pollen, tree seeds, and tree fungal networks. Given that they are sessile—rooted in place—trees depend on the wind to scatter their pollen spores into the air. Birds, in turn, disperse tree seeds to new locations, dropping them in flight, digesting fruit and passing the seeds out elsewhere, or like jays storing fruit and seeds in disparate areas to eat later. Birds also inadvertently carry barbed or sticky seeds on their feet and bodies, an adhesive process known as epizoochory. When a colleague gifted Charles Darwin the limb of a red-legged partridge, a ball of earth remained stuck to it for three years. Darwin broke open the ball, added water, and set it beneath a bell glass. He later discovered that more than eighty plants had grown from it, including at least five different species.

This holistic "hitching" is apparent, too, in the manner that trees in the forest communicate through vast mycorrhizal (fungus-root) networks, a phenomenon explored in Suzanne Simard's, *Finding the Mother Tree*. In these ways, it could be said that trees "transplace" themselves—inhabiting dispersed locales and places at once—across many miles of land as they develop and take on a diffused, disseminated, and porous identity, something loosely akin to Indra's Net, a metaphor for interpenetration, interdependent origination, and inter-being[38] found in Vedic and Mahayana Buddhist philosophy.[39] As Richard Powers observes of trees, "A thing can travel everywhere, just by holding still."[40]

In *The Songs of Trees*, a work that examines a dozen of the world's most beautiful trees, biologist David Haskell speaks of ecological aesthetics as entailing the perception of beauty in "sustained, embodied relationships" within a living community. It involves an "ethic of belonging" and necessitates incarnate interactions, which include both the human and non-human. Beauty is not "titillating prettiness or sensory novelty."[41] Rather, it is an experience that requires ongoing attention and active listening as well as something like what Iris Murdoch designates as "unselfing"—stepping outside the narrow confines of one's self to encounter other beings and worlds in a non-possessive way. According to Murdoch, this dissolution is not deliberative or willful. Rather, it is a kind of "self-forgetful pleasure" that occurs by attending to the life of trees, animals, and stones.

Using the Ponderosa Pine to explore these ideas, Haskell claims the tree "senses, integrates, weighs . . . the world that combines external and internal intelligence" because it is linked to fungi and bacteria through its roots and leaves.[42] The Ponderosa houses a network that is at once electrical, chemical, and hormonal even if its ability to communicate is slower than the nervous systems of animals. Trees are "masters of integration, connecting, and unselfing," dialoguing in effect with the world around them like "Platos of biology."[43] Another emblematic tree is the banyan, which stretches its tendrilous limbs and aerial roots physically downward to the earth as well as upward to the sky, connecting the beyond with the below. Naturalist John Ryan characterizes banyans as "spiritual mediators" and "religious conduits" as well since they have helped to spread Buddhist thought throughout India, Japan, Indonesia, and Thailand.[44]

A version of this way of looking at trees is "connective beauty." From this vantage, natural objects are beautiful because of their relation to other things, which either make them beautiful or enhance their existing beauty. Ronald Moore distinguishes two forms that can occur: *juxtaposition* (a physical relation) and *association* (a mental relation). Thus, a tree may appear to be more beautiful to us if we associate it with a relative who has died or a house we grew up in. Place memory and time come into connective play. By contrast, we might find a very different tree beautiful because it hangs gently over and is juxtaposed with a lovely pond full of fish, ducks, and swans. In both instances, there emerges a complex dynamic of parts and wholes.[45]

A key expression of a holistic framework is provided by Aldo Leopold in his influential land ethic, where it is condensed into a pithy maxim: "A thing is right when it tends to preserve the integrity, stability, and beauty of the biotic community. It is wrong when it tends otherwise."[46] Of what we might term relational aesthetics, Leopold adds: "Our ability to perceive quality in nature begins as in art with the pretty. It expands through successive stages of the beautiful to values as yet uncaptured by language."[47] American poet Robinson Jeffers also expressed a holistic conception of beauty: "The parts change and pass, or die, people and races and rocks and stars, none of them seems to me important in itself, but only the whole. This whole is in all its parts so beautiful, and is felt by me to be so intensely in earnest, that I am compelled to love it." He adds, "It seems to me that this whole alone is worthy of the deeper sort of love."[48]

One question that arises about this way of looking at trees concerns how far such connections extend. Does the beauty of trees, necessarily include or, alternatively, exclude the architecture of a building with which they are often visually linked, for example? Does it include the gardens, parks, and yards where trees grow? And are some connections simply reveries, the play of the imagination, or associated flights of fancy?

4. Beautility

Another way to appreciate trees is through their transformation into objects for human use or consumption—as well as the other-than-human services they provide when we include birds, sloths, squirrels, snakes, ants, and other creatures who make their nests and homes in trees or find their food supplies on or around them.[49] From this perspective, arboreal beauty arises through utility, and what potentially emerges might be styled as "beautility" (beauty + use). It is not so much the tree or forest that is valued holistically, or the parts appreciated intrinsically, but rather the instrumental use, pragmatism, or purpose to which a tree is put.

Art and craft frequently converge and commingle here, as when we enjoy both the simple beauty and practical use of a wooden mallet in the workshop, a rolling pin in the kitchen, a handcrafted chair in the dining room, a finely sculpted banister along the stairs, or a baseball bat on the playing field. Trees are thereby relocated into the human sphere and domesticated within our households. They are also, in a sense, interiorized in our bodies when we dine on pears, apples, figs, cherries, or a multitude of nuts. From trees, we obtain dyes and drugs, ointments and incense, resins and varnishes, gums and glues, fibers, fruit and fuel, paper and paints, and much more. Trees have been whittled, molded, shaped, and cut into weapons, writing instruments, utensils, houses, ships, and furniture, among many other objects.

In most cultures and countries, we find an overlapping aesthetic fascination with and selective use of trees. The Neem, for example, is one of the most important trees in India and is referred to as the "village pharmacy" because of its wide use in traditional medicine. In the southwestern part of the United States, mesquite has provided housing timber for native desert dwellers as well as lumber for corrals, fencing, tools, and household items. Ethnobotanist Gary Nabham celebrates the tree's beauty, which he finds is linked collaboratively to its utility. "Mesquite's architectural elegance, its fragrance, taste, and texture all spell beauty to me, writ large in the desert," he says, noting, "It is not merely useful."[50]

A potential danger with this viewpoint arises when trees are seen mostly—or only—in deeply instrumentalist and anthropocentric terms, when their utility is not counter-balanced by a respect or reverence tethered to their beauty. Use slips easily into abuse as well as over-use. Thoreau thus observes:

> I have been into the lumber-yard, and the carpenter's shop, and the tannery, and the lampblack factory, and the turpentine clearing; but when at length I saw the tops of the pines waving and reflecting the light at a distance high over all the rest of the forest, I realized that the former were not the highest use of the pine. It is not their bones or hide or tallow that I love most. It is the living spirit of the tree, not its spirit of turpentine, with which I sympathize, and which heals my cuts.[51]

The Giving Tree by Shel Silverstein provides an instructive fictional story in this regard when a tree continually gives to a young boy who merely takes throughout his developing life—apples to eat and sell for money, bark in which to carve his initials, a house made from branches, and a boat constructed from the trunk—until at long last the happy tree is but a stump upon which the child, now an old man, can rest.[52]

The flip side of utility is uselessness. In Taoism, an uncarved block (樸) of wood is a key material image connoting our supposed original nature, which can be shaped, cut, or sculpted into different expressions or simply left alone in its pristine condition. In this way, we might come to see a very different whole in trees as well as the value of emptiness and the delight in "letting be"—in short, the appreciative "use" of the beautifully unused or useless, as in the protection of an old growth or uncut "virgin" forest.[53]

5. Suchness

"A dewdrop hanging for a split-second—that is bonsai," remarks Julian Velasco, the curator of the Brooklyn Botanic Garden's bonsai collection.[54] Implicit is this observation is another way to appreciate a tree—that is, to see it in its relative immediacy, its simple "is-ness," its direct "thus-ness," its plain-spoken "suchness." In contrast to a utilitarian perspective, the "message" of tree *is* the tree itself. The tree is not a symbol; it is not a representation; and it is not an eternal or ideal form. The tree does not point beyond itself to an abstract realm or Platonic essence. Its beauty is found in its particularity and givenness.

Tathātā (Sanskrit: तथाता) is the Buddhist term meaning "suchness" or "thusness," and it suggests a reality that is largely absent of conceptual formulations and free of sharp distinctions between subject and object. When a tree is perceived as *tathātā*, it is merely "thus" and not other to or completely independent from us. Like the Buddha, who was referred to as *Tathāgata*—one who has attained suchness—a tree could be said to embody the three Buddhist marks of existence: *anicca* (impermanence); *anatman* (no- or not-self), and *dukkha* (suffering). It can also conceivably be viewed in terms of *shunyata* (emptiness) and *idaṃpratyayatā* (specific conditionality).

The tree is tree-ing, we might say, if we "verb" the noun, an article of speech that can surreptitiously both substantialize entities and overly-objectify organisms. Instead, we can perceive trees in processual terms, through change—via an ongoing arising, coming-to-be, and eventual cessation—in their dependent origination and their interdependence with a forest community should they thrive within one.

This point is further evidenced within Buddhism by the classic work *The Gateless Gate*, where we find: "A monk asked Joshu [Zhaozhou] "Why did Bodhidharma come from the West? Joshu [Zhaozhou] said, "The cypress [or oak] tree in the courtyard [garden]." One way to read this kōan (or instructive riddle) is that it calls attention to the simple "thereness" and "suchness" of the tree, its being-as-it-is. As one commentator puts it, the "response is not unlike Van Gogh's irises or Cezanne's apples. To know the irises as Van Gogh knew them, or the apples as Cezanne knew them, one must be the irises, be the apples." Moreover, "In Zen it is said one should sit like an oak tree with its roots deep into the ground, its branches lost in the sky, immutable, whole. If one has done this one will have no difficulty with Zhaozhou's oak tree in the garden, and one will know the radical difference between thereness and overthereness. Zhaozhou's oak tree is everywhere."[55]

There are at least four ways to encourage an appreciation of trees in their givenness or suchness. The first and most important is simply spending time with them, getting to know their particular or peculiar qualities, meditating under them, perhaps even discovering their individual character. A friend of mine who teaches at Haverford College discusses with his class the works of poets such as Rainer Rilke, Marianne Moore, and William Carlos Williams, figures who have written about trees. Afterward, he asks his students to adopt a tree on campus, spend time with it, and then compose poetry about it. Later in the semester, the students walk the campus grounds as a group, gather in turn beneath each chosen tree, and listen to the student's poem devoted to it.[56]

Haiku is a second well-honored method of appreciating the natural world and, in this case, trees. Described aptly as a stone thrown into the pool of a listener's mind, this art form encourages us to attend to what presents itself in its coming to light and phenomenal showing. Haiku is usually tied to the seasons and to natural phenomena such as birds, flowers, mountains, and plants, particularly cherry and plum trees in the East. In short, it can bequeath us in a precise condensed expression the who, what, where, and when of a given thing, "thing-ing," or being. Here are three illustrative haiku with tree themes: (i) "Leaves falling / Lie one on another. / The rain beats on the rain;" (ii) "Blossoms on the pear—/ and a woman in the moonlight / reads a letter there;" and (iii) "A fallen leaf / Returning to the branch? / butterfly."[57] Two additional short poems by Ikkyū Sōjun (1394–1481) that resemble haiku provide supporting examples:

Void in Form: "When, just as they are, / White dewdrops gather / On scarlet maple leaves, / Regard the scarlet beads!"

Form in Void: "The tree is stripped, / All color, fragrance gone, / Yet already on the bough, / Uncaring spring!"[58]

Cultivating and embracing the Japanese aesthetic of *wabi-sabi* (侘寂)—*wabi* means "subdued" or "austere" and *sabi* means "rustic patina"—is a third valuable approach to appreciating a select group of trees. Very roughly, it connotes beauty in imperfection, incompleteness, or impermanence. Through a *wabi-sabi* perspective, we can better value odd and unusual trees that deviate from a cultural norm, ideal form, or more classical appearance: asymmetrical trees; trees with scars, burns or wounds; ghost trees; dead or dying trees; petrified wood, as well as denuded trees in winter, or trees with an abject, solitary, or austere beauty. The Dragon's Blood trees of Yemen, the baobab of Madagascar, the silk cotton trees of Cambodia, the Pirangi Cashew trees of Brazil, and the Wollemi pine of Australia are all instances of rare, exotic, atypical, or bizarre forms that also challenge our ways of seeing. We might even speculate whether there are distinct "personalities" of some trees that communicate a unique or eccentric style to the forest or larger world. The cultivation of and care for bonsai, for example, can be emblematic of a *wabi-sabi* aesthetic because these miniature trees are associated with loneliness, simplicity, asymmetry, sublimity, weathered textures, twisted wood, and tranquility.[59]

A final possible way to grasp the suchness of trees is to see them as beings capable of awakening, striving toward the light and a form of enlightenment. Through their growth, blooming, and flowering, they are potential or incipient buddhas, beings who bud and become aware over time. Since trees are sessile, they exhibit great proficiency in simply sitting or just standing there, practicing stillness, beautiful posture, and effortless verticality, something like *zazen* (seated meditation) or, alternatively, either *vrksasana* (tree pose) when upright and growing or *shavasana* (corpse pose) when fallen and horizontal, to use yoga references. As the French poet and critic Paul Valéry once put it in his "Dialogue of the Tree," "I say that if someone on Earth does meditate, it is the Plant."[60]

Although there are many merits to this way of looking at trees, one challenge for the aesthetic framework involves the issue of mediation. Do we, in other words, ever fully experience a tree directly and in an unmediated manner? Is our perception, to one degree or another, always filtered through forms of cultural, psychological, or biological influences about our beliefs, needs, desires, fears, or blindnesses?[61]

6. Surface and Sensual Qualities

The sensual and surface qualities of a tree are often what first attract and engage us in formative encounters with them. Here, the human sensorium is drawn to a rich aesthetic reservoir that appears in arboreal form. The colors of leaves are a snare for our eyes. Flowering buds entice not only insects and birds but draw our noses to them as well. Fruit and nuts provide tasty treats for us in addition to fodder for scavenging squirrels and other creatures. The sounds of birds in the branches, the rustling of wind in the leaves, and the cool, calm silence of the woods generate the notes, rhythms, and quiet pauses for the "songs" and "music" of trees. The texture of bark encourages us to touch, hold, or climb trunks and outstretched limbs. Beauty is thereby tied closely to the varying aesthetic qualities of a tree's sensual appearance, its disclosure in the forest, the way it stands, sways in the breeze, or shows off its garb in autumn and spring.

The beauty of leaves is due in large part to their changing colors, which commences when trees stop generating chlorophyll, a sun-absorbing molecule necessary to photosynthesis that provides leaves with a green hue. But these colors are dependent upon the immanent mortality of the foliage. Most people tend emotionally and physiologically to prefer green or red trees to purple, yellow, or orangish brown trees given these differences may be cues about the survival features of a habitat.[62] As autumn arrives, deciduous trees perform their annual striptease, divesting themselves of their cover and "clothing." "Death is the mother of beauty," Wallace Stevens astutely observes, and this point is especially fitting in the forest, wherein deceased or dying trees become hosts for new life.[63] Standing dead trees or "snags" provide homes for woodpeckers and other creatures, while rotting nurse logs can take hundreds of years to fully disappear, during which time they nourish their local surroundings.

Thoreau waxed poetic about tree leaves, particularly in his essay "Autumnal Tints," where he speaks of the leaf in terms of a fruit and focuses on the connections between its color and its maturity or ripening. "It is pleasant to walk over the beds of these fresh, crisp, and rustling leaves. How beautifully they go to their graves! how gently lay themselves down and turn to mould!—painted of a thousand hues, and fit to make the beds of us living."[64] For Thoreau, falling autumn leaves, which transform the earth into a kind of lovely cemetery, "teach us how to die," but even more significantly through their fluttering beauty and colorful extravagance, they inspire us to appreciate life, especially given that their demise provides sustenance for coming generations: "How beautiful, when a whole tree is like one great scarlet fruit full of ripe juices, every leaf, from lowest limb to topmost spire, all aglow, especially if you look toward the sun! What more remarkable object can there be in the landscape? Visible for miles, too fair to be believed. If such a phenomenon occurred but once, it would be handed down by tradition to posterity, and get into the mythology at last."[65] Of red maples in late autumn, he observes: "On causeways I go by trees here and there all bare and smoke-like, having lost their brilliant clothing; but there it lies, nearly as bright as ever, on the ground. . . . A queen might be proud to walk where these gallant trees have spread their bright cloaks in the mud. I see wagons roll over them as a shadow or a reflection, and the drivers heed them just as little as they did their shadows before."[66]

There exists, too, a full menu of tree and forest smells ranging from petrichor, an earthy aroma that emerges after it rains, to a cyanide compound in black cherry bark that smells like bitter almonds. Camphor trees, which possess a fragrant wood, by comparison produce a pungent smell and have medicinal and insecticidal properties. Their oil repels moths and can be used for therapeutic chest rubs. Some camphor trees in fact are embraced within Shinto, where they are wrapped with a sacred rope and considered to be home to *kami*, hidden spirits. A coniferous forest often retains a piney scent, akin to a mix of sap, candied orange peel, and sugar. These odors derive from bitter-tasting essential oils called terpenes and help freshen the air with their anti-microbial and antibacterial qualities. Tree fragrances, particularly those produced by flowers, are important for attracting pollinating insects, too. With a lively fusion of scientific detail and poetic nuance, David Haskell discloses the many ways that we might learn to better appreciate and connect primally with trees through our olfactory sense, especially given that smell is so closely bound to our emotional life and childhood memories. Like a Proustian madeleine, the sweet and spicy aroma of oak-casked whiskey, the wet vegetative tang of the horse chestnut seed, the successive whiffs of Ponderosa pine bark, leaf litter, or woodsmoke, and the distinct scents of newly printed books—as well as old musty ones—can delight us sensually and even transport us to the deep recesses of a mature forest or the "lost time" of a vanished landscape. As Haskell puts it, "Amid the smell of healthy trees, we feel at home. Leafy odours of vigorous trees signal productive habitats and human well-being. The absence of such balm sets us on edge."[67]

Taste is allied closely with smell, and eating the fruit and nuts of a tree involves all the other senses as well. Sap from more than two dozen species of maple trees can be tapped and then boiled to remove the water and concentrate the sugar to create "wild food" in the form of syrup for pancakes, waffles, and desserts, a process first developed by Indigenous people of North America.[68] Like smell and taste, the haptic sense of touch is an integral, if undervalued, aesthetic phenomenon. Bark is roughly like the "skin" of trees, if we invoke a human analogy. It provides a waterproof layer that contains and protects internal organs. As bark ages and weathers, it wrinkles like human skin and drops off. There are many patterns, shapes, and textures to this outer covering—just as there are to the forest carpet—and we can often identify and then further appreciate trees by their kinds of bark. Pitch pines, for example, develop thick insulation, while American beech maintains a more youthful "complexion." As we run our hands across scarred bark, it tells stories of fire, infections, extreme weather (e.g., frost ribs), and other woes, whereas smooth bark does not allow organisms to grasp or move upon it easily.[69] The Rainbow Eucalyptus displays perhaps the most colorful and striking of all kinds since the tree sheds its bark to display a neon green layer that ages into a panoply of bright stripes: pinks, purples, blues, reds, and oranges.

Climbing trees is often a form of exploratory play, especially for children, one that teaches balance, grit, and ingenuity. It is also an enterprise that relies on the silent "sixth sense" of bodily proprioception. Robert Frost's poem "Birches" celebrates youthful swinging on these thin pliable trees and draws a lesson for the poet as a much older man when he imagines climbing "black branches up a snow-white trunk / Toward heaven, till the tree could bear no more, / But dipped its top and set me down again / That would be good both going and coming back."[70] As our own senses and aesthetic sensibility mature, we grow to appreciate the supporting curves of cedar chairs, the solid sounds of a sharp kitchen knife clicking against a stiff chopping block, and the reassuring grip of a well-honed wooden tool, straight-grained hard rock maple pool cue stick, or persimmon-headed golf club in our hands.

When a tree falls in the forest and no human being is around to listen, it surely still makes a sound—and thereby provides a plausible answer to the perennial philosophical conundrum—for the simple reason that there are many other organisms present to experience the event, linking percept with perceiver in the process. In his poem "The Sound of Trees" Frost reflects on the possible interpretations of the noises that trees make with their swaying near his home, relating them to his personal dilemma of whether to remain in one place like the trees or set forth on a journey. "They are that that talks of going / But never gets away; / And that talks no less for knowing, / As it grows wiser and older, / That now it means to stay."[71] In the end, the speaker in the poem decides to take their advice, "set forth," and "be gone."

What sounds or songs, however, do trees truly make, if any? Despite its relative silence, the forest encourages us to take notice of minute movements, flickering images in the sun, shadows crawling up and down trees, the muffled rustling of leaves underfoot, and the muttering of wind in the branches. There is a clear, if indistinct, soundscape that emerges when we listen attentively and even a form of music that seems to arise if we stretch the meaning of the term. *Matsukaze* (松風), for example, is the Japanese word for "song of pines," which describes the melodic chorus of these trees. Birds, too, thrive within the edifice and extended perceptual field of many trees to generate and generously share many beautiful tunes both in the forest ecosystem and human community.

Wood, of course, is one of the main ways that we keep an everyday connection with the forest. Several key distinctions are worth noting here. One is between heartwood and sapwood. Heartwood is the fibrous substance that has died but because of its genetic structure is resistant to decay. Usually older, harder, and darker, it forms the discolored circles at the center of a tree's trunk, branches, or cross-section. Sapwood, by contrast, is the living wood between the bark and heartwood that carries water from roots to branches to leaves as well as stores the tree's sustenance. A second distinction is between hardwood, which comes from trees with broad leaves like the oak or birch, even though the wood is not in every instance hard, and softwood such as cedar or balsa, which derives from conifers and can sometimes be harder than certain hardwood trees, as is often the case with the yew.

Inspired by Merleau-Ponty and Thoreau, Galen Johnson adopts a phenomenological approach to exploring the aesthetics of wood, wherein he perceives a potential convergence of aesthetic and sensual pleasure. Johnson extols the sensuousness of wood and handmade wooden objects, including their acoustics—"wood sings"—and aromas, which involve the "resurrection of the scents of the forest." He observes: "The wooden surface is a tactile, sensuous membrane that meets us as a rough or smooth texture, close kin with the skin of the human body."[72] Along the way, Johnson points out that there are communities of wood and wood working such as the Shakers, from whom we might learn. One less noticed form of wood, however, is the sinuous tree root. "The root is the mysterious tree, it is the subterranean, inverted tree," notes phenomenologist Gaston Bachelard.[73] At the boundary of the worlds of earth and air, the root—part serpent, part claw; part hair, part rock; part wood, part filament—moves sluggishly in two directions, depending upon whether our dreams send it downward toward the dead or bend and bear it toward the heavens.

7. Ambience

Sometimes we encounter trees not as single organisms or individuated beings but less discretely and distinctly, more diffusely. We saunter through an arboreal stand in a hazy mist or navigate through it in fog. We hike in the cloud forests of Costa Rica, Ecuador, Sri Lanka, or Columbia. We amble through the woods at dusk or in early morning when sunlight is dim, the air is damp, and our vision is obscured. Or we listen quietly at night to owls while sitting around a campfire in a grove of pines. At such times, surrounding spires of wood appear to lose their solidity, individuality, and clarity. They seem to dissolve into something more atmospheric. Our aesthetic experience, in turn, grows immersive, less cognitive, more affective. As a sensibility, an attunement to ambience discloses dimensionality and depth. It also suggests intimacy as our separate sense of self softens and melts away.

As literary and ecological theorist Timothy Morton observes, ambience "suggests something material and physical, though somewhat intangible, as if space itself had a material aspect."[74] This description might fit a camping scene at dawn or twilight when the sun is low to the horizon, angling through the trees. Applying equally to music and sculpture, ambience surrounds "on both sides" (from the Latin root *ambo*) as the experience of being ensconced in the forest suggests. At times, the woods can almost feel like an underwater world—with its cool damp air, shady and silent moving forms, and moist earth with spongey plants beneath our feet. Ambience displays other characteristics that we routinely find in engagements with forest phenomena, including *tone* (the way matter vibrates to generate a mood or feel, as in walking through the woods on frozen snow in winter), the *timbral* (the quality of physical sounds like birdsong in flowering spring trees), the *Aeolian* (arriving from no distinct source like an autumn wind murmuring through pines), and the *medial* (contact created in the midst of something, as for example a fox bathing in a pool of sunlight in a forest glen).[75]

Shinrin-yoku (森林浴) is a Japanese expression meaning "bathing in the forest atmosphere" or taking in the woods through one's senses. Forest bathing suggests an immersive experience and an ambient encounter with trees in terms of a shifting field of being-ness. Forest air appears fresher, cleaner, and healthier than other air we regularly breathe. Spending time in the woods lowers our blood pressure and heart rate. It improves our immune system, reduces stress hormones, and helps our overall health. Such benefits likely derive in part from phytoncides, essential oils that inhabit wood and plants, and that trees give off to protect themselves against insects and germs.[76]

Crown shyness is another ambient aesthetic phenomenon found in species of trees such as the Japanese larch, black mangrove, lodgepole pine, and eucalyptus in which their crowns come near to but do not quite touch one another—a form of arboreal "social distancing" so to speak. Instead, these trees create canal-like and jigsaw puzzle openings with their branches, perhaps to slow the speed of leaf-eating insects, prevent damage during heavy storms and winds, or better share exposure to light, including even plants on the ground—a possible example of convergent evolution and both inter- and intra-species cooperation. The empty and open spaces not just the materiality and physical presence of the tree assume aesthetic significance. "These trees are magnificent," Rilke writes, "but even more magnificent is the sublime and moving space between them, as though with their growth it too increased."[77] In this way, the interstitial air and wind contribute to forest beauty. Indeed, we come to appreciate the vast canopy and "second story" world that moves high above our heads but often goes unnoticed until we gaze consciously upward, glide through the branches suspended on a zipline, or scale trees to enjoy a panoramic view. While ambience is a viable way to better appreciate the arboreal world, one challenge for this approach to looking at trees is that it can tend to defy discursive expressions.[78] In other words, it might generate dream-like states and be difficult to put into words or communicate to others.

8. Stories

Humans have long been fascinated by tales—both fictional and factual—involving trees and forests. Siddhartha Gautama sits under a Bodhi

Tree and achieves enlightenment. Newton is struck by a falling apple and discovers gravity. The sages of China find wisdom and beauty in trees, which also provides inspiration for Eastern poets and painters. Hansel and Gretel are abandoned in the woods. Nathaniel Hawthorne's "Young Goodman Brown" sets off on an odd errand into the forest. The family patriarch in Gabriel García Márquez's *One Hundred Years of Solitude* is tied to a chestnut tree after he goes mad. And a host of humans are transformed into trees in Ovid's *Metamorphoses*, including Daphne who is changed into a laurel to escape the lust of Apollo; Cyparisus who is converted into a cypress so that he may grieve the death of his pet deer; and the couple Baucis and Philemon who become entwined oak and linden trees for eternity as a reward for their hospitality to disguised gods.

In Italo Calvino's novel *The Baron in the Trees*, a twelve-year-old boy refuses to eat a plateful of snails and in protest climbs up a knobby holm oak tree, never to descend again, spending his entire life in numerous treetops, where he hunts, fishes, marries, fights forest fires, and wins the respect of scientists and philosophers throughout Europe.[79] Even upon the vast sea, the tall mast of the ship and Ahab's wooden leg take on arboreal significance in Melville's *Moby Dick*. Barefoot in pauper's clothes with a tin pot for a cap, John Chapman, more widely known as Johnny Appleseed, plants nurseries throughout Pennsylvania, Ohio, Illinois, and Indiana. Because Chapman opposed grafting, the apples he grew were likely not intended for eating but instead used only for making cider. As food writer Michael Pollan suggests, Johnny Appleseed was welcome in cabins throughout the Midwest because he was carrying the gift of alcohol to the frontier as an "*American* Dionysus."[80]

"Storytelling reveals meaning without committing the error of defining it," observes Hannah Arendt. We are invariably drawn to the power of stories, and even continue to tell them to ourselves as we sleep and dream. In *Wired for Story*, Lisa Cron points out that "Story, as it turns out, was crucial to our evolution—more so than opposable thumbs. Opposable thumbs let us hang on; story told us what to hang on to."[81] And one thing, of course, we've clung to in our history as a species is trees. Stories provide us with a shared experience in a fragmented culture; they help bind us together; and they assist us in seeing phenomena as parts of a greater, more integrated whole. As one of the oldest art forms that may have originated around a glowing campfire but now extends to novels, myths, plays, and film, stories provide adaptive advantages that enable us to survive. They permit us to work out many scenarios in life with little risk and low cost; they offer us a way to communicate practical and memorable information across cultures and generations; and they encourage us to explore and examine the beliefs, perspectives, and values of other people.[82]

In their own way, trees also tell stories. They convey to us what has happened and what is presently unfolding in the land around them, including below the ground, in the canopy, and through the material flows in the soil. They "speak" to each other about insects, water, humidity, sunlight, and much else. They hold memory in their concentric rings and through their witnessing of events over long stretches of time.[83] As if to further ballast this point, we speak curiously both of an "overstory" and an "understory" in the forest, unconsciously acknowledging in our language the role of arboreal time and narrative.

The very word "tree" is related to "truth" through the proto-Indo-European root *deru*, meaning to be firm, solid, or steadfast, and it suggests the aspirational sense of seeking light and enlightenment in "the above." Indeed, every tree has a truth to share. Leaves are intricate and ordered maps that can be read and studied. Like animal hands or paws, their shapes, lines, and veins help to tell us who they are, how they've been, and where they might be going.

In the process, these arboreal tales help to communicate "storied residence" in the land, a kinship and belonging to the larger biotic community and one of the greatest stories ever told—namely, the epic account of evolution. This way of seeing and listening to trees also suggests the merits of a narrative view of environmental aesthetics, which relates events in time to place in a manner that can satisfactorily explain seasonal changes or the amazing vertical lifespan—and horizontal afterlife—of a branching woody organism.

Here, we can point as well to the close connections between the library—the place where stories are collected, organized, and stored—and the forest from which books historically originate and still depend. "Library," in fact, is related to the Latin *liber*, which was originally "the inner bark of trees" and perhaps derives from the proto-Indo-European root meaning "leaf" or "rind." As Gary Snyder points out in a short essay called "The Forest in the Library" both are highly developed, complex, and intelligent information sharing systems and sites of concentrated consciousness.[84] Astronomer Carl Sagan has noted, too, how books are composed from trees. A book "is an assemblage of flat, flexible parts (still called 'leaves') imprinted with dark pigmented squiggles. One glance at it and you hear the voice of another person—perhaps someone dead for thousands of years."[85]

Consider briefly two stories, one fictional and the other more factual, that highlight some of these points about arboreal narratives. First, in Richard Powers's *The Overstory*, members of the Hoel family photograph a single Chestnut tree over the course of many successive generations. This focal practice not only provides a sense of the life of an individual evolving tree through a great span of time but also documents a given genealogical tree—a changing clan via the frame of a stationary growing plant—and the community of people who grow up, mature, and die beneath its watchful limbs. We are offered, in effect, an aperture into deeper time and an entrance into a larger encompassing narrative: an economic depression, a world war, and regional poverty, as well as minor human triumphs and travails. Powers writes: "The generations of grudge, courage, forbearance, and surprise generosity; everything a human being might call the *story* happens outside his photos' frame. Inside the frame, through hundreds of revolving seasons, there is only that solo tree, its fissured bark spiraling upward into early middle age growing the speed of wood." And later, he writes: "Three-quarters of a century dances by in a five-second flip. Nicholas Hoel thumbs through the stack of a thousand photos, watching for those decades' secret meanings . . . It's all encoded somehow in that animated tree, the gatherings in each season . . . Nicholas feels the years peel off like steamed wallpaper."[86]

A second story features the ginkgo trees of Hiroshima, Japan. Ginkgo, which are dioecious—some male, others female—and embraced by Pure Land Buddhists, have survived for two hundred million years, including an asteroid strike that killed dinosaurs. For Will Matsuda, a photographer and writer based in Portland, ginkgo provide the most meaningful connection to Hiroshima and the loss of his relatives because the trees are some of the only living entities to endure the horrendous effects of the atom bomb. Gingko grow roots deep into the soil and are exemplars of resilience. In Japan, survivors of the bomb are referred to as "hibakusha," which is similar to the name given to the surviving trees: "hibakujumoku." As Matsuda notes, "Some of the original trees are still alive today, and—like many human survivors—they and their descendants are scattered across the globe." One survivor, who was only ten years old when the bomb killed her mother and other relatives, moved to Oregon and worked with an organization, Green Legacy Hiroshima, that plants the seeds of surviving ginkgo in the United States. "I can't grow my mother," she says. "I can't grow my cousin. But the tree, I could."[87] This power of trees to persevere and even to thrive after disasters has inspired similar stories related to survivor trees following the Oklahoma City bombing in 1995 and the 9/11 attack in New York City in 2001. In the former instance, an eighty-year-old American elm was nurtured back to health and became a living memorial for the city, while in the latter tragedy, a battered "Ground Zero" Callery pear tree recovered and is now a destination for many pilgrimages.[88]

9. Seasonality

The beauty of trees is greatly conditioned by the season in which they appear, wax, wane, or dissolve into the ground or background of a landscape. Their leaves, branches, and bark can draw attention to and magnify key dimensions of the "rounded year": winter, spring, summer, and autumn, or, alternatively, wet and dry seasons. In the forest, we take note of seasonal changes in color, sound, scent, and temperature as well as the animals that alight to our senses. Spring and summer are marked by the expansion of heat and light, while in fall and winter the arboreal world contracts as life grows cold, dormant, and quieter, retreating underground or migrating elsewhere.[89]

In temperate regions, we grow aware of winter's arrival by noticing the bare branches of trees when they are missing leaves or ballasted by snow. The woods are relatively silent this time of year, too. In spring, green replaces winter whites and browns in deciduous forests. Ephemerals emerge on the thawing ground. The understory starts to promenade itself. "Spring too, very soon! / They are setting the scene for it—plum tree and moon," says Bashō in a poignant haiku.[90] Here, we see the tree framing both time and place. Blooming cherry trees in Japan are especially emblematic of seasonal change in this regard—augurs of the terminus of winter. In summer, trees are obliged to respond to the pressures of heat. On sweltering days, they suck up to 130 gallons of water. During autumn, we witness the loss of leaves but the arrival of mushrooms on the forest floor. Squirrels, mice, and jays diligently collect food around or upon the columns of wood that tower around them.

In short, sightings of specific trees, animals, and other plants become omens for us of the passage of seasonal time: apples fruiting in autumn, bees pollinating in spring; sunflowers stretching toward the sun in summer.

The seasons emplace time and provide a sense of temporality to place. Time is given shape as a concrescence of local forms and atmospheric forces. The budding magnolia trees in a park, for example, embody and express it more touchingly and beautifully than the paper calendar on a kitchen wall. The seasons, in turn, offer traces of their presence or passing in the arboreal world, signatures of time in tree rings or wind-tugged leaves lured across the ground and sky as if on kite strings. The year is thereby bound together in the land, anchored in the ground by all sorts of species of coniferous and deciduous life. Thoreau in fact goes as far to claim that a place is not complete until it possesses trees to mark the seasons, and that they are as important as a town clock. "Let us have willows for spring," he suggests, "elms for summer, maples and walnuts and tupelos for autumn, evergreens for winter, and oaks for all seasons."[91]

10. Emotions

The influential art critic Clive Bell once declared that the beginning point for all aesthetic perspectives is "the personal experience of a peculiar emotion."[92] Emotional states ranging from madness to melancholy are thus attributed on a regular basis variously to artworks, artists, and audiences, with one of the challenges being the identification of the exact source, scope, and effects of such emotions. Within the art world, views based on emotions are usually associated with an expressive theory of aesthetics and often find their roots and inspiration in Romanticism.

In the natural world, however, emotional states are not usually located in the phenomena themselves—since there is no creative artist and no resulting artwork when we look at or speak, for example, of a baobab tree or waterfall. Rather, we acknowledge that trees and other natural entities possess the capacity to evoke feelings, passions, sentiments, affections, and moods *within us*. They inspire or calm us. They seduce us to their trunks, leaves, or limbs and even help us to fall in love, including quite possibly with trees themselves. They precipitate fear or anxiety. They assist us in learning trust, as when a young child ventures out on a swaying branch or spends a stormy night sleeping in a treehouse. They amaze, bewilder, distract, annoy, and surprise us. We delight in their presence when we picnic beneath grand or gnarled trees and experience ecstasy when we swing from a rope looped high in their branches.

Poet William Blake remarked that "The tree which moves some to tears of joy is in the eyes of others only a green thing that stands in the way."[93] For many of us, though, the weeping willow, for example, stimulates wistful emotions, especially sorrow. The changing colors of leaves contribute capriciously to our moods, whether it is the joyous arrival of spring or the woeful eclipse of summer. Trees routinely offer us sensual pleasure by way of either their constitutive parts or composite whole. Through luscious fruit, comforting shade or refuge, stimulating views and prospects, and places to nap, including even eternal rest in a tree-lined cemetery, we experience and associate positive emotions with them. Forests, too, generate feelings of awe, wonder, and mystery. And such emotions widely give way to spiritual, metaphysical, and mystical feelings, though they can comfortably remain secular, occupying an interstitial place between the domains of science and religion.

It is helpful to note that "emotion" is related to the French word *émouvoir*, which means "to stir up." In this regard, trees can easily embody or express an "arousal model" of aesthetic appreciation. According to this perspective, we are "moved" by the natural world in its many outcroppings and shifting forms. From this vantage, science-based views of the natural world do not always engage our feelings, which are legitimate ways of interacting with the environment.[94]

Martha Nussbaum has written of the intelligence of emotions as discerning and discriminating responses that reveal what is of value to us individually or socially, including compassion, empathy, grief, loneliness, and love.[95] In this sense, it might conceivably be the case that our emotional responses to trees which are flourishing or, alternatively, being threatened and cut down can reveal meaningful ethical judgments about the beauty, power, fragility, and vulnerability of forests and the natural world, especially when set in a nuanced narrative context that shows them intersecting with our own lives and livelihoods.

The philosophical work of Alphonso Lingis, which takes up and explores "dangerous emotions" as well as "imperatives" that lie outside the narrow confines of the human mind, might help us to further grasp the ways in which trees possess a more active agency and influence upon us and the surrounding world than we initially presume or imagine.[96] A beautiful or abject looking tree may summon us to look at it, listen to it, or climb it. Another tree may call forth a kind of command to respect it, speak with it, or protect it. This is perhaps what occurred when Julia Butterfly ascended Luna, a two-hundred-foot-tall ancient California redwood, remaining there for 738 days before coming down. Or what happened when the women of the Chipko movement embraced and defended trees in India. In this way, aesthetic experience can possess a form of intensity—as does a strong fragrance—that solicits a qualitative response and responsibility on our part, and a corresponding movement from the perception of arboreal beauty to ecological duty.

11. Moral Beauty

The relationship between aesthetics and ethics—between beauty and duty—is admittedly complex, but there often does appear to be a close connection between the two realms of value, including our judgments about the natural world and especially trees. Emerson, for example, observed that "All high beauty has a moral element in it."[97] And Thoreau proclaimed, "The perception of beauty is a moral test."[98]

Many individual species of trees have rooted themselves in our cultural lives and collective minds, where we attribute to them various virtues or, less occasionally, vices in the case, for example, of trees used for human hangings or forests associated with dread, danger, and evil in literature, myth, and folklore. More positively, we often gather around an evergreen during winter holidays. The oak provides us with shade and inspiring images of endurance, vigor, reliability, or strength. The redwood and sequoia suggest majesty and grandeur. Poplars and birches connote refinement or grace; the cypress intimates melancholy; and the plane tree signals grandeur.

Thoreau located an ethical grain in the arboreal realm when he declared that nothing "stands up more free from blame in this world than a pine tree," pointing to the nobility of a species that resides in the "ancient rectitude and vigor" of natural surroundings.[99] He was clearly fascinated by trees, treating them as akin to neighbors, "distant relations," and even friends. Thoreau often walked as many as ten miles in winter to "keep an appointment" with a birch, beech, or pine tree with whom he was "an old acquaintance" and no doubt returned to his writing desk with a story to share, one that that aided in the composition of *Walden* and the journals he diligently kept. Trees inspired the muse in Thoreau and fired his lyrical imagination; they kept his scientific mind occupied with matters related to classification, seed dispersal, and forest succession; they provided philosophical insights about form, matter, and movement; and they offered him spiritual comfort as "shrines" that intimated great mysteries in the cosmos.

In this regard, the social authority and influence of trees emerges when they are fashioned into moral metaphors and material images. Michael Pollan identifies several cultural species that inhabit the western worldview, including the Political Tree, the Romantic Tree, the Colonial Tree, and the Puritan Tree. Puritans, for example, have tried to cut and clear trees to redeem nature, while romantics might worship trees to restore culture.[100] The sylvan sphere occupies our minds as a realm upon which we project our anxieties, desires, and fears. Forests are "shadows of civilization," enigmatically offering sites of danger, darkness, and asylum for lawbreakers as well as generating places of reverence, enlightenment, and revelation. "In the forest the animate may suddenly become inanimate, the god turns into a beast, the outlaw stands for justice, Rosalind appears as a boy, the virtuous knight degenerates into a wild man, the straight line forms a circle, the ordinary gives way to the fabulous."[101]

If individual trees or clusters of them embody or express forms of beauty, forests are more likely to be instances of the sublime. A forest is a realm routinely engendering at once both wonder and existential worry, or at least discomfort—a peculiar sense of awe coupled with the suspicion of something awful to come, as when a violent storm, hurricane, tornado, or tsunami strikes. The sublime is an encounter beyond that which is simply beautiful. Its sheer magnitude can generate feelings of our own smallness and finitude in a vast universe, as well as provide us with an experience of amazement and a curious kind of pleasure.

Kant identified two forms of the sublime: the mathematical, which involves being overwhelmed by prodigious size, and the dynamical, whereby we are astounded by enormous force. We might say that whereas daylight is beautiful in its capacity to "charm" us—and that is the period when we usually observe trees—night is more sublime to the extent it can morally or aesthetically "move" us. The sheer immensity of a large forest is beyond our capacity to fully comprehend it and, along with its near boundlessness, eerie silences, and seeming formlessness, it can cause us to oscillate swiftly between aesthetic and emotional extremes.

12. Sacredness

Trees, which hold a special status in most cultures, were once considered to be the wooden spines and sacred spires of the earliest forest shrines, especially in places like ancient Greece, where they were sometimes protected by law as precincts of the divine (*hieron temenos*). Throughout the world, selected tree species, and especially individual instances of them, are held in high esteem. Their beauty is linked closely with deep reverence: the Tree of Life in the Hebrew Bible, the Tree of Jiva and Atman in Vedic scripture, the *shinboku* (神木) believed to be inhabited by kami in Shinto shrines, the Oaks of the Celtic Druids, and the trees of the *I Ching* (*Book of Changes*), among them.

In India, daily prayers are offered to the pipal (*Ficus religiosa*), aka fig or Bodhi, often addressed to Vishnu, the protector deity. In Varanasi, India, worshippers at several temples circumambulate the pipal seven times and wrap colored threads around the tree or provide offerings as a sign of care. Some Hindus worship the pipal as an embodiment of the three major deities: Vishnu (the trunk), Brahma (the roots), and Shiva (the branches). The emperor Ashoka even erected a temple to the east of the most famous Bodhi Tree. All such trees of this kind are considered sacred by Buddhists as well as many Hindus and Jains, but only those propagated from the original tree are recognized as fully special. This first and most famous tree has been regenerated many times over the centuries in what we might creatively call *tree-incarnation* (arboreal reincarnation) since the tree continues to endure in some sense beyond death in a form philosopher Alfred North Whitehead termed "objective immortality."

Tree marriage has also been a widespread historical practice by people in India given that many believe in sacred arboreal powers—to help with fertility problems, to mitigate suffering, or to connect with the souls of ancestors or the unborn.[102] More recently in Mexico, some women are marrying trees as a legal, ecological, and political protest against logging. In the Redwood National and State Parks of northern California, there even exists a beautiful "Cathedral Tree"—nine trees that grew together in a circle around a mother tree stump—beneath which Easter services are held each year and weddings regularly occur. In Kerimäki, Finland, I visited the largest wooden church in the world. Constructed in the 1840s and seating more than three thousand people, it lies near a beautiful, pellucid lake. The church is a masterwork of carpentry and a celebration of the beauty of wood with its many arches, pews, galleries, columns, beams, and domes, a transformation of the forest into hallowed architecture.

The association between trees and a sense of the sacred is a perennial one. In his classic work *The Golden Bough*, James Frazier identifies the many cultures—from the Celts, Germans, and Greeks to the Ojibwa, Koreans, and Chinese—who have considered trees to be divine or populated their woods with gods. From an outpost in the Sierra Mountains, John Muir thus spoke in a spiritual vernacular of the woods:

> A few minutes ago every tree was excited, bowing to the roaring storm, waving, swirling, tossing their branches in glorious enthusiasm like worship . . . Every hidden cell is throbbing with music and life, every fiber thrilling like harp strings, while incense is ever flowing from the balsam bells and leaves. No wonder the hills and groves were God's first temples, and the more they are cut down and hewn into cathedrals and churches, the farther off and dimmer seems the Lord himself.[103]

The sentiment was echoed by Emerson, who proclaimed, "In the woods, we return to reason and faith."[104] This belief in animate wood or inspirited trees has frequently led to prohibitions on the use or abuse of many groves, helping to preserve them for posterity. In this regard, Gary Snyder points to a close conjunction in the land—the soil, forest, waterholes, and mountains—of the good, the wild, and the sacred, to which we might reasonably add the beautiful.

The comparison of forests to temples, museums, and cathedrals is illustrative and apt because it helps to reveal the aesthetic and ecological value of these realms and points toward a possible reservoir of the sacred. The forest is nature's most magnificent museum, and it is an exultation of a lofty living sphere that has taken long periods of time to be assembled or, more exactly, self-assembled. There is beauty, even if there is no visible artist at work here. An arboretum serves similarly as a kind of gallery for trees, a place where they are identified, admired, and protected for their various aesthetic forms and biotic value, though we need unfortunately to add that forests themselves are increasingly prone to becoming less like museums and more like mausoleums—realms of the dead, dying, or extinct.

We require more than just singular sites of the sacred—individual trees such as a five-thousand-year-old Bristlecone Pine—which are roughly akin to monasteries in the human world. Instead, we need to create and preserve "eco-steries," wide and wild places, expanses of wooded land—rainforest in particular—that are considered ecologically valuable and worthy of protection. Here, one could appeal analogically to the importance of transitioning from an Endangered Species Act in the United States—which attempts to preserve individual species—to an Endangered Habitat Act, which would likely protect many thousands of different species.

An ancient forest, observes Snyder, is "a place of organisms, a heaven for many beings, a temple where life deeply investigates the puzzle of itself."[105] Hermann Hesse speaks similarly of trees as sanctuaries: "Whoever knows how to speak to them, whoever knows how to listen to them, can learn the truth. They do not preach learning and precepts, they preach, undeterred by particulars, the ancient law of life . . . When we are stricken and cannot bear our lives any longer, then a tree has something to say to us: Be still! Be still!"[106] But perhaps we should be patient in identifying what counts as sacred for, as Snyder advises, it might be best to let the land inform and apprise us. "The cry of a Flicker, the funny urgent chatter of a Gray Squirrel, the acorn whack on a barn roof—are signs enough," he suggests.[107]

13. Imagination

Sometimes, we perceive things not as they are but as we are. Seeing becomes "seeing as" when it is channeled through a fertile imagination, which serves as an aesthetic filter for our senses and experience. We stroll through a forest, park, or cemetery in winter, and the dark outlines of denuded trees appear as our grandparents, as wild animals, as menacing skeletons or witches, as peculiar creatures holding hands, or as the patterns produced by an x-ray of a human nervous system or brain. Our minds encourage and embrace these flights of fancy and forms of personification, thereby making the world more accessible to us.

Joan Maloof proclaims, "To really feel a forest canopy one must use different senses, and often the most useful one is the sense of imagination."[108] Emerson likewise praises the role of imagination in perceptions of beauty:

> Things are pretty, graceful, rich, elegant, handsome, but, until they speak to the imagination, not yet beautiful. This is the reason why beauty is still escaping out of all analysis. It is not yet possessed, it cannot be handled. Proclus says, "it swims on the light of forms." It is properly not in the form, but in the mind. It instantly deserts possession, and flies to an object in the horizon. If I could put my hand on the north star, would it be as beautiful? The sea is lovely, but when we bathe in it, the beauty forsakes all the near water. For the imagination and senses cannot be gratified at the same time. Wordsworth rightly

speaks of "a light that never was on sea or land," meaning, that it was supplied by the observer.[109]

The genius of the imagination lies in revealing the conversion of everything into something else. "Facts which had never before left their stark common sense, suddenly figure as Eleusinian mysteries. My boots and chair and candlestick are fairies in disguise, meteors and constellations."[110]

Building on a tradition initiated by Kant, environmental philosopher Emily Brady identifies four kinds of imagination that operate with respect to the natural world and that we in turn might apply to appreciating trees more specifically. First, *exploratory* imagination involves free contemplation of objects, as when we walk by a gnarled tree and see it as an elderly man's face full of bark-like wrinkles. Second, *projective* imagination entails "seeing as" and adding on to an image, as when we envisage a canopy of trees as kind or sinister toward us while camping beneath them. Third, *ampliative* imagination encourages inventiveness, visualization, and creative leaps. It is active and more penetrating than other forms of imagination. Thus, we might expansively "see" in a single acorn the oak into which it will grow, the squirrel who carried and dropped it, the ensuing rain and soil that will nourish it, and even a succession of woods that might emerge from it. Finally, *revelatory* imagination allows larger aesthetic truths to be revealed; it is where we carry perceptions to their limits, as when we detect the immense powers of the earth through the contemplation of a lightning storm, gushing waterfall, or rapidly spreading wildfire in a forest.[111]

Imagination may even arrive in the very guise of a tree itself because it is able to conjoin above and below as well as the real and the dreamed. The tree, as Bachelard shows through the exploration of material images, is a force of integration because it can be "everywhere at once." Such an arboreal image is expansive and inclusive—of the roots and the boughs. It becomes the cosmological tree, the tree that embodies or symbolizes the universe.[112] Nevertheless, one challenge for this framework is that it can possibly lead to misrepresentations, fictions, or even dangerous associations if we forget the science, lose sight of the facts, or disconnect too much from the material world through free play of the imagination. Hence, there is need for a syncretic perspective that combines art with science.

The work of some contemporary artists attests to the role of imagination with respect to an aesthetic of trees. These figures typically transform trees into something resembling their natural forms but also other than what they initially appear to be. We, in turn, look at trees with fresh eyes, or perhaps notice them for the very first time. Even the simple act of wrapping a tree with yarn, ribbons, or prayer flags serves to call attention to it, to delimit, and to foreground the oft hidden background. It functions as a form of framing, as when we walk with a camera and engage in active looking. Thoreau thus remarks: "Two or more hemlocks on opposite sides of a brook make the most beautiful frame to a waterscape, especially in a deciduous wood, where the light is somber and not too glaring."[113]

We close this investigation of arboreal aesthetics with a cursory consideration of a few examples of tree art that focus on sculptural and site-specific creations. This work builds indirectly on an influential tradition in the west that includes an engagement with trees in the photography of Ansel Adams, the poetry of writers from Robert Frost to Seamus Heaney, and the paintings of Anselm Kiefer or Vincent van Gogh. Such representation or transfiguration of trees by ecologically sensitive artists helps us to better appreciate and protect arboreal specimens and the forests in which many of them dwell.

As he has done with stone, ice, water, soil, light, snow, and other elemental material, Andy Goldsworthy magically fashions stunning evanescent "earth works" out of leaves, branches, roots, and entire trees to reveal the many qualities of wood and to evoke primal earthly forces of growth, change, time, and decay. "Wood Line," for example, is a sinuous sculpture that speaks to and "draws" a particular place, a eucalyptus grove in the Presidio in San Francisco. It consists of a curving line of large eucalyptus branches that snake their way for 1,200 feet along the forest floor, providing a sharp contrast with the vertical trees above and an object for children to play upon before the wood eventually sinks back into the soft earth.[114] In other works, Goldsworthy explores the entrails of a tree, creates beautiful wooden arches, suspends trees in stone walls, generates delightful geometric images with colorful leaves, offers a floating "gift" of circled branches fashioned in a salmon hole to the rising tide and embracing sea, and wends a 2,300-foot stone divide around trees and saplings in a sculpture park in Storm King, New York.

An especially eye-catching tree sculpture by a different artist, Roxy Paine, is a forty-five-foot tall, eight-ton work entitled "Graft," part of a series she calls "Dendroids," a term that suggests tree-like branching. Constructed of stainless steel, "Graft" glistens as a silver object that stands out in the sun, both at once alluring and unalive, thus generating a range of responses from intrigue and delight to concern and anxiety. One side of the artificial tree features orderly branches that rise upward in a predictable fashion, while the other side appears twisted and fraught, thereby uncomfortably marrying or "grafting" classical imagery with romantic associations.[115]

In another provocative piece called "Tree Logic," Natalie Jeremijenko inverts six live trees and suspends them from a truss to show their dynamic growth over time. Although they hang upside down, the trees still grow away from the earth and toward the sun, generating unusual shapes in the process that cause us to question our settled perceptions and ideas of what a tree is and how it appears—in a manner loosely like Duchamp's inversion and relocation of a urinal from a bathroom (low and base) to a museum (high and celebrated) to create his incendiary artwork *Fountain*.[116]

By contrast, Olga Ziemska constructs tree sculptures from reclaimed wood and metal. Her "Stillness in Motion" series presents striking images of women made from local material. One depicts an arresting silhouette of a woman built from willow branches and wire and trailed by flowing branches. Another work called "Mind Eye" shows a large human head in the Dolomites of Italy through which one can view the surrounding mountains. And a third entitled "The tree told me so . . ." involves birch logs, mirrors, branches, and sand beautifully arranged in a serpentine shape inside of a church in the Czech Republic. Ziemska also fashions large oval eyes out of wood and creates long vertical poles with plaster fingertips and hands on their end that rise to the sky in a forest stand, summoning the viewer to listen, look, or touch the surrounding trees.

Lastly, Caroline Wendling's "White Wood" (2014) is notable for both its size and the fact that it is a living environmental artwork. In essence, it is a deciduous woodland created by the Scottish community of Huntly and Wendling. It consists of seven hundred planted trees, including forty-nine oak saplings from acorns derived from Joseph Beuys's earlier (1982) project in Kassel, Germany. In brief, the project explores ideas connected with layered temporalities, forest regeneration, public participation, ecological scale, and deep time in the Anthropocene and, according to one critic, engages themes such as "mesh" and "enchantment" developed respectively by environmental theorists Timothy Morton and Jane Bennett.[117]

Conclusion

We've seen there are multiple approaches to appreciating trees and forests. It's reasonable to believe, though, that humans are often disposed to look for what nonhumans can "give" to us, or what we might conceivably "take" from them. While the most insightful, accurate, and beautiful modes of viewing the natural world may necessitate developing something like what Thoreau calls "different intentions of the eye," some of the habitual ways we look at trees still tend to proceed in a one-sided manner as well. We might, however, turn this one-directional perspective around to empathetically or imaginatively consider how trees "look" at—listen to, touch, and sense—us; to wonder about what we give to them, if anything at all; or at least to reflect upon what such thought experiments could imply. In doing so, it's possible that a more respectful and better-informed connection with trees could emerge over time.

In a remarkable passage in *I and Thou*, Martin Buber contemplates a tree, noting that we could potentially look at this living organism as a picture; see it in terms of its form, movements, and membership in a species; or regard it through its mathematical properties and natural laws. But until we are "drawn into a relation," the tree remains an "It"—a thing, an object, or our possession through appropriative perception. When the important transition occurs, however, we develop a more reverential "I-Thou" (or "I-You") relationship and dialogue with the tree as opposed to an objectifying "I-It" interaction and monologue. Such a transformation does not mean we must surrender other ways of looking and forms of contemplation. Rather, we can still perceive the tree in terms of "its form and its mechanics, its colors and its chemistry, its conversation with the elements and its conversation with the stars," but now the tree "confronts" us corporeally and "has to deal with" us as we deal with the tree—"only differently."[118] Such a *relationship* involves *reciprocity*. It also usually entails a meaningful and irreducible *encounter* not just a personal *experience*, and this is when we truly begin to see and perhaps understand and even care for or love the tree.

There appears in fact to be a form of reciprocity built into many kinds of seeing wherein that which is observed looks back and beholds us in one way or another. Merleau-Ponty shares an illustrative observation from painter Paul Klee: "In a forest, I have felt many times over that it was not I who looked at the forest. Some days I felt that the trees were looking at me, were speaking to me . . . I was there, listening." Klee adds, "I think the painter must be penetrated by the universe and not want to penetrate it . . . I expect to be inwardly submerged, buried. Perhaps I paint to break out."[119] Merleau-Ponty refers to this intertwining and reversibility of perception as a *chiasm*, a comingling and crossing of the seer with the seen. With trees, it is almost as if we might conceive of the knots (burls), for example, in their trunks, limbs, and bark as incipient eyes, organs of perception that look back at us.[120] Rilke offers us a poetic perspective broadly akin to that of Merleau-Ponty, for whom "vision is the meeting, as at a crossroads, of all the aspects of Being."[121]

> Space, outside ourselves, invades and ravishes things:
> If you want to achieve the existence of a tree,
> Invest it with inner space, this space
> That has its being in you. Surround it with compulsions,
> It knows no bounds, and only really becomes a tree
> If it takes its place in the heart of your renunciation.[122]

I have tried in this chapter to show the various interrelated and mutually reinforcing ways of appreciating the beauty of the arboreal world. In this effort, I have provided a pluralistic and syncretic account that draws equally upon science and the arts along with a range of subjective, intersubjective, and more objective aesthetic views. I have explored the form, function, and uses of trees and revealed how they can be seen at once in their individual "givenness" as well as their broader holistic, ambient, and seasonal dimensions. I have pointed to the significance of the surface and sensual features of trees—including qualities perceived through smell, touch, and sound—and suggested that the stories we tell about them, the emotional responses we feel toward them, and the virtues we attribute to them are important routes through which to discover aesthetic value. We can find beauty, too, in the spiritual and imaginative manners that we behold or creatively represent trees.

Understanding what draws us to trees can assist us in responding to the ecological crisis and worldwide deforestation and perhaps move us from a sensibility involving arboreal beauty to a sense of sylvan duty and even a sustainable focus on environmental policy. It required 350 million years for evolutionary forces to assemble the world's great forests. It has taken far less time for us to disassemble most of these magisterial realms where the great wealth of tree species on the planet make their homes. Let's work to value, appreciate, and protect the earth's trees and forests! The Buddha, the Lorax, and the women of the Chipko movement in India, among many others, would surely agree.[123]

Notes

1. Richard Powers, *The Overstory* (New York: W. W. Norton, 2018), 50.
2. Botanists generally consider bamboo to be a grass rather than a tree, but culturally, especially in the East, it has often been regarded as a tree.
3. On the two main models of environmental aesthetics, see the work of Allen Carlson (the cognitivist model) and Arnold Berleant (the engagement model). For example: Allen Carlson, *Aesthetics and the Environment* (London: Routledge, 2000) and Arnold Berleant, *Living in the Landscape* (Lawrence: University Press of Kansas, 1997).
4. Ronald Moore, *Natural Beauty: A Theory of Aesthetics Beyond the Arts* (Toronto: Broadview Press, 2008), chap. 2.
5. Jiddu Krishnamurti, *Freedom from the Known* (San Francisco: HarperSanFrancisco, 1969), 25.
6. Holmes Rolston, "The Aesthetic Experience of Forests," in Allen Carlson and Arnold Berleant, eds., *The Aesthetics of Natural Environments* (Toronto: Broadview Press, 2004), 188.
7. Ralph Waldo Emerson, "Beauty" in *The Conduct of Life* in *Ralph Waldo Emerson Collection: Collected Essays and Lectures* (Independently Published, 2021), 437.
8. Friedrich Nietzsche, *On the Genealogy of Morals* part III, sect. 12, trans. Walter Kaufman and R. J. Hollingdale (New York: Vintage Books), 119.
9. Moore, op. cit., 12.
10. See also James H. Wandersee and Elisabeth E. Schussler, "Preventing Plant Blindness," *The American Biology Teacher* 61, no. 2 (Feb. 1, 1999), 82–86.
11. Powers, *The Overstory*, op. cit., 423.
12. Wallace Stevens, "Thirteen Ways of Looking at a Blackbird," *The Collected Poems of Wallace Stevens*, ed., Holly Stevens (New York: Vintage, 1990), 93.
13. In a consideration of the beauty of trees, we should keep in comparative mind the aesthetics of the aerial domain, which quietly interfaces with and affects the arboreal realm. In a very cursory way, the aerial world is daily more accessible to most of us than the woods or deep forest. It is also a region marked by more regular and pronounced perceptual change than the comparatively stable, earth-bound arboreal realm. Whereas we might observe trees more easily through a lens that separates and delimits their shapes, sizes, and boundaries, the sky usually requires more active "framing" to view its contents and fleeting "moods." Trees tend to possess a larger range of color; they are more commonly subject to alteration by human hands; and they show greater particularity to our eyes, while the aerial domain is often more monochromatic, largely absent in design, and less discrete in appearance. Again, these differences should not be exaggerated too far, especially since the aerial and arboreal spheres are adjoining and interact

in intricate ways with one another. See David Macauley, "Head in the Clouds," *Environment, Space, Place* 2, no. 1 (Spring 2010): 145–82.

14. This interpretation and application of "form" to trees admittedly differs in some ways from more traditional views of form and formalism in aesthetic theory and art.

15. Plato, *Philebus,* 64e, translated R. Hackforth in *The Collected Dialogues of Plato,* ed. Edith Hamilton and Huntington Cairns (Princeton, NJ: Princeton University Press, 1961).

16. Plato, *Sophist* 228a, translated F. M. Cornford in *The Collected Dialogues of Plato,* op. cit.

17. Aristotle, *Poetics,* 1450b35ff, trans. Ingram Bywater in Richard McKeon, ed., *The Basic Works of Aristotle* (New York: Random House, 1941).

18. See, for example, Liliana Curcio, "The Geometry of Beauty" in *Faces of Geometry*, eds., Paola Magnaghi-Delfino, Giampiero Mele, and Tulia Norando (Springer, 2021), 101–14.

19. Henry David Thoreau, quoted in Andrew McCarthy, "Whatever the Problem, It's Probably Solved by Walking," *New York Times*, March 25, 2023.

20. It is worth noting that at least one theorist, Adriana Cavarero, has contested and critiqued the notion of *homo erectus* (upright man) and a preferential link between *ars philosophica* (the philosophical tree) and uprightness. She points to Carl Jung, Kant, the glorification of the phallus, masculinity, and the notion of *orthos* (straight-ness as right or correct) as relevant in this regard. The salient point is that it makes sense to pay heed to less celebrated aspects of trees and natural phenomena. See Adriana Cavarero, *Inclinations: A Critique of Rectitude* (Stanford, CA: Stanford University Press, 2016).

21. Gary Snyder, *Practice of the Wild* (San Francisco: North Point Press, 1990), 138.

22. Jared Farmer, *Elderflora: A Modern History of Ancient Trees* (New York: Basic Books, 2022).

23. Johann Wolfgang von Goethe, cited in *Goethe: Scientific Studies* in *Goethe: Collected Works*, Vol. 12, ed. and trans. Douglas Miller (Princeton, NJ: Princeton University Press, 1988), 327. See also Heather I. Sullivan, "Goethe's 'Leaf' and Scales of the Anthropocene versus the Geological." plantphilosophy.org.uk/j-w-goethe-philosopher-botanist

24. Thoreau, *Walden*, ed. Brooks Atkinson (New York: Random House, 1937), 273–75.

25. For a philosophical exploration and defense of the relation between function and aesthetic value, see Glen Parsons and Allen Carlson, *Functional Beauty* (Oxford: Oxford University Press, 2008).

26. Annie Dillard, *Pilgrim at Tinker Creek* (New York: Bantam Books, 1975), 114.

27. Janine Benyus, *Biomimicry: Innovation Inspired by Nature* (New York: Quill, 1997), chap. 3.

28. Colin Tudge, *The Tree: A Natural History of What Trees Are, How They Live, and Why They Matter* (New York: Crown Publishers, 2005), xvi.

29. Judith H. Heerwagen and Gordon H. Orians, "Humans, Habitats and Aesthetics," in Stephen Kellert and Edward O. Wilson, eds., *Biophilia Hypothesis*, 138–72. The study compared trees in African savannas with those in Japanese gardens. We might keep the point about flowers in mind on Valentine's Day; it's quite possibly our evolutionary ancestry is speaking to us through plants.

30. Joan Maloof, "Measuring the beauty of forests," *International Journal of Environmental Studies* 67, no. 3, 431–37.

31. In the study, men rated the older forests more beautiful than women did.

32. L. M. Arthur, "Predicting Scenic Beauty of Forested Environments: Some Empirical Tests," *Forest Science* 23, no. 2: 151–59. and T. C. Brown and T. C. Daniel, "Progress in Predicting the Scenic Beauty in Forested Landscapes," *Forest Science* 32, no. 2: 471–87.

33. Michael Pollan, *The Botany of Desire: A Plant's Eye View of the World* (New York: Random House, 2001), 75.

34. Denis Dutton, *The Art Instinct: Beauty, Pleasure, and Human Evolution* (New York: Bloomsbury, 2009).

35. Emerson, "Beauty," op. cit., 437.

36. Emerson, "Nature," *The Portable Emerson*, ed. Carl Bode (New York: Penguin Books, 1981), 18.

37. John Muir, *My First Summer in the Sierra* (Boston: Houghton Mifflin Co., 1911), 110.

38. Thich Nhat Hanh illustrates interbeing with an arboreal and aerial simile he names "Clouds in Each Paper." "If you are a poet, you will see clearly that there is a cloud floating in this sheet of paper. Without a cloud, there will be no rain; without rain, the trees cannot grow; and without trees, we cannot make paper. The cloud is essential for the paper to exist. If the cloud is not here, the sheet of paper cannot be here either. So we can say that the cloud and the paper inter-are." Thich Nhat Hanh, quoted in Barbara O'Brien, "Inter-being: The Inter-existence of All Things," *Learn Religions* website, March 6, 2017.

39. In some ways, this points toward a kind of cosmic ecology. Or perhaps a "radically" reworked notion of Deleuze and Guattari's rhizomes, a nonlinear network that links any point to any other point, though they critique trees and arborescent models.

40. Richard Powers, *Overstory*, op. cit., 3.

41. David George Haskell, *The Songs of Trees: Stories from Nature's Great Connectors* (New York: Penguin Books, 2017), 148–53.

42. Haskell, op. cit., 152.

43. Haskell, op. cit., 153.
44. John Ryan, "Banyan" in John C. Ryan, Patricia Vieira, and Monica Gagliano, eds., *The Mind of Plants* (Santa Fe, NM: Synergetic Press, 2021), 23.
45. Ronald Moore, *Natural Beauty*, op. cit., 178ff.
46. Aldo Leopold, "The Land Ethic," in *A Sand County Almanac* (New York: Oxford University Press), 240.
47. Leopold, "The Land Ethic," 96.
48. Robinson Jeffers, *The Wild God of the World: An Anthology of Robinson Jeffers*, ed., Albert Geppi (Stanford, CA: Stanford University Press, 2003), 189.
49. The male bowerbird is arguably one of the great artists of the forest, who fuses beauty with utility in creating aesthetically pleasing nests to attract a female mate. See David Rothenberg, *Survival of the Beautiful: Art, Science and Evolution* (London: Bloomsbury, 2012).
50. Gary Nabham, *Mesquite: An Arboreal Love Affair* (Chelsea, Vermont: Chelsea Green Publishing, 2018), 171.
51. Thoreau, *The Maine Woods* (New York: Penguin Classics, 1988), 165.
52. Shel Silverstein, *The Giving Tree* (New York: Harper and Row, 1964).
53. *The Tao Te Ching*, trans. Stephen Mitchell (New York: HarperCollins, 1988). For example, "The world is formed from the void, / like utensils from a block of wood" (chapter 28).
54. Julian Velasco, quoted in Katherine Roth, "Bonsai for Beginner: Be Patient," *Providence Journal*, May 31, 2014.
55. *The Gateless Gate*, trans. Kôun Yamada (Boston: Wisdom Publications, 2004), case 37. In terms of the commentary given by Albert Low, see Meredith Hotetsu Garmon, *Hotetsu's Zen Blog*, January 2, 2017.
56. See Breena McBride, "A Poetic Tribute to Haverford's Trees" (April 26, 2010). www.haverford.edu/college-communications/news/poetic-tribute-haverfords-trees
57. Nancy Wilson Ross, *The World of Zen* (New York: Vintage Books, 1960), 126, 117, and 126, respectively for the haiku.
58. Lucien Stryk and Takashi Ikemoto, eds., *Zen Poetry* (New York: Grove Press, 1995), 31.
59. On bonsai gardening in relation to Gilles Deleuze's philosophy of becoming, see Jayson Jimenez, "Becoming Bonsai, Becoming Carer," *Environmental Philosophy*, Vol. 20, No. 1, 1–24.
60. Paul Valéry, *Dialogue de l'arbre*, Paris, Gallimard, 1945, trans. by W. McCausland Stewart, in J. Mathiews, ed., *The Collected Works of Paul Valéry*, Vol. 4 (Princeton, NJ: Princeton University Press, 1989). Valéry adds: "What you perceive of a shrub or a tree is only the outside and instant, offered up to the indifferent eye, which only skims the surface of the world. But to spiritual eyes the plant presents not just a simple object of humble, passive life, but a strange will to join a universal weaving."
61. Harold Bloom's literary criticism is relevant in this regard, wherein he speaks of a misreading of one's predecessors. Wordsworth's Yew tree, for exam-

ple, stands in anxious relation and often hidden mediation to the trees of earlier poets. See Bloom, *The Anxiety of Influence* (London: Oxford University Press, 1973).

62. A. J. Kaufman and V. I. Lohr, "Does Plant Color Affect Emotional and Physiological Responses to Landscape?" *Acta Horticulturae* 639, 229–33.

63. Wallace Stevens, "Sunday Morning," *The Collected Poems of Wallace Stevens*, ed., John Serio and Chris Byers (New York: Vintage Books, 2015), 71.

64. Thoreau, "Autumnal Tints," in *The Natural History Essays*, ed., Robert Sattelmeyer (Salt Lake City: Peregrine Smith, 1980), 157–58.

65. Thoreau, "Autumnal Tints," 147.

66. Thoreau, "Autumnal Tints," 153–54.

67. David Haskell, *Thirteen Ways to Smell a Tree* (London: Gaia, 2021).

68. For a relevant contemporary exploration, see Robin Wall Kimmerer, *Braiding Sweetgrass: Indigenous Wisdom, Scientific Knowledge, and the Teachings of Plants* (Minneapolis, MN: Milkweed Editions, 2015), chap. 7.

69. Peter Wollhebin and Jane Billinghurst, *Forest Walking* (Vancouver: Greystone Books, 2022), 34–41.

70. Robert Frost, "Birches" in Harry Thomas, ed., *Poems about Trees* (New York: Alfred A. Knopf, 2019), 202.

71. Robert Frost, "The Sound of Trees" in Frost, *Mountain Interval* (Rahway, NJ: Henry Holt, 1931), 75.

72. Galen Johnson, "Forest and Philosophy: Toward an Aesthetics of Wood," *Environmental Philosophy* 4, nos. 1–2 (Spring and Fall, 2007): 59ff.

73. Gaston Bachelard, *La Terre et les rêveries du repos* (Paris: Jose Corti, 1948), 291.

74. Timothy Morton, *Ecology without Nature: Rethinking Environmental Aesthetics* (Cambridge, MA: Harvard University Press, 2007), 32.

75. Morton, *Ecology without* Nature, 32ff.

76. Yoshifumi Miyazaki, *Shinrin Yoku: The Japanese Art of Forest Bathing* (Portland: Timber Press, 2018).

77. Rainer Maria Rilke, letter, quoted in Gaston Bachelard, *The Poetics of Space*, trans. Maria Jolas (Boston: Beacon Press, 1969), 201.

78. Cheryl Foster, "The Narrative and the Ambient in Environmental Aesthetics" in Carlson and Berleant, eds., *The Aesthetics of Natural Environments*, op. cit., 205.

79. Italo Calvino, *The Baron in the Trees*, trans. Archibald Colquhoun (San Diego, CA: Harcourt Brace Jovanovich, 1959).

80. Michael Pollan, *The Botany of Desire*, op. cit., 39.

81. Lisa Cron, *Wired for Story* (Berkeley, CA: Ten Speed Press, 2012), 1.

82. See Dennis Dutton, *The Art Instinct*, op. cit., especially pages 109–24 on the survival benefits of storytelling.

83. See John Ryan, "'Old Trees Hold Memory,'" chapter 6 in the present volume.

84. Gary Snyder, *A Place in Space* (Washington, DC: Counterpoint, 1995), 199–204.

85. Carl Sagan, *Cosmos* (New York: Ballantine Books, 2013), 295.

86. Richard Powers, *The Overstory*, op. cit., 16–18.

87. Will Matsuda, "The Trees That Survived Hiroshima," *New York Times*, May 5, 2023.

88. Jill Jonnes, *Urban Forests* (New York: Penguin Books, 2016), chaps. 17 and 22.

89. See Luke Fischer and David Macauley, eds., *The Seasons: Philosophical, Literary, and Environmental Perspectives* (Albany, NY: SUNY Press, 2021).

90. Bashō, quoted in Nancy Wilson Ross, *The World of Zen*, op. cit., 117.

91. Thoreau, in *H.D. Thoreau: A Writer's Journal*, ed. Laurence Stapleton (New York: Dover, 1960), 187.

92. It is important to note, however, that Clive Bell's theory of aesthetics focused on what he called "significant form," which he separated from beauty. Works of art that elicit aesthetic emotions possessed the quality of significant form. Clive Bell, *Art* (New York: Frederick A. Stokes Company Publishers, 1913), 3.

93. William Blake, selection from letter, 1799 in *The Portable Blake*, ed. Alfred Kazin (New York: Penguin, 1977), 179.

94. See, for example, Noel Carroll, "On Being Moved by Nature: Between Religion and Natural History," in Salim Kemal and Ivan Gaskell, eds., *Landscape, Natural Beauty and the Arts* (Cambridge: Cambridge University Press, 1993), chap. 12.

95. Martha Nussbaum, *Upheavals of Thought: The Intelligence of Emotions* (Cambridge: Cambridge University Press, 2001).

96. Alphonso Lingis, *The Imperative* (Bloomington: Indiana University Press, 1998) and *Dangerous Emotions* (Berkeley: University of California Press, 2000).

97. Emerson, "Beauty," op. cit., 442.

98. Thoreau, *The Writings of Henry David Thoreau* (Boston: Houghton Mifflin and Co., 1906), Vol. X, chap. 2, 126.

99. Henry David Thoreau, *Journal*, Dec. 20, 1851, quoted in Thomas, ed., *Poems about Trees*, op. cit., 31.

100. Michael Pollan, *Second Nature: A Gardener's Education* (New York: Delta, 1991).

101. Robert Pogue Harrison, *Forests: The Shadow of Civilization* (Chicago: University of Chicago Press), x.

102. Vijaya Nagarajan, "Rituals of Embedded Ecologies: Drawing *Kōlams*, Marrying Trees, and Generating Auspiciousness," in Christopher Key Chapple and Mary Evelyn Tucker, *Hinduism and Ecology* (Cambridge, MA: Harvard University Press, 2000), 453–68. See also William Meredith's poem, "Tree Marriage" in Harry Thomas, ed., *Poems About Trees*, op. cit., 230.

103. John Muir, *My First Summer in the Sierra*, op. cit., 196.

104. Emerson, "Nature," *The Portable Emerson*, op. cit., 11.
105. Gary Snyder, *Practice of the Wild*, op. cit., 96.
106. Hermann Hesse, *Wandering: Notes and Sketches*, quoted in Maria Popova, "Hermann Hesse on What Trees Teach Us about Belonging and Life," *The Marginalian*, n.d., accessed August 7, 2023.
107. Snyder, *Practice of the Wild*, op. cit., 96.
108. Joan Maloof, *The Living Forest* (Portland, Oregon: Timber Press, 2017), 13.
109. Emerson, "Beauty," op. cit., 442.
110. Emerson, "Beauty," op. cit., 442.
111. Emily Brady, "Imagination and the Aesthetic Appreciation of Nature," in Carlson and Berleant, eds., *The Aesthetics of Natural Environments*, op. cit., 161–64.
112. Bachelard, op. cit., 300.
113. Thoreau, quoted in Richard Higgins, *Thoreau and the Language of Trees* (Berkeley: University of California Press, 2017), 26.
114. Andy Goldsworthy, *Wood* (New York: Abrams, 1996).
115. See Jill Jonnes, *Urban Forests*, op. cit., xiii–xv.
116. See Natalie Jeremijenko, Tree Logic. https://massmoca.org/event/natalie-jeremijenko
117. See Alan Macpherson, "Art, Trees, and the Enchantment of the Anthropocene: Caroline Wendling's *White Wood*." *Environmental Humanities* 10, no. 1 (2018), 241–56.
118. Martin Buber, *I and Thou*, trans. Walter Kaufmann (New York: Charles Scribner's Sons, 1970), 58. Note Buber's continued use of "it" and "its" in his description even while seeking alternative descriptions of and relationships with the tree, a challenge I have wrestled with as well.
119. Maurice Merleau-Ponty, "Eye and Mind" in *The Primacy of Perception*, ed., James M. Edie, trans. Carleton Dallery (Evanston, IL: Northwestern University Press, 1964).
120. On the eyespots that exist on many organisms like butterfly wings and the possibility that entities from peacocks and moths to mirrors and the sun seem to look back at us, see James Elkins, *The Object Looks Back: On the Nature of Seeing* (New York: Simon and Schuster, 1996). As Elkins put it, "To see is to be seen, and everything I see is like an eye, collecting my gaze, blinking, staring, focusing and reflecting, sending my look back to me" (51).
121. Merleau-Ponty, *The Primacy of Perception*, op. cit., 188, translation altered.
122. Ranier Maria Rilke, untitled poem, quoted in Gaston Bachelard, *The Poetics of Space*, op. cit., 200.
123. A much shorter version of this chapter was presented to the Comparative and Continental Philosophy Circle in Bogota, Columbia, in May 2023. I wish to thank Eric Orts and Laura Pustarfi for their helpful comments on my work.

11

Do Trees Sing?

DAVID ROTHENBERG

If a tree. If a tree falls. If a tree falls in a forest and no one hears it, does it make a sound?

Why is it that a tree falling in a forest is among the most famous stories in philosophy? Oddly, it's about trees, not humans. It occurs in the forest, not a location that people usually visit. So why is this scenario remembered so well and so fondly?

I believe the thought experiment suggests that we humans desperately wish to be needed in the world and also want to comment upon it. We truly desire the world to require our presence, not only for us to name and number everything but also to announce it all into existence—to being there.

We sing the world into existence, writes philosopher Martin Heidegger. You've got to praise the mutilated world, observes poet Adam Zagajewksi.

If you hear the whole world as music, it's a lot more amiable, beautiful, mysterious, and elusive. Ordered but not too orderly; organized but not too exact in its message.

We never fully know what music means.

Nature is *The Great Animal Orchestra*, says Bernie Krause. *Earth's Wild Music* intones Kathleen Dean Moore. While browsing in a bookstore in Cambridge, England, I find that everything is singing, including works entitled *The Song of the Seal* and *The Song of the Swamp*, not to mention *Where the Crawdads Sing*.

It's amazing; my heart's beating; it's all in a rhythm. *Everything* sings. Except it doesn't.

Yes, now I'm a typical philosopher pulling the wings off butterflies. No wonder we lose so many friends.

Don't get me wrong. I am also a musician who makes music with nature. I play live with sprossers, sisichaks, magicicadas, cachalots, and slightly musical coneheads. Exactly for that reason, I don't use the word "song" lightly.

If there are *Songs of Trees*—the title of another book—I really want to hear them. But do these tunes truly exist?

Clearly, we want nature to be musical. If the sounds around us are perceived as music, it's all more beautiful, resonant, and meaningful but also more accessible. Music, however, is not simply a language; it does not need to be decoded or translated. Its beautiful order simply resounds.

Sound becomes music if someone says it is. The music hunter is claiming, "Here you go, *take* this sound as music, consider it as such. Listen to where it gets you."

Wind rustles through trees. Leaves fall. Ride your bicycle upon the wet leaves. Climb the tree, run your hand on the bark. Wait: put your ear to the trunk—can you hear anything? Maybe not. Hydrophone in the trunk, root to the skies. Movement of fluids, low rumble. How much sound is really there?

All roots interconnect, liminal intelligence. Knowledge not like human thought but still apparent. The trees *know*. So much. We hear the rustle, the wind, the crackle. We want to hear more than is there.

Electrical impulses. Flowing up and down. Trees can be tracked, data comes out. Data can be turned into sound. *Any* sound. Thus, the tree sings. The tree too is a musician.

Plant scientist Monica Gagliano is not convinced of this kind of tree music:

> Devices which assign a musical voice to plants and make them "sing" have been around since the seventies. These are nothing more than multimeters that measure electric current . . . . They have been modified so that they detect the impedance from a leaf to the root system and then use a MIDI interface to arbitrarily assign musical notes to different ranges of voltage

values. These gadgets have become increasingly popular and may be quite appealing at first, as they appear to create a tangible connection between the human and the plant by claiming to offer a direct experience of the plant "voice" and in the same case, stretching it further to plant intelligence and consciousness. Sadly, the sounds emitted by these devices are not the sounds emitted by the plant.[1]

This is quite a strong statement from a very unusual scientist who some have described as a "plant whisperer." She is no purely traditional creator of hypotheses and collector of data but rather a truly intuitive thinker who believes that the subjects of her research, at first coral reef fish, and now terrestrial plants, do communicate with her, in their own honest ways, that do not involve turning electrical impulses into familiar sounding electronic melodies. Her warning, which is buried in the footnotes of her fascinating book *Thus Spoke the Plant*, really should be taken seriously. In fact, she articulates most clearly a worry I have had for years about these kinds of sounds.

An artist tells you their work is about this or that, and information from the natural world informs what we see or hear. But we usually take this information on faith, especially if the resulting work doesn't sound much like the source from which it is supposed to emerge. In the case of data being transformed into music, this process is called "sonification." It's the audio equivalent of visualization, where images are created to reveal hidden structures in data.

This process can certainly produce cool tunes, and sometimes it can be useful in revealing patterns that otherwise we would not know are there. But there is a fine line where the purported story behind a phenomenon takes over, and we run wild with the metaphor.

Thus: trees sing. The music of trees. The music of the spheres. The sounds of gravitational waves and black holes. Swamp song. Seal song. Rabbit song. Worm song. All sound great, but I'm not sure they really exist.

I love music and sound too much to take it all on faith.

How does this play out with a work I deeply respect, David Haskell's *The Songs of Trees*? Are songs actually there? With Monica's admonishment in mind, I review some of the fine-sounding examples on David Haskell's website, which accompanies the book.[2]

The first two sounds he includes are examples of sonification: "Twigs have a daily heartbeat as water pulses through them. I measured this 24-hr cycle with a sensor, then used a computer to make the cycle audible to human ears. We hear the twig's diameter changing in the notes of an electronic piano. The fatter the twig, the higher the note." The result is a flight-of-the-bumblebee-like fast piano in exact regular time, clearly a sonified example of changing data. Not really a sound from the tree, but a listenable example of natural processes. The data does make sense as music, sure, but the piano sound? Arbitrary. A bit of sleight-of-sound.

Afterward, Haskell seems to be *hunting* for songs from his trees. I applaud him for this, actually. Sound is a powerful metaphor, taking in data instead of looking for it or calculating. He listens to the rain on trees. He sticks a hydrophone into a trunk on a palm tree next to the beach. You hear the ebb and flow of the water. He does the same on a street tree during the year he lived in New York City. Quite a change. The tree transmits subway noises, children playing. Skeptical passersby. We imagine the wood listens. It is muffled, indistinct, unsatisfying but inducing of wonder.

In Colorado, he places an ultrasonic sensor on a Ponderosa twig and then transposes the rhythms down into something we can hear. In a way, this is my favorite. He compresses twelve hours into forty seconds, and a clear rhythm appears. These clicks come from unhearable pops the twigs make. So, I feel they are actually there. Sonographically, a rhythm is produced. Is this then an actual song from the tree?

I asked Haskell about the exact regularity, since over twelve hours sped up there is a precise rhythm that emerges. Here's what he said to me: "The clicks are from a constructed click track whose tempo corresponds to the slope of the graph. The *graph* was the real data. The clicks are an unsatisfactory rendition. The regularity is an artifact. Actually listening to real-time ultrasound from trees without drilling into them proved beyond my abilities for this project."[3] In other words, the rhythm reveals the rate of change, like a derivative in calculus, and it is not a tiny snap coming from the twig itself. But it *sounds* so tree-like. It's what we want to hear. "Far more successful," Haskell continues, "were my accelerometer explorations, say of the beech tree." How the wood *feels* or *senses* the wind pass over its roundness: "The tree's cells are shaken (not stirred) and any insect in the twig could detect the vibrations through its feet." The noise gently rustles. It sounds a bit like we would hear the wind, but then again, we never hear wind. We only hear wind when it touches something, moves something, passes through something.

Haskell then moves to the more metaphorical songs, the notion of the tree interconnected to its environment. The song of the tree does not

Do Trees Sing? | 295

Figure 11.1. Sonogram made from David Haskell's ultrasonic ponderosa pine sounds, beyond the range of human hearing. *Source*: Created by David Rothenberg.

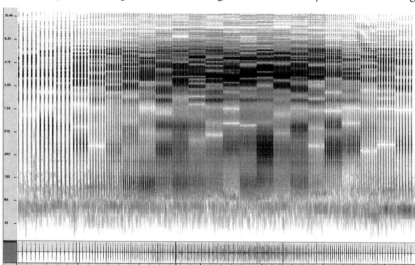

come from the tree; it is all the sounds surrounding the tree, that need the tree, and that the tree needs:

Balsam fir, boreal forest in western Ontario:

"A forest's intelligence emerges from many kinds of interlinked clusters of thought. Nerves and brains are one part, but only one, of the forest's mind." Bird song in the boreal forest in summer. Recorded next to the balsam fir.

Or:

Green ash, Sewanee, Tennessee:

"The tear in the canopy caused by the tree's fall created an inverted geyser of light. After a year under the abundant flow of photons, what were small herbs have turned into bushes." Hooded warbler and others singing from dense undergrowth along the fallen ash's trunk.[4]

So, the songs of trees may very well be the music we hear around trees, in the midst of trees, of other creatures inspired by trees. But the world wants to listen to the world. We dream of joining in.

Autumn is in full swing outside my window. Tiny birch leaves petal down from their branches, each day falling more and more, yellowish green colored. Adjacent maples and dogwoods are already red. Do the different-colored leaves possess varied sounds? Haskell's attentiveness has led me to ask such questions, ones I will be unable to answer.

I still want the trees to make sound. I still don't know if they do. It is the ultimate philosophical conundrum. If it falls in the forest and no one listens, does the tree in fact make a sound? Why does this famous image ring so loud in the annals of philosophy?

In Sam Green's live performance film, *32 Sounds*, inspired by *32 Short Films about Glenn Gould* and also Simon McBurney's *The Encounter* on Broadway, the audience in the theater wears special headphones while a film is shown on stage along with live music, and Sam speaks a monologue about sound, memory, recording, mixtapes, and old technology versus new technology.

Probably the most beautiful sequence in the film is a massive tree falling silently in the forest. Then foley artist Saori Tsukada is shown with broken plates, sheets of metal, and giant brooms conspiring to make the proper sound we would expect to hear and that we need to witness for it to exist. The tree performs only as we perform.

Composing, performing, and listening, asked John Cage: what could these three activities *possibly* have to do with one another? This coming from a man whose composition *Child of Tree* involved the composer on stage struggling to break down a tree too strong for him to do so. I will never forget the spectacle of seeing the master up on stage at the New England Conservatory in 1990 struggling to snap the twigs of that tree.

If a tree is broken up on a concert stage, it is certainly making music. It is music if the composer tells you it is, asks you to consider the situation as music, if only while it is happening.

Thus, the trees sing if you want them to. Or to paraphrase Zen Buddhist Dōgen, speaking of mountains walking, "if you can't hear it, you can't sing yourself."

I'm not, however, advocating song shaming. I *want* you to be skeptical of all this, like Monica Gagliano. Let us not forget that she is *not* some dyed-in-the-wool strait-laced scientist. No, this is the researcher whose study subjects—the fish in coral reefs—started talking to her one day and told her to get out of the water, go up on land, and stop killing animals in the name of knowledge. The fish themselves told her to dry herself off and start studying plants.

She deeply believes in the communicative agency of the vegetable world and has written several papers calling for a new science of plant bioacoustics to emerge. And since then it has in fact emerged.

Why then does she rail against sonification, against the transformation of electrical impulses from the trunks, stems, and twigs into wonderful music of vast human invention? Remember what she said above: "Beware of the tendency to stop listening to the plants, and to substitute their real communication with your imagination of how we humans would like the plants to sound."

It is easy for us to stop listening to the wonders around us, and to hear only what we expect to hear.

But the real phenomenologist watches out for this problem and waits for nature to change its mind about us, to surprise us, to even *speak* with us in the ways it knows to speak and the ways we are able to hear.

If the tree does not change you, then you are not hearing the music of the tree. Because tree music is not immediately our music. It should be something alien, but welcoming. Opening our ears to the world should change us. After the songs of trees, our songs should no longer be the same.

There are many examples of music composed of electrical impulses from plants in the way Gagliano is warning us against. We musicians are taught not to criticize our fellow sonic explorers, but I will provide one example of what she would not approve: music by Karel Hacker, which is supported by the Merck Corporation.

Hacker attaches sensors to ferns and leaves, and these impulses trigger his modular synthesizer setup.[5] Note that the music he creates, fine modular synth stuff, is *not* coming from the plants. The sensors on the plants merely supply triggers that set off the usual synthesizer sounds. This is exactly what troubles Gagliano, and she is firm about it:

> There is a simple reason why such an approach to plants has no integrity. Just consider this: *humans also produce electricity and can be plugged into such devices and made to "sing."* However, nobody would believe that the sound coming from such a device is in fact the voice of the human. However, in the case of plants, we are misled into believing that the sound coming from the device is in fact a plant's voice.

Like the human, plants have their own voice, and there is no need to use electrical signals to produce a surrogate voice. While such devices may have had their place in the seventies, their immature anthropocentric approach is disrespectful, as it overrides the agency of the *other* (the plant) and as such, *reveals the same abusive mind-set responsible for the disregard and the destruction of plants and nature.*

The "music of plants" may be portrayed as a scientific exploration into the communicative world of plants and may seem to carry the promise of deepening our understanding of plant perception and intelligence, but our ignorance is dangerous. For those who care not to ignore but look and listen beyond the surface, you will soon realize that this approach to plants is *far* from enlightening.[6]

Not only is Gagliano unimpressed by such plant-triggered electronica, she finds it abusive and insulting!

I once asked David Haskell what microphone I should use to listen to trees. His answer: "No mic. Just ears. Repeat as necessary. This is my main method."[7]

Despite all the technology he has tried, Haskell is above all a listener, and a chronicler. He wants us to tune into the possibilities for actual, immediate experience. He has certainly made fine sonifications and interesting recordings. But these techniques themselves can also take us away from nature.

The trees are singing for us. That is, if we are able to listen, and are ready to discover what we do not expect to hear.

One need not agree with this conclusion, and of course we can use many sources of inspiration, electrical or conceptual, to goad us into music. But do consider that some approaches may be better, and others worse. If we are afraid of passing aesthetic judgment on creative phenomena, we have lost any criteria for quality in culture.

I hope you don't mind considering such opinions and judgment here. Go out and listen to trees, listen deeply, but always question what you hear.

Notes

1. Monica Gagliano, *Thus Spoke the Plant* (Berkeley, CA: North Atlantic Books, 2018), 230.

2. David Haskell's website of sonic examples for *Songs of Trees* can be found here: https://dghaskell.com/compilation.
3. Personal correspondence via email, 1 November 2022.
4. https://dghaskell.com/compilation
5. Karel Hacker, "In tune with nature." www.emdgroup.com/en/company/curiosity/in-tune-with-nature.html
6. Gagliano, *Thus Spoke the Plant*, 231.
7. Personal correspondence via email, 10 August 2022.

Trees and Ethics

Figure I.7. A cat in an apple tree, Arcata, California. *Source*: Photo by David Macauley.

Interstice

Apple

Trees give it all away, don't they?

This is not our world with trees in it. It's a world of trees where humans have just arrived.

The best arguments in the world won't change a person's mind. The only thing that can do that is a good story.

Before it dies, a Douglas-fir, half a millennium old, will send its storehouse of chemicals back down into its roots and out through its fungal partners, donating its riches to the community pool in a last will and testament. We might well call these ancient benefactors *giving trees*.

We're living at a time when claims are being made for a moral authority that lies beyond the human. . . . People up and down this coast are risking their lives for plants. I read a story last week—a man who had his legs sheared off by a machine he tried to chain himself to.

—Richard Powers, *The Overstory*

In the illustrated children's story *The Giving Tree* by Shel Silverstein, an apple tree generously sustains a young boy, who matures during the story into an adult and eventually an elderly man. Through a lifetime, the tree gives him fruit, bark, branches, and wood for various purposes until finally all that remains is a vestigial stump upon which the old man sits. The tale may be interpreted in different ways, but it leads us to wonder, "What, if anything, do we humans give trees in return for their many gifts?" Are we often simply "takers" in our interactions with the more-than-human world? In the case of the apple and other domesticated plants, it is fair to acknowledge our cultivation of and care for selective flora; however, with most other species the answer is less clear and even disconcerting, especially since we pose a grave danger to forests and biodiversity worldwide.

The apple is among the most beloved fruits on the planet, and the tree has been domesticated for thousands of years, having journeyed from Central Asia along the Silk Road in Europe and on to North America, where it was introduced by colonists in the seventeenth century. It has been bred for an assortment of traits, including color, size, firmness, acidity, and sugar content. In *The Botany of Desire: A Plant's-Eye View of the World*, Michael Pollan argues that through our desire for sweetness the apple has become one of four plants, along with the tulip, potato, and marijuana, that have helped to transform civilization. There are now more than eight thousand cultivars of this fruit, including Granny Smith, Winesap, McIntosh, Golden Supreme, and Red Delicious, many of which are used to produce culinary delights ranging from apple pies, apple sauce, and apple butter to cider, smoothies, and juices. To reach our plates as food, apples must be cross-pollinated, and honeybees are among the most common and reliable participants in this process.

There exists a rich cultural, mythological, and religious history associated with apples and apple trees. This tapestry includes Adam and Eve's ingestion of the forbidden fruit; the ancient Greek bond between apples and Aphrodite (to throw an apple at another was to declare one's love); Newton's falling apple and the discovery of gravity; Cézanne's still-life paintings of the humble fruit along with his bold proclamation, "With an apple I want to astonish Paris"; Johnny (Appleseed) Chapman's tree plantings throughout the Midwest; Snow White's poison apple; William Tell's splitting of an apple perched atop his son's head with a crossbow; and students traditionally gifting the fruit to their favorite teachers.

Among philosophers, Martin Heidegger spoke highly of the apple tree in a "face-to-face" meeting he had with one. Poets, too, have long been fond of the tree and its fruit. In "After Apple-Picking," Robert Frost prepares for winter sleep with the scent of apples near and knows that in dreaming he will "keep hearing from the cellar bin / The rumbling sound / Of load on load of apples coming in." On a different seasonal note, William Cullen Bryant counsels us to plant apple trees to enjoy "Buds, which the breath of summer days / Shall lengthen into leafy sprays; / . . . Boughs where the thrush, with crimson breast, / Shall haunt and sing and hide her nest; / . . . Sweets for a hundred flowery springs / To load the May-wind's restless wings, / . . . Fruits that shall swell in sunny June, / And redden in the August noon."

In what follows, Mara Miller considers the virtues of "wise trees" in East Asian traditions and their relevance for the ethical life of humans, while James Hatley explores arboreal values and the power of storytelling through his encounters with ponderosa pines in Montana. Many challenges arise concerning our moral relationships with trees. When is it permissible, for example, to cut one down? Are some trees more valuable than others? Do trees have interests and, if so, should they be ascribed rights? And how can we improve our own lives by attending to the values in the plant world? Some of these issues are raised or addressed in the forthcoming chapters.

—David Macauley

12

The Ponderosa Pines of Gold Creek
Discerning Arboreal Values for an All-too-Human World

James Hatley

> If your mind were only a slightly greener thing, we'd drown you in meaning.
>
> —Richard Powers, *The Overstory*

On the Way to Trees

In coming to know of Ponderosa pines, one can do worse than to begin by becoming mindful of their waters. So often one approaches the knowing of all manner of things under the sun, including trees, via a frontal attack. One says to oneself, "Let's bring one to mind, right now, so we can begin to say things about it." This is the logic of field books and manuals of identification, the world conveniently reduced to a series of entries in a text, each one pinning down a living kind on the page for the reader's impatient access and immediate gratification. But if ecology has taught the humanities anything at all of value, certainly it is how any living kind is entangled in innumerable circuits of becoming who it is via how others are. The very approach then that one takes to any living kind matters. Frontal is usually not the best bet. It does not leave enough room for a proper introduction.

Figure 12.1. Ponderosa pines. *Source*: Photo by James Hatley.

Let one begin then, more humbly and with greater deference, by attending to the waters of a particular creek by the name of Gold Creek, where Ponderosas reside. Let one do so, keeping in mind not only the flow of these waters directly visible to the eye but also those deeper invisible channels seeping and percolating through the stony mountain soils underneath one's feet. For one of the innumerable ways to understand the significance of a Ponderosa pine is to consider how it too serves as a moment in this immense hydrological movement, diverting upward the otherwise downward flow of Gold Creek's waters, elevating some part of them into great columns of cellulose towering over a forest floor. By means of this operation, some part of Gold Creek reenters the atmosphere intact through the pine's respiration. But what otherwise remains is transformed through the alchemy of photosynthesis and metabolic processes into the very sap and body by which a Ponderosa is constituted as it is. This includes a subtle, sweet odor, discernible if one scratches the bark. The smell is often described as similar to vanilla, or butterscotch, or cinnamon, although in fact it is precisely that of a Ponderosa.

One could do worse then than to consider these waters by which Ponderosas are finding their way into life. But in how these waters have come to be christened "Gold Creek," complications immediately ensue. In the first place, in Montana more than one watershed carries the name of "Gold Creek." In fact, within just an hour or two of Missoula, at least three are to be found, one immediately to the east flowing into the Blackfoot River, another further to the southeast flowing into the Clark Fork, and a third directly south but to the west flowing into the Bitterroot. Perhaps the most famous of these is upstream from the town of Drummond on the Clark Fork, the site where gold was first discovered and briefly mined in what would later become the territory and then state of Montana. This "Gold Creek" even has its own Wikipedia page. Whether this matters to the creek is unclear.

But these were not the waters that occupied the thoughts of Tarn and Cathy Ream as we drove along steep slopes teetering over a canyon through which the lower reaches of one of the other Gold Creeks, the one flowing into the Blackfoot, was to be found. Cathy and Tarn, mother and daughter, have spent a good portion of their lives in the company of this particular instantiation of Gold Creek. They have strong feelings about it and stories to tell.

Cathy, who holds a doctorate in zoology, helps her donkey Zeb from the trailer, while she discusses the plight of the trees in this watershed. In the late 1980s the forest was razed by the Plum Creek Timber Company, which clearcut the entire drainage in more or less one fell swoop. In this way a leveraged buyout was financed that left the business and its lands in the hands of Wall Street profiteers.[1] The environmental and economic mayhem caused by this act, Cathy notes ironically, had at least one bittersweet outcome: after a fire a decade later, the deep canyon through which Gold Creek flows near its outlet was no longer hidden by a green, impenetrable canopy of lodgepole and ponderosa pine. In the wake of clearcutting and its aftermath, a great rocky gorge had emerged from shadows into the light of day for all to see.

But it's not for the sake of looking down into a denuded abyss that I have been invited along. Rather, I have been enlisted by Cathy and Tarn to accompany them on their current pilgrimage to Primm Meadow, a grove of ancient Ponderosas that mercifully avoided being logged out in the 1980s, even as all about them a forest was succumbing to the chainsaw. Tarn and her family have been frequenting the grove off and on for decades, and for the last several weeks Tarn has been reminiscing about earlier visits, in part for the pure joy of remembering them and in part to prepare me to take part in the one now being planned.

I sensed in her words a depth of feeling for, of involvement in this place that in turn arrested me, warned or cautioned or alerted me, even before I had seen it for myself, that something was afoot there that required attentiveness on my part too. This was not just another walk in the woods. The meadow was a place that had over the years commanded a loyalty from Tarn and Cathy, a promise of return such that the very tempo of their lives, the way they were moving through time, would be incomplete without it.

Tarn and Cathy are hardly the first people to fall in love with these trees. Primm Meadow gets its name from a family, and particularly a woman who lived in the shadows of this grove for most of her life. She is buried there, in fact. Her name is Mahalia Jane Primm. Richard Manning describes the grove named after her as populated by "behemoths . . . hundreds of them, five feet across at the base, more than one hundred feet tall, more than five hundred years old, trees whose roots clutch the same soil that once held the roots of a woman's life."[2] By many accounts, it was the love of Mahalia for this grove, along with her insistence of living in its company even unto her death, long after her husband had abandoned their homestead, that deterred Plum Creek from stripping away its great pines along with the rest of the trees of this watershed.

And so, amidst the wreck and ruin of the watershed, a stately grove still stands. We move toward it in fits and starts, as Zeb pauses here and there to sample an array of grasses still dotting the earth in mid-September. A lot is to be learned about the different living things upon which one's footsteps are finding their way by following carefully the appetites of one's donkey.

What's in the Name?

How we name things matters. For instance, might we not name these waters after beaver instead of gold? Why not Beaver Creek? Indeed, beaver are now making a comeback here, damming up a series of ponds in the creek's middle reaches, a development that is finally to be encouraged, thanks to the intervention of the Nature Conservancy in cooperation with the state of Montana after the watershed was logged out by Plum Creek. Certainly naming an actual creek after a creature who finds its way here precisely in order to elaborate the nature of these waters, to share in their blessing and to extend it in a manner for which that creature is uniquely suited, should be a good thing.

But heretofore, during the time of Western settlement, any beaver who might have appeared in these waters would have been quickly rooted out. For all too many, this policy of non-toleration still ought to be the case. Tarn and Cathy point out where one beaver pond was recently trapped out by someone keeping a watch on such things. For that person, and for those with whom they are in league, the waters of Gold Creek would be better off if they never again welcomed a single beaver. From this viewpoint, this blessed, spunky critter is to be understood as a plague, a pestilence. The very gesture then of renaming this creek so that its ancient alliance with beaver might not only be recognized but also sustained is to be summarily refused. The creek is better off populated by the ghosts of beaver rather than being home to the real, living thing.

Again, how we name things matters. For instance, more than a few "Gold Creeks" are scattered not only across the landscape of the western United States but also across the face of the entire planet. There is one in Australia, another in Nevada, a third in British Columbia, a fourth in Alaska. It turns out that the name "gold" has been repeatedly and indiscriminately assigned to watersheds subdued by colonialism, rendering them unilaterally in terms of their most valued contribution to mercantile economies of exploitation. The waters then are named for that which will actively and incessantly be removed from them, their treasure hoard of metal. The particular instantiation of Gold Creek where I now find myself, like so many of the others, is named as a site of looting. This act of naming in turn is a symptom of what Linda Hogan diagnoses in colonialism as "a hatred of life itself, of fertility and generation" that suffers from an incapacity "to receive the best gifts of land, not gold or pearls or ownership, but a welcomed acceptance of what is offered."[3]

Another sort of naming of the waters and their watersheds is contemplated by Linda Hogan in her essay "What Holds the Water, What Holds the Light." There she reminds her readers that determining the appropriate name for an earthly element—or a living kind, for that matter—is a crucial part of our human vocation. We need, she argues, to be very careful about how we name things and how we intone those names, once they have emerged into the light of day. We are always already speaking for more than ourselves. As a result, nothing less than the healing of our skewed relationship with other lives, both human and more-than-human, is at issue. This requires, Hogan argues, modes of language in which we read others and are read by them not only via their explicit words but also "via gesture, stance, facial expression, scent."[4] Modes of language are called for in which we are in the very first instance enveloped in a communication with other humans and other living kinds from which we cannot step back.

In her essay, Hogan sets out to celebrate the dappling of desert sandstone with ephemeral pools of water after a heavy downpour. "Along the way," she writes, "my friend and I stopped at a cluster of large boulders to drink fresh rain collected in a hollow bowl that had been worn into stone over slow centuries. Bending over the stone, smelling earth up close, we drank sky off the surface of water."[5] Here the genius of the waters of a particular country, of a certain place under the sun, to shape and orient one's all-too-human doings emerges in Hogan's speaking of them. Hogan's very search for the words that would name these waters involves one's being called into attentiveness to them. One recognizes how one's speaking of them has been invited from beyond one's own capacity as merely human to have done so meaningfully. In this way, one's naming of the waters involves necessarily that one becomes their witness. In this way, the waters emerge in their creative agency to bless those who would come into proximity to them.

What particularly appeals to me about Hogan's approach is how the naming of the waters occurs not only via a single inert word or phrase but also via active complexes of naming, in which the waters enfold and are enfolded by all that they serve to bless and be blessed by. As a result, the naming of the waters inevitably involves the telling of stories that emerges through the particular dispensation of the waters in a particular place, such as the story Hogan tells about a plain clay pot keeping water cool in her kitchen, stories not understood primarily through their masterful structuring of a narration but rather as a humbling immersion into socialization, a receptive being with another living element that invites humans into ongoing interchange with it. In this way, naming brings humans into a larger biotic and abiotic community, not simply with the others of one's own kind but also with all the other others with whom one is called upon to share one's world.[6] In this way, naming is inherently polyvocal, gathering into intercourse the many voices of the creaturely, so that the expression of a community's investment in a particular creature becomes manifold and differentiated, as well as permeated with gratitude and responsibility.

Hogan struggles with how our practices of evoking the living things and elements of this world have inevitably been perverted by the colonial language of commerce and trade, a language whose "ears . . . do not often hear the songs of the white egrets, the rain falling into stone bowls."[7] To these might one not also add, in the case of Gold Creek, beaver and belted kingfishers, the flat mammalian tails of the former slapping the waters in a gathering dusk, the harsh rattles of the latter calling out in summer's early light over waters cloaked in rustling, green thickets of alder and willow?

A Saying That Listens

The creatures inhabiting a more-than-human living world demand to be heard in a language that has ears to listen to them. The way that Hogan puts this—that language itself must have ears to hear—is both unusual and authoritative. Her point, as I take it, is not only metaphorical but also ethical. It claims not merely that language itself is pregnant with meaning but also that it invokes a fundamental gesture, a pivot of inflection, by which the very things of this world are to be in their first instance witnessed as striking us with their meaning. In a language with ears, hearing is already implicated in any saying that might arise. We speak then, whether of trees, or kingfishers, or mules, or fellow humans, for that matter, only in the aftermath of our having been invoked by them; our very words emerge as a witness to that which already has claimed those words from beyond our own ken to have authored them.

Insofar as our speaking is always already indebted to those to whom and of whom we would speak, it is to be understood in a Levinasian sense as saying (*le dire*). For Levinas, saying involves a mode of address immersed in its orientation to another, in which one attests in a humility without reservation, in a gratitude beyond any exchange of gifts, that one is attendant upon that other. In our saying, we are not the masters of creation but its impoverished servants and ever watchful witnesses. "This witness," Levinas writes, "is not reducible to the relationship that leads from an index to the indicated. . . . It is the meaning of language, before language scatters into words." As he puts it a few sentences earlier, "[Saying] is thus exposing of the exposure, saying that does not say a word, that signifies, that as responsibility, is signification itself, the one-for-the other."[8]

Our saying of the waters in this sense is not to be understood as an indexical event, whether quantitative or qualitative, in which one announces in one's own voice certain aspects or values, no matter how admirable, that we have ascertained pertain to the waters and that which only afterward are to be communicated to the hearing of others. In speaking indexically we might point to a particular body of water and report that it is "glimmering." But in our saying, as opposed to our speaking, one finds the very breath by which one's voice resonates as bearing a meaning; this glimmering, is not, in the first place, one's own.

One finds that before one could have spoken anything at all, one could never have said enough. One says "glimmering" in such a way that this very saying acknowledges how it already is in peril of betraying that for whom it would speak. In this recognition of the second order of one's speaking, one finds in one's very saying of the world and its denizens that one is already in the position of having been inspired from beyond one's own ken in one's speaking. One finds that before one can claim one's speaking as one's own to master, it has already been offered for the sake of others in a mode of witness.

Perhaps another way to put this is that a language that has ears is involved in ongoing gestures of an etiquette, of an "after you, sir,"[9] in which the priority of the significance of she who is to be named is registered in its very saying as that name. One speaks politely, with attentiveness and care, regarding how the other might hear one's saying of the other. Further, as suggested by Sol Neely, for Levinas, this etiquette occurs in how one hears not only the human but also the more-than-human approach of another:

> The sounds and noises of nature disappoint when they are not heard from the point of view of the utterance, when they remain mired in the tranquility and materiality of things at rest, registered only in the medium of sound with all its aesthetic self-sufficiency. In contrast, it is the social relation—the irreducible kinship relation expressed by "all my relations"—the utterance itself of ancestry and place by which the noise and sounds of nature are at last heard through an inspired eco-phenomenology.[10]

The "after you, sir" is amended then so that it might also be heard as "after you, oh waters," and "after you, oh kingfisher." In the troubling naming of a watershed by settlement peoples as "gold creek," we have already considered how the very speaking of that particular name in those particular circumstances is shorn of etiquette and so becomes demeaning to that which has been so named. The waters of gold creek thus find themselves encaged in a language without ears.

This vulnerability of these waters to being demeaned in our very saying of them deserves careful, discerning consideration. This is also true of donkeys and kingfishers and Ponderosa pines and all the other earthly elements and living kinds, which is to say, the creaturely, who both bless and are blessed by these waters. Human beings too! Neely would remind us that the very etiquette of hearing creaturely others involves one as a matter of course in an ethic of translation. And when translation goes awry, a violence is inflicted upon these others that proves to be both uncanny and subtle, even as it threatens to become immense and world shattering.

The creaturely discernment that is called for involves not only the paring down of one's own language so that it might not import, at least too facilely, one's all-too-human perspectives into how other living things make sense of their world, but also the provocation of one's language so that it is disrupted and interrupted by other ways of saying that would not have emerged without the approach of others, whether human or more than human. The language of creaturely discernment is both empty and florid, a manifestation interrupted by revelation. Here, the pressure of a creaturely ethics, its interruption of things as usual, proves itself to be anarchical, which is to say it invites the emergence of values that could not have been anticipated through one's own way of life.

One place where the work of creaturely discernment might alight within our human ways of language can be found in Van Dooren and Rose's now canonical account of lively ethnography, in which they argue for modes of storytelling that render others, whether human or more-than-human, "fleshly and thick on the page" and in the process "give rise to proximity and ethical entanglement, care and concern."[11] In this endeavor, any clear and distinct demarcation between what is real and what is narrated is rejected. Rather one cultivates "patternings, risky co-makings, speculative fabulations,"[12] as Donna Haraway has put it, in which the stories we tell prove to be already of the world understood as verb, as ongoing creative activity, rather than as a container with fixed boundaries in which we deposit our speaking.

Ultimately, these lively modes of storytelling situate our all-too-human ethical life in a scene awash with more-than-human modes of sentience and responsiveness. In these circumstances, one finds the very words emerging in one's mouth (and the images arising in one's envisioning) alive with provocations to one's responsibilities in regard to the world that exceed what would have been possible to have been registered through human means alone. In the wake of these provocations we are called upon to cultivate actively what Van Dooren and Rose understand as "the arts of becoming-witness,"[13] arts that owe much to a post-Levinasian notion of anarchical responsiveness and responsibility.

A Grove of Trees

How might it be, then, that one is called upon not only to welcome into one's world that living kind which is named as Ponderosa Pine but also to acknowledge how they too might welcome (or not!) one's all-too-human kind into their world? And how might this occur in a moment on this planet when the very weathers are shifting, as climate change deepens its hold upon the life ways of a vast array of living kinds including Ponderosas? These questions have been lurking in the waters of Gold Creek since the opening lines of this chapter, as I have recounted how Cathy and Tarn guided me toward our meeting with a grove of trees at Primm Meadow. This annual pilgrimage, no matter how informal it might be, invites one to entertain pressing and fundamental questions regarding how one is to be oriented toward oneself, toward others, toward one's world. And these questions in turn are asked with a strong sense of the pressing need for one's own reorientation—for healing, for renewal, for consolation—particularly so in our time, permeated as it is by mounting peril to all living things.

When the world is running amuck, go find a grove of trees. Across a variety of cultures, trees have offered companionship and protection, as well as instruction and ministry to those who seek refuge and solace, not to mention truth and insight. Oedipus looks for shelter in a sacred grove at his life's end. Kukai, the originator of Shingon Buddhism, establishes a locus of pilgrimage and spiritual development on Koyasan, a mountaintop populated with towering groves of cypresses and cedars. In the Biblical account of creation, none less than the Most High plants a garden for the first human, a grove of diverse trees selected to be pleasing both in their sight and their fruit, a verdant garden watered by four rivers—Pishon, Gihon, Tigris, and Euphrates. Much more recently, Annie Dillard, in her *Pilgrim at Tinker Creek*, frequents the groves of great sycamores lining the creek's waters and is stopped cold in her tracks one evening by a backyard cedar, as it becomes a tree of lights catching the setting sun and soaring over "grass that was wholly fire, utterly focused and utterly dreamed."[14]

As our small group enters the grove, we become quiet. Each of us slowly threads their way through the towering, cinnamon-colored trunks as these in turn, solidly implanted into the earth, take in, in their needle-ladened green heights, the midday sun of late summer. I am in awe. Partly it's the mass, and partly it's the height. And partly it's just how old, how long these trees have been making their home here. As Dillard puts it, "They last, taproot and bark, and we soften at their feet."[15]

But it's also how the open spaces between them invite human visitors in. The meadow is unabashedly a parkland, a place for interspecies sociality and mingling, particularly of the sort in which humans can readily participate. Zeb too seems to be happy in these circumstances as he, now unburdened of his passenger, takes a breather and dines on a liberal mix of greens carpeting these grounds, even in the dryness of September.

That such a parkland would exist in this rocky and arid environment is in itself a sort of miracle. "The forests of Montana," Richard Manning observes, "cling to mountain slopes only because of monumental caprice and catastrophe . . . The odds are against trees growing here because the land is dry and hard."[16] Indeed, the very earth of this region has only recently emerged into the light of day, as a regime of glaciation, which sheathed this watershed in ice for over a hundred thousand years, has given way in the last ten thousand or so to a somewhat warmer, even if still arid, climate. Not unsurprisingly in such circumstances, the soils here are often but "a skiff of dirt" poised on "ice ground gravel."[17] Only the geologically recent intervention of a thick layer of ash deposited from a massive volcanic eruption occurring about eight thousand years ago has endowed this dirt with sufficient nutrients to support the forests that have now found their way into this landscape.

Further, water does not linger here. What little rain does fall in this watershed with its steep, rocky slopes, is quickly spirited away by gravity. As if to underline this fact, the not-so-distant rush of the waters coursing down the West Fork of Gold Creek permeate the quiet environs of Primm Meadow. Whoever walks these mountains quickly learns that its waters for the most part are either swift or non-existent. One becomes attuned to a stone-fed silence punctuated by the distant echoing of torrents.

Yet Ponderosas have learned to find and conserve water in a place where there is little to be had. A seedling in this meadow might be only three inches in height after a year, yet its taproot would be eight times as long.[18] As a result of its deep and spreading root systems, Ponderosas are able to grow to their full height even in arid circumstances. Further, they are more adept than other conifers at closing the pores (stomates) of their needles to prevent water loss during hot weather.

During the nineteenth century, Ponderosa pines were a new thing under the sun to settlement culture, and, in fact, were only given their scientific name—*Pinus ponderosa*—in 1829 by Scottish explorer David Douglas. Fiedler and Arno note that Douglas "named it . . . after the Latin *ponderosus*, meaning heavy, weighty, and significant."[19] Also known as Yellow Pine by settlers, this tree was the prize of these forests for those intent on exploiting newly occupied lands for their strongest and most useful timber. Over decades, masses of Yellow Pine were harvested up and down the Blackfoot watershed, and then floated down the river to be milled at Bonner. Railroad ties and trestles, shoring timbers for mines, and beams and siding for the houses in which the miners, as well as a wide assortment of loggers, ranchers and townspeople lived, all of these and more were built with the wood of these trees. Across the Western United Sates, Yellow Pine, like the yellow gold for which Gold Creek is named, made fortunes and sustained commercial empires, of which Plum Creek Company is a recent if somewhat diminished example. The truth of the matter is that Plum Creek's irresponsible treatment of this watershed's forests was only the latest chapter in a hundred-year-long story of scraping these mountains clean of their greatest trees.

But where is the language with ears that would hear Ponderosas otherwise than as a commodity, which is to say otherwise than as an undifferentiated stream of a set of potentially useful qualities to be consumed endlessly for our all-too-human ends? Or to put it more provocatively: where and when exactly is the language in which Ponderosas might be given a say in the matter of their co-habitation with our own living kind? And so the question strikes me anew: what might the Ponderosas of this grove be to me, and I to them? And with that question lies an invitation to participate in the polyvocality of naming that signals any living thing's entrance into meaning. How might I be invited, even charged, by these trees to speak? In what way, do I find myself claimed?

It strikes me, as a I consider these questions, that I have lived in the company of Ponderosas my whole life and learned hardly anything about them in that time. My ignorance mirrors a complaint one hears often about the citizens of settlement culture, that the trees and grasses in whose company one lives are generally perceived as a diffused ambience, a green blur against a blue or cloudy background of sky.[20] This plight is in fact generally the case not only for the average citizen but even for, for instance, my students in environmental studies.

We so often name and love trees, then, without really knowing them. But even in this paucity of understanding the magnificence of this living kind interrupts our ignorance with at least its very size and age. For even if the world remains a green blur to many who travel through these forests, that blur resolves, as we walk into it, into massive, unnamed beings, swaying with the weathers, persisting in their greenness through terrible snows, living in an arc of time that stretches far beyond one's own tenancy on the face of the earth. Whoever they are, they exceed us.

But these trees also call upon us to recognize much more than their massive size and the lengthy arcs of their temporal existence. For these Ponderosas, as do all arboreal living kinds, constitute a distinctive way of life. As a way of life they possess modes of agency, developed and honed through generations of evolutionary adaptation that render them precisely skilled at being who they are in the circumstances in which they find themselves.

Burning Creation

This watershed burns. That this is so should not be surprising to anyone who pays attention to these things. For untold millennia preceding European settlement, the Salish, Kootenai, and Kalispel peoples of this region consciously employed fire to sculpt forests that already were dependent, even before humans showed up, on fire for their flourishing. Primm Meadow is itself the outcome of such careful and knowing interaction over generations of humans with Ponderosas. Long before European settlers arrived here, Indigenous peoples transformed the grove into parkland that was maintained by regular, selective burnings that would rejuvenate desired plants and keep lodgepole pines and Douglas firs from crowding in among the Ponderosas. Mahalia Janet Primm, then, served as one link in a long chain of human caretakers, only the most recent of which were settlers.

Yet settlement culture, and particularly its foresters, newly minted in their expertise in silviculture, resisted for around a century the irrefutable fact concerning not only the inevitability but also the necessity of fire in these mountains. As Fiedler and Arno point out, American research in the development of forestry science was fixated on European practices of caring for trees, practices that were attuned to a wetter climate with more fertile soils.[21] From the perspective of Europe, a forest that burns is a forest that is wasted. In spite of the resistance of not only Indigenous peoples but also, surprisingly, at least some of the more insightful capitalist bosses of early big lumber companies in the Montana West, a Forest Service policy prohibiting all forest fires, even in stands of Ponderosa pines who clearly benefited from frequent low-intensity fires, carried the day, at least until recently.[22]

Two stories now need to be retold, stories relayed to me that day in the grove by Cathy and Tarn, stories that now are passed on to the reader. Both of these have to do with an element of arboreal life that heretofore has remained in the background of this discussion, namely that most trees are eminently flammable and find themselves as a life form often subjected to incendiary events. Indeed, as the title of this chapter suggests, the world in which trees live in general and Ponderosas in particular is a world in which one is called upon to tell the story of a living kind whose way of life involves being burnt alive. Or at least regularly singed, if one is a healthy Ponderosa living in a healthy ecosystem. Indeed, of all the trees of the Montana West—Douglas fir, red cedar, lodgepole, limber pine, larch, white pine, and all the rest—Ponderosas are the most prone to finding themselves in the midst of a fire, one every decade or so, even without human intervention.

But a word of warning: the telling of the story of Ponderosa's relationship with fire is complicated by the increasingly powerful modes of human interaction with a more-than-human living world. Currently, the ways of life of just about everything under the sun are finding their previous holds upon their place in the world threatened. Not only the impact of industrial logging pervades this grove and its surrounding forests but also increasingly the effects of global climate change. So even if, as a sign posted in Primm Meadow tells its visitor, "fire is as natural to western forests as floods are to free flowing rivers,"[23] one must also keep in mind that the fire regimes of these forests are undergoing an intensification that is a human artifact. In the thirty years since the logging out of this watershed by Plum Creek, the fire season in the Montana West under the influence of Global Climate Change has lengthened by an average of forty to eighty days.[24] Massive swaths of forests located not only in western North America but also in Siberia, the Amazon, and southeast Australia are increasingly vulnerable to explosive fire events due to the increased length of the fire season, and also, at least in some cases, to milder winters paradoxically affecting negatively the health of trees.[25] Even increased rainfall in the spring is contributing to a more incendiary landscape as the intensified growth in that season adds to flammable material for a lengthened fire season of late summer and early fall.

The intensification of the fire season has been wreaking havoc on forests that were already being pushed to the limit by over-harvesting and, ironically, a century of fire suppression. In the summer of 2003, just a few decades after the massive clearcutting by Plum Creek, the Primm Mineral fire burned over twenty-four thousand acres of forest in the Gold Creek watershed. All around Primm Meadow today, stands of charred snags, remnants of a forest that was growing in after the regime of clearcutting in the 1980s, stretch in all directions up and down the mountain slopes.

And yet the meadow itself remains untouched, its great trees still green and thriving. A sign placed in the middle of the grove by the Nature Conservancy, not far from the grave of Mahalia Primm, explains: "Wildfire roared through Gold Creek in 2003. Smoke blocked the sun. Towering flames engulfed entire stands of trees. Then something extraordinary happened when the fire entered Primm Meadow. The wall of flames dropped to knee-height, and the centuries-old ponderosas survived—once again. Swept along by the pines' own kindling of needles, cones and bark flakes, the flames crept through the meadow."[26] This story of the meadow's resilience in the midst of so much else going wrong is heartening. One can understand why Cathy and Tarn, as so many others in this area, treasure this place. Indeed, revere it.

But this offering of our reverent regard for this grove is permeated with irony. For we now live in a time when pilgrimages to a sacred grove necessarily become fixed on the vulnerability of the grove itself to depredation and neglect. We make pilgrimage, then, for the very sake of being able at all to make a pilgrimage. The Primm Meadow grove offers its visitor not so much a place of safety and repair as one in which the very vulnerability of trees and their groves to the consuming energies of planetary exploitation is brought into focus. The continued existence of sacred groves altogether is at issue here. As one appreciative blogger puts it, "Primm Meadow: A cathedral of pines amidst the apocalypse."[27]

Now that we have reached the grove, Cathy is ready to share a second story that occurred in that same season of fire in 2003. She relates how she visited here a few months after the blaze had been quenched, in early October, and witnessed a remarkable if troubling image, one that stays fixed in her mind. As she entered the grove, she noticed that one of its trees, likely one that was already doing poorly, perhaps diseased or aged, had not only succumbed to the flames but also, months later, smoke, welling up from the smoldering depths of the earth, was still pouring out of the tree's hollowed char of a snag, as if it were a great chimney. Cathy offers this image up for meditation, leaving those who hear of it to draw their own conclusions. I sense an intricate network of roots ranging deep into the earth, still burning, cooking the earth itself until the very life of the soil is baked away, until every inch of the tree's mass is carbonized, rendered into ash and charcoal.

This image now sticks with me. When I meditate upon its hold upon me, at least two thoughts come to mind. In the first I find myself in awe of how these great trees instantiate a unique form of life, one differing radically from my own, even if ultimately we are, as all living, earthly things, to some degree related. I think of this tree's needles over centuries drinking in carbon dioxide from the atmosphere and transforming it, through the power of photosynthesis, into the cellulose that had become the very body of this tree. This way of life, so foreign to my own, cautions me not to presume I understand all that is provoked for my consideration by it.

Just imagining my all-too-human body as that of Cathy's smoldering tree gives me the shivers. Certainly this thought of an arboreal metamorphosis consumed in flames adds a distinct twist to Ovid's already haunting story of Daphne, a human transformed into a laurel tree festooned with green leaves, permeating the airs with a sweet smell. Daphne's plight might be strange and terrifying, yet still wondrous, inspiring. But humans are not comfortable at all with the notion of metamorphosing into a tree as it goes up in smoke in a forest succumbing to flame. That we too are flammable, even in our fully human form, is perhaps one of the most disturbing thoughts a human might think. In no way could one counsel a society of our own living kind in which one would regularly submit the majority of one's fellow citizens, at least while still living, to flames so that in turn our coming generations might be given room to grow and be nourished. Yet this is precisely the way in which at least some species of trees operate, limber pines for example.

Cathy's burning tree, then, invites those humans who would think upon it into creaturely discernment of its meaning, of how it announces what is of value through its distinctive way of life and how we in our instantiation as a living kind nevertheless find ourselves claimed by this.

This is to say, humans are called to a discernment that ponders modes of anarchic differentiation, of the welling-up of values that cannot be anticipated through our own all-too-human way of life, of meanings that transcend our own capacity to affirm them directly as our own, for our all-too-human ends. We do not mean to live in the same way a tree does, and this is a good thing for both sides of that equation.

This realization in turn leads to the second thought promised above. For precisely our attempt to orchestrate a living world in which only human values are taken into account has led inexorably to one in which trees are increasingly burning indiscriminately, as if they themselves were merely passive elements in a machinery gone horribly wrong. Cathy's tree in these circumstances serves as a troubling symptom foretelling the fate of forests undergoing intensified fire regimes that would no longer renew the soil in which trees grow but rather leave it sterile, incinerated to its very roots.[28]

The challenge we face in such circumstances is to remember and honor the ancient entanglement, eons thick, of trees with fire, one that honors all elements of this entanglement, remaining mindful of the dignity of another living kind for whom burning, even to its quick, is a way of life. In the era of the Pyrocene, as has been described by Stephen Pyne, the tendency has been to tell stories about fire that resist its entanglement with the other living kinds.[29] Instead we have been sharing our accounts of a world characterized by, as Anthony Weston puts it, its "desolation," which is to say, a world in which only human agency is recognized and matters. Consumed by a self-absorption with our own living kind, we have been, Weston charges, "driving ourselves into loneliness, funneling both our sociality and our sensibility into the closed circle of human life alone."[30]

The practice of lively ethnography, to which this chapter has aspired, if only in fits and starts, would provide at the very least a diagnosis of the widespread refusal characteristic of our time to cultivate the arts necessary to our becoming a witness to a more-than-human living world. To counter our desolation, we are being called upon to become circumspect regarding how the particular, even peculiar, values revealed in the ways of life of the arboreal living kinds (among all the other living kinds sojourning on the face of the earth) escape at every turn a thinking that would specify and pin down their shape, epistemologically and ontologically, and so merely provide a guidebook to them. Indeed, the very eagerness to see these values in terms that are transparent to one's all-too-human way of understanding them involves a surreptitious rejection of the very categories of inspiration and revelation by which this communication, this saying between humans and trees, might more meaningfully proceed.

Inspiration begins not in curiosity but in deference. And for this reason, prayer is called for. Even now, as the words of this chapter are being set out to circulate among the human readers of this volume, let us acknowledge another audience hovering in proximity, a certain grove of trees, for which the snows of winter are dissipating, even as glacier lilies and shooting stars are emerging into bloom with arnica and arrowleaf balsam root to come soon after. Lupine too. At this very moment, pileated woodpeckers are at work mining the bark of the pines for grubs, as a diversity of living kinds work out their ways of life on the western fork of Gold Creek. Let us keep in mind that the trees of Primm Grove are not indifferent to these all-too-human words that are being offered here on their behalf.

The greatest danger is not only that the arboreal world, as we have come to know it, will be fundamentally altered by our actions, and so overtaken by an anthropogenic regime of fire, as terrible as this might be. Rather, we also should be increasingly wary as our saying of this our more-than-human world is being consumed by our very inattentiveness to the stake that the other living kinds have in our incendiary affliction, in this our age of the Pyrocene.

Notes

1. For a lively and in-depth account of the corporate shenanigans that led to this outcome, see Richard Manning, *Last Stand* (New York: Penguin Books, 1991).

2. Manning, *Last Stand*, 41.

3. Linda Hogan, *Dwellings: A Spiritual History of the Living World* (New York: W. W. Norton & Company, 1995), 44.

4. Hogan, *Dwellings*, 57.

5. Hogan, *Dwellings*, 42–43.

6. In regard to these "other others," see Levinas's discussion of the third party as a category of discursive involvement. Through it, one is called upon to attend to how one's being called to offering one's voice uniquely for the sake of another is to be supplemented by one's addressing how that offering affects all the "other others" beyond the one claiming one's voice or witness. In that discussion, Levinas understands the third party as a category comprising (all) other humans (Emmanuel Levinas, *Otherwise than Being*, 281). But another sort of third party is being contemplated above, one that involves beyond humans, all other living kinds, which is to say, all other creatures, the more-than-human.

7. Hogan, *Dwellings*, 46.
8. Levinas, *Otherwise than Being, or beyond Essence*, Alphonso Lingis, trans. (Pittsburgh: Duquesne University Press, 1999), 151.
9. Levinas, *Otherwise than Being*, 117.
10. Sol Neely, "On Becoming Human in Lingit Aani: Encountering Levinas through Indigenous Inspirations." *Environmental Philosophy*, 13, no. 1 (Spring 2016): 83–104, on 102. Also, see this recent discussion filling out important implications to Neely's Indigenous reading of Levinas: Kaleb Cohen. "Making the Hands Impure: On the Role of Orality in Becoming Responsible for the More-Than-Human World." *Nature and Its Unnatural Relations*, edited by Alain Beauclair and Josh Toth (Lanham, MD: Lexington Press), 2024.
11. Deborah Bird Rose and Thom Van Dooren, "Lively Enthography." *Environmental Humanities* 8, no. 1 (May 2016), 89.
12. Donna Harroway,"String Figures: Multispecies Muddles, Staying with the Trouble." Paper presented at the University of Alberta. March 24, 2014. Quoted in "Lively Ethnography," 89.
13. Rose and Van Dooren, "Lively Enthography," 89.
14. Annie Dillard, *Pilgrim at Tinker Creek* (New York: Harper's Magazine Press, 1974), 33.
15. Dillard, *Pilgrim at Tinker Creek*, 101.
16. Manning, *Last Stand*, 44; David Haskell, *The Songs of Trees: Stories from Nature's Great Connectors* (New York: Viking, 2017), 131.
17. Manning, *Last Stand*, 44.
18. Carl E. Fiedler and Stephen F. Arno, *Ponderosa: People, Fire, and the West's Most Iconic Tree* (Missoula, MT: Mountain Press Publishing Company, 2015), 46.
19. Fiedler and Arno, *Ponderosa*, 40.
20. Christian Diehm, "Staying True to Trees: A Specific Look at Anthropocentrism and Non-Anthropocentrism," *Environmental Philosophy* (Fall 2008): 3–16, on 7.
21. Fiedler and Arno, *Ponderosa*, 75–76.
22. Fiedler and Arno, *Ponderosa*, 71.
23. Words transcribed from a sign in Primm Meadow on September 8, 2022.
24. W. Jolly, M. Cochrane, P. Freeborn, et al.,"Climate-Induced Variations in Global Wildfire Danger from 1979 to 2013. *Nature Communications* 6, no. 7537 (2015), https://doi.org/10.1038/ncomms8537. See also, "How Years of Fighting Every Wildfire Helped Fuel the Western Megafires of Today." *The Conversation*, August 2, 2021. https://theconversation.com/how-years-of-fighting-every-wildfire-helped-fuel-the-western-megafires-of-today-163165
25. Stefan H Doer et al., "Climate Change: Wildfire Risk Has Grown Nearly Everywhere—But We Can Still Influence Where and How Fires Strike." *The Conversation*, June 30, 2022. https://theconversation.com/climate-change-wildfire-risk-has-grown-nearly-everywhere-but-we-can-still-influence-where-and-how-fires-strike-185465

26. Words transcribed from a sign in Primm Meadow on September 8, 2022.

27. Shirley Atkins, "Primm Meadow: A Cathedral of Pines amidst the Apocalypse." Treesource. June 25, 2017. https://treesource.org/travel-through-trees/montana-primm-meadow-ponderosa-pines. Accessed January 21, 2023.

28. See, for example, Fiedler and Arno's account of the June 2010 Schultz fire in Arizona. Modest in its size—only 15,000 acres—but catastrophic in its outcome, the blaze not only wiped out "virtually all trees over broad areas" but also left the soil severely burned and disturbed. Fiedler and Arno, *Ponderosa*, 120.

29. Stephen Pyne, "The Planet Is Burning," *Aeon*. Accessed March 23, 2023. https://aeon.co/essays/the-planet-is-burning-around-us-is-it-time-to-declare-the-pyrocene

30. Anthony Weston, *Back to Earth: Tomorrow's Environmentalism* (Philadelphia: Temple University Press, 1995), 85.

13

Wise Trees

Exemplars in the Arts of East Asia

MARA MILLER

Many wise historical figures such as Aristotle[1] and Isaac Newton have been inspired by trees, as was the Buddha, who found enlightenment after meditating beneath a tree for many days. Trees impress us with their longevity and sheer size, which make them valuable as markers, even witnesses, to history.[2] There is in fact a natural relationship between age and wisdom since wisdom is often acquired as one grows older, even by means of the process of aging, and since wisdom can help us make decisions that contribute to a long, good life. One of China's most famous and wise poets, Du Fu (also spelled Tu Fu, 712–770),[3] wrote several poems on the thatched hut he built after becoming a "withdrawn" gentleman. He chose his spot largely because of the trees: "I constantly desire to escape to Nature. / I am fond of wine and love wind-blown bamboos; /When I choose a dwelling, it must have woods and a spring." In his "Song of My Nan Tree Uprooted by the Storm" (760), he tells us:

> By the river stood a nan tree in front of my thatched hut;
> Old folk told me that it was two hundred years old.
> It was entirely for this that I cleared and chose the site;
> In the fifth month I already imagined autumn cicadas.

From the southeast came a whirlwind, shaking the earth . . .
The trunk still struggled to resist the storm; . . .
Did Heaven intend its roots to be torn from the depths?
My nature loved the old tree by the blue waves,
Spreading over the bank a green canopy.
Peasants often lingered in fear of snow and frost; . . .
A tiger topped, a dragon overthown, it lies in the brush;
Tear tracks' bloody marks fall down my breast.
When I have a new poem, where shall I recite it?
The thatched hut now is without distinction.

The relationship between trees and human beings, however, is much deeper, historically, biologically, and psychically than even all of that. We originated in trees; scientists have recently discovered that the fractures in the limbs of the primate fossil named Lucy, one of our earliest known ancestors,[4] are similar to the kind of injury that results from falling out of trees. Paleontologists also now recognize the great importance of our ancestors' reliance on the provision by trees of shade and shelter for home-building, a benefit that continues to help birds, insects, and mammals, including human beings, today. Even in what is sometimes called "First Nature"[5] (the pre-agricultural world), trees offered nourishment, material for fuel, building, and tools—means by which we still survive and flourish.

Cultures in China, Japan, and Korea have since earliest times gone further: in many cases, they see trees and forests as divine or at least as deeply spiritual beings. In East Asia, especially Japan, in contrast to the threatening symbolic realms of European fairy tales and myths, trees and forests are considered sacred. Sacred trees (*goshinboku*) are endemic in Japan,[6] such as the two-thousand-year-old camphor (*Cinnamomum camphora*) at the Kinomiya Shinto Shrine in Atami, Japan; the Sakonno sakura (cherry); and Ukonno tachibana (a wild native citrus tree) standing on each side of the stairway of the Shishin-den main hall of Gosho, the imperial palace in Kyoto. Sacred forests and their products are highly revered, as I was told by the craftsman hanging the new paper in the teahouse at Shofuso Japanese House and Garden in Philadelphia during its 2007 renovation. They are studied and protected by Japan's Society for the Study of Ancient Groves.[7]

~

But what distinguishes East Asian perspectives from other views is the degree to which trees are viewed as wise. Here, the practical, aesthetic, moral/ethical, metaphysical, and spiritual dimensions of the arboreal world converged in multiple social contexts, both folk cultures and the elite literati culture, and in the three so-called "axial-age" religions of Buddhism, Confucianism, and Daoism, often with significant overlap or cross-currents among them and, in spite of vast cultural differences among them across the countries of East Asia.

Can wisdom exist in trees? Many in East Asia think so. Is this more than just perception or projection of their desired inner qualities? What would wisdom be like in arboreal beings? We must first inquire, however, about the meaning of this claim, and then the very nature of wisdom itself. How do we know it, or recognize it?

Wise Trees: What Can This Mean?

Over centuries, trees in Japan, China, and Korea have been perceived—and honored, even emulated—for their wisdom. Trees inspired people who sought virtue, righteousness, and the good life. The custom continues today with representations in painting, in theatre in the form of the pine tree painted on the Noh stage to confer gravity to the proceedings, and in poetry, literature and other media, including television.[8]

What can this peculiar phrase "perceived as wise" mean? It is more than poetry. It is not simply a case of fanciful language. It is far from an instance of the pathetic fallacy, the attribution of human emotions and responses to inanimate things, about which literary critic I. A. Richards asked, so trenchantly of a poem plagued by "predominating pathetic fallacies," if it is claimed that trees "worship, arise, [and] run": "Is this mysticism, humbug, or the mere raving of a fanatic?"[9] Whether his criticism, that trees don't do those things, is valid or not, these are not the sorts of things asserted about—or attributed to—wise trees.

The trees represented in these contexts are more than merely emblems, visible signs of something abstract but usually fairly easily specified (e.g., "justice"). They are far deeper than metaphor, the figurative use of one word to represent another based on some actual similarity. The very word "represent" in this context can be misleading since we must recognize that it operates on two levels: the representing of trees in a poem or painting, and the representing that trees themselves are understood to perform in our case: namely embodying or conveying wisdom, age, virtue, and so on. It goes farther than allegory as well, since, first, while the meaning of allegory is typically described as "hidden," it is nonetheless, like "emblem," easily stated, and second, in allegory there is a relatively simple one-to-one correlation between the signifier and the referent. In the case of psychoanalyst Carl G. Jung's usage, by contrast, what makes something a symbol is that its meaning is capable of nearly infinite adumbration over a lifetime or more—even centuries.

If so, these representations of trees are symbols in Jung's sense, that is, a psycho-spiritually profound cultural resource and way of thinking or feeling that both transcends the individual and connects her with others (for Jung, all humanity); one that is capable of almost infinite adumbration and reverberation. As Jung puts it:

> a symbol is the intimation of a meaning beyond the level of our present powers of comprehension:
>
> > A symbol remains a perpetual challenge to our thoughts and feelings. That probably explains why a symbolic work is so stimulating, why it grips us so intensely, but also why it seldom affords us a purely aesthetic enjoyment. A work that is manifestly not symbolic appeals much more to our aesthetic sensibility because it is complete in itself and fulfills its purpose.[10]

Trees as symbols are part of an ontology of integration with nature that reaches to the very ground of being-ness and the meaning of our own being.[11]

Ways Trees Are Wise: Association

Part of the reason we may see trees as wise is reinforced by straightforward association. The story of the Buddha's enlightenment under the Bodhi Tree traveled from India to China with Buddhism during the Han period (206 BC–220 AD). A thousand years later, a Buddhist monk, Myōe Shōen (1173–1232), was famously painted meditating in a tree.

Figure 13.1. Buddhist monk Myōe Shōnin meditating in a tree. *Source*: Anonymous, 13th c. Kozanji (Temple). Public domain.

Within several centuries of Buddhism's arrival, Daoist and Confucian wise men, especially those who became exemplars for future generations, came to be associated with trees as well. They took inspiration from both the trees and those exemplars identified with them, and they emulated them, as shown in a poem by Li Ruhua that identifies six trees with six Confucian gentlemen who were renowned for their wisdom and virtue:

> The tall catalpa, straight and towering, is like Lu Zhonglian.
> The lonely pine, high and haughty, is like Kong Beihai.
> The old juniper, quiet and elegant, is like Pang Degong.
> The ancient locust, obstinate and proud, is like Xi Shuye.
> The high wutong, quiet and restful, is like Tao Yuanliang.
> The sparse fir, cold and stern, is like Wang Wugong.[12]

Painter-poet Huang Gongwang inscribed on a painting by Ni Zan (Ni Ts'an, 1301–1374) a poem (thereafter entitled *Six Trees*):

> Distant cloudy mountains range across the autumn river;
> Nearby, ancient trees huddle by the sloping shore.
> Six gentlemen stand facing one another,
> Upright, straight, outstanding, and unbending.[13]

Significantly, Tao Yuanming (T'ao Yuan-ming, aka Tao Qian, T'ao Ch'ien, 365–427) is shown in a painting, *T'ao Yuan-ming's Ode on "Homecoming"* by Li Tsai, a full millennium later (1424), under pine trees.[14] Confucian scholars' retreats are snuggled beneath the embrace of pines.

(Lady) Murasaki Shikibu (973–after 1014) is reputed to have written *The Tale of Genji* at Ishiyama-dera Temple, under pines of course.

And forests typically surround mountain monasteries, whether they are Daoist or Buddhist. They inhabit palaces and villas.

As we saw with Du Fu's nan tree earlier, such visual and poetic associations of wise trees with wise men implies the trees are capable of the physical, intellectual, spiritual, and moral.

In East Asia, the practical uses of trees blend into the aesthetic and the spiritual realms of the arts, which in turn facilitate deep spiritual growth;[15] pine soot is made into cakes for calligraphy ink and wood stain; pomegranate dyes clothing and stains wood; trees such as bamboo[16] "are used for making paper, to help the life of the mind, and for making flutes, to help the life of the emotions"[17]—and for implements in the tea ceremony, flower arranging, gardens, and other arts, as well as for food.[18]

Figure 13.2. *Enjoying the Moon in a Riverside Cottage*, Ike no Taiga, 1765. *Source*: Philadelphia Museum of Art. Public domain.

Figure 13.3. *Murasaki Shikibu writing the* Tale of Genji *at Ishiyama-dera (Temple), overlooking a garden beneath pine trees*. *Source*: Private collection of the author.

Figure 13.4. Pine trees at Itsukushima Shrine (c. 693), temple and palace of the Taira (Heike) family, Miyajima, Hiroshima Prefecture, 2003. *Source*: Photo by Mara Miller. Public domain.

The trees themselves, as living support systems, came to be seen as protectors and exemplars of virtues and qualities productive of an ideal life, an essential component for longevity. (Compare naturalist John Hay's observation: "Trees refuse defeat, growing back again, rooted in timelessness."[19])

Arborist and writer William Bryant Logan reports:

> The fine British arborist Neville Fay outlined the seven ways that this regeneration can happen: One of the reiterations at the base of the trunk can make its own root system and its own new trunk. . . . An old scaffold branch can do the same. Or the tree may completely resprout from the basal root system, rising again from the ground up. Or the tree's lowest branches may strike the ground, root where they hit, and generate a new tree. Or a small-diameter trunk can form right inside

the decaying ancient one and there make a fresh start. Or new roots may start in the hollow at the base of the tree, and touching ground, they may generate a new trunk and crown. Finally, the tree may fall right over, its lateral branches turning into new trees.[20]

As a result of these complex processes, trees come to be associated with wise men. (I use the male term advisedly: while women throughout East Asia did become literati [*wen-jen, bunjin*], the custom took centuries to include women, the role and its practices were far more rare for women, they rarely if ever served in an official capacity, and women had a different set of historical exemplars and ethical standards.)

The Seven Sages of the Bamboo Grove, for example, are a group of friends, mostly Daoist literati scholars and poets, living in China around 225–275 BCE.

They are usually shown among bamboo, where they pursue the activities that characterized the life and temperament of scholars: playing

Figure 13.5. Bamboo grove at the Suzhou Museum designed by I. M. Pei + Pei Architects, Suzhou, China, 2006. *Source*: Photo by Mara Miller.

and listening to the musical instrument called the *qin*, practicing *qingtan* (pure conversation), playing the board game called *weiqi*, lighting incense, and drinking. The Seven Sages became famous not only for their publications and their official service but for their wisdom and virtue in retiring from the public service that was required of all Chinese scholars when that public life proved itself too corrupt or disappointing. (Poetry-writing and other arts went along with scholarship and public service.)

What is the relation between their wisdom and virtue and the bamboo that surrounds them? No one, so far as I know, argues that it was the bamboo that made them wise. Nor does bamboo by itself, in a painting, for instance, necessarily represent the Seven Sages (as irises so often represent the "Eight-Plank Bridge" chapter of the Japanese *Tales of Ise*). Yet to one who knows the literature and art, a bamboo grove near a residence or tea house will inevitably call to mind the Seven Sages; one may find oneself feeling one is living among them, living with them. The sound of bamboo rustling in the wind is a cherished aesthetic experience; one can enjoy it because one knows it will not break in the wind. So it makes a good windbreak, and confers a sense of protection that expands to represent safety and the comforts of home: "A home by the stream faces water flowing west, / Bamboos and trees, high and low, obscure mountain paths."[21]

Did the bamboo also facilitate the Sages' ongoing practice of wisdom? Perhaps make it possible? Did it do so in virtue of its example?

Trees as an Embodiment and Manifestation of Wisdom in East Asia

Thus far this chapter has argued that in China, Korea, and Japan trees are widely understood as wise because they both symbolize wisdom and are historically associated with wise men. But the relation between trees and wisdom in East Asia is much deeper, going beyond symbolism or association: trees *embody* qualities that comprise wisdom, and they make them manifest so that we can perceive them—and emulate them.

Because their wisdom is embodied in their modes of being and ways of living, their inability to formulate it directly to us in human language is immaterial. Trees are teachers of the important virtues, exemplars if you will, like the great moral heroes.

Two species, pines and bamboo, are especially prized for their virtues. Pines are able to grow in the harshest, most adverse circumstances. Bamboo can bend with the wind, a flexibility that is similarly valuable in the personal and especially professional life of human beings. Others join them: the plum tree, producing the first flowers to emerge after winter, and so prized for temerity in facing adversity, together with pines and bamboo, are known in literati culture and beyond as the "Three Friends of Winter;" like the "Four Gentlemen" (chrysanthemum, bamboo, orchid, plum), which recur over centuries in countless paintings and poems.

Problems with Wisdom in Trees

Our Western search for wisdom comes from the ancient Greeks, and the ancient Greek philosophers are notoriously logocentric. Paradigmatically, when we think of wise individuals, we imagine asking them questions, as in the cartoons of a person climbing a mountain to consult a guru, or their giving advice or teaching in verbal discourse, like Socrates in the Platonic Dialogues.

Trees don't speak; they don't even have language. How can they be wise, without speaking, without *telling* us what to do, how to behave?

There are two answers to this challenge.

First, scientists are discovering trees do possess language; it is just not human language.[22] That is, they have means of communicating within themselves (in the sense in which neuroscientists and others speak of cells communicating) and among themselves, with other plants, and even with animals, using systems that are complex and structured. Their language is physical, not oral. Naturalist John Hay sees it somewhat differently, though: that trees are themselves the expression: "Trees are central to earth's expression, in depths of silence, torrents of energy."[23]

The second answer is that spoken and written (human) language is only one of our human communication systems. It is particularly useful for consciousness and for communication with ourselves, but written and spoken language are not the only ways human beings communicate, even with each other. Visual and other arts, body "language," natural physical actions or reactions, costumes, our home décor, our choice of cars, all communicate—effectively, constantly, and sometimes far more than we would like.

It is important to remember that not all of what we communicate via these means, even via language construed more narrowly, is conveyed *deliberately*. Effective communication may be unintentional, and therefore it is not always communication of *knowledge* (on the part of the person transmitting the message). Knowledge is also not dependent on consciousness. Muscular knowledge, knowledge of many bodily functions, rarely requires conscious awareness; similarly we often act on knowledge we have forgotten, or never become aware of at all.

Like knowledge, wisdom need not depend on consciousness or intention. While some views of wisdom see it as highly theoretical and a function of (human) language, John Hay suggests language is not necessary for knowing, much less for wisdom: "Trees stand deep within a kind of knowing that surpasses human knowledge. . . . What speech is there, you wonder, in their communion with the earth? . . . In their presence, you may become aware of a greater, planetary silence that defines the unknown, if only because it refuses to answer when invoked."[24] Certainly we know many things without being able to put them into language; much of our "knowing how" is of this kind, as is knowledge that is unconscious or pre-liminal, to use phenomenologist Alfred Schutz's term.[25] This perspective allows for the recognition of non-linguistic (somatic, visual/artistic, neurological, biochemical) and unconscious or pre-liminal knowledge not only in ourselves but in information systems, other animals, and plants.[26]

Trees arguably possess knowledge and wisdom that is like this and in this way.

Gardeners and farmers likewise know that their plants are constantly "telling" us what they need or want—sharing their biological interests—through changes in color, vibrancy, posture (drooping), and so on.

Is this wisdom about what is necessary for their lives?

Wisdom seems to imply agency, conscious awareness, choice, and deliberation. If so, trees may not be wise. Yet recent discoveries by researchers suggest not only that trees actively communicate[27] but that, as agents, trees are more dynamic agents than we commonly suppose.[28]

Both these capabilities bear important implications for the possibility of wisdom in trees. Recent findings suggest that trees manifest at least two of the ten crucial dimensions of wisdom presented below: acting on an ability to go beyond immediate interests and needs, taking—or at least *acting as if* they are taking—the long view, and going beyond their own interests, intellectually and practically. This apparent capacity might be construed as commensurate with Buddhists' second great virtue, compassion, understood, especially in East Asia, to apply to *all* living things. It may even be that trees "understand" other points of view, and even (taking it further) can empathize. (As with human beings and other animals, however, recognizing differences among individuals and between species is imperative, given that not all species of trees, or all individuals within a species, are alike.)

The East Asian Context: Literati Culture and Landscape

Valuing of trees as wise in East Asia is closely, but not exclusively, linked with literati culture. The Seven Sages mentioned above are early progenitors of China's elite literati culture, which spread, with significant changes, to Korea and Japan. It grew out of two deeply entrenched sets of values, customs, and institutions. First was the writing system (later adopted by the Japanese and Koreans, ill-suited though it was to their languages), consisting of tens of thousands of ideograms; this was foundational. Second was the Chinese civil service system based on writing and literate culture, developed much later, which depended on a high level of education in the Confucian classical literature. The writing could be carved on stone, wood, or wet clay or written with a brush in ink on paper or silk. Complex as it was, it demanded years of close study, primarily of poetry, philosophy, and history, which were transmitted over two and a half millennia or more which became the basis for the civil service. Education, the civil service, and the Chinese ethical system were deeply Confucian, but during the Song Dynasty, Confucianism, Buddhism, and Daoism came to be philosophically and practically integrated in various ways, through what is known as the "Song Synthesis."

Out of the various philosophical combinations arose a diverse and creative "literati" (*wen-jen*) culture that nourished the arts of calligraphy, poetry, and painting as forms of recreation and delight, but also of personal intellectual and spiritual development.

∼

Trees are part of the landscape. Two main currents enlivened the appreciation of landscape in classical literati culture. First, landscape, as mountains and rocks, embodies the foundational forces of the cosmos, conceived from earliest times as the oppositions yin and yang (female and male, guest and host, ruler and subject, cold and hot, etc.), thought to structure all natural and human/social interactions. (Opposites though they are, yin and yang are not mutually exclusive, but support and give rise to one another; nor are they associated with good and bad.) In one Chinese painting, *Trees and Rocks*, art historian Wen Fong describes the interplay of forms as "a series of richly interacting large-and-small, high-and-low, front-and-back, dry-and-moist, spiky-and-smooth yin-yang relationships. . . . with thickening-and-thinning brushstrokes, . . . [evincing] thorough mastery of nature's 'principles' in pictorial representation.' "[29] As historian of Chinese painting Richard Barnhart put it: "The hills and rivers, changeless settings for brief lives, were conceived then as embodiments of ultimate intelligence and virtue. In the words of the classic Confucian text *Chung Yung*, or 'Doctrine of the Mean,' 'nature is vast, deep, high, intelligent, infinite and eternal.' . . . The idea of nature is the idea of eternity, order, and structure; the embodiment of virtue and morality, and a constant reminder of the Tao [currently transliterated Dao] of existence."[30]

Figure 13.6. *Early Spring* by Guo Xi (Kuo Hsi 1020–1090), signed and dated 1072. *Source*: National Palace Museum, Taipei. Public domain.

The continuity of reciprocity (or integration) of landscape and trees, cosmos or Dao, and individual human beings is revealed in a poem by Tang Yin (T'ang Yin, 1470–1524) on his 1516 painting *Whispering Pines on a Mountain Path*:

> In front of Mount Nü-chi, traversed by wild paths,
> The sound of the whispering pines harmonizes closely with that of the waterfall.
> As I listen quietly with total attention,
> I feel the spirit of Tao rising within me.[31]

Figure 13.7. *Landscape for Zhao Yipeng*, after Tang Yin (Chinese, 1470–1524), late 15th–early 16th century. *Source*: Metropolitan Museum of Art. Public domain.

Many of Tang Yin's paintings show scholars' secluded huts protected by pines.

In addition, literati arts extoled the virtues and pleasures of landscape as a realm of freedom, where one may escape from the office into nature, whether gardens or the mountains, to experience a sense of expansion into the universe, as opposed to the often-grueling work in the civil offices with its sometimes-corrupt expectations.

As far back as the fourth century such escapes from work, in two forms, involved trees and landscape (literally "mountains [and] water"). First, individuals made excursions into the countryside, either alone (with a servant), to visit friends, or with a small group of companions such as the Lanting (Orchid Pavilion) poetry party memorialized in a preface to the poetry the friends composed, written by Wang Xizhi (Wang Hsi-chih, 303?–361?).

Wang Xizhi's *Lanting Xu (Preface to the Poems Composed at the Orchid Pavilion)* celebrated a gathering of scholars who drank and wrote poetry in an idyllic mountain setting, surrounded by pines and other trees. Inspiring generations of scholars, based on its sense of freedom from the cares of officialdom and the enjoyment of like-minded comrades, it has been evoked repeatedly in paintings and garden settings.

Figure 13.8. *The Orchid Pavilion Gathering*, Yamamoto Jakurin (1721–1801), 1790. Source: Wikimedia Commons. Public domain.

Second, many scholar-officials retired early to their family estates, including Wang Wei (699–760), considered the progenitor of literati landscape painting with his portrayal, after his retirement, on a long handscroll of his home estate. Pines figure prominently in it, comprising a depiction that inspired countless artist-poets over the next twelve and a half centuries and facilitated both the artistic practice and the association of trees with wisdom and wise men.

Wang Xizhi himself is another such example, shown as he watched geese at his lakeside pavilion in a portrait by Qian Xuan (Ch'ien Hsuan, 1235–1305).

Wang Xizhi is credited with the invention (or discovery) of the possibilities of cursive calligraphy for personal expression, in which the individual strokes within a written character may be linked graphically,

Figure 13.9. *Wang Xizhi Watching Geese*, Qian Xuan (1239–1301), Chinese, ink painting with color, c. 1295. *Source*: Metropolitan Museum of Art. Public domain.

without the brush being lifted from the silk or paper, as was previously required (and still prevalent in scripts for official purposes and seals). This innovation made personal expression possible not simply in the content of the text but in the very form of the calligraphy, and thus gave rise to calligraphy as a new art, with new potential—potential that was carried over into painting. Wang Xizhi's insight was said to have been inspired by the geese he watched whose flight and swimming never left gaps from one location to another—hence the significance of the pose Qian Xuan selected for him.[32] He is thus considered a founder of the literati tradition. But he is also one of its most important exemplars.

Remembering our Seven Sages, note as well the grove of bamboo on the far shore of the image. Given the curves of the bamboo to both the right and left, the wind in which they bow must be coming *toward* it—and him. He doesn't give way. He is a literati cultural hero not only for this discovery, and the model his own calligraphy inspired (one can to this day buy scarves and table runners with reproductions of the sole extant example of his calligraphy), but for his virtuous retirement.

Similarly, Tao Qian (T'ao Ch'ien, or Tao Yuanming [365–427]) retired from official service and then farmed, drank, cultivated chrysanthemums, wrote poetry, and was chosen by Du Fu as his "mentor." The celebration of retreats such as Wang's, Tao's, and Du Fu's beneath his nan tree generated a third means of "escape" from daily rigors, annoyances, and corruption: painting and writing poetry about trees. From such paintings, which one is to "enter" through the imagination, we can absorb the benefits of the trees and their wise example.

Barnhart's description of how this works in a paradigmatic landscape painting, *The Riverbank*, could almost be a summary of Daoist-Confucianist metaphysics of the Dao and yin-yang, and its view of the role of human beings:

> The interaction of mountains and water is the very essence of *shan-shui* ("mountains and water"), the Chinese concept of landscape. In Chinese art, mountains do not exist without water. "The wise find pleasure in the waters, the virtuous find pleasure in mountains," wrote Confucius, a little enigmatically but certainly suggesting something fundamental to his concept of ideal existence. There is a wholeness in the cycle of creation, life, and growth reflected in the eternal struggle of mountains and water: the mountains rise into the sky,

water falls from the sky, washing over the mountain, moving it re-building it. On one level of interpretation this incessant symbiotic relationship is the subject of *The Riverbank* as it is of most Northern Sung landscape paintings. Translated into a formal mode, the water is openness—moving space that joins the sky to establish the only counterbalance to the solid mass of rock and mountain. . . . one becomes aware of continuous interaction, observes the movements within its structure, one becomes aware of continuous interaction, of interpenetration, and finally of the inextricable union of earth and water, the two primal elements. Growing from their union are the trees, grasses, flowers, and shrubs of the landscape; tall pines in the high mountains; gnarled, windswept deciduous species joining the pines in the foreground; dark bamboo in the sheltered valleys. With the trees our scale narrows, our focus on the dimension of life sharpens as we draw away from the cosmic vastness of mountains and water toward the relative vulnerability of trees, which are born, grow, flourish, decay, and die, as do all the living things of earth. We are thus brought to the final elements of the landscape, its human dimension.[33]

An important caveat: with East Asian painting, poetry, and thinking about landscape, it is almost impossible not to oversimplify. The variety, complexities, and nuances of the arts and philosophies and individuality of the painters' characters are easily underestimated, though they make understanding of art, trees, nature, and their relations to human life truly symbolic (in Jung's sense). Our shared existential conditions and our responses to trees make it possible to see trees as wise and as similar to ourselves in our most successful aspects. They also make it possible to use our painting, calligraphy, and poetry about trees and the landscape to express emotion, from the most transient to the most abiding and definitive. As Fong says, comparing Ni Zan's painting with the printed version in Ni's manual:

> Although the calligraphy of this inscription [on the painting] compares closely with that of The Six Gentlemen, the painting has a completely different overall appearance. The rock forms, covered with seemingly careless, almost messy strokes and horizontal dots, reflect an educated taste for childish daubing.

For Ni Tsan brushwork, here delightfully playful (*hsi/xi*), is painting the blending of the various kinds of brushstrokes to reveal not only the true landscape, but also the anxious feelings of the artist. The painting records the moment when transient emotion becomes pure feeling (ch'ing/qing), combining urgency with detachment, a characteristic that is uniquely Ni Tsan's.[34]

The Meaning and the Value of Wisdom

Elsewhere I proposed a list of the kinds of awareness, behaviors, and attitudes that comprise common-sense notions of wisdom as it relates to nuclear weapons and energy.[35] Although the list is not exhaustive, it is useful here because the features are broadly applicable across a wide range of domains: child-raising, education, relationships, warfare, and financial investment. These traits can be called "practical wisdom."

Wisdom, it should be noted, can inhere in individuals, but also in populations, workforces, and institutions, and it can apply to decisions and actions too.

There are, it seems, at least ten crucial dimensions of wisdom, many of which are exhibited by trees. Without anthropomorphizing, and hewing closely to ordinary views of the arboreal world, we can see that trees exhibit some aspects of wisdom. Points 1, 4, 7, 9, and 10 are most likely to apply to trees; specific applications to trees are italicized:

1. The ability to go beyond immediate interests and needs, and to take the long view.

2. The ability to go beyond one's own and/or one's group's interests and subjective point of view; to understand—or take into account—other perspectives, to empathize, even when one cannot agree with or accommodate these views.

3. The ability to combine knowledge from varied contexts, to make connections and recognize applicable similarities—and differences;

4. The ability to hold off on action until the time is appropriate, a sensitivity to what the ancient Greeks called *kairos*, the awareness of the need to carefully time certain actions

(such as planting, harvesting, or attacking in war) within a larger context (not just a date, but the weather, or the arrival of one's supplies or the actions of one's enemies; see *Ecclesiastes* 3:1–8: "To everything there is a season . . . .).["][36] *Trees "act" in accordance with the seasons, or, rather, with the weather, which might otherwise sabotage growth with unseasonable frosts and thaws.*

5. Self-knowledge, the ability to recognize one's own strengths and weaknesses, virtues and flaws, and even morally neutral qualities of character, to take them into consideration and relate them to the problem at hand.

6. Recognition of one's own "baggage"—the way one's personal history and the lessons already learned affect one's thinking, emotions, and reactions.

7. Taking responsibility for one's own actions (past and future). *While it might seem odd to speak of trees acting responsibly, they do frequently offer food, shelter from the elements, escape routes from enemies, views for hunting, and support for homes, as well as myriad other materials for plant, animal, and human survival.*

8. The ability to recognize where or when general rules of knowledge do *not* apply to a local or specific variation.

9. Discerning and sometimes setting boundaries when something is not relevant or appropriate. *Trees largely ignore what is not relevant to them.*

10. Knowing when to refrain from acting, to delay gratification. Wisdom has both an inherent action dimension—and an *in*action dimension, the capacity to refrain from acting when that is what is called for, the *wuwei* of Daoism, in view of long-term benefits and benefits to others or the larger community.[37] *Trees recognize where the general rules of their (tacit) knowledge base do not apply due to local or specific variation, without trying to exceed their natural limitations. This is often called "enlightened self-interest." Here, too, trees wait until the time is right for every stage of their development and for most of their responses to stimuli.*

While these points have been conceptualized for the context of distinctively modern dilemmas and crises, they are familiar age-old, life-and-death capabilities and situations. Many can be seen as different ways of looking at the traditional virtues, or character traits, like patience, tenacity, and altruism or love. We commonly understand wisdom not simply as a cognitive state or set of attributes but as an ability to *act* or *refrain from acting* in certain ways—to behave in accordance with these "larger" views, to forego immediate gratification in lieu of long-term benefits to others or the larger community.[38]

The list above suggests several themes relevant to wisdom in trees. First, time plays an important role: "planning" for the future, "learning" from our own past, delaying "gratification" (enlightened self-interest). Many trees by their nature last longer than we do, fifty to hundreds or even several thousand years, and their extended time-scale predisposes them to both the long-range considerations and building on—though not necessarily being *conscious of*—the past. (I am not yet prepared to defend consciousness in trees.)

In addition to temporal issues, wisdom seems to require considering not just ourselves but others. Moreover, just like mammal and insect species who might live in herds, hives, or packs as well as being solitary, trees have different modes of individuality, collectivity, and community existence, not just the readily identifiable models with which we are familiar.

Whether in human beings or in trees, we value wisdom also because it confers authority (though it is only one of several ways this quality can be conveyed), and authority communicates for those who encounter it both a feeling of confidence in themselves and a sense of security in the world and their situations.

Wisdom in Trees

Understanding wisdom in trees requires rethinking the relationship between the individual (formerly or vernacularly defined by its single trunk and/or its genetic make-up) and its group. Studies of trees show that our assumption that each tree stands unique and alone is faulty. Coppices are extensions of a single original that has been cut. Some apparent "individuals" comprise vast assemblages of trees which are linked genetically and historically across miles. The new shoots of one bamboo, the *Bambusa nana*, emerge at the center of the clump during the winter and around the edges in the summer, thus keeping the old stems warm or cool as desirable, making an association with filial piety natural.[39] Even the death of a tree in nature may not be simply the end of an individual but also the beginning of a process of living and dying for others; new trunks may emerge from the old. As writer Verlyn Klinkenborg tells us, "A tree that dies in the woods never really dies. . . . a tree in the woods takes nearly as long to die as it takes to live. What we call death—suddenly going horizontal—is merely a midpoint to a tree."[40] Understanding wisdom in trees requires a different model of the relationship of the individual to the collectivity or community than we are familiar with.

Trees focus more easily on their community (when they have one) than do human beings or even animals. While altruism is a notable feature of human individuals and societies, and has been documented in animals as well,[41] human beings do not—cannot—take it for granted; indeed, a good deal of the attention and efforts of religion globally has focused on teaching and fostering altruism in one guise or another.

With trees, extending themselves to others comes naturally. But chemists and biologists speak of self-recognition by cells; trees' cells certainly possess this capacity, termed "self-/non-self-discrimination" in the plant signaling and behavior literature. And trees such as black walnuts protect themselves from encroaching plants that would utilize their resources by exuding poisons. How should we understand "the self" of a tree? Is it not, at the least, analogous to the "self" of a cell, which is able to recognize those similar to and different from "itself?"

The Meaning of Wisdom in the East Asian Wisdom Traditions

Given the diversity and complexity of the wisdom traditions in East Asia, it is impossible here to provide even a cursory outline of the forms of wisdom that are thought to be exhibited by trees, much less to broaden our discussion of this crucial concept to include the wisdom of ancient Greek and Biblical sources. We can, nonetheless, note a few relevancies that trees evince.

It may be easiest to make the case for Daoism, where immersion in the Dao, the "Way" of the cosmos/natural order, by means of *wuwei*, neither action nor inaction, is the principal objective. Contemporary Daoist scholar Ronnie Littlejohn explains that Daoists "have preferred to focus on understanding the nature of reality, increasing their longevity. Fundamental Daoist ideas and concerns include *wuwei* ('effortless action'), *ziran* ('naturalness'), how to become a *shengren* ('sage') or *zhenren* ('perfected person'), and the ineffable, mysterious *Dao* ('Way') itself."[42] While one might take issue with trees "*preferring*" to "becom[e] a sage or perfected person" (I do not claim to know their intentions—it is hard enough to know my own!—but, then, their ability to succeed as sages is precisely what is at issue in this chapter!), it is not hard to recognize that trees exhibit effortless action, naturalness, and that, whether they "understand" the nature of reality and the "ineffable, mysterious Dao ('Way') itself," they do conform to it. Does this not suggest a mutual relationship between our Seven Sages with the bamboo that surrounds them?

Daoism may also help us with the problem of trees not sharing human language discussed above. The value of knowing without explicating linguistically is attested by the Daoist tradition. According to Lao Tzu (6th–5th c. BCE), "He who knows does not speak. He who speaks does not know. . . . Become one with the dusty world. This is called profound identification."[43] The last sentiment is echoed by Confucian scholar, Xunzi (Hsün-tzu, 340–145 BCE), who, for all his divergence from the Daoists, "suggested that one needs to go through three stages to cultivate the mind: emptiness, unification, and stillness."[44]

Buddhism provides another perspective on wisdom in trees. For example, when pines and bamboo are lauded for withstanding harsh conditions, is this not an illustration of three of the Buddha's Four Noble Truths? First, that suffering is inevitable and ubiquitous; second, that suffering is caused by craving or desire; and third, that there is a way out of suffering, which we can achieve by relinquishing our attitudes of desire and fear (attachment). (The fourth truth, that there are ways to end suffering, namely, by means of the Eight-Fold Path, seems to me less relevant to trees, but one might make the case.)[45]

Yet it is Confucianism, with its concern for society—and for the individual within a society that is often as harsh as nature—that insists most strongly on the ways trees manifest values consistent with wisdom, in order to survive harsh conditions. These may be transitory, like the winds that force bamboo to bend (instead of breaking, blowing over, or uprooting like other trees), or permanent, like the impoverished basic circumstances of a pine growing in a cliff-side rock. Such forces, such conditions, are seen as analogous to the ones in which human beings must live and work. The concern is largely with ethics and the aspects of wisdom that are useful to, or becoming in, scholar-officials like Wang Xizhi, Tao Yuanming, and Du Fu. Yet as Du Fu's poem suggests, they are helpful to anyone whose life includes difficulties.

Wise Trees: Peach

In a similar vein, peaches may be taken as reminders of Daoist values and beliefs. The peach is a sacred symbol in Daoism, implying longevity and more: in the legendary land of "Peach Blossom Spring," by Tao Yuanming, a fisherman gets lost and discovers a paradisical land filled with peach trees where families and children live without fear, famine, and conflict, a freedom and harmony suggestive of wisdom (after returning home, the fisherman is never able to find his way back, of course).[46]

In the culminating scene of the anime film *Kung Fu Panda*, when the ancient sage transmits his wisdom to the beloved young panda hero, the pair sits on a high cliff deep in the mountains beneath a flowering peach tree (reminding us of Daoist values) whose physical beauty illustrates life-giving wisdom itself. Kung Fu Panda's inspirational peach is part of a documented tradition nearly two millennia old of trees that embrace an ideal life for their human beings.

Figure 13.10. *Peach Blossom Spring*, Zhang Hong, Chinese, dated 1638. *Source*: Metropolitan Museum of Art. Public domain.

352 | Mara Miller

Wise Trees: Pines and Poetry

Except for pollarding—a pruning method that controls the size and shape of a tree—Western ideals of arboreal beauty (derived from Aristotle) insist each tree should be allowed to grow according to its inherent (ideal) form, with pines, for instance, forming a virtual cone (picture a Christmas tree). The opposite applies in East Asia, where the anomalies reflecting the deprivations, challenges, and vicissitudes of its life story are more fully appreciated.

Lu Gueimeng (also transliterated Lu Kuei-meng) explains the reasoning behind the love of pine trees. Notice how the musings begin with a painting:

> A Taoist devotee came from Tientai and showed me a picture called "Grotesque Pine."
>
> It was indeed a terrifying sight: the roots of the pine coming out from a cave, crawling spirally up along the edge of a crag. Its trunk was exceedingly massive, but stunted, not more than four or five feet in height; its foliage was thick and luxuriant, so that trunk, branches, and leaves huddled together gave one the impression of an injured dragon, a lame tiger, or a tied and caged man of great strength. I was asked if I could explain how a pine tree could be so warped and twisted.

Figure 13.11. *Hawk-Eagle in a Pine Tree*, Soga Nichokuan (act. C. 1625–1660). One of a pair of six-panel folding screens; ink on paper. *Source*: Museum of Fine Arts, Boston. Public domain.

He has begun by describing the tree's physical appearance but soon moves to the environmental forces that caused it:

> In reply, I said: "Why should there be any abnormality in the growth of trees and grasses?" If they have the right kind of soil and climate, untrammeled by anything external, they always stand upright and flourish. Pines and cedars, being more hardy than most trees, should be better able to withstand adversity. The pine that we are looking at had the misfortune to have issued from a cave, handicapped by all the impediments to growth. How can it be expected to extract itself from its environment? In spite of the setbacks in its early days, it was able to preserve a certain *righteous* spirit. When it attained maturity, it put up a *brave* struggle with the rocks. However, the *opposing forces* were too much for it. Accumulated *agonies and frustrations* found expression in its gnarled and knotted form, and the world calls it a grotesque tree.

With the shift to an ethical discourse (italicized above), he prepares the analogy to human life:

> How is this different at the human level? Heaven endows a person with talents and when they are not appreciated, he feels dejected and withdraws. Then he matures and gathers wisdom, but finds himself jostled and deprived by the powers that be. Then he breaks out in gorgeous and impassioned art, and the world calls him an eccentric person. Alas! When a tree is curbed it becomes deformed, which is the only way for it to express itself. When a person is deprived, he becomes eccentric, which is the only way for him to distinguish himself. "Is this not a case of all's well that ends well?" The Taoist devotee declared, "Well said! Why not write a eulogy for me." So I wrote this:
>
>> A pine grows in shady crags:
>> A grotto its prison, a cave its scourge.
>> It suffers from depression
>> Which results in deformity.
>> It becomes so unsightly
>> That even the spirits and ghosts

> Think it quite incredible.
> A Taoist devotee marvels at it
> And forthwith records it
> In weird shapes and words.
> I being a leader among eccentrics
> Have pleasure in writing this eulogy.[47]

Note the contrast with the Aristotelian and Platonic ideal. As much as it is a biological explanation, it is also a moral analysis, reflecting the customs of the culture—the agonies and frustrations, deprivations, and lack of appreciation "felt" by the tree are felt by scholar-officials (and perhaps monks as well)—meant to be resisted by those who cultivate themselves philosophically and artistically. Such acts give life to those standards derived from philosophical reflection. The tree withstands adversity, preserves a righteous spirit, needs to express itself—and deserves a eulogy. (Eulogy, from the ancient Greek, literally means "happy or fortunate" "words.")

The interpenetration of pines with the Confucian gentleman ideal emerges again and again. The tenth-century master Zhing Hao (Ching Hao) said, tall pine trees "possess the virtuous air of a gentleman."[48] Daoist scholar and painter Huang Gongwang (Huang Kung-wang, 1269–1354), at a scholarly gathering in Suzhou, inscribed on Ni Zan's 1345 small hanging scroll *The Six Gentlemen* (which shows no men, only pines) the poem:

> Distant cloudy mountains range across the autumn river;
> Nearby, ancient trees huddle by the sloping shore.
> Six gentlemen stand facing one another,
> Upright, straight, outstanding, and unbending.[49]

Wise Trees: Bamboo and the Painting of Bamboo

Bamboo is renowned for its ability to bend in the wind.

It continues not just to live but to thrive through even the fiercest storms; its thin leaves don't tear. The protection bamboo offers as a wind barrier is both physical and symbolic, which may account for its presence in so many paintings of the bodhisattva Kwan-yin (Jp., Kannon), an incarnation known for compassion toward anyone who asks for protection.[50] Botanist and scholar Edwin T. Morris tells us:

Figure 13.12. *Bamboo in the Wind*, Yi Jeong (artist name Taneun, 1541–1626). *Source*: Metropolitan Museum of Art. Public domain.

The bamboo, like the pine, had many symbolic associations. The literati found that this versatile plant had many admirable qualities: it was strong but resilient; it grew in measured segments, showing a sense of limit and propriety; it would remain green in winter; it grew in clumps, evincing clan feeling; it produced no flowers in the spring, so would not compete with others; and it grew rapidly, a model of self-development. . . . [The poet] Su Tung-po [1030-1101, Su Dungpo, aka Su Shih] said that without bamboo in the surroundings, it would be hard to practice morality.[51]

Rarely mentioned is the emotional range captured by the movement of those branches, trunks, and leaves. It can be soft, gentle, seemingly sad or wistful, or perhaps even melancholy. But it can also be exuberant and gay. Artists have captured it all.

Does it do this for us? Perhaps by reminding us of the Sages' example, perhaps by other means: the soothing sound of its rustle in wind, the unostentatious color, the oh-so-slight startle we get when the trunks of adjacent bamboo clack against each other.

I speak here as one who has twice lived among bamboo. I can hardly claim it made me wiser. Yet it certainly paved the way. It soothed me at a time of great turmoil in my life. It enlivened my—our—aesthetic sense, our feeling that life is worth living and enjoyable even when difficult and frightening. It brought me into a daily awareness of my links to ancestors, literary, artistic, and philosophical if not genetic, those whom Alfred Schutz calls "predecessors," thus extending my awareness of my place in the social world, relieving it of its gruesome constrictions by impending deadlines and dreaded appointments.

The Seven Sages, beloved of literati, became one of the best-known East Asian models for the ethical man, and mentors via the imagination for countless others such as Wang Xizhi and Tao Yuanming, also associated with trees and retirement to gardens and landscape, who have been celebrated in the arts throughout China, Japan, and Korea for fifteen hundred years.[52]

Painting Again

This power, which we can call the power of association, is such that even painting them, an act that reflects human wisdom, also contributes to its development. (Painting, along with poetry and calligraphy were known as "the three perfections.")[53] As Li Rihua (1565–1635), wrote on a painting of bamboo to be given as a gift:

> To paint bamboo is to sweep away vulgarity;
> Without vulgarity there is no need to sweep.
> He has his mind set to leave vulgarity behind,
> Even though he is surrounded by vulgar roots.
> This gentleman is not a vulgar one;
> Morning and evening he supports himself by planting and
>   digging;

> He is addicted to the taste of brush and ink;
> He takes food only to avoid being hungry;
> He is not attracted to profits;
> Nor to the power of fame.
> This gentleman's cultivation is tasteful;
> The bamboo's movement is also graceful.
> To each other neither is vulgar;
> They should be friends forever.[54]

This view surely contributes to the proliferation of paintings of wise trees and other plants that is especially engrained in the Confucian literati tradition but is also widespread among Daoists, Buddhists, and others.

The Mustard Seed Garden, an illustrated seventeenth-century printed painting manual mass-produced in China that also became popular among literati artists in Japan, taught methods of painting trees, rocks, people, and things; the "Four Gentlemen" (orchid, bamboo, plum and chrysanthemum); "grasses, insects, and flower plants;" and "feather-and-fur and flowering plants." Its "Book of the Bamboo" shows the intimate relations among artistic practice, the subject matter of painting (trees), and wisdom:

> Unless heart and idea are attuned, there can indeed be no good results. It is essential to have serenity, something that can arise only from a tranquil soul. Avoid making stems like drum sticks. Avoid making joints of equal length. Avoid lining up the bamboo like a fence. Avoid placing the leaves all to one side. Avoid making them . . . like the fingers of an outstretched hand, or like the crisscrossing of a net, or like the leaves of the peach or willow. At the moment of putting brush to paper or silk, do not hesitate. From the deepest recesses of the heart should come the power that propels the brush to action.[55]

The creation of painting manuals goes back centuries. In 1350, the incomparable painter of landscape Ni Zan (Ni Ts'an, 1301–1374) made one. Regarding a composition of bamboo with two trees, Ni Zan says:

> For the larger tree the brushwork should be soft, so that its branches look tender; for the smaller tree the brushwork should be ancient, so that it looks archaic. If the larger tree is seen from the front, the smaller tree should grow to one side. . . . In painting trees the space between them may be filled with

bamboo, which need not be done with too much precision. But if the trees are seen on a sunny day, then they should be matched with sunny bamboo. This means the bamboo leaves should all point upward.[56]

For him, painting of trees should reflect, as does his poetry, the seasons and the weather, as well as his own mood. His inscription on that same illustration reads:

> I once tied my boat near the cottage at Fu-li,
> Where the green river and white gulls stirred my melan-
>   choly thoughts.
> I shall remember the two trees on the south bank,
> How the blue-green bamboo clings, after rain, like morning
>   glories.[57]

Case Study: Dōgen's Self-Portrait as a Plum Tree

Dōgen (1200–1253), the incomparable Zen monk, abbot, philosopher, poet, innovator in food aesthetics, and one of the greatest minds the world has known, also wrote autobiographical poetry. In one of his "Verses of Praise on Portraits of Himself," we find:

> Old plum tree, old plum tree,
> A long time nurturing spring in every branch and leaf,
> The function of the immovable ground is clear in each
>   detail;
> The samādhi of adornment is in each and every dust.
> On top of the staff are no knots at all;
> On his sitting cushion is the body in ten directions. . . .
> Entering a tiger's cave,
> He laughed at words from the lips of Daxiu.
> A stubborn rock dwelling in the mountains,
> He's a senile old fool in the monastery.[58]

In comparing himself to an aged plum tree, Dōgen is summoning a botanical analogy and a powerful aesthetic image that would have been familiar to all his readers. But it is also a symbol for human life and wisdom that had been in use throughout East Asia for centuries. In these regards, the plum functions much like the equally familiar bamboo and pine tree. All three are esteemed for their ability to withstand hardship, to survive storms, and persevere in harsh environments; indeed, it is the interaction of pines and plums to their sometimes seemingly impossible living conditions that creates their interesting shapes of gnarled, twisted, and knotted branches—their beauty, their uniqueness—a quality that is immediately apparent to any viewer.

Commentators point out that " 'Knots' indicates both knots or knobs of branches and also sections, segments [of bamboo, for instance], categories, stages, junctions, or junctures. The staff without knots shows the oneness beyond discrimination of stages of Dōgen's teaching." The very feature that leads to the plum's unique and individual beauty, in a painting or in life, is here, in the person Dōgen cast aside: he has—as those who know his philosophical works such as Shōbōgenzō, can attest—transcended the usual human condition.

Beyond all this, however, is the choice of a plum. The similarities between plums and pines in life stories, including their resulting shapes and aesthetic appeal, are profound. As global culture reveals, the wonderful thing about pines, and the reason pines are cherished as Christmas trees, is that they are evergreen. It is even their vernacular name. They do not represent rebirth but resilient continuation because they stay greenly alive all year, no matter how bitter the cold.

Plums, by contrast, do not. From a temporal point of view, plums are at the opposite end of the scale. Keenly sensitive to the first indications of warmer weather and longer hours of sunlight, they are among the first flowers to emerge in the spring, often while snow is still on the ground. The shape of their branches has been determined through decades of living, but their blossoms are of the moment and what a moment to celebrate it is! Plums, furthermore, like orchids and vegetables, are celebrated for possessing the socially desirable "ineffable quality of understatement (p'ing-tan)," as Alfreda Murck delightfully puts it.[59]

We can see how the poem expresses Dōgen's sense not only of who he is but of how he fits into the larger scheme of things: his Zen lineage, the whole of nature, the entire universe or cosmos and thus also Buddhist teaching as a whole.[60] His self-abnegation in the final two lines, which is close to ironic, both provides biographical information and situates him cosmologically in the real physical world even as the metaphor of the rock undercuts the entire biological analogy he had developed until then.

Conclusion

There are many questions facing us in the Anthropocene as we destroy life on Earth faster than we can even report on it, much less document its demise. Michael Pollan, speaking of a maple tree he recently planted, calls it "a frail thing to burden with so much reflection."[61] Maybe so, but the East Asian tradition suggests it is our use of trees as metaphor, that is to say, solely as a function of language rather than as vital, existential components of our lived experience, that is a problem, that is the "frail thing," not the myriad strengths trees embody.

This chapter traces the ways many people, indeed whole subcultures, in East Asia understand trees as wise, using complex processes of representing trees in the arts to convey trees' capacities for witnessing, enduring, growing, flourishing, and providing for others. Wise trees, as we have seen, offer many benefits to human beings. They can inspire us. They can show us the good life and how to be ethical, connect with others, and live a long time. They provide models to emulate. They protect us—physically, from wind, rain, heat—and psychologically, offering a barrier against a world that can seem hostile. They offer ways to communicate the otherwise ineffable.

Because they manifest virtues that we need to cultivate and absorb, trees can serve as models to emulate, as beings whose simple presence can reassure us, comfort us, and make a better life possible for us, as they do for their animal and plant companions. As John Hay suggests, "It may be that the less we are able to attribute to trees, the more impoverished we become; it is a kind of deforestation of the spirit. They have a superhuman quality that cannot be diminished."[62] It seems that East Asian painting and poetry about trees have much to offer if we need to replenish the spirit.

It is clear we still have much to learn from trees. What that is, and whether we can manage to do it, remain open questions.

Notes

1. Aristotle famously illustrated his theory of the Four Causes by analyzing the development of acorns into trees. See Zachary Fruehling. www.zacharyfruhling.com/philosophy-blog/aristotle-acorns-and-oak-trees-on-stunted-growth-real-mentorship-and-how-to-cultivate-a-fully-developed-human-being#:~:text=The%20ancient%20Greek%20philosopher%20Aristotle,cultivation%2C%20nurturing%2C%20and%20environment

2. Diane Cook and Len Jenshel, *Wise Trees* (New York: Abrams, n.d. [after 2017]). See also Robin Lloyd, "Trees Have the Potential to Live Indefinitely," *Scientific American*, December 24, 2021. See also, for example, the State of Hawaii's legislation on Hawaii's "exceptional trees:" For the purposes of this section, "exceptional trees" means a tree or stand or grove of trees with historic or cultural value, or which by reason of its age, rarity, location, size, esthetic quality, or endemic status has been designated by the county committee as worthy of preservation. Exceptional trees may be designated generally by biotaxy or individually by location or class." www.capitol.hawaii.gov/slh/Years/SLH1975/SLH1975_Act105.pdf

3. Transliteration practices for Chinese changed in the 1970s–1980s; I use the recent spellings except in quotations that used the earlier ones, but in all cases, on first use, I offer the alternatives within parentheses.

4. Regarding Lucy's bone fractures, see Adam Hoffman, "Did a Fall From a Tree Kill Lucy, Our Famous Ancestor?" *National Geographic*, August 29, 2016, www.nationalgeographic.com/science/article/lucy-tree-fall-human-ancestor. Basic research on Lucy is cited in Caitlin M. Schrein, "Lucy: A Marvelous Specimen." *Nature Education Knowledge* 6, no. 7 (2015): 2. www.nature.com/scitable/knowledge/library/lucy-a-marvelous-specimen-135716086/#:~:text=Lucy%2C%20a%203.2%20million%2Dyear,in%201974%20in%20Hadar%2C%20Ethiopia.&text=The%20fossil%20locality%20at%20Hadar,288)

5. "The Three Natures" is the name of a model derived from a distinction proposed by Cicero and developed in the mid-1500s, Bartolomeo Taegio and Jacopo Bonfadio: "First Nature" is the wild; "Second Nature" is agriculture (and, for Hunt, urban developments); and "Third Nature" is The Garden. It has been used by garden theorist John Dixon Hunt in his *Greater Perfections: The Practice of Garden Theory* (London: Thames and Hudson, 2000), 30, and by philosopher David Fenner and horticulturalist Ethan Fenner in their book on the aesthetics of gardens and gardening. David Fenner and Ethan Fenner, *The Art and Philosophy of the Garden* (New York: Oxford University Press, 2024).

6. Sacred groves are found around the world; see *Encyclopedia.pub*, a peer-reviewed open-access "simple scholarly reference on scientific topics and concepts, https://handwiki.org/wiki/Religion:Sacred_grove. Also see: https://arboretum.harvard.edu/stories/eternal-forests-the-veneration-of-old-trees-in-japan

7. On Japanese forests, see Eric J. Cunningham, *The Unseen Forest: Spectacles of Nature and Governance in a Japanese National Forest, A Dissertation Submitted to . . . the University of Hawaii* . . . , December 2012; Glenn Moore and Cassandra Atherton, "Eternal Forests: The Veneration of Old Trees in Japan," *Arnoldia* 77, no. 4 (May 18, 2020). https://arboretum.harvard.edu/stories/eternal-forests-the-veneration-of-old-trees-in-japan; Yasuhiro Kotera, "Sacred Forests: The Ecological Power of Reverence," December 22, 2021; and Minakata Kumagusu, "*Chinju no mori*, or the sacred forests that surround Shinto shrines." www.nippon.com/en/column/g00415 and www.theearthandi.org/post/sacred-forests-the-ecological-power-of-reverence

8. Many episodes of *Soko Ga Japan*, such as that aired in Honolulu on KIKU TV Wednesday, November 9, 2022, feature sacred trees.

9. I. A. Richards, *Practical Criticism* (New York: Harcourt, Brace & World, Inc.), 91.

10. C. G. Jung, "On the Relation of Analytical Psychology to Poetry," from "*Über die Beziehungen der analytischen Psychologie zum dichterischen Kunstwerk*," *Seelenprobleme der Gegenwart* (from Zurich: Rascher, 1931) and "Psychology and Literature" (from "Psychologie und Dichtung," *Gestaltungen des Unbewussten*) (Zurich: Rascher, 1950), 76, ß118 and 76–77, ß119.

11. See the essays in J. Baird Callicott and Roger T. Ames, eds., *Nature in Asian Traditions of Thought: Essays in Environmental Philosophy* (Albany, NY: SUNY Press, 1989).

12. Quoted by Chu-tsing Li, *The Chinese Scholar's Studio: Artistic Life in the Late Ming Period: An Exhibition from the Shanghai Museum*, Chu-tsing Li, James C. Y. Watt, editors (New York: the Asia Society Galleries, published in association with Thames and Hudson, 1987), 20–21.

13. Fong, op cit., 116. The painting, from 1345, is his fig. 108.

14. This is in a detail of the painting ("Sitting by a Limpid Stream Composing Poems"). See Fong, op. cit., 136, figs. 123 and 123a.

15. On the relation of arts like poetry, painting, tea ceremony and calligraphy to spiritual development, see Robert E. Carter, *The Japanese Arts and Self-Cultivation* (Albany, NY: SUNY Press, 2008); and "The Moral Dimension of Japanese Aesthetics" (extensively revised version of the article previously published in *The Journal of Aesthetics and Art Criticism* [Winter 2007]) in *Re-Thinking Aesthetics: The Role of Body in Design*, ed. Ritu Bhatt (Routledge, 2013): 158–80.

16. Bamboo are grass, of course, not trees, but in East Asia they are seen as trees by most non-botanists due to their size, verticality, and single trunk with branches. Klinkenborg points up the similarity to ourselves as well: "The sense of kinship is real. Like trees, we are vertical and branching. We poke upward on the horizon. We breathe with them in a shared cycle." Klinkenborg, *Wise Trees*, 11.

17. Edwin T. Morris, *The Gardens of China: History, Art, and Meanings* (New York: Charles Scribner's Sons, 1983), 170.

18. Craig Clunas's *Fruitful Sites: Garden Culture in Ming Dynasty China* provides ground-breaking work not only on aesthetics and literary and cultural symbolism but on the practical and commercial products of these gardens (Durham, NC: Duke University Press, 1996).

19. John Hay, "The Autumn Trees," in *Old Growth* (Northampton, MA: *Orion* magazine, 2021), 89–93, on 92.

20. William Bryant Logan, "The Things Trees Know: A look inside their secret lives," in *Old Growth* (Northampton, MA. *Orion* magazine, 2021), 25–38, on 35. One of these processes is even known as "phoenix regeneration," 37. Also: Peter Wohlleben, *The Hidden Life of Trees: What They Feel, How They

Communicate—Discoveries from A Secret World (Greystone Books, 2015), David Suzuki Institute Book, 2016.

21. Poem by painter Shen Zhou (Shen Chou) on one of his paintings. Fong, op. cit., 149.

22. See Luke Fischer's essay in this book's section on "Language in Trees," "Speaking Trees: From the Language of Nature to Arboreal Communication," and Richard Grant, "Do Trees Talk to Each Other? A controversial German forester says yes, and his ideas are shaking up the scientific world," in *Smithsonian Magazine*, March 2018. www.smithsonianmag.com/science-nature/the-whispering-trees-180968084/#:~:text=Trees%20share%20water%20and%20nutrients,Scientists%20 call%20these%20mycorrhizal%20networks. Also: Richard Schiffman, "'Mother Trees' Are Intelligent: They Learn and Remember," *Scientific American*, May 4, 2021.

23. Op. cit., 89.

24. Op. cit., 89.

25. I distinguish the terms by following psychoanalyst Sigmund Freud and philosopher Alfred Schutz, where unconscious material is semi-deliberately obscured and accessible only indirectly, and preliminal is part of ordinary life that I choose not to attend to: the fact that I am thirsty while writing this, for example.

26. For reasons of space, I omit *understanding*, an intermediate step I propose between the original DIK and wisdom.

27. Peter Wohlleben, *The Hidden Life of Trees* (Greystone Books, 2015). For a more cautious view, see Stephanie Pappas, "Do Trees Really Support Each Other through a Network of Fungi?: Trees Communicate and Cooperate through a Fungal Web," *Scientific American*, February 13, 2023; and Kathryn Flinn, "The Idea That Trees Talk to Cooperate Is Misleading," *Scientific American*, July 19, 2021.

28. See notes 22 and 25.

29. Fong, 123. I disagree with him when he says it "offers no revelation of cosmic significance."

30. Richard Barnhart, *Along the Border of Heaven: Sung and Yuan Paintings from the C. C. Wang Family Collection*, New York: Metropolitan Museum of Art, 29–30.

31. Quoted in Fong, op. cit., 154.

32. In the Metropolitan Museum of Art, New York: www.metmuseum.org/TOAH/HD/yuan/ho_1973.120.6.htm

33. Barnhart, op. cit, 30, 33.

34. Fong, op. cit., 118.

35. Mara Miller, "Atomic/Nuclear Weapons and Energy Technologies (ANWETs): The Need for Wisdom," in *Practical Wisdom in the Age of Technology: Insights, Issues and Questions for a New Millennium*, Dalal, Ali Intezari, Marty Heitz, eds. (New York: Routledge and Gower, Publishing: Series: The Practical Wisdom in Leadership and Organization Series), 101–17. www.ashgate.com/default.aspx?page=638&series_id=622&calcTitle=1&forthcoming=1G

36. While our current American mindfulness and "wisdom" industry stresses being-in-the-*present*, wisdom requires keen sensitivity to the *kairos* of the different time-orientations: *is this* the time to be present, or to take action based on the future? The full set of Biblical examples reads:

To every thing there is a season, and a time to every purpose under the heaven:

> A time to be born, and a time to die; a time to plant, and a time to pluck up that which is planted;
> A time to kill, and a time to heal; a time to break down, and a time to build up;
> A time to weep, and a time to laugh; a time to mourn, and a time to dance;
> A time to cast away stones, and a time to gather stones together; a time to embrace, and a time to refrain from embracing;
> A time to get, and a time to lose; a time to keep, and a time to cast away;
> A time to rend, and a time to sew; a time to keep silence, and a time to speak;
> A time to love, and a time to hate; a time of war, and a time of peace.
> —*Ecclesiastes* 3: 108, King James version, from Bible Gateway, www.biblegateway.com/passage/?search=Ecclesiastes%203&version=KJV

37. Miller, op. cit., 102.
38. Miller, op. cit., 102.
39. Morris, op. cit., 170.
40. Verlyn Klinkenborg, Introduction, in *Wise Trees* (New York: Abrams, n.d. [after 2017], 9.
41. In my cat Sarashina, for instance—though definitely not in another of my cats, Kaji. I have witnessed two coyotes chasing food for and protecting their mate, who was injured.
42. Ronnie Littlejohn, "Daoist Philosophy," *The Internet Encyclopedia of Philosophy*, ISSN 2161-0002, https://iep.utm.edu/, 2.23.23. https://iep.utm.edu/daoismdaoist-philosophy/ It is less clear that other values such as "ordering life morally, practicing rulership, and regulating consciousness and diet" apply to trees.
43. Lao Tzu, *Tao-te Ching*, chapter 56, in Wing-Tsit Chan, *The Way of Lao Tzu (Tao-te ching), Translated, with introductory essays, comments, and notes by Wing-Tsit Chan* (Upper Saddle River, NJ: Prentice Hall, 1963), 199; https://terebess.hu/english/tao/chan.html adapted from Chapter Seven, "The Natural Way of Lao

Tzu," *A Source Book in Chinese Philosophy* (Princeton, NJ: Princeton University Press, 1963). https://terebess.hu/english/tao/chan.html

44. Hsing Yun, Venerable Master. *The Four Noble Truths: The Essence of Buddhism* (Fo Guang Shan International Translation Center, 2014), 28. www2.hawaii.edu/~donnab/religion/The%20-four-noble-truths_by_Fo_Guang_Shan_Temple_Master_Hsing_Yun.pdf

45. They are found in every source on Buddhism; here they are from Hsing Yun, op. cit., 1.

46. *Anthology of Chinese Literature, Volume I: From Early Times to the Fourteenth Century*, edited by Cyril Birch (New York: Grove Press, 1965), 167–68. ©1965 Grove Press.

Countless paintings and now videos of this legend are available. http://afe.easia.columbia.edu/ps/china/taoqian_peachblossom.pdf

47. Lu Guimeng (also transliterated Lu Kuei-meng), "Preface to a Eulogy on a Grotesque Pine," quoted in T. C. Lai, *Noble Fragrance: Chinese Flowers and Trees* (Kowloon and Hong Kong: Swindon Books, 1977 or 1985), 7–9.

48. Quoted by Wen C. Fong, in Wen C. Fong, Alfreda Murck, Shou-chien Shih, Pao-chen Ch'en, and Jan Stuart, *Images of the Mind: Selections from the Edward L. Elliott Famly and John B. Elliott Collections of Chinese Calligraphy and Painting at The Art Museum, Princeton University*. The Art Museum, Princeton University, 1984, 116.

49. Fong, op. cit., 113–14, 116. Calligraphy and painting are shown in fig. 108, p. 114.

50. See for example Gakuo's ink painting of Water-Moon Kannon (Bodhisattva Avalokiteshvara), framed by bamboo in the Cleveland Museum of Art, in Michael R. Cunningham, Stanislaw J. Czuma, Anne E. Wardwell, and J. Keith Wilson, *Masterworks of Asian Art* (Cleveland: Cleveland Museum of Art in association with Thames and Hudson, 1998).

51. Morris, op. cit., 170.

52. Quoted by Chu-tsing Li, *The Chinese Scholar's Studio: Artistic Life in the Late Ming Period: An Exhibition from the Shanghai Museum*, Chu-tsing Li and James C. Y. Watt, eds. (New York: the Asia Society Galleries, published in association with Thames and Hudson, 1987), 20–21.

53. This Daoist/Confucianist recognition of the spiritual power of art seen here is not entirely dissimilar to that expressed in the Lotus Sutra of Mahayana Buddhism, where making a Buddhist work of art, by copying the sutra, shaping a Buddha statue in the sand, or painting a Buddha, contributes to one's journey to Enlightenment.

54. Quoted by Chu-tsing Li, op. cit., 21.

55. Morris, op. cit., 170. There are good reasons for this connection between an ability to paint and the (emotional and literal physical) heart: the technology

of ink painting. The ink renders correction impossible, while the suppleness of the brush reveals the slightest hesitation or tremor.

56. Fong, op. cit., 117–21 (fig. 111–13), translated from National Palace Museum, Taipei, comp. *Ku-kung shu-hua lu (A Descriptive Catalogue of the Painting and Calligraphy in the National Palace Museum*, Vol. 3 (Taipei: National Palace Museum, 1965), 20–21.

57. Fong, op. cit., 118; illustrated with the trees in his figs. 111 and 113.

58. *Dogen's Extensive Record: A Translation of the Eihei Kohroku*, translated by Taigen Dan Leighton and Shohaku Okumura, from which these poems are taken (Somerville, MA: Wisdom Publications, 2004), 601.

59. Alfreda Murck, "Paintings of Stem Lettuce, Cabbage, and Weeds: Allusions to Tu Fu's Garden," *Archives of Asian Art*, XLVIII (1995), 32–47.

60. "'The body in ten directions,'" the commentators tell us, "is short for 'the entire world in ten directions is the true human body,'" a principle Dōgen both discusses philosophically and astonishingly is able to make the set of relationships visually and linguistically evident by means of his choice of characters and their arrangement, in *Shōbōgenzō* and elsewhere.

61. Michael Pollan, "Norway Maple: Trees as Metaphor," in *Old Growth* (Northampton, MA: *Orion* magazine, 2021), 171

62. Hay, op. cit., 92.

Legal and Political Trees

Figure I.8. Eucalyptus, El Cerrito, California. *Source*: Photo by Laura Pustarfi.

Interstice

Eucalyptus

> Trees is soul people to me, maybe not to other people, but I have watched the trees when they pray, and I've watched them shout and sometimes they give thanks slowly and quietly.
>
> —Bessie Harvey, in *Black Art, Ancestral Legacy*

> Municipal gum, it is dolorous
> To see you thus
> Set in your black grass of bitumen—
> O fellow citizen,
> What have they done to us?
>
> —Oodgeroo Noonuccal, *Municipal Gum*

Eucalyptus trees are invited invaders. They were brought to California during the gold rush from Australia with the hope they would provide a fast-growing resource that could be used either ornamentally or as timber for furniture and construction. On the west coast, however, they have tended to spread widely and to become twisted tough wood when dried—thus undermining their economic value—though they function well as windbreaks on farms and along highways. They also typically take over surrounding soil, turning it acidic, which then makes it more difficult for other plants to survive and flourish. Eucalyptus generates a brusque crunch underfoot, and their dry yet pliable leaves and pod-like seeds can pierce even the most resilient shoes. Their pungent scent might capture or even accost one's senses on a woodland walk.

The tree in the adjacent photo is a Blue Gum Eucalyptus (*Eucalyptus globulus*), which is native to southern Australia, where they are used to make dyes, pulpwood, and didgeridoos, an Aboriginal wood instrument.

A fresh-fallen leaf from this tree might serve as a kind of fancy feather should you desire one for your hat. These trees, however, have usurped land once occupied by native California plants and animals, thus posing a challenge to local biodiversity. Currently, such areas hold wild stands of eucalyptus between the residing oaks, redwoods, and pines. Although the trees are presently cultivated, there are now arguably fewer reasons for them to remain or proliferate other than the fact they have become a noticeable part of the existing landscape. Fierce battles have been fought in northern California over their continued presence and their apparent threat to native tree and animal species, along with their high susceptibility to fire.

Trees like the eucalyptus bring to the fore legal and political questions concerning the proper relationships and best affiliations between the arboreal world and human society. Intertwined with ethical considerations like those raised in the previous section of this book are matters involving how trees move about and root themselves with human assistance in an increasingly globalized and border-permeable world, as well as concerns about their contested existence within intersecting human social and political spheres. Should non-native species be protected even if some might be considered "useless," as Sam Mickey proposes in the next section, following the Chinese Daoist philosopher Zhuangzi? And how might issues tied to arboreal personhood impact such debates over the composition and control of wooded lands, a topic Eric Orts explores in his chapter. These controversies highlight at the broadest level our complex connections to trees and forests.

—Laura Pustarfi

14

Philosophers with a Peculiarly Instructive Aversions toward Trees

SAM MICKEY

In an age of ecological destruction and mass extinction, what would a philosopher have to say to a tree? According to Erazim Kohák, "the first thing a philosopher says to a tree is 'Sorry.'"[1] That expression of remorse is based on a "shocked recognition"—the recognition that nonhuman existence has more vitality and value than has been assumed throughout the predominantly anthropocentric history of philosophy, and the shock that philosophy is complicit in "the ruthless devastation of nature" and "the agony of our nonhuman kin."[2] Kohák is talking about philosophy in its European and Anglo-American expressions, so-called Western philosophy. He is not referring to Indigenous philosophy or Buddhist philosophy or other philosophies for which anthropocentrism is less common. A cursory glance at major figures in Western philosophy seems to support Kohák's statement.

Whether it was done intentionally or not, philosophers have built and maintained ideological support systems for arboreal destruction, giving credence to motivations and justifications for treating trees as mere objects, as resources to be used, or as a passive background against which human affairs take place. However, this is not the whole story. It is also the case that thinkers in this philosophical tradition have provided means for resisting and transforming those ideological support systems. Indeed, sometimes a philosopher will do both at the same time: supporting *and* undermining the chauvinistic promotion of human interests over trees. To show how that works, this chapter covers a few ostensibly egregious examples of philosophers who express an aversion toward trees: Socrates talking about trees as if they have nothing to teach him; Jean-Paul Sartre writing of a chestnut tree that embodies the nauseating absurdity of existence; and Gilles Deleuze and Félix Guattari expressing weariness of trees, as if trees have received far too much conceptual attention and should now be replaced by another botanical paradigm, the rhizome. These thinkers are not anthropocentric, or at least not simply so, but they clearly express an aversion to trees, a sort of "arborophobia," to adopt a term from Canadian poet Nancy Holmes.[3]

If philosophical ideas can be sufficiently ambiguous as to be capable of undermining what they support, perhaps philosophical arborophobia could be capable of somehow undermining ways of thinking that are denigrating and destructive to trees. Perhaps thinking of trees as useless can, in a certain sense, become a way of protecting trees from overuse and abuse, undermining any inclination to think of trees primarily or exclusively as usable objects. Maybe considering trees as useless is not something for which philosophers must apologize. To explore this possibility, more is needed than a critique of arborophobia. A great abundance of critiques show how philosophers have been complicit in devaluing the natural world, including the objectification, instrumentalization, and backgrounding of trees and other nonhumans. Valid though the critiques may be, there remains the task of branching out to make new connections. You could call this postcritical thinking, as in the "second naïveté" or "second faith" to which Paul Ricoeur refers, designating an interpretive stance informed by critique (the hermeneutics of suspicion) but not limited to it: "The contrary of suspicion, I will say bluntly, is faith. [. . .] the second faith of one who has engaged in hermeneutics, faith that has undergone criticism, postcritical faith."[4]

The term "postcritical" originated with Michael Polanyi, for whom "the critical framework" has "burnt away," and our task now is "to restore the balance of our cognitive powers," including beliefs, tacit knowledge, "intellectual passions, the sharing of an idiom and of a cultural heritage, affiliation to a like-minded community."[5] Postcritical interpretation directs attention away from many reading strategies that have become standard among scholars. Rita Felski gives a list of what postcritical thinking does *not* do: "subject a text to interrogation; diagnose its hidden anxieties;

demote recognition to yet another form of misrecognition; lament our incarceration in the prison-house of language; demonstrate that resistance is just another form of containment; read a text as a metacommentary on the undecidability of meaning; score points by showing that its categories are socially constructed; brood over the gap that separates word from world."[6] Felski defines the task of postcritical thinking this way: "Interpretation becomes a coproduction between actors that brings new things to light rather than an endless rumination on a text's hidden meanings or representational failures."[7]

Focusing less on failures and more on illuminative coproduction, postcritical thinking stands against "purity politics," which "attempts to meet and control a complex situation that is fundamentally outside our control," shutting down "the field of possibility that might allow us to take better collective action against the destruction of the world in all its strange, delightful, impure frolic."[8] Purity politics is "a de-collectivizing, de-mobilizing, paradoxical politics of despair."[9] Always pointing out the ecological failures of philosophers is simply disempowering. Never moving beyond critique, theory grows cynical, as Peter Sloterdijk observes in his *Critique of Cynical Reason*, where he proposes a more life-affirming sensibility: cheekiness. That which is "cheeky" (*frech*) is not just naughty, irreverent, amusing, or insolent, but more fundamentally, it is "brave, bold, lively, plucky, untamed, ardent."[10] Cheeky theory is an impure, strange, delightful frolic.

The term "postcritical" can be confusing and misleading, as are so many words with a prefix that has gone postal (e.g., postmodernism, postcolonialism, and poststructuralism). Erecting a post in front of critique seems too divisive, too antagonistic toward critique. What would be something more lively, plucky, and strangely delightful? It would be something conducive to connection and coproduction, something closer to a "poetics of relation," to use Édouard Glissant's phrase. A poetics of relation is not "expressed through a procession of trajectories, itineraries succeeding or thwarting one another, but explodes by itself and within itself, like a network, inscribed in the self-sufficient totality of the world."[11]

When speaking about trees and to trees, a tree-shaped way of speaking would seem fitting for a poetics of relation. Postcritique can give way to what Hannah Cooper-Smithson calls "arboromorphic poetics," wherein "boundaries become hedgerows—spaces of relation, innovation, and growth."[12] Creativity and critique are not in opposition. Rather, "critical writing is creative; creativity is critical."[13] Arboromophic poetics builds networks, rooting and branching, even with philosophers who seem averse to arboreal existence. Trees might not need an apology, *pace* Kohák. Maybe carefully crafted connections matter more, even those born of disinterest, dislike, or disgust. Could there be something about the aversions toward trees in Socrates, Sartre, and Deleuze/Guattari that points toward a deeper affinity? That affinity would be strange and unexpected, making a philosophical dislike of trees appear as a way of protecting trees. Furthermore, it would be particular to these philosophers, not generalizable to an affinity hidden in all negative statements about trees. In other words, if these seemingly arborophobic philosophers have a creative connection with trees, that would be peculiar in both senses of the word: strange and particular.

For an arboromorphic poetics, even philosophers who appear hostile to trees can express an affinity for trees. It depends how everything mixes together, as in Emanuele Coccia's metaphysical exploration of the ways trees and other kinds of plants make shared atmospheres—times and spaces of mixture—through which life creates environments that mix in atmospheric conditions that support more life, "as though being in the world meant above all to 'make atmosphere.'"[14] Rationality comes not from cynicism or from separation and dissociation but from the dynamics of mixing. "Rationality is a matter of forms, but form is always the result of the movement of a mixture that produces variation, change."[15] With this sense of rationality, the point is not to critique Socrates, Sartre, and Deleuze/Guattari for their aversions toward trees. The point is to seek out arboromorphic mixtures they might have propagated.

A Tree with Nothing to Teach

Consider what Socrates says in Plato's *Phaedrus*. The dialogue opens with Socrates asking Phaedrus whither he is coming and going. Phaedrus answers that he is going to take a walk outside the city, following the advice of Lysias, with whom Phaedrus had been conversing in the city prior to seeing Socrates. Socrates asks what they were conversing about, and Phaedrus says that he will share a speech that Lysias gave, but only if Socrates comes along for this walk, to which Socrates assents. On their walk, Socrates realizes Phaedrus is hiding a scroll under his cloak with "the actual discourse" [*ton logon auton*] written on it, so Socrates suggests they look for somewhere to sit so Phaedrus can read the speech to him, and

Phaedrus points out a "very tall plane tree" in the distance, suggesting it as a suitably shady and grassy spot for them.[16] They proceed to walk there.

Different species of plane trees can be found throughout the northern hemisphere. In North America, the American sycamore (*Platanus occidentalis*) is a common example. It has broad leaves and can grow up to twenty to thirty meters tall. It is a good shade tree, as Phaedrus observes. Plato's choice of this tree species—a plane tree, not an oak, fir, or other shade tree—is perhaps not incidental. The term "plane tree" (*platanon*) derives from the Greek word *platus*, in reference to the "broad" leaves of this type of tree. *Platus* is also the etymological root of the name Plato (*Platon*), which was supposedly given to him because of his broad chest and shoulders. The plane tree, like Plato's writings, is the site of a philosophical question about the difference between speech and writing.

When they arrive at the tree, Socrates remarks on how delightful the place is, even noticing that it is a sacred place, appreciatively telling Phaedrus that he has "guided the stranger most excellently" (230c). Phaedrus says Socrates is indeed like a stranger when he's in the country, observing that Socrates seems to never go outside the city walls. Socrates offers this explanation: "You see, I am fond of learning [*philomathes*]. Now the country places [*khoria*] and the trees [*dendra*] won't teach me anything, and the people [*anthropoi*] in the city do. But you seem to have found the charm [*pharmakon*] to bring me out" (230d). Trees and country places are too far from the presence of people and their speech (*logos*) for it to be of any use for Socrates in his love of learning. Learning requires dialogue, so he stays in the city, unless he is drawn out by the right *pharmakon*—a word with many meanings, including "drug," "charm," "medicine," and "poison." The *pharmakon* that brought Socrates out to *khoria* and *dendra* is a written speech, a substitute for the speech that Phaedrus heard directly from Lysias. This association between drugs (*pharmaka*), places (*khoria*), and writing illuminates Socrates' attitude toward trees (*dendra*).

In short, Socrates says three things: (1) he learns only from people, (2) places and trees won't teach him anything, and (3) he is spending time in the country only because Phaedrus drugged him with scrolls. That sounds anthropocentric, but this focus on humanity is due to a deeper commitment, centered on speech (*logos*). Plato's dialogues favor the presence of *logos* in conversations over its absent and ambiguous appearances in trees, places, drugs, and writing. Plato is indeed logocentric, to use Derrida's sense of the word, which David Gunkel defines succinctly: "A way of thinking about thinking and language that gives central importance to the spoken word as the first signifier—'first' in terms of both sequence and status—and thereby differentiating it from writing, which, by comparison to speech, is a secondary and derived representation or image. For Derrida, this way of thinking defines an entire epoch that others have called '(Western) metaphysics.'"[17] Speech involves pure, self-sufficient, unambiguous presence, whereas writing is a *pharmakon*—an ambiguous substance that is both cure and poison. Writing can cure a deficiency in memory, but it can also facilitate dependency and thus poison one's ability to remember. With ambiguity and dependency, writing is a drug tainting the self-sufficient presence sought in Plato's dialogues and throughout the history of Western metaphysics.[18] Yet, those dialogues and that history would not exist without writing.

Writing simultaneously undermines logocentrism while rendering its history possible. *Khora* ("place") functions similarly. Figuring prominently in the cosmology of Plato's *Timaeus*, *khora* is an undulating openness, a dynamic spacing within which ideal forms are imprinted onto the material world. *Khora* shakes up the form/matter binary while also making room for it. It resembles chaos. Derrida cautions against associating chaos with *khora* because chaos is often viewed negatively as destructive and terrifying. Identifying chaos with *khora* imposes "the anthropomorphic form and the pathos of fright."[19] *Khora* is chaotic but not like an undifferentiated abyss that must be controlled and dominated to maintain order. Chaos is not opposed to the order of the cosmos but is the openness necessary to keep the cosmos moving and changing. That resembles chaos theory, where chaos refers to dissipative systems. Far from equilibrium, they generate pattern and order. As Ilya Prigogine and Isabelle Stengers say in their groundbreaking work on this topic, chaotic "fluctuations and changes at the local levels of a system" generate "its instability and complexity but, importantly, also guarantee its order and regularity at the macrolevel."[20]

The *Phaedrus* brings all these figures into one scene with the plane tree. It is through the *pharmakon* of writing that Socrates is brought out to *khoria* and *dendra*. Useless for learning because lacking in *logos*, the plane tree clearly connects to *khora*, the *pharmakon*, writing, and perhaps even the broad-shouldered writer himself, *Platon*. The point here is not to unmask the systems of oppression at work in logocentrism, which establishes hierarchies that prioritize mind over body, humans over nonhumans, reason over emotion, and masculine over feminine. The point is not to reject Plato or Western metaphysics. Derrida is often mistaken for rejecting Platonism and rejecting metaphysics. He clearly states otherwise. "I have insisted again and again that I am not rejecting metaphysics. I do not 'reject' metaphysics. Not even Platonism. Indeed, I think there is an unavoidable necessity of re-constituting a certain Platonic gesture."[21] The task of metaphysics is never finished, never rid of supplements, differences, absences, ambiguities, and uncertainties, but that does not mean metaphysics and its concomitant hierarchies are bad or something that should or could be avoided. Rather, it means that metaphysical commitments are provisional and open-ended, amendable, able to be criticized, and more importantly, transformed.

What, then, of Socrates finding trees useless for learning? He is expressing logocentrism, which entails a speech/writing hierarchy that correlates with other binary oppositions, like identity/difference, presence/absence, citizen/stranger, culture/nature, human/nonhuman, masculine/feminine, and so on. His logocentrism sounds arborophobic. Uncomfortable being outside the city, and unwilling or unable to learn from trees, Socrates expresses an anxiety about the place of trees in philosophy. However, to simply unmask the anxieties in a text would be an exercise in critique. If the text is read from the perspective of arboromorphic poetics, there is something instructive about Socrates' aversion to trees. Socrates is situating trees among figures like *khora*, *pharmakon*, and writing, destabilizing while also structuring the limits of his love of *logos*. Perhaps Socrates is acknowledging the limits of metaphysics, letting trees be, not forcing them to speak, not attempting to gain direct access to them, not dominating or exploiting them. Is Socrates safeguarding trees from assimilation into human evaluations and rationalizations? Perhaps the first thing a philosopher says to a tree is, "You do not have to play into a teacher/student hierarchy with me or engage me in dialogue," or more simply, "You can just exist," or more simply still, "You exist." To offer a tree an apology (*apologia*), regardless of how noble its admission of distress and regret, is still placing the tree into a logocentric frame rather than branching out into an existential affirmation.

An Absurd Tree

Another philosopher who might say "You exist" to a tree is Sartre, specifically considering his 1938 novel *Nausea*, where the absurd superfluousness of existence is disclosed to the main character (Antoine Roquentin) through an encounter with a chestnut tree. Chestnut trees are deciduous trees highly valued for their fruit (chestnuts) and wood, but the chestnut tree in this novel resists all words and classifications, occasioning an existential epiphany. Although the emotional valence of this encounter is deeply negative, the absurdity of the tree can be read as a protective gesture, like Socrates' dismissal of any tree teachings. These trees are off limits from human appraisals, evaluations, and rationalizations.

Roquentin is an academic, a historian to be precise, and throughout the novel he is clearly going through an existential crisis. As he puts it, "I exist, that's all. And that trouble is so vague, so metaphysical that I am ashamed of it."[22] The existence of things disgusts him in a weird way, provoking the titular nausea, which he describes as a "sweetish sickness" when reflecting on the feeling of a pebble in his hands.[23] The nausea intensifies throughout the book, as he continues having anxious responses to things, culminating in the revelation of a chestnut tree while he is sitting on a bench in a park, when "suddenly, suddenly, the veil is torn away."[24] At this point, the nausea has become so ubiquitous that he identifies with it. "I no longer have to bear it, it is no longer an illness or a passing fit: it is I."[25] Words and reference points fall away, as Roquentin is frightened, "alone in front of this black, knotty mass, entirely beastly."[26]

This arborophobia opens onto a vision of existence. The sheer existence of the tree appears *de trop*, translated as *"In the way."*[27] While not inappropriate, much is missed in that translation. *De trop* literally means "too much," connoting that which is superfluous, excessive, extra, unnecessary, and useless. It is absurd, as Roquentin observes: "The word absurdity is coming to life under my pen."[28] Shortly before the encounter with the chestnut tree, he noted his own superfluousness, saying "my place is nowhere; I am unwanted, *de trop*," but now this exorbitant absurdity overflows the boundary between self and world. Roquentin becomes the tree. "I *was* the root of the chestnut tree," he realizes.[29] This absurdity "was there on the trunk of the chestnut tree . . . it was *the* chestnut tree."[30]

> We were a heap of living creatures, irritated, embarrassed at ourselves, we hadn't the slightest reason to be there, none of us, each one, confused, vaguely alarmed, felt in the way in relation to the others. *In the way*: it was the only relationship I could establish between these trees, these gates, these stones. [. . .] And I—soft, weak, obscene, digesting, juggling with dismal thoughts—I, too, was *In the way*. [. . .] *In the way*: I was *In the way* for eternity.[31]

To say that a being is *de trop* is to say that it is irreducible, underivable from any other being: "things are entirely what they appear to be—and behind them . . . there is nothing" (96, *Nausea*). The idea of being *de trop* for eternity is not just something Roquentin thinks. It is a core concept in Sartre's famous work of phenomenological ontology, *Being and Nothingness*, published about five years after *Nausea*. "Being-in-itself is never either possible or impossible. It *is*. This is what consciousness expresses in anthropomorphic terms by saying that being is superfluous (*de trop*)—that is, that consciousness absolutely can not derive being from anything, either from another being, or from a possibility, or from a necessary law. Uncreated, without reason for being, without any connection with another being, being-in-itself is *de trop* for eternity."[32] Just as the absurdity of the chestnut tree dissolves the boundary between Roquentin and the tree, so does superfluousness overflow the boundary between being (the in-itself) and the nothingness of consciousness (the for-itself). "Just as my nihilating freedom is apprehended in anguish, so the for-itself is conscious of its facticity. It has the feeling of its complete gratuity; it apprehends itself as being there for nothing, as being *de trop*."[33]

Even more so than Plato's writing about Socrates and the plane tree, Sartre's writing about Roquentin and the chestnut tree seems blatantly arborophobic, on one hand, while also exemplifying arboromorphic poetics, on the other. The chestnut tree is frightening, absurd, and useless, which sounds quite bad from a critical perspective. For a relational poetics it sounds weirdly tactful, expressing a terrifying encounter whereby absurdity becomes a conduit for connecting with the tree while leaving the tree intact—untouched and unbothered by vacillations of rational inquiry. Leaving trees be—without *logos*, without reason, without usefulness—is a way of connecting with them by affirming their irreducibility. It requires resisting the urge to make trees useful to philosophical rumination or useful to anything or anyone at all.

Tiresome Trees

Could it be the case that including trees in thought and theory precludes a poetics of relation, inhibiting the formation of diverse and complex connections across boundaries? What if tree theory severely restricts creative, diverse modes of engagement with trees? Deleuze and Guattari suggest something along these lines with their declaration, "We're tired of trees. We should stop believing in trees, roots, and radicles. They've made us suffer too much."[34] They see trees as the epitome of hierarchy, exemplifying a clear distinction between top and bottom, in contrast to the gnarly complexity of rhizomes, which grow horizontally and send out roots and shoots from their nodes. Examples include ginger, bamboo, irises, and violets, which are all similar tubers (e.g., potatoes) and bulbs (e.g., garlic and onions). They grow variously below ground, above ground, or on the surface, non-hierarchically crossing above with below and horizontal with vertical.

Deleuze and Guattari are not upset about actual trees. Trees are an abstract analogue for hierarchies, and they can be found everywhere: a corporation, a monarchy, a pyramid scheme, a family, an evolutionary process, and many other places. The sentence trees of linguistics are a clear example, where everything contained in the subject and predicate of a sentence is superseded by the syntactical rules of the sentence, represented by an S symbol. Deleuze and Guattari are weary of "Chomsky's grammaticality, the categorical S symbol that dominates every sentence."[35] In contrast to Chomsky's generative syntax, Deleuze and Guattari sound closer to the generative semantics of George Lakoff, for whom language is not a hierarchical system dominated by syntactical rules. With generative semantics, it is not that there are no diagrams of sentences. There are sentence trees, but they are exceedingly naughty, extending to and through many levels of meaning, making diagrams messier and more provisional.[36]

For generative syntax, language is determined not by rules governing sentence structure, but by meaning, which is intrinsically metaphorical. Mapping domains of meaning onto one another (e.g., time is money; love is a journey), metaphor is conjunctive articulation. This is how the rhizome operates for Deleuze and Guattari, through "a logic of the AND": "the rhizome is the conjunction, 'and . . . and . . . and . . . 'This conjunction carries enough force to shake and uproot the verb 'to be.'"[37] More than a matter of linguistics, the rhizome gets to the very root of metaphysics, undermining the priority of Being, subordinating "is" to "and," extending outside Being to interbeing. Deleuze elaborates on this point in his dialogue with Claire Parnet.

> The whole of grammar, the whole of syllogism, is a way of maintaining the subordination of conjunctions to the verb to be, of making them gravitate around the verb to be. One

must go further: one must make the encounter with relations penetrate and corrupt everything, undermine being, make it topple over. Substitute AND for IS. A *and* B. The And is not even a specific relation or conjunction, it is that which subtends all relations, the path of all relations, which makes relations shoot outside their terms and outside the set of their terms, and outside everything which could be determined as Being, One, or Whole. The AND as extra-being, inter-being.[38]

Deleuze and Guattari want to connect the unambiguous linearity of arborescent systems back into the dynamics of complex systems. In other words, they are replacing dualistic systems with nondualistic systems, which of course ends up in another dualism, that between dualism and nondualism. They realize that their nondualistic rhizome can easily become "a new or different dualism."[39] Indeed, it is inevitable, as Derrida said of the inevitability of repeating the Platonic gesture of positing binary oppositions and prioritizing one term over another. As with Derrida, Deleuze and Guattari seek ways that binaries undermine themselves, uprooting their own foundation. "We invoke one dualism only in order to challenge another," proposing a model "that challenges all models" while realizing that dualisms and hierarchies are "the furniture we are forever rearranging."[40]

Binaries happen, but some binaries are preferable to others. Even though the rhizome is opposed to trees, it is positioned that way to challenge all dualisms, all models, including any philosophical, economic, or legal model that would devalue or degrade arboreal existence. The rhizomatic aversion to trees ends up undoing the very rhizome/tree opposition it supposes. Hierarchical and non-hierarchical dynamics enter into conjunctive relationships, becoming mutually immanent. "There are knots of arborescence in rhizomes and rhizomatic offshoots in roots." With this mutual immanence in mind, what initially seems like an arborophobic statement, "We're tired of trees," can better be engaged as a performance of arboromorphic poetics. Deleuze and Guattari use negativity to challenge negativity. They play with aversion as a way of branching out, challenging thinking to make creative connections. Indeed, Cooper-Smithson invokes the rhizome in her description of arboromorphic poetics. "Form is entangled, nonlinear, rhizomatic," as "we dig for interdisciplinary connections across all species of written matter. Textual relationships are grafted, planted, tended, grown."[41]

Useless Trees

Socrates' plane tree, Sartre's chestnut tree, and the tiresome trees of Deleuze/Guattari have something in common. They are presented negatively, particularly in a way that can be framed in terms of uselessness: useless for learning, existentially useless (*de trop*), and useless for creatively conjunctive rhizomes. Yet, what seems like sheer negativity leads toward creative connections. Useless trees become strangely useful. They become rhizomes, growing across and outside the limits of language and metaphysical hierarchy. Deleuze and Guattari call this the "wisdom of the plants: even when they have roots, there is always an outside where they form a rhizome with something else—with the wind, an animal, human beings."[42] That outside is the place of the AND, where Being is uprooted. That uprooting does not simply negate Being. It exposes it to connectivity, inter-being, without which no events could occur at all. What looks like the negation or disappearance of logocentric truth (the presence of Being) also opens a space of that truth to appear. Derrida puts it this way: "The disappearance of truth as presence, the concealment of the present origin of presence is the condition of any (manifestation of) truth."[43]

The aversions that Socrates, Sartre, and Deleuze/Guattari express about trees point toward a background condition for any manifestation of arboreal truth. However strange, nauseating, or tiresome it may be, the exorbitant superfluousness of trees renders philosophical reflections on trees possible. It is their uselessness that makes them useful. Along these lines, what looks like a branch of philosophical arborophobia in Western philosophy can be productively juxtaposed with the ancient Chinese philosopher, Zhuang Zhou, commonly known as Zhuangzi, which is also the name of a principal text of Daoism attributed to him. In the opening chapter, Zhuangzi converses with a philosopher named Huizi, talking about an old oak tree. Huizi says the tree's trunk "is too gnarled and bumpy to apply a measuring line to, its branches too bent and twisty to match up to a compass or square. You could stand it by the road, and no carpenter would look at it twice. Your words, too, are big and useless, and so everyone alike spurns them."[44] Zhuangzi responds: "Now you have this big tree, and you're distressed because it's useless. Why don't you [. . .] relax and do nothing by its side, or lie down for a free and easy sleep under it? Axes will never shorten its life, nothing can ever harm it. If there's no use for it, how can it come to grief or pain?"[45]

Uselessness protects the oak tree. Furthermore, the useless is not only protective. It is the very ground of the usefulness of trees and of the whole earth, as Zhuangzi points out:

> "A man has to understand the useless before you can talk to him about the useful. The earth is certainly vast and broad, though a man uses no more of it than the area he puts his feet on. If, however, you were to dig away all the earth from around his feet until you reached the Yellow Springs, then would the man still be able to make use of it?"
> "No, it would be useless," said Huizi.
> "It is obvious, then," said Zhuangzi, "that the useless has its use."[46]

Uselessness maintains sustainability and renewability. Uselessness here is not simply the opposite of use. It is outside of use because it is its regenerative, relational ground. It is an "efficacious uselessness."[47] This uselessness does not indicate a lack of potential for use or value. It is a productivity that exceeds use. It is out-of-order or out-of-use, beyond use yet not reducible to the useless as opposed to useful.

This generative uselessness resembles what Sara Ahmed calls "queer use," whereby something that is out-of-use can be reused, find a new use, or find a new user who was not intended to use it, like when an out-of-use mailbox becomes a nest for birds.[48] Queer use finds potentials lingering in the background, waiting to be seen, heard, released from what is given. "To queer use is to make use audible, to listen to use, to bring to the front what ordinarily recedes into the background," what ordinarily seems unordinary, improper, or a waste of time.[49] One can detect rhizomatic resonances as Ahmed describes how queer use can lead to an outside, to "the creation of an exit point, opening a door to allow something to escape, can lead to more and more coming out."[50] Queer use is conjunctive creativity, opening use to greater variety of possibilities: "it is collective and creative work; it is diversity work."[51] As diversity work, queer use can be thought of as what the process-relational philosopher Erin Manning calls an "ethos of a pragmatics of the useless," where that which is useless according to dominant norms—notably, whiteness and neurotypicality—becomes a site for the creation of novel values outside the scope of anything given, anything known, anything substantive.[52]

A pragmatics of the useless is about collective, creative work to facilitate a greater abundance and diversity of values. Talking about the pragmatic use of the useless might sound annoyingly paradoxical, but there is a reason for that. As artist and writer Jenny Odell puts it in her reflection on Zhuangzi's use of the useless tree, "it's not a paradox for the sake of being a paradox: rather, it's merely an observation of a social world that is itself a paradox, defined by hypocrisy, ignorance, and illogic," such that "a man attempting a humble and ethical life would certainly appear 'backward': for him, good would be bad, up would be down, productivity would be destruction, and indeed, uselessness would be useful."[53] This paradox is expressed in the ironic title of Odell's book. In an overactive society of destructive economic growth, "a plan of action" bears the title "How to Do Nothing."[54]

For Odell, the useless oak tree represents "resistance-in-place"—forming oneself into "a shape that cannot so easily be appropriated by a capitalist value system."[55] She is specifically interested in political resistance to the attention economy, where attention to digital information and virtual worlds becomes a commodity, the value of which is measured in things like clicks, views, retweets, likes, and follows. Along with political resistance, there are two other aspects of doing nothing: contemplative and ecological. The contemplative side involves reclaiming attention in a way that lets go of ossified habits and opens to more receptive relationships with one's thoughts, feelings, and actions. Contemplative practices are not about attaining some sort of virtuosity. They are described more accurately as practices for letting go, releasing habits, resembling "an *unlearning* rather than a learning."[56] Perhaps Socrates has nothing to learn from trees because he is unlearning with them.

The ecological side of doing nothing is about recuperating creative relationships with one's nonhuman neighbors and kin. Talking about trees as if they are tiresome, nauseating, and useless for learning can be a way of doing nothing with trees: contemplating the inexplicable mystery of their existence, building ecological intimacy with trees through nonverbal (non-logocentric) contact, and resisting the assimilation of trees into the horizons of utility, commodification, and progress. This entails resisting all forms of instrumentalization that reduce trees to objects of human use. It entails resistance to logocentrism and the various hierarchies involved with the history of metaphysics, even including hierarchies that seek to honor intrinsic value over instrumental value. For a pragmatics of useless trees, even the most well-intentioned and well-formed hierarchies should be treated as provisional, calling for ongoing dismantling and repurposing to foster a greater abundance and diversity of arboreal relationships.

Notes

1. Erazim Kohák, "Speaking to Trees," *Critical Review* 6, no. 2–3 (1992): 376.
2. Kohák, "Speaking to Trees," 375.
3. Nancy Holmes, *Arborophobia* (Edmonton: University of Alberta Press, 2022).
4. Ricoeur, Paul. *Freud and Philosophy: An Essay on Interpretation*, trans. Denis Savage (New Haven, CT: Yale University Press, 1977), 28. "The second naïveté [. . .] is postcritical and not precritical; it is an informed naïveté." Ibid., 496.
5. Michael Polanyi, *Personal Knowledge: Towards a Post-Critical Philosophy* (Chicago: University of Chicago Press, 1958), 266.
6. Rita Felsky, *The Limits of Critique* (Chicago: University of Chicago Press, 2015), 173.
7. Felsky, *The Limits of Critique*, 174.
8. Alexis Shotwell, *Against Purity: Living Ethically in Compromised Times* (Minneapolis University of Minnesota, 2016), 7–9.
9. Shotwell, *Against Purity*, 9.
10. Peter Sloterdijk, *Critique of Cynical Reason*, trans. Michael Eldred (Minneapolis: University of Minnesota Press, 1987), 103.
11. Édouard Glissant. *Poetics of Relation*, trans. Betsy Wing (Ann Arbor: University of Michigan Press, 1997), 195.
12. Hannah Cooper-Smithson, "Arboromorphism," *Environmental Humanities* 14.1 (2022): 235.
13. Hannah Cooper-Smithson, "Arboromorphism," 235.
14. Emanuele Coccia, *The Life of Plants: A Metaphysics of Mixture*, trans. Dylan J. Montanari (Medford: Polity Press, 2018), 45.
15. Coccia, *The Life of Plants*, 109.
16. Plato, *Phaedrus*, trans. Albert A. Anderson (Millis: Agora Publications, 2009), 229a.
17. David J. Gunkel, *Deconstruction* (Cambridge, MA: MIT Press, 2021), 142.
18. For Derrida's detailed analysis of Plato's *pharmakon*, see "Plato's Pharmacy" in Jacques Derrida, *Dissemination*, trans. Barbara Johnson (Chicago: University of Chicago Press, 1981), 61–171.
19. Jacques Derrida, *On the Name*, ed. Thomas Dutoit, trans. David Wood, John P. Leavey, Jr., and Ian McLeod (Stanford, CA: Stanford University Press, 1995), 103.
20. Ilya Prigogine and Isabelle Stengers, *Order Out of Chaos: Man's New Dialogue with Nature* (New York: Bantam Books, 1984), 206.

21. Jacques Derrida, "Response to Baldwin," in *Arguing with Derrida*, ed. Simon Glendinning (Malden: Blackwell Publishers, 2001), 105.

22. Jean-Paul Sartre, *Nausea*, trans. Lloyd Alexander (New York: New Directions, 1964), 105.

23. Sartre, *Nausea*, 10–11.

24. Sartre, *Nausea*, 126.

25. Sartre, *Nausea*.

26. Sartre, *Nausea*, 127.

27. Sartre, *Nausea*, 129.

28. Sartre, *Nausea*.

29. Sartre, *Nausea*, 122, 131.

30. Sartre, *Nausea*, 135.

31. Sartre, *Nausea*, 128–29.

32. Jean-Paul Sartre, *Being and Nothingness: A Phenomenological Essay on Ontology*, trans. Hazel E. Barnes (New York: Washington Square Press, 1984), lxvi.

33. Sartre, *Being and Nothingness*, 84.

34. Gilles Deleuze and Félix Guattari, *A Thousand Plateaus: Capitalism and Schizophrenia*, trans. Brian Massumi (Minneapolis: University of Minnesota Press, 1987), 15.

35. Deleuze and Guattari, *A Thousand* Plateaus, 7.

36. "At one end, some Generative Semanticists argued that language was one big schmoosh, with no place at all for borders, even in principle; sound was at one end of the linguistic continuum, meaning at the other, and a small group of uniform rules knit them together. At the other end, Chomsky's camp, the Interpretive Semanticists, seemed to be boundary fetishists." Randy Allen Harris, *The Linguistics Wars: Chomsky, Lakoff, and the Battle Over Deep Structure*, 2nd ed. (New York: Oxford University Press, 2021), 10.

37. Deleuze and Guattari, *A Thousand Plateaus*, 25.

38. Gilles Deleuze and Claire Parnet, *Dialogues*, 2nd ed., trans. Hugh Tomlinson and Barbara Habberjam (New York: Columbia University Press, 2002), 57.

39. Deleuze and Guattari, *A Thousand Plateaus*, 20.

40. Deleuze and Guattari, *A Thousand Plateaus*, 21.

41. Cooper-Smithson, "Arboromorphism," 235.

42. Deleuze and Guattari, *A Thousand Plateaus*, 11.

43. Derrida, *Dissemination*, 168.

44. Zhuangzi, *The Complete Works of Zhuangzi*, trans. Burton Watson (New York: Columbia University Press, 2013), 6.

45. Zhuangzi, *The Complete Works of Zhuangzi*.

46. Zhuangzi, *The Complete Works of Zhuangzi*, 231.

47. John S. Major, "The Efficacy of Uselessness: A Chuang-Tzu Motif." *Philosophy East and West* 25 (1975), 266.

48. Sara Ahmed, *What's the Use? On the Uses of Use* (Durham, NC: Duke University Press, 2019), 34.

49. Ahmed, *What's the Use?*, 198.
50. Ahmed, *What's the Use?*, 215.
51. Ahmed, *What's the Use?*, 229.
52. Erin Manning, *For a Pragmatics of the Useless* (Durham, NC: Duke University Press, 2020), 76.
53. Jenny Odell, *How to Do Nothing: Resisting the Attention Economy* (Brooklyn: Melville House, 2019), xvi.
54. Odell, *How to Do Nothing*, xi.
55. Odell, *How to Do Nothing*.
56. Francisco J. Varela, Evan Thompson, Eleanor Rosch, *The Embodied Mind: Cognitive Science and Human Experience* (Cambridge, MA: MIT Press, 1993), 29.

15

Trees as Legal Persons

Eric W. Orts

A fool sees not the same tree as a wise man sees.

—William Blake

I grew up in a farmhouse in southeastern Ohio, and an old sugar maple grew at the same time in our backyard. My father slung an old tire over a branch to make a swing for us kids. We had outdoor picnics in the summer under its shade. The tree was enormous with many thousands of leaves throwing off oxygen. House guests remarked on how well they slept in their room with a window looking out into the tree. Sugar maples (*Acer saccharum*) can live from three hundred to four hundred years, and so it is quite possible that this sugar maple had been living since before the founding of the United States.[1] We will never know for sure, though, because my parents sold the house and its property (including the tree) when they retired, and one of the first things the new owner did was cut down the great sugar maple. Nobody to my knowledge counted the rings to gauge its age.

In the law, this majestic tree—so valuable for many purposes—is treated simply as an item of human property.[2] Unless a tree is located in a government-protected park or preserve, its owner may generally do anything with it.[3] Cherish it or burn it. Enjoy its shade or cut it into lumber.

Admire the scale of its carbon dioxide intake and oxygen production, or destroy it as a risk to human-built structures.

This received wisdom, however, is beginning to change. Increasingly, the flexible legal category of "persons" is being extended to recognize and to protect different parts of the natural world. This chapter considers whether and to what extent we should recognize trees as legal persons too.[4]

The chapter builds on a classic contribution in the legal literature: Christopher Stone's "Should Trees Have Standing?"[5] Stone grappled with the question of who can and should be able to speak for the natural environment (including forests and trees) in court. More recently, Gwendolyn Gordon revisited the idea of "environmental personhood" and found an increasing number of examples used in the United States and around the world.[6] An important dimension of this movement has also been the influence of Indigenous peoples and religious traditions, such as in New Zealand, Bolivia, Ecuador, and India.[7]

I defend the proposition that we should expand the flexible legal category of persons beyond "real fictions" like business and nonprofit corporations to include other natural entities in the world such as rivers, coral reefs, endangered species, animals living in the wild, domesticated animals, forests, and even individual trees.[8] I do not advocate that the same level of protection for the lives of human beings should extend to non-human living beings. There are nevertheless good reasons to extend legal recognition even to individual trees as legal persons in some cases. The sugar maple I remember fondly from my childhood, for example, may have deserved some measure of legal process before its summary execution.[9] So too may many other beautiful, valuable trees and forests with which we human beings share our planet.[10]

Treating at least some trees as legal persons respects the complex web of life on which we all depend. At the outset, however, allow me to recognize a danger of misinterpretation. To say "trees are legal persons" risks provoking an emotional reaction from many who tend to view the world only in anthropocentric terms. "To confer rights onto some new 'entity,'" Stone observed, may often "sound odd or frightening or laughable."[11]

Here, I argue pragmatically that the usefulness of according legal personality to trees and other non-human living beings does not require adopting a biocentric rather than anthropocentric point of view.[12] It's true that our legal systems should highly value trees in part for their intrinsic value—especially those, like my family's old sugar maple or thousand-year-old redwoods and sequoias of California, that inspire a respect akin to what we feel for human elders or ancestors. Jared Farmer aptly describes these kinds of trees as "elderflora."[13] At the same time, we should also value trees for the practical ends of protecting the natural world in our own human interests, and those of our descendants, against existential threats to our global environment, including the climate emergency and biodiversity losses.[14] Respecting trees and forests, and better protecting them, can provide a partial solution to these existential threats, following a philosophy of taking one conscious step at a time toward sustainability.[15]

Not Only People Are Persons: The Flexibility of Legal Fictions

To begin with, it is important to emphasize that the legal concept of "persons" is not synonymous with what philosophers call "natural kinds" of "people."[16] We can understand people as consisting of all presently living human beings, the extant members of the species of *homo sapiens*. It is common in everyday language and in philosophy to refer to people also as individual persons. However, it is the law, an artificial social institution designed by and for people to organize themselves in the world, that designates various people to be "persons" with recognized rights.[17]

The law does not always recognize even all people as legal persons. In some of the most tragic chapters in human history, some people were not counted as legal persons at all, such as in the notorious *Dred Scott* decision by the United States Supreme Court in 1857. This case held that enslaved or freed people classified as "negroes of the African race" had zero constitutional rights, triggering the Civil War to resolve, or to begin to resolve, this dispute.[18] As notoriously, the original U.S. Constitution counted each enslaved human being as three-fifths of a person to calculate representation in an all-white male House of Representatives, but gave these enslaved people no legal rights, again lasting until after the Civil War.[19] Indigenous people were entirely excluded as well.[20]

Or consider examples of legal personhood with respect to the human life span, namely, when life as a "person" begins or ends. In *Roe v. Wade*, the Supreme Court decided to draw the line at fetal viability for constitutional purposes, allowing for regulation to protect a human fetus as a person (against the needs or wishes of its mother) when a fetus could survive independently outside the womb.[21] Then, fifty years later, the

Court overturned *Roe* and enabled the regulation of a human fetus as a person at conception.[22] Many states are now racing to impose anti-abortion laws. In Ohio, the legislature passed a statute forbidding any abortion when the heartbeat of a fetus can be detected, with no exceptions even for incest or rape.[23] A number of states are going even further, adopting laws recognizing "fetus personhood" which will, for example, criminalize all abortions as murder.[24]

At the other end of the life span, legal questions arise about when we human beings have the legal authority to end our own lives. The law recognizes the right to give another person this power and authority in advance of the possibility (increasingly, the likelihood) that many of us will, because of an accident, disease, or old age, become unable mentally or physically to make end-of-life decisions for ourselves. Controversy surrounds whether people should have a legal right to die when facing a deadly illness or other declining physical or mental condition.[25] After life, the law empowers a person to transfer property (an estate) via the legal instruments of a will and testamentary trusts to individual or organizational persons who survive them.[26]

In the middle stages of our lives, the law makes determinations about competence: at what age, for example, may an individual vote, serve in the military, drive a car, sign a contract, purchase alcohol, or run for political office? In other words, people are legally recognized as "persons" separately for different kinds of rights and responsibilities. A child, for instance, does not have "standing" to defend or assert their own rights but instead depends on a parent or other appointed guardian for legal representation.

Some people have more rights than others depending on the happenstance of place and nationality. People recognized as citizens living in a recognized nation-state, for example, are persons with rights that non-citizens (pejoratively called "aliens") do not have. Non-citizens can be prevented from entering a country's territory—or, if illegally present without a visa or other permission, they can be deported. Non-citizens are restricted in what kinds of constitutional and other legal rights they may claim when residing in a country.[27]

The importance of the concept of persons in the case of citizens relates to another use of the idea of a legal person: the recognition of organizational persons such as nation-states and corporations. The United States of America and the People's Republic of China do not exist as "natural kinds," powerful as they may seem in the world. They are legal and political inventions, as are all nation-states and other government entities ranging from small towns and rural counties to the United Nations or the World Trade Organization.[28] Under international and national laws, the world's nation-states are treated as legal persons. The United States, for example, can bring or defend lawsuits as a legal person both internationally and as a party in domestic courts. It has legal "standing."[29]

In a similar manner, business or nonprofit organizations can gain recognition as legal persons that have standing to represent interests of human beings that construct, organize, and fund them.[30] In Gordon's felicitous words, "corporate personhood [is] quicksilver; it seems an endlessly adaptable concept."[31] This flexibility can be abused to commit fraud, evade taxes, or commit other crimes.[32] Overall, though, the legal creations of nation-states and corporations as persons are socially useful, and rightly representative of collective human desires and interests. We therefore continue to believe in these imaginary persons and make them real as part of the legal matrix of our social world.[33]

Why not then create similar legal fictions to include parts of the natural world, including trees and forests? If the law can treat a ship made from wood as a legal person, why not extend a legal fiction to trees themselves in certain circumstances?[34] This is the question Stone asked in 1975, repeated and extended by Gordon in 2018.[35] Elizabeth Kolbert renewed attention to the question recently in *The New Yorker*.[36] Following their leads, we should answer: yes, trees should have standing, and at least sometimes we should recognize them as legal persons.

In fact, we do so in many ways already. Even treating trees as human property means that people acting as property-owners may protect them, just as we do animals such as livestock or our companion dogs and cats. Governments also act to protect trees, forests, rivers, and other eco-systems through the creation and policing of national parks and other government-owned land, as well as through laws, such as the Endangered Species Act, pollution control regimes, and local zoning ordinances. In one recent example, the U.S. government has exerted strenuous efforts to save the sequoias (*Sequoiadendron giganteum*) from destruction by climate-intensified wildfires.[37] Legislation can also empower nonprofit organizations or Indigenous groups to act as guardians in the representation of nonhuman living entities.[38]

The argument here, then, is not so radical or unusual as it may sound at first. We already treat trees as legal persons in many respects, and these precedents should be expanded.

A Philosophical Turn toward Recognizing Trees as Persons

One immediate objection to the idea to treat trees or other non-human entities in the natural world as legal persons is to say that it does not correspond to everyday understandings of the meaning of "person," or to a conception of the legal system as designed to advance the interests and rights of people and not non-human animals, plants, or other life.

In the Western philosophical tradition, John Locke's view of the "person" has held sway. For Locke, a "person" means "a thinking intelligent being, that has reason and reflection, and can consider itself, as itself, the same thinking thing, in different times and places."[39] The key for Locke is self-consciousness. "When we hear, smell, taste, feel, meditate, or will any thing," he explained, "we know that we do so."[40] Locke recognized an oak as having an "individual life" and "identity" separate from the general category of trees or other species of oaks.[41] However, he reserved an attribution of moral status and standing to self-reflecting human beings who, like himself, can move around with consciousness from place to place.

Until relatively recently, contemporary Western philosophers followed Locke's lead. Harry Frankfurt, for example, argued that a "person" requires having a consciousness or mind capable of making deliberative choices about actions, counting out other nonhuman species.[42] At least since Peter Singer's landmark book *Animal Liberation*, however, the boundaries of Locke's definition have been pushed philosophically to include other sentient animals, including various kinds of apes (the evolutionary cousins of *homo sapiens*) and other mammals including livestock and animal companions, as well as some wild animals.[43] Whales and dolphins have self-consciousness and communication abilities equivalent (or close) to those of human beings.[44] The scientific study of the senses has opened new horizons in understanding the internal worlds (*Umwelten*) of many animals who perform far beyond the sensory abilities of people along a number of dimensions.[45]

New science is stretching the boundaries about how we think of trees and other plant species as well. Trees, we now know, have senses that are similar to sight, smell, touch, and hearing. When a tree falls in the woods, a lot of other trees notice! They communicate with each other, and at least some species have the ability to act collectively in response to external threats.[46] Whether the "thinking" in the root, trunk, and leaf systems of trees approximates brain activity in animals is an open question, but a closer affinity than previously thought between trees and other plants (*Plantae*) with the animal kingdom (*Animalia*) has been demonstrated.[47] Contrary to Locke's assumption, trees even move from place to place—though in generational migrations and much more slowly than animals like us, though the global climate disruption has lately accelerated their pace.[48]

One objection to expanding the category of persons to include non-human living beings is that doing so would create moral confusion. Human beings are the primary holders of moral rights and responsibilities, so this argument goes, and to consider non-human animals or a plant like a tree to be a person blurs the philosophical boundaries of the concept. As one philosopher has recently argued:

> When one applies the concept of personhood to nonhuman entities, the concept of personhood loses much of its utility. Much of the meaning of personhood is distorted or diluted when the idiom of personhood is used to articulate the metaphysical, moral, and legal statuses of whales, mice, pigs, chickens, mosquitoes, trees, lakes, and so forth, and the opportunities for distortion or dilution are many: the reconceptualization of animal features as human-like ones, the importing of reasons to care for intrinsically valuable entities into reasons to care for persons, and the utilization of metaphysical views for grounding moral ones and of moral ones for grounding legal ones. Even if a focus on personhood is neither utterly worthless nor positively harmful, one may legitimately wonder if these efforts (whether they reconceptualize personhood or place it on a pedestal) do not impoverish philosophical investigations instead of opening up interesting new ways of thinking about the diversity of beings inhabiting our world.[49]

The main problem with this argument is that the received understanding of the word "person" to refer only to human beings privileges our own species in a manner that has become detrimental to existence of many others—which, given the interdependence of life, then threatens our own existence as a "species being" too.[50] In other words, it is no longer tenable in terms of the long-term prospects for the well-being of our own species to conceive of the moral universe of living beings to include only homo sapiens. It is insufficient to object that changing one's conceptions of the world to accord with an updated scientific and philosophical understanding of it would cause "confusion."[51]

One helpful clarification in understanding the rights and responsibilities of human and non-human living beings derives from an argument provided by Christine Korsgaard. It is a mistake, Korsgaard suggests, to assume that recognizing a non-human living being as a moral person means that it necessarily has rights *and* responsibilities. She describes a living being as having "an end in itself," along Kantian lines, in both "an active and a passive sense."[52] Human beings can act rationally and self-reflectively, and we can use reason to understand mutual moral rights and responsibilities for our actions. This does not mean, however, that only people have moral rights in the "passive sense" as "ends in themselves." Non-human living beings can and sometimes should be recognized to have some rights (such as to live free of wanton human destructiveness), even when they cannot conceive of or bear reciprocal moral responsibilities or duties.[53]

In premodern times, human societies and legal systems often attributed responsibilities to non-human animals such as rats, pigs, or insects for "wrongs" that they were alleged to have committed against human beings.[54] We know now that most non-human living beings cannot exercise reflective reasoning or use language sufficiently to bear moral responsibility. (Some of our fellow mammals, such as orangutans and some whales, might qualify as exceptions.)[55] This does not mean, however, that non-human living beings cannot be understood as having passive moral standing and therefore, to some extent, rights.[56]

As Korsgaard argues, Immanuel Kant was wrong to say that laws preventing cruelty to animals were justified only because of the effects the cruelty might have on human attitudes and behavior.[57] If someone maliciously kills my dog Butterbean, for example, it is not only a wrong to me as his owner, though I would also surely suffer because I love my dog. Killing Butterbean would be a crime akin to murder primarily because it would violate his own right to life. Along similar lines, Joseph Vining remarks that "a widening sense of animals as having intrinsic worth, even individuality" means that "the law's leaving virtually untouched this vast area of animal suffering at human hands is more and more anomalous," leading to proposals regulating against the unnecessary suffering of factory-farmed animals, including through an expansion of the criminal law.[58]

A similar rationale extends to cover the lives of some plants including individual trees. Replace my dog in the hypothetical above with a centuries-old tree growing in my backyard, such as an old sugar maple, which I may also cherish. If someone destroys this tree to inflict emotional or economic harm on me, that's a moral wrong to me—but it is also a wrong-in-itself to kill a beautiful living being such as an elder tree for no good reason.[59]

The right to life of plants is of course often and continuously balanced against our own rights to live—such as whenever I want to make a salad. We should nevertheless recognize plants as having an intrinsic value in themselves, as well as an instrumental value to us. Plants, including trees, are not created to exist only as commodities for our use and consumption; they are an integral and irreplaceable part of the interdependence of life on our planet. In this sense, they have a systemic or eco-systemic value. This is one good reason that in many traditions we say a grace or prayer before meals in gratitude for the food (even if only vegetarian) that we are blessed to have and to eat.

We should therefore treat trees and forests in a manner that not only maximizes the production of wood for our use as lumber and paper, or the production of oxygen and carbon sequestration, but that also respects the moral lives of trees and the ecological value of forests. *Homo sapiens* co-evolved with trees, and we have opposable thumbs and the ability to climb easily because of this fact.[60] Trees are correctly described as the "lungs of the planet."[61] The collective production of oxygen by more than three trillion trees balances (though imperfectly) the massive collective production of carbon dioxide by eight billion people.[62] Estimates vary, but on average it takes seven to nine trees to produce a sufficient amount of oxygen for one person to live.[63] To say trees provide us only with these "ecosystem services," though, radically misapprehends their full value.[64] In particular, long-lived trees or "perdurables" can teach us by example the value of long-term thinking and an ecological perspective.[65]

This is not to say that expanding conceptions of moral and legal persons to include other non-human life will be easy or straightforward. As shown above, the use of "person" to describe human beings is not easy or straightforward either. Treating non-human beings, including trees, as persons too, however, means extending a basic level of moral respect and recognition to other life forms that compose the "we" who inhabit the Earth.

Extending this kind of recognition and respect to include a conception of non-human rights is also significantly limited. We can count out—and simplify—the exercise with respect to many rights that we recognize for human beings alone. For example, moral and political rights of "freedom of speech or assembly" or voting rights "designed to protect our autonomy and our right to live according to our own values" are not implicated with respect to trees or forests.[66] To say that a tree is a person with some measure of rights and moral standing is not to say that a tree has a right to vote. A business corporation has no right to vote either.

Speaking generally, we should loosen the boundaries that we have drawn to privilege the human species from the rest of creation. We are not so comparatively smart or special as we too often have historically liked to think (though there has no doubt been an evolutionary value to a species-centric cultural focus, until now).[67] For our own survival and well-being as a species, we need to expand our understanding of intelligence to include many other kinds of life. As James Bridle argues,

> From bonobos shaping complex tools, jackdaws training us to forage for them, bees debating the direction of their swarm, or trees that talk to and nourish one another . . . the non-human world seems suddenly alive with intelligence and agency. It's a trick of the light of course: these other minds have always been here, all around us, but Western science and popular imagination, after centuries of denial and inattention, are only just starting to take them seriously. And taking them seriously requires us not only to re-evaluate our idea of intelligence, but our idea of the entire world.[68]

In response to this new and expanding understanding, we should not only populate novels and other artistic forms of expression with references to non-human beings including trees, such as in Richard Powers's *The Overstory*.[69] We should increase our appraisal of moral responsibility to trees and the natural world in general.[70] This means that we should continue to expand our legal systems to include trees as persons, because they are "more than just a commodity."[71]

How to Treat Trees as Legal Persons

"Legal personhood is not binary; it is not a yes-or-no proposition," Gwen Gordon points out. "The differentiation of legal rights and responsibilities starts, not ends, at the question of whether something may or may not be considered a person in the meaning of a statute."[72]

The firmament of our human-centered universe would not fall if we began to recognize more trees, as well as other non-human parts of the natural world, as legal persons deserving of some protection. The development of law should follow the development of moral and ethical views, as it has done in the past.[73]

Distinctions can and must be made. Consider again the example of my dog Butterbean. I have legal ownership of him and a corresponding duty to care for him. Laws against cruelty to animals restrict my treatment of him. He does not have a right—and I do not have a right to exert on his behalf—to enter a local bar in Philadelphia. Arguably, he should (as he would in France), and Butterbean does have the right—or I have a right to exercise on his behalf—to come into my office at the University of Pennsylvania which has designated itself as having "pet friendly" policies. Butterbean does not and should not have a right to vote, drive a car, drink a beer, carry a gun, or enter into a contract.

Similarly with trees: we may condition the ownership of property or the development of real estate on zoning or other requirements to protect trees by giving them some basic rights to be heard in court or, more precisely, to give human agents the power to raise an issue in court regarding their provisional rights to life. Several years ago, for example, a plan for a new public school in my neighborhood in West Philadelphia involved cutting down a number of trees. To satisfy concerned neighbors, the development plan preserved many of the larger trees—and a special outdoor structure for children's education in a tree-filled area was included in the final landscape design. In this sense, my neighbors acted effectively as representatives of these trees and their value to us as neighbors and to future generations.

Consider also an example from the recent Korean television series, the *Extraordinary Attorney Woo*. In one episode, a small town was fighting the development of a new road from Seoul that would divide it. A large, five-hundred-year-old hackberry tree (*Celtis koraiensis*) would have had to be destroyed to accommodate the road. In the end, the protagonist lawyers uncovered a politically motivated oversight that foiled an earlier attempt to designate the tree as a national monument, so the case was won.[74] In real life, there is now a movement to designate the actual tree used in the TV show as a protected monument.[75]

Recognizing some trees, such as this ancient hackberry, as having a legal personality would allow for the appointment of designated representatives to represent the tree's interests in court. At first, this approach may seem far-fetched, but consider that our legal system allows for the appointment of a *guardian ad litum* for other purposes in individual litigations, such as child custody hearings or other cases in which a human person cannot represent themselves. Why not for landmark trees or other non-human living beings?[76] In some cases, for example, the U.S. government may step in: such as the Forest Service acting to protect endangered sequoias and other trees from wildfires, or the National Oceanic and Atmospheric Administration acting as a statutory trustee to protect fish, marine mammals, and their eco-systems.[77] Or consider a heart-wrenching counter-example: the failure of the Forest Service to protect the oldest known tree on Earth—granting a permit in 1964 in Nevada to a doctoral student to cut down a bristlecone pine with a chainsaw to see how old it was. The tree was killed to confess to human beings that it was more than 4,900 years old.[78]

For particularly valuable trees and stands of forest, we could extend the designation of legal personality to allow groups of people other than the government to act to protect them. The "public ownership" of national parks and forests need not equate to "government ownership." As Stone long ago envisioned, recognition of legal standing can be extended to groups other than the government who may be particularly well-suited to represent the rights and interests of trees and forests.[79] Germany recognizes some representations of this kind by designating government-qualified nonprofit organizations as legal representatives for particular non-human entities, such as forests, rivers, or protected wilderness supporting a complex living eco-system.[80] Examples in the United States may include recognizing nonprofit "riverkeepers" to have standing to advocate for the health of different river systems.[81]

A critic might respond that to give individual trees or other non-human living beings legal standing as a "person" would open the proverbial floodgates of litigation. However, again as Stone recognized, this claim is "too easily exaggerated."[82] Legal claims must be based on some recognized grounds of authority and empowerment, not simply generalized assertions of "harm." Lawyers also "value their time too much to throw it away," and good lawyers don't come cheap.[83]

Even if a marginal increase in litigation would occur, there is no reason today to privilege economic development that is destructive to the natural world against legal process. As Gordon also observed, we do not worry much about the multiplication of corporate entities, even though the treatment of them have become "an incoherent, inconsistent wildebeest" in the law.[84] Courts nevertheless make sense of the complex, multi-faceted persons that are citizens, corporations, and nation-states. There is no reason they cannot make sense too of non-human animals, trees, and forests as legal persons in appropriate cases.

One last important concern is political. Giving trees legal standing, according to this view, might give rise to derogatory labels such as "tree-hugger."[85] This political reaction would undermine environmentally positive goals, on this view, by violating common understandings about moral value as primarily human-centered and human-defined. In other words, to treat trees as legal persons would be counter-productive from a pragmatic point of view of protecting both human beings and our environment.[86]

There is some merit in this concern, but on balance a greater recognition in the law, as well as philosophy, of the value of trees as living beings would press the cause of environmental protection forward: in the interest of human beings as well as trees and forests. One problem today in mobilizing support for responding to large global threats such as climate disruption and biodiversity loss lies in the very scale of the challenges. The sheer size of the problems can be numbing and stultifying. Focusing on saving one old tree or a stand of trees can be grounding for many individuals, and this moral and political grounding may grow into support for larger political actions to protect the natural environment. Saving trees, in other words, can make a real difference.

The "fragility of things," as political theorist William Connolly writes, recommends a reconsideration of "the very idea of a person" as having only "an image of human uniqueness." As in tending the health of a forest, we may sometimes need conceptually to "burn out sections of undergrowth and replace it with new plantings." Then, the "very trajectory of what counts as progress may take a turn" toward a "care for being" and "an ethic of cultivation."[87]

Corporations have representatives that "speak" for them, the often-complex assemblages of human rights and interests unified in business legal structures.[88] Similarly, representatives can speak for trees as a legal persons: flexibly, and not dogmatically.[89]

Conclusion

A few years ago, my wife and I decided to cut down—and kill—a large Norway maple (*Acer platanoides*) that had been growing for many years, at least a century according to its tree rings, outside of our townhouse on a quiet Philadelphia block. Not only did it provide shade in the hot Philly summers and a home for squirrels and songbirds, but one stout branch had been used for a number of years to hang a piñata for local children to whack down during our annual block party. My son developed an attachment to the tree at a young age: its leaves shading and throwing off oxygen directly into his third-floor bedroom. However, our neighbors worried for several years that the tree was in decline and tilted toward falling on their houses (or maybe ours) in a storm. We resisted these entreaties as long as the tree remained healthy. Then, when it became clear that some branches were indeed dying and the trunk was being attacked by insects, we paid for the tree's removal.

To treat this tree as a legal person may have added another step to the process. A tree-protective zoning ordinance might have required a permit to remove the tree (which would no doubt have been granted with alacrity under the circumstances). Perhaps the outcome of such an imagined process would have been different if the tree were fully healthy and in the prime of life, but the needs of human beings (and the risks to our homes), as well as the added consideration that the Norway maple is an invasive species, would have made this particular legal question a no-brainer.[90]

As Christopher Stone recognized, "to say that the natural environment should have rights is not to say anything as silly as that no one should be allowed to cut down a tree."[91] We should nevertheless raise the bar with respect to zoning ordinances and other legal measures to protect landmark trees—as well as the trees growing in forests, especially old growth forests that serve as deep carbon sinks and support a large diversity of other species as well as our own.[92]

It's true that greater protections of the rights and interests of non-human living beings may impede some kinds of economic development—such as clear-cutting forests or clearing land for new real estate projects—but as species beings it would be better for us to slow down.[93] The breakneck speed of human economic development, especially over the past several centuries, now imperils the ecological equilibrium of our planet. There are limits to economic growth as an overall social objective.[94] Like trees—or J. R. R. Tolkien's Ents—perhaps it would be better for us to think and act more slowly—more arboreally and with greater wisdom.[95]

Notes

1. D. A. Tirmenstein, "Acer saccharum," in USDA Forest Service, Fire Effects Information System (Aug. 5, 2022). www.fs.fed.us/database/feis/plants/tree/acesac/all.html

2. The traditional view is that trees are treated as a part of real property unless "severed" from it and sold as personal property like rocks, coal, or "similar easily removed products of the earth." "Property–Trees–Severance," *Harvard Law Review* 13 (1899): 225.

3. Zoning laws may also restrict the destruction of trees, but they have been relatively lax in the United States. In Pennsylvania, for example, the practice of forestry is allowed by state statute in all zoning districts, though with reasonable administrative restrictions, such as to prevent erosion or clear-cutting and to promote good forestry management. See, e.g., *Chrin Bros. v. Williams Township Zoning Hearing Board*, 815 A.2d 1179 (Pa. Commonwealth 2003).

4. As discussed further in this chapter, there is an overlap between legal and philosophical understandings of the category of "persons." My main focus will be primarily on legal persons, but it will refer to some extent to philosophical discussions as well.

5. Christopher D. Stone, "Should Trees Have Standing?—Toward Legal Rights for Natural Objects," *Southern California Law Review* 45 (1972): 450–501. See also Christopher D. Stone, "Should Trees Have Standing? Revisited: How Far Will Law and Morals Reach? A Pluralist Perspective," *Southern California Law Review* 59 (1985): 1–154. For a collection of other essays, including the original, see Christopher D. Stone, *Should Trees Have Standing? Law, Morality, and the Environment* (Oxford: Oxford University Press, 3d ed., 2010).

6. Gwendolyn J. Gordon, "Environmental Personhood," *Columbia Journal of Environmental Law* 43 (2018): 49–91. I am indebted to Gwen, an insightful friend and colleague whom we have lost, like a great and wise tree, too soon. I imagine Gwen's spirit now communing with the Te Aroha, an eight-hundred-year old pohutukawa tree revered by the Māori in New Zealand. See Diane Cook and Len Jenshel, *Wise Trees* (New York, Abrams, 2017), 66–67. As well as a legal scholar, Gwen was an anthropologist who had observed the Māori whose treatment of "environmental persons" informed her work. She would have also been pleased to see the recent legal development, supported by the Māori and other indigenous people, declaring whales to be "legal persons" to protect them. Remy Tumin, "In Move to Protect Whales, Polynesian Indigenous Groups Give Them 'Personhood,'" *New York Times*, Mar. 29, 2024. www.nytimes.com/2024/03/29/world/australia/whale-personhood-polynesia-maori.html

7. Gordon, "Environmental Personhood," 53–57; see also James Bridle, *Ways of Being: Animals, Plants, Machines: The Search for a Planetary Intelligence*

(New York: Farrar, Straus, and Giroux, 2022), 266–68; Matthew Hall, *Plants as Persons: A Philosophical Botany* (Albany, NY: SUNY Press 2011), 99–117.

In ancient Greece and other philosophical and religious traditions, trees and other non-human natural entities were regarded as divine, each having their own genius loci or guardian spirit. Christopher D. Stone, *The Gnat Is Older Than Man: Global Environment and the Human Agenda* (Princeton, NJ: Princeton University Press, 1993), 237–39; Lynn White, Jr., "The Historical Roots of Our Ecological Crisis," *Science* 155 (1967): 1203–7, on 1205. See also Hall, *Plants as Persons*, 17–35, 73–98, 119–35 (reviewing competing views among ancient Greek philosophers as well as in Buddhist, Hindu, and Pagan traditions); David Macauley, *Elemental Philosophy: Earth, Air, Water, and Fire as Environmental Ideas* (Albany, NY: SUNY Press, 2010), 94–95 (observing that the "association between trees and a sense of the sacred is a perennial one" throughout the world). Also "a shared feature of Indigenous North American spiritual traditions is that they all 'have a sacred center at a particular place, be it a river, a mountain, a plateau, valley, or other natural feature. . . .'" Amitav Ghosh, *The Nutmeg's Curse: Parables for a Planet in Crisis* (Chicago: University of Chicago Press, 2021), 34 (quoting Vine Deloria, Jr.).

8. A real legal fiction refers to various constructions and conceptions in the law which are imagined or invented artificially into existence, but then become "real" by virtue of their instantiation into everyday social practices that are enforced by legal rules and institutions, including courts. Business corporations, contracts, property, and many other structures and concepts of the law are composed largely of "legal fictions," but they are no less "real" because we believe in them and act as if they are real because the laws says so, and people follow and believe in the law. See, e.g., Eric W. Orts, *Business Persons: A Legal Theory of the Firm* (Oxford: Oxford University Press, rev. ed., 2015), 30–51. For a classic on the topic, see Lon L. Fuller, *Legal Fictions* (Stanford, CA: Stanford University Press, 1967).

9. Given its age and size, for example, perhaps the sugar maple could have been recognized as an historical landmark or some other specially protected category. One method of preserving a tree without designating it as a legal person is to create a municipal park to protect it, which converts the tree and the land supporting it into public property. For example, see the Landsdowne Sycamore, which is 350 to 400 years old and protected by a local park in Pennsylvania for its historical and natural value. www.monumentaltrees.com/en/usa/pennsylvania/delawarecounty/9799_theintesectionofwycombeandlacrosseave/. For city ordinances designed to protect "special trees," including "heritage, historic, and landmark" trees, see T. J. Swiecki and E. A. Bernhardt, "Guidelines for Developing and Evaluating Tree Ordinances" (Vacaville, CA: Phytosphere Research). http://phytosphere.com/treeord/heritage.htm

10. As philosopher Christine Korsgaard observes, "we" is a collective pronoun usually used to refer only to ourselves and fellow human beings, perhaps sometimes including future generations, when we write, do art, or engage in

public action. A scientific and philosophical appreciation of what might be called the interdependent web of life, however, has led many to question whether "we" should refer to all living beings that inhabit the Earth, including other animals and plants such as trees. Korsgaard elevates the scope of moral philosophy beyond the anthropocentric focus of Immanuel Kant and others to include non-human animals as "fellow creatures" deserving moral recognition and respect, though she does not go so far as to include trees and other plants (though leaves this question open). Christine M. Korsgaard, *Fellow Creatures: Our Obligations to the Other Animals* (Oxford: Oxford University Press 2018), 3–5, 23–25, 199–201. Recent anthropological and other scientific work suggest that "we" should include other living beings in the world, returning to an older style of "thinking like a forest." Eduardo Kohn, *How Forests Think: Toward an Anthropology Beyond the Human* (Berkeley: University of California Press, 2013); Ben Rawlence, *The Treeline: The Last Forest and the Future of Life on Earth* (New York: St. Martin's Press, 2022), 261–68. In Bridle's words: "*We share a world*. We hear, plants hear; we all hear together. We all feel the same sun, breathe the same air, drink the same water. Whether we hear the same sounds in the same way, whether they are meaningful to us in the same way, is beside the point. We exist, together, in the shared experience and creation of the more-than-human world." Bridle, *Ways of Being*, 69–70 (original emphasis).

11. Stone, "Should Trees Have Standing?" 455. A possible cautionary example is that a political campaign for the U.S. Senate has recently targeted trees and money spent by the federal government in protecting them. See Dana Milbank, "Herschel Walker's Anti-Tree Campaign Is Genius," *Washington Post*, Aug. 23, 2022, www.washingtonpost.com/opinions/2022/08/23/herschel-walker-anti-tree-gaffes (quoting Walker's comments, including: "[A] lot of the money is going into trees. You know that, don't you? It's going into trees. We've got enough trees. Don't we have enough trees around here?"). Yet Walker lost the election (to Senator Raphael Warnock), so perhaps the trees had the last laugh.

12. See Andrew Light, "Taking Environmental Ethics Public," in *Environmental Ethics: What Really Matters, What Really Works*, eds. David Schmidtz and Elizabeth Willott (New York: Oxford University Press, 2002), 556–66 (advocating a similar pragmatic approach to environmental philosophy and policy).

13. Jared Farmer, *Elderflora: A Modern History of Ancient Trees* (New York: Basic Books, 2022).

14. On the climate emergency, see, e.g., Timothy M. Lenton et al., "Climate Tipping Points—Too Risky to Bet Against," *Nature*, 575/7784 (November 2019): 592–95. On the loss of biodiversity, see Elizabeth Kolbert, *The Sixth Extinction: An Unnatural History* (New York: Picador 2015).

15. For one scientific primer on the relationship of forests, trees, climate, and biodiversity, see Ian Thompson, et al., "Forest Resilience, Biodiversity, and Climate Change: A Synthesis of the Biodiversity/Resilience/Stability Relationship

in Forest Ecosystems" (United Nations Secretariat of the Convention on Biological Diversity, 2009), www.cbd.int/doc/publications/cbd-ts-43-en.pdf. And on taking one step at a time, there is no better guide than Thich Nhat Hanh: "When we breathe in and out and hug a beautiful tree, we are in Heaven. . . . When we are truly alive, we can see that the tree is part of Heaven, and we are also part of Heaven. The whole universe is conspiring to reveal this to us, but we are so out of touch that we invest our resources in cutting down the trees. If we want to enter Heaven on Earth, we need only one conscious step and one conscious breath." Thich Nhat Hanh, "Beyond Birth and Death," Lion's Roar, Sept. 17, 2020. www.lionsroar.com/beyond-birth-and-death

16. Alexander Bird and Emma Tobin, "Natural Kinds," *The Stanford Encyclopedia of Philosophy* (Spring 2022) (Edward N. Zalta ed.). https://plato.stanford.edu/archives/spr2022/entries/natural-kinds

17. Orts, *Business Persons*, 30–51 (providing general background on the nature of "legal persons"). The law is also informed by theoretical and empirical considerations, including those derived from everyday observations and philosophical analysis.

18. *Dred Scott v. Sandford*, 60 U.S. 393 (1857).

19. U.S. Constitution, art. 1, § 2 (superseded by the Thirteenth, Fourteenth, and Fifteenth Amendments).

20. For an historical summary with references, see Eric W. Orts, "Senate Democracy: Our Lockean Paradox," *American University Law Review* 68 (2019): 2047–56.

21. 410 U.S. 113 (1973). The time of fetal viability changes in accordance with medical technology.

22. *Dobbs v Jackson Women's Health Organization*, 597 U. S. 215 (2022).

23. Jane Mayer, "Goodbye, Columbus," *New Yorker* (Aug. 15, 2022): 22.

24. Kate Zernike, "Activists Push to Get Fetuses Person Status," *New York Times*, Aug. 22, 2022, A1.

25. For an overview including compelling examples, see David L. Sloss, Note, "The Right to Choose How to Die: A Constitutional Analysis of State Laws Prohibiting Physician-Assisted Suicide," *Stanford Law Review* 48 (1996): 937–73. In the United States, physician-assisted suicide is not yet recognized as a constitutional right. See *Vacco v. Quill*, 521 U.S. 793 (1997); *Washington v. Glucksberg*, 521 U.S. 702 (1997).

26. One may question the extent to which human societies should allow the dead hand of the past to rule the future in this manner, and limitations on the duration or size of bequests are therefore often imposed, such as the rules against perpetuities in the law of trusts and estates (limiting the number of generations a will's provisions may extend) or the imposition of hefty estate taxes. In the world of trees, of course, there is no such thing. In old-growth forests, the death of an ancient ancestor is immediately followed by an explosion of new growth by younger

trees. See, e.g., Peter Wohlleben, *The Hidden Life of Trees: What They Feel, How They Communicate*, trans. Jane Billinghurst (London: HarpersCollins 2016), 25–36.

27. See Stone, "Should Trees Have Standing?" 450–51 (recounting the historical expansion of rights of children, women, Blacks, American Indians, prisoners, and aliens). See also Selya Benhabib, *The Rights of Others: Aliens, Residents, and Citizens* (Cambridge: Cambridge University Press, 2012).

28. For a historical treatment of the rise of nations replacing empires, see Benedict Anderson, *Imagined Communities: Reflections on the Origin and Spread of Nationalism* (London: Verso, rev. ed. 1983); Ernest Gellner, *Nations and Nationalism* (1983) (Ithaca, NY: Cornell University Press, 2d ed., 2009).

29. The legal and moral concepts of "persons" and "standing" are closely linked. See Korsgaard, *Fellow Creatures*, 93–96. Legally, standing means simply having the attribute of a "person" recognized as sufficient to be a party or other formal participant in a judicial or other legal proceeding. There are various legal procedural and substantive restrictions on standing that I do not discuss here.

30. Orts, *Business Persons*, 9–51.

31. Gordon, "Environmental Personhood," 50.

32. For recently documented examples of the misuse of corporate forms, see Katharina Pistor, *The Code of Capital: How the Law Creates Wealth and Inequality* (Princeton, NJ: Princeton University Press, 2019).

33. I've argued elsewhere that we often underestimate the flexibility of laws that create and govern the many "business persons" with which we have populated our cultural landscape. Orts, *Business Persons*. The same is true of artificial political persons. The European Union and the United Nations are examples of possible emerging alternatives to nation-states as a primary default form of artificial organization.

34. Oliver Wendell Holmes, Jr., *The Common Law* (Little Brown 1881) (New York: Legal Classics Library reprint ed. 1982), 26–27 ("It is only by supposing the ship to have been treated as if endowed with personality, that the arbitrary seeming peculiarities of the maritime law can be made intelligible, and on that supposition they at once become consistent and logical.").

35. Stone, "Should Trees Have Standing?;" Gordon, "Environmental Personhood." See also Christiana Ochoa, "Nature's Rights," *Michigan Journal of Environmental and Administrative Law* 11 (2021): 39–86.

36. Elizabeth Kolbert, "Testing the Waters: Should the Natural World Have Rights?" *New Yorker*, Apr. 18, 2022, 16–20.

37. Joshua Partlow, "California's giant sequoias are burning up. Will logging save them?" *Washington Post*, Aug. 16, 2022, www.washingtonpost.com/climate-environment/2022/08/16/giant-sequoias-fire-mariposa-grove (discussing regulatory alternatives and noting that, in only a few years, six of the seven largest wildfires in California history have destroyed approximately one-fifth of all of the large sequoias on Earth).

38. Writing thirty-five years after his original article, Christopher Stone canvassed many ways in which personhood and standing have been extended to non-human living beings and natural entities. Stone, *Should Trees Have Standing?*, 49–62, 159–76. See also Gordon, "Environmental Personhood," 60–62; Ochoa, "Nature's Rights," 71–85. Of particular interest, Stone's ideas seem to have borne fruit in New Zealand, where legislation now empowers the Māori people to legally represent land preserves and a large river system. See Bridget Williams, "Reconceptualizing Entrenched Notions of Common Law Property Regimes: Māori Self-Determination and Environmental Protection Through Legal Personality for Natural Objects," 26 *Buffalo Environmental Law Journal* 26 (2019): 163–88.

39. John Locke, *An Essay Concerning Human Understanding* (London: E. Holt) (1689), chap. XXVII, § 9, 225.

40. Locke, *An Essay Concerning Human Understanding*, chap. XXVII, § 9, 226.

41. Locke, *An Essay Concerning Human Understanding*, chap. XXVII, § 4, 222.

42. Harry G. Frankfurt, "Freedom of the Will and the Concept of a Person," *Journal of Philosophy* 68 (1971): 5–20; see also Korsgaard, *Fellow Creatures*, 41. For less demanding philosophical concepts of a person, see P. F. Strawson, *Individuals* (London: Methuen, 1959), 101–2; A. J. Ayer, *The Concept of a Person* (New York: St. Martin's, 1963), 82 (both cited by Frankfurt). See also Amélie Oksenberg Rorty, "The Transformations of Persons," *Philosophy* 48 (1973): 261–75 (providing expanded social and cultural notions of persons). For a disruptive account that disputes the view that people are unified or integrated persons over their entire lifetimes, see Derek Parfit, *Reasons and Persons* (Oxford: Oxford University Press, rev. ed., 1987), 197–347.

43. Peter Singer, *Animal Liberation: A New Ethics for Our Treatment of Animals* (New York: Harper Collins, 1975). Other influential philosophical contributions in a similar or related direction around this time include those by J. Baird Callicott, Stephen Clark, Kenneth Goodpaster, Mary Midgely, Arne Naess, John Passmore, Tom Regan, Holmes Rolston, and George Sessions. See Peter Hay, *Main Currents in Western Environmental Thought* (Bloomington: Indiana University Press, 2002), 27–45, 57–59.

44. Mark Peter Simmonds, "Intelligence in Whales and Dolphins," in *Global Guide to Animal Protection*, ed. Andrew Linzey (Urbana: University of Illinois Press, 2013), 43–44.

45. Ed Wong, *An Immense World: How Animal Senses Reveal the Hidden Realms Around Us* (New York: Random House, 2022), 7–13. For example, there are now recognized to be more than the five senses, including the ability of some creatures to sense warm-body heat or electromagnetic fields, and a higher order of smell unavailable to humans (just ask your dog).

46. Wohlleben, *The Hidden Life of Trees*, 6–13. See also Daniel Chamovicz, *What a Plant Knows: A Field Guide to the Senses* (New York: Scientific American

Books, 2012) (arguing that plants have sentience given their responsiveness to light, sound, taste, touch, and other stimuli); Daniel Chamovicz, "Plants Are Intelligent, Now What?," *Nature Plants* 4 (2018): 622–23 (observing that plants have communications and signaling systems, and arguing that we should not get hung up on definitions of "intelligence" or not).

47. See Anthony Trewavas, "Aspects of Plant Intelligence," *Annals of Botany* 92 (2003), 1–20 (providing details on various aspect of plant communications, behavior, and intelligence, and indicating various directions for further research, such as understanding how maristems in plants may approximate brains in animals). In arguing that plants may have a "final good" sufficient to root them (so to speak) in moral standing along with animals, Korsgaard observes that "[t]he difference between the plant's tropic responses and the animal's actions might even, ultimately, be a matter of degree." Korsgaard, *Fellow Creatures*, 200. Cf. Kohn, *How Forests Think* (extending philosophical insights from Charles Pierce to examine various non-human methods of communication, representation, thinking, and conceptions of other living "selves" in the world).

48. Bridle, *Ways of Being*, 123–25 (observing that whole forests are now in motion responding to climate change in the largest migration since the Ice Age); Rawlence, *The Tree Line*, 5 (observing the tree line in the northern hemisphere is now moving hundreds of feet every year owing to global climate disruption). As Shakespeare might have said, the wood has begun to move, and not just from Macbeth's perspective! See Macauley, *Elemental Philosophy*, 98.

49. Jonas-Sébastien Beaudry, "Are Animals Persons? Why Ask?" *Journal of Animal Ethics* 9 (2019): 6–26, 8.

50. On our self-conception as a "species being," which includes our relationship to other species, see Korsgaard, *Fellow Creatures*, 48–50, 67, 193–94.

51. Beaudry, "Are Animals Persons?" 14, 17. I mean "science" broadly, including not only the physical sciences but also disciplines such as anthropology, history, and political science. Non-anthropocentric philosophies run quite deep in history. The threat posed by deforestation and lack of respect for trees, for example, was recognized in ancient China, Greece, and likely elsewhere. See, e.g., Yi-Fu Tuan, "Our Treatment of the Environment in Ideal and Actuality," *American Scientist* 58 (1970): 244–49.

52. Korsgaard, *Fellow Creatures*, 141–45.

53. Cf. Korsgaard, *Fellow Creatures*, 110 (giving the example of how one can meaningfully argue that every dog deserves—or has a right—to a good home). To be clear and fair, I'm extending Korsgaard's argument here regarding rights to include at least some plants such as old trees as well as non-human animals in a manner that she may not agree with.

54. See Bridle, *Ways of Being*, 251–52 (recounting "a long tradition of animal trials and executions in medieval Europe and colonial America" showing how people "believed that animals bore responsibility for their alleged crimes"). See

also William Ewald, "Comparative Jurisprudence (I): What Was It Like to Try A Rat?" *University of Pennsylvania Law Review* 143 (1995): 1889–2149.

55. See Meilan Solly, "Orangutans Are the Only Non-Human Primates Capable of 'Talking' About the Past," *Smithsonian Magazine*, Nov. 15, 2018, www.smithsonianmag.com/smart-news/orangutans-are-only-non-human-primates-capable-talking-about-past-180970827 (on orangutans); R. Douglas Fields, "Are Whales Smarter Than We Are?," *Scientific American* (in Mind Matters, Jan. 15, 2008), https://blogs.scientificamerican.com/news-blog/are-whales-smarter-than-we-are (on whales).

56. In philosophical terms, one might distinguish here between "moral agents" who act with intelligent other-regarding intentions and "moral patients" who cannot, but who nonetheless deserve some level of serious moral consideration by moral agents. See Tom Regan, *The Case for Animal Rights* (Berkeley: University of California Press, 1983), 151–56; Evelyn Pluhar, "Moral Agents and Moral Patients," *Between the Species* 4 (1988), 32–45. https://philpapers.org/rec/PLUMAA

57. Korsgaard, *Fellow Creatures*, 77–169. Cf. Mary Midgley, "Duties Concerning Islands" (1983), reprinted in *Environmental Ethics*, 71–81, 75–77 (criticizing Kant on this score, though expressing some reservations about extending the concept of rights).

58. Joseph Vining, "Animal Cruelty Laws and Factory Farming," *Michigan Law Review First Impressions* 106 (2008): 123–27. https://repository.law.umich.edu/cgi/viewcontent.cgi?article=1121&context=mlr_fi

59. For an extended historical account of different species of trees that produce individuals respected by many cultures as the equivalent of wise ancestors, see Farmer, *Elderflora*.

60. See Macauley, *Elemental Philosophy*, 96. See also Colin Tudge, *The Tree: A Natural History of What Trees Are, How They Live, and Why They Matter* (New York: Crown, 2005), xvii (pointing out the fact that without trees "our species would not have come into being at all").

61. See, e.g., UN Environment Program, World Conservation Monitoring Center, "Restoring forests, the lungs of the planet" (July 2021). www.unep-wcmc.org/en/news/restoring-forests—the-lungs-of-the-planet

62. The approximate 3.1 trillion trees on Earth measures out to about 422 trees per person. Robert Krulwich, "The Earth Has Lungs. Watch Them Breathe," *National Geographic* (Mar. 9, 2016), www.nationalgeographic.com/science/article/the-earth-has-lungs-watch-them-breathe. It is the global industrial-scale human mining and burning of fossil fuels for energy that throws this balance out of whack, producing the climate crisis.

63. Luis Villazon, "How many trees does it take to produce oxygen for one person?" *BBC Science*, (undated). www.sciencefocus.com/planet-earth/how-many-trees-does-it-take-to-produce-oxygen-for-one-person. Accessed May 19, 2024.

64. For various criticisms of the concept and framing of "ecosystem services," see Matthias Schröter et al., "Ecosystem Services as a Contested Concept: A Synthesis of Critique and Counter-Arguments," *Conservation Letters* 7(6) (2014): 514–23.

65. See Farmer, *Elderflora*, 23–29. Farmer writes: "Perdurable [trees] are more than service providers. They are ethical gift givers. They invite us to be fully human—truly sapient—by engaging our deepest faculties: to venerate, to analyze, to meditate. They expand our moral and temporal imaginations." Farmer, *Elderflora*, 23.

66. Korsgaard, *Fellow Creatures*, 7.

67. For the case against "human superiority," see Korsgaard, *Fellow Creatures*, 9–15, 53–74.

68. Bridle, *Ways of Being*, 10–11.

69. Richard Powers, *The Overstory: A Novel* (New York: W. W. Norton & Co., 2018). Cf. also Amitav Ghosh, *The Great Derangement: Climate Change and the Unthinkable* (Chicago: University of Chicago Press, 2016) (criticizing contemporary literature, especially novels, for tending to omit environmentally essential topics such as the climate emergency).

70. For an early influence in this direction, see Hans Jonas, *The Imperative of Responsibility: In Search of an Ethics for the Technological Age* (Chicago: University of Chicago Press, 1984). For an argument that theories of a social contract should be similarly expanded, see Michel Serres, *The Natural Contract*, trans. Elizabeth MacArthur and William Paulson (Ann Arbor: University of Michigan Press, 1995) (originally published in French in 1990).

71. Wohlleben, *The Hidden Life of Trees*, 241–45.

72. Gordon, "Environmental Personhood," 50.

73. See Jedediah Purdy, "Our Place in the World: A New Relationship for Environmental Ethics and Law," *Duke Law Journal* 62 (2013): 857–932.

74. "A Tale about Sodeok-dong," *Extraordinary Attorney Woo*, episodes 7 and 8 (Netflix 2022).

75. Haley Yang, "Tree Featured in 'Extraordinary Attorney Woo' to be Considered for Natural Monument," *Korea JoongAng Daily*, July 28, 2022, https://koreajoongangdaily.joins.com/2022/07/25/ entertainment/television/Extraordinary-Attorney-Woo-woo-youngwoo-Attorney-Woo-hackberry-tree/20220725111820730.html. Two other Korean hackberry trees were previously designated natural monuments.

76. Stone, "Should Trees Have Standing? Revisited," 2, 25–34.

77. Stone, *Should Trees Have Standing?* 166.

78. Farmer, *Elderflora*, 349–60. Posthumously, the tree was named Prometheus.

79. Stone, "Should Trees Have Standing?" On the larger idea of guardians for future generations and the global commons in international law, see Stone, *Should Trees Have Standing?* 103–14, 130–32.

80. Stone, *Should Trees Have Standing?* 68.

81. Stone, *Should Trees Have Standing?* 166 (discussing riverkeepers designated for the Delaware River, the Hudson River, and the San Francisco Bay). For an example, see the Delaware Riverkeeper Network, www.delawareriverkeeper.org. Accessed May 19, 2024.

82. Stone, "Should Trees Have Standing? Revisited," 2–7.

83. Stone, *Should Trees Have Standing?* 165–66.

84. Gordon, "Environmental Personhood," 63. We should indeed worry much more than we do about the misuse of corporate entities. See, e.g., Pistor, *The Code of Capital*.

85. It's not clear how "tree-hugger" became derogatory. The origin of the term appears to be a reference to villagers in India in 1730 who died while hugging trees in a vain attempt to prevent them being cut down for a palace. These tree-huggers were killed, but subsequent legal action prevented future logging from taking place. Bryan Farrell, "Where Did the Phrase 'Tree-Hugger' Come From?" *Earth Island Journal* (Jan. 12, 2012), www.earthisland.org/journal/index.php/articles/entry/where_did_the_word_tree-hugger_come_from. A contemporary parallel seems to be playing out as of this writing on the outskirts of Atlanta where a forest is being cut down for a "Cop City" training facility. Adeel Hassan and Sean Keenan, "What Is 'Cop City'? The Atlanta Police Center Protests, Explained," *New York Times*, Mar. 7, 2023, www.nytimes.com/article/cop-city-atlanta-protests.html; Sean Keenan and Rick Rojas, "'Cop City' Prosecutions Hinge on a New Definition of Domestic Terrorism," *New York Times*, Feb. 26, 2024. www.nytimes.com/2024/02/26/us/cop-city-domestic-terrorism.html

86. Light, "Taking Environmental Ethics Public."

87. William E. Connolly, *The Fragility of Things* (Durham, NC: Duke University Press, 2013), 131.

88. Orts, *Business Persons*, 41–45.

89. Gordon, "Environmental Personhood," 88–91.

90. The Norway maple was first introduced to North America from Europe by John Bartram, the famous arborist, in Philadelphia in 1756, and he began to offer it for sale. It was planted for its hardiness in urban and other human-built environments, but the species soon escaped to the wilds, as trees often have a habit of doing. *Plant Invaders of Mid-Atlantic Natural Areas* (National Park Service/U.S. Fish and Wildlife Service, 4th ed., 2010), "Norway maple." www.invasive.org/alien/pubs/midatlantic/acpl.htm

91. Stone, "Should Trees Have Standing?" 457. Concerns about "ethical extensionism" have merit, but there is good reason to think that distinctions can be made in theory and practice, such as, for example, by estimating relative sentience of living beings when considering how to treat them. See Kai M. A. Chan, "Ethical Extensionism under Uncertainty of Sentience: Duties to Non-Human Organisms without Drawing a Line," *Environmental Values* 20 (2011): 323–46.

92. For an example, see the controversy over an "Olympic oak" competing with plans for development in Los Angeles. Tim Arango, "In Los Angeles, a Tree With Stories to Tell," *New York Times*, May 28, 2022, www.nytimes.com/2022/05/28/us/in-los-angeles-a-tree-with-stories-to-tell.html. Note also that it is better environmentally to let dead trees rot in place as a source of sustenance for an "outrageous diversity" of other life rather than to cut them down, at least when it is safe to do so. See Margaret Roach, "Dead Tree? Don't Rush to Chop It Down," *New York Times*, May 19, 2024, RE9.

93. Greater recognition of rights and interests of trees and other non-human living beings could also provide greater leverage for many different groups of people to act at various social levels to preserve the global climate. See Eric W. Orts, "Climate Contracts," *Virginia Environmental Law Journal* 29 (2011): 197–236.

94. See, e.g., Julie Livingston, *Self-Devouring Growth: A Planetary Parable as Told from Southern Africa* (Durham, NC: Duke University Press, 2019).

95. See Matthew Dickerson and Jonathan Evans, *Ents, Elves, and Eriador: The Environmental Vision of J.R.R. Tolkien* (Lexington: University Press of Kentucky, 2006), 119–44.

Afterword

The Sequoia Archipelago

Don Hanlon Johnson

Several years ago, while on a teaching trip to Japan, I had a particularly revelatory experience about the role of trees in human consciousness. It happened in the hills above Kyoto where Buddhism first emigrated from China. The trails above the Zen monasteries dating back to the eighth century were crowded with pilgrims. Our path suddenly came upon a grove of old-growth Sequoias, the genus that encircles the northern Pacific from the middle of California up the coast through Alaska to Kamchatka down to China, Korea, and Japan. The Japanese pilgrims each stopped and bowed before these giants.

I live in that crescent, a two-mile walk from my home to Muir Woods National Monument, a canyon filled with old-growth redwoods. The human behavior in Japan was dramatically different from California. Unlike here where the Old Ones stand quietly unclothed in their magnificence fenced-off from by a paved trail, the Japanese trees were touchable and circled by thick colorful ropes, signaling something sacred, which evoked gestures of reverence from the walkers.

That manifest difference is certainly due in part to the very different attitudes cultivated within Shinto and the Biblical traditions. In Japan, the divine manifests in the natural worlds of streams, rocks, winds, and trees, all of which deserve reverence as much as we who exist within and among these forces of nature. The Biblical traditions certainly honor the Earth as something to be cared for as but a station on the immortal soul's journey toward an eternal refuge. However, in itself the Earth is not essentially implicated within our spiritual lives.

Certainly, it would be a mistake to judge one people or religion as more enlightened than another. Japanese have denuded the ancient trees more extensively than Americans. And overflowing groups of walkers through Muir Woods are typically struck by awe and appreciation for these wise old beings. Everywhere along the Northern Pacific crescent the forests have been butchered to satisfy human needs with little, if any, reverence. It is right to honor activists like Julia Butterfly Hill who have endangered their lives to protect what is left of these forests from the corporate greed of the lumber companies. And yet, there is something about the Japanese public expression of reverence that is helpful in bringing to the fore a more palpable sense of the wisdom offered us by these majestic beings. There is something powerful in engendering effective communities about a shared acknowledgment that these are more than materials for human shelter and wealth, but also for our souls. Shinto, like the many Earth-honoring spiritual traditions of Indigenous peoples in the Americas, are examples of ways of transcending the political conflicts that make it so hard to create a widely shared force to nurture what is given us. And to transcend the endless so-called "rational" debates about projected dangers, where we must learn to live with the always ambiguous claims of science, deflecting us from going forward with serious transformations of our destructive pathologies.

I was inspired to title this afterword by Aleksandr Solzhenitsyn's revolutionary book about the chain of Soviet prison camps that used to stretch out through Siberia to the far east where the Sequoias live. That chain was populated with creative courageous dissidents who, like the Redwoods, carried forward in their silence the deeper human values that Stalin was intent on destroying, many of whom survived to carry on their works as guides for how to stand firm in one's hopes and values in the presence of severe attempts to muffle their voices. But, like those courageous survivors, an end of captivity leaves difficult challenges about how and where to go now that some bonds of thinking about our existence on this planet have been broken. We are faced with the complexities of dealing with centuries of oppressions, neglect, unchecked greed, and outright mistakes of otherwise well-intentioned judgments about how to live sustainably and justly in this amazing home in which we find ourselves. In reflecting on the lessons from the residues of the 2024 election, it is clear that many of us who have engaged in addressing the ecological emergencies have neglected to our peril the often desperate needs of salaried laborers and their families, such as those left behind in the decline of the lumber industry. This volume of intricate and thoughtful reflections on one small part of this monumental challenge is itself a step toward solutions, a model of how to work together more effectively, addressing the whole picture before us. Perhaps we will be helped in this task by learning from the trees themselves: how to be more quiet with each other swaying in the wind, letting our common roots join theirs in reaching down into the earth itself for strength and balance, reaching for the light.

Figure A.1. Don Hanlon Johnson. *Source*: Photo by Don Hanlon Johnson.

Suggestions for Further Reading

Philosophy of Tree and Plant Life

Abbott, Sarah. "Approaching Nonhuman Ontologies: Trees, Communication, and Qualitative Inquiry." *Qualitative Inquiry* (2021): 1–13. doi.org/10.1177/1077800421994954

Aloi, Giovanni, and Michael Marder. *Vegetal Entwinements in Philosophy and Art: A Reader.* Cambridge, MA: MIT Press, 2023.

Calvo, Paco, and Natalie Lawrence. *Planta Sapiens: The New Science of Plant Intelligence.* New York: W. W. Norton, 2023.

Casey, Edward S., and Michael Marder. *Plants in Place: A Phenomenology of the Vegetal.* New York: Columbia University Press, 2023.

Diehm, Christian. "Staying True to Trees: A Specific Look at Anthropocentrism and Non-Anthropocentrism." *Environmental Philosophy* 5, no. 2 (2008): 3–16.

Di Paola, Marcello. *The Vegetal Turn: History, Concepts, Applications.* Cham, Switzerland: Springer, 2025.

Goethe, Johann Wolfgang von. *The Metamorphosis of Plants.* Spain: MIT Press, 2009.

Grusin, Richard, ed., *The Nonhuman Turn.* Minneapolis: University of Minnesota Press, 2015.

Hall, Matthew. "How Plants Live: Individuality, Activity, and Self." *Environmental Philosophy* 17, no. 2 (2020): 317–45. https://doi.org/10.5840/envirophil20211797

Irigaray, Luce and Michael Marder. *Through Vegetal Being: Two Philosophical Perspectives.* New York: Columbia University Press, 2016.

Kohák, Erazim V. *The Embers and the Stars: A Philosophical Inquiry into the Moral Sense of Nature.* Chicago: University of Chicago Press, 1984.

Macauley, David. *Elemental Philosophy: Earth, Air, Fire, and Water as Environmental Ideas.* Albany, NY: SUNY Press, 2010.

Maher, Chauncey. *Plant Minds: A Philosophical Defense.* New York: Routledge, 2017.

Marder, Michael. *Time is a Plant.* Leiden: Brill, 2023.

Marder, Michael. *The Philosopher's Plant: An Intellectual Herbarium.* New York: Columbia University Press, 2014.
Marder, Michael. *Plant-Thinking: A Philosophy of Vegetal Life.* New York: Columbia University Press, 2013.
"Michael Marder and Gary Francione Debate Plant Ethics." *Columbia University Press Blog*, March 6, 2013. https://cupblog.org/2013/03/06/michael-marder-and-gary-francione-debate-plant-ethics
Miller, Elaine P. *The Vegetative Soul: From Philosophy of Nature to Subjectivity in the Feminine.* Albany, NY: SUNY Press, 2002.
Nassar, Dalia. *Romantic Empiricism: Nature, Art, and Ecology from Herder to Humboldt* Oxford: Oxford University Press, 2022.
Nassar, Dalia, and Margaret Barbour. "Tree Stories: The Embodied History of Trees and Environmental Ethics." *Cultural Politics* 19, no. 1 (2023): 128–47.
Nealon, Jeffrey T. *Plant Theory.* Stanford, CA: Stanford University Press, 2015.
Ryan, John Charles. "Passive Flora? Reconsidering Nature's Agency through Human-Plant Studies (HPS)." *Societies* 2 (2012): 101–21.
Sandford, Stella. *Vegetal Sex: Philosophy of Plants.* London: Bloomsbury Academic, 2023.
Theophrastus. *Enquiry into Plants.* Cambridge, MA: Harvard University Press, 2003.
Wood, David. *Thinking Plant Animal Human: Encounters with Communities of Difference.* Minneapolis: University of Minnesota Press, 2020.

Tree and Plant Intelligence

Chamovitz, Daniel. *What a Plant Knows: A Field Guide to the Senses.* New York: Farrar, Straus, and Giroux, 2012.
Chamovitz, Daniel A. "Plants are Intelligent; Now What?" *Nature Plants* 4, no. 9 (2018): 622–23. doi:10.1038/s41477-018-0237-3
Coccia, Emmanuele. *The Life of Plants: A Metaphysics of Mixture.* Medford, MA: Polity Press, 2019.
Crowther, T. W., H. B. Glick, K. R. Covey, C. Bettigole, D. S. Maynard, S. M. Thomas, J. R. Smith, et al. "Mapping Tree Density at a Global Scale." *Nature* 525 (September 1, 2015): 201–5.
Darwin, Charles, and Francis Darwin. *The Power of Movement in Plants.* London: John Murray, 1880.
Falik, Omer, Perla Reides, Mordechai Gersani, and Ariel Novoplansky. "Self/Non-Self Discrimination in Roots." *Journal of Ecology* 91, no. 4 (Aug. 1, 2003): 525–31. doi:10.1046/j.1365-2745.2003.00795.x
Gagliano, Monica, Charles Abramson, and Martial Depczynski. "Plants Learn and Remember: Let's Get Used to It." *Oecologia* 186, no. 1 (2018): 29–31. doi:10.1007/s00442-017-4029-7

Karban, Richard. *Plant Sensing and Communication*. Chicago: University of Chicago Press, 2015.
Kimmerer, Robin Wall. *Braiding Sweetgrass: Indigenous Wisdom, Scientific Knowledge, and the Teachings of Plants*. Canada: Milkweed Editions, 2013.
Mancuso, Stefano. *The Nation of Plants*. New York: Other Press, 2021.
Mancuso, Stefano and Alessandra Viola. *Brilliant Green: The Surprising History and Science of Plant Intelligence*. Washington, DC: Island Press, 2015.
Montgomery, Beronda L. *Lessons from Plants*. Cambridge, MA: Harvard University Press, 2021.
Myers, Natasha. "Conversations on Plant Sensing: Notes from the Field." *NatureCulture* (2015): 35–66.
Pollan, Michael. *The Botany of Desire: A Plant's Eye View of the World*. New York: Random House, 2001.
Trewavas, Tony. "Plant Intelligence: An Overview." *BioScience* 66, no. 7 (Jul. 1, 2016): 542–51. doi:10.1093/biosci/biw048

Arboreal Personhood

Bird-David, Nurit. "'Animism' Revisited: Personhood, Environment, and Relational Epistemology." *Current Anthropology* 40, no. S1 (1999): S67–S91.
Hall, Matthew. *Plants as Persons: A Philosophical Botany*. Albany, NY: SUNY Press, 2011.
Puleo, Thomas J. "Incorporating Nonhuman Subjectivity into World Society: The Case of Extending Personhood to Plants." In *Modern Subjectivities in World Society: Global Structures and Local Practices*, edited by Dietrich Jung and Stephan Stetter, 211–27. Cham, Switzerland: Palgrave Studies in International Relations, 2019.
Stuckey, Priscilla. "Being Known by a Birch Tree: Animist Refigurings of Western Epistemology." *Journal for the Study of Religion, Nature, and Culture* 4, no. 3 (2010): 182–205.

Arboreal Ethics

Federal Ethics Committee on Non-Human Biotechnology. *The Dignity of Living Beings with Regard to Plants: Moral Consideration of Plants for their Own Sake*. Berne, Switzerland: Federal Ethics Committee on Non-Human Biotechnology, 2008.
Kallhoff, Angela, Marcello Di Paola, and Maria Schörgenhumer. *Plant Ethics: Concepts and Applications*. Routledge Environmental Humanities. 1st ed. Vol. 1. Milton: Routledge, 2018. doi:10.4324/9781315114392

Stone, Christopher D. *Should Trees have Standing?: Law, Morality, and the Environment*. 3rd ed. New York: Oxford University Press, 2010.

Trees and Aesthetics

Balog, James. *Tree: A New Vision of the American Forest*. New York: Sterling, 2004.
Cook, Diane, and Len Jenshell. *Wise Trees*. New York: Abrams, 2017.
Fenner, David, and Ethan Fenner. *The Art and Philosophy of the Garden*. New York: Oxford University Press, 2024.
Galen A. Johnson. "Forest and Philosophy: Toward an Aesthetics of Wood." *Environmental Philosophy* 4, no. 1–2 (2007): 59–76. doi:10.5840/envirophil200741/26
Gibson, Prudence. *The Plant Contract: Art's Return to Vegetal Life*. Boston: Brill, 2018.
Goldsworthy, Andy. *Wood*. New York: Abrams, 1996.
Holten, Katie. *About Trees*. Berlin: Broken Dimanche Press, 2016.
Holten, Katie. *The Language of Trees: A Rewilding of Literature and Landscape*. Portland, OR: Tin House, 2023.
Lima, Manuel. *The Book of Trees: Visualizing Branches of Knowledge*. New York: Princeton Architectural Press, 2014.
Macpherson, Alan. "Art, Trees, and the Enchantment of the Anthropocene: Caroline Wendling's White Wood." *Environmental Humanities* 10, no. 1 (2018): 241–56.
Maloof, Joan. "Measuring the Beauty of Forests." *International Journal of Environmental Studies* 67, no. 3 (2010): 431–37. https://doi.org/10.1080/00207231003676113
Nakashima, George. *The Soul of a Tree: A Woodworker's Reflections*. New York: Kodansha International, 1981.
Rolston, Holmes. "The Aesthetic Experience of Forests." In *The Aesthetics of Natural Environments*, edited by Allen Carlson and Arnold Berleant. Toronto: Broadview Press, 2004.
Salonius, Pippa, and Andrea Worm, eds. *The Tree: Symbol, Allegory, and Mnemonic Device in Medieval Art and Thought*. Turnhout, Belgium: Brepols Publishers, 2014.

Trees and Plants in Literature

Calvino, Italo. *The Baron in the Trees*. Translated by Archibald Colquhoun. San Diego, CA: Harcourt Brace Jovanovich, 1959.
Concilio, Carmen, and Daniela Fargione, eds. *Trees in Literature and the Arts: HumanArboreal Perspectives in the Anthropocene*. Lanham, MD: Lexington Books, 2021.
Gagliano, Monica, John Charles Ryan, and Patricia Vieira. *The Language of Plants: Science, Philosophy, Literature*. Minneapolis: University of Minnesota Press, 2017.

Hall, Matthew. *The Imagination of Plants: A Book of Botanical Mythology*. Albany, NY: SUNY Press, 2020.
Higgins, Richard. *Thoreau and the Language of Trees*. Berkeley: University of California Press, 2017.
Le Guin, Ursula K. *The Word for World is Forest*. New York: Tor, 1972.
Macauley, David. "Fabulism: A Forest Fantasy" In Macauley, *Flights of Philosophical Fancy*, blog. https://davidmacauley2003.wordpress.com/2020/01/04/fabulism-a-sort-of-fantasy
Powers, Richard. *The Overstory*. New York: W. W. Norton, 2018.
Ryan, John C., and Glen Phillips. *Seeing Trees: A Poetic Arboretum*. Montrose, CO: Pinyun Publishing, 2020.
Silverstein, Shel. *The Giving Tree*. New York: Harper and Row, 1964.
Thomas, Harry, ed., *Poems about Trees*. New York: Alfred A. Knopf, 2019.
Thoreau, Henry David. *Faith in a Seed*. Edited by Bradley P. Dean. Washington, DC: Island Press, 1993.
Thoreau, Henry David. *The Maine Woods*. New York: Penguin Classics, 1988.
Tolkien, J. R. R. *Tree and Leaf*. Boston: Houghton Mifflin Company, 1989.

Human Experience with Trees

Canton, James. *The Oak Papers*. HarperOne, 2021.
Gibson, Prudence. *The Plant Thieves: Secrets of the Herbarium*. Sydney, Australia: NewSouth Publishing, 2023.
Gagliano, Monica. *Thus Spoke the Plant: A Remarkable Journey of Groundbreaking Scientific Discoveries and Personal Encounters with Plants*. Berkeley, CA: North Atlantic Books, 2018.
Haskell, David George. *The Forest Unseen: A Year's Watch in Nature*. New York: Penguin Books, 2012.
Haskell, David George. *The Songs of Trees: Stories from Nature's Great Connectors*. New York: Penguin Books, 2017.
Hogan, Linda. *Dwellings: A Spiritual History of the Living World*. New York: W. W. Norton, 2007.
Kaza, Stephanie. *The Attentive Heart: Conversations with Trees*. New York: Shambhala, 1993.
Louv, Richard. *Last Child in the Woods*. Chapel Hill, NC: Algonquin Books, 2008.
Luoma, Jon R. *The Hidden Forest: The Biography of an Ecosystem*. Corvallis: Oregon State University Press, 2006.
Maathai, Wangari. *Replenishing the Earth: Spiritual Values for Healing Ourselves and the World*. New York: Doubleday, Random House, 2010.
Maathai, Wangari. *The Greenbelt Movement: Sharing the Approach and the Experience*. Nairobi: Environment Liason Centre International, 1988.
Roy, Sumana. *How I Became a Tree*. New Haven: Yale University Press, 2021.

Ryan, John C., Patrícia Vieria, and Monica Gagliano. *The Mind of Plants: Narratives of Vegetal Intelligence*. Santa Fe, NM: Synergetic Press, 2021.

Simard, Suzanne. *Finding the Mother Tree: Discovering the Wisdom of the Forest*. New York: Knopf, 2021.

Wohlleben, Peter, and Jane Billinghurst. *Forest Walking*. Vancouver: Greystone Books, 2022.

Trees, Forests, and Society

Cone, James H. *The Cross and the Lynching Tree*. New York: Orbis Books, 2011.

Farmer, Jared. *Elderflora: A Modern History of Ancient Trees*. New York: Basic Books, Hachette Book Group, 2022.

Fischer, Luke, and David Macauley, eds. *The Seasons: Philosophical, Literary, and Environmental Perspectives*. Albany, NY: SUNY Press, 2021.

Haberman, David. *People Trees: Worship of Trees in Northern India*. New York: Oxford University Press, 2013.

Harrison, Robert Pogue. *Forests: The Shadow of Civilization*. Chicago: University of Chicago Press, 1992.

Jones, Owain, and Paul Cloke. *Tree Cultures: The Place of Trees and Trees in their Place*. New York: Berg, 2002.

Jonnes, Jill. *Urban Forests: A Natural History of Trees and People in the American Cityscape*. New York: Penguin Books, 2016.

Kohn, Eduardo. *How Forests Think: Towards an Anthropology Beyond the Human*. Berkeley, CA: University of California Press, 2013.

Maloof, Joan. *The Living Forest*. Portland, OR: Timber Press, 2017.

Maloof, Joan. *Teaching the Trees: Lessons from the Forest*. Athens: University of Georgia Press, 2007.

Maser, Chris. *Forest Primeval: The Natural History of An Ancient Forest*. Corvallis: Oregon State University Press, 2001.

Nadkarni, Nalini. *Between Earth and Sky: Our Intimate Connections to Trees*. Berkeley, CA: University of California Press, 2008.

Preston, Richard. *The Wild Trees*. New York: Random House, 2008.

Rival, Laura. *The Social Life of Trees: Anthropological Perspectives on Tree Symbolism*. New York: Berg, 1998.

Robbins, Jim. *The Man Who Planted Trees*. New York: Random House, 2015.

Rutkow, Eric. *American Canopy: Trees, Forests, and the Making of a Nation*. New York: Scribner, 2012.

Shiva, Vandana. "Vandana Shiva: Everything I Need to Know I Learned in the Forest." *YES! Magazine*, February 10, 2020. www.yesmagazine.org/issue/nature/2019/05/03/vandana-shiva-seed-saving-forest-biodiversity

Subramaniam, Banu. *Botany of Empire: Plant Worlds and the Scientific Legacies of Colonialism*. Seattle: University of Washington Press, 2024.

Tudge, Colin. *The Tree: A Natural History of What Trees Are, How They Live, and Why They Matter*. New York: Three Rivers Press, 2007.

Williams, Michael. *Deforesting the Earth: From Prehistory to Global Crisis*. Chicago: University of Chicago Press, 2003.

Wohlleben, Peter. *The Power of Trees: How Ancient Forests Can Save Us If We Let Them*. Greystone Books, 2023.

Critical Views on Plant Studies

Firn, Richard. "Plant Intelligence: An Alternative Point of View." *Annals of Botany* 93 (2004): 345–51.

Hamilton, Jennifer. "Bad Flowers: The Implications of a Phytocentric Deconstruction of the Western Philosophical Tradition for the Environmental Humanities." *Environmental Humanities* 7, no. 1 (2015): 191–202. doi:10.1215/22011919-3616398

Taiz, Lincoln, Daniel Alkon, Andreas Draguhn, Angus Murphy, Michael Blatt, Chris Hawes, Gerhard Thiel, and David G. Robinson. "Plants Neither Possess Nor Require Consciousness." *Trends in Plant Science* 24, no. 8 (2019): 677–87.

Contributors

Daniel O'Dea Bradley is a professor of philosophy at Gonzaga University in Spokane where he lives with his wife, Roisin Lally, and three daughters, Laura, Maria Anne, and Ciara. His teaching and research hinges on the tension between a phenomenology of the sacred and a hermeneutics of suspicion. While not forgetting the contributions of the iconoclasm of the twentieth century, he tries to open philosophy to think the sacredness of being, thereby allowing for dialogue with Native American thought, liturgical and sacramental religion, and environmental ethics. Trees have always been a central part of Dan's life. He and his family live surrounded by apple and cherry trees on the very southernmost spur of the Selkirk mountains at an ecological border where Douglas Fir and Ponderosa Pine forests morph into the grasslands of the Palouse. They spend their summers in a tiny remnant of ancient oak forest in the west of Ireland. And he visits the cedar-hemlock forests of the northwest coast any chance he gets!

Kimberly Carfore, PhD, is a professor in both the Environmental Studies and Theology & Religious Studies Departments at the University of San Francisco. She is the founder of Wild Women, a Bay Area nonprofit whose goal is to empower and educate women in the outdoors. She teaches ancestral skills with a focus on friction firemaking, specifically the bowdrill and flint & steel methods. In this way, her relationship with trees involves the practice of creating fire through material relations with Buckeye, Cedar, Sage, and Cottonwood. This practice maintains balance. Dr. Carfore is the co-chair of the Religion and Ecology unit of the American Academy of Religion. She serves on the Advisory Board for the Yale Forum on Religion and Ecology for ecojustice and ecofeminism. Her most recent publication is an article titled "Ecofeminist Theology: Intersectional Justice and Plumwood's Philosophical Animism" published in the *SAGE Journal of Feminist Theology*.

Edward S. Casey is Distinguished Professor of Philosophy at SUNY Stony Brook. He is past president of the American Philosophical Association (Eastern Division) and was the chair of the philosophy department at Stony Brook 1990–2001. He is the author of twelve books, among them *Imagining, Remembering, The Fate of Place, Getting Back into Place, The World at a Glance, The World on Edge*, and (most recently) *Turning Emotion Inside Out: Affective Life Beyond the Subject*. He is co-author with Michael Marder of *Plants in Place: A Phenomenology of the Vegetal*.

Luke Fischer is a philosopher and poet based in Sydney, Australia. His various writings focus on interconnections among poetry, philosophy, art, and the environment (including trees). Fischer's books include the monograph *The Poet as Phenomenologist: Rilke and the 'New Poems'* (Bloomsbury, 2015) and the poetry collections *A Gamble for my Daughter* (Vagabond Press, 2022), *A Personal History of Vision* (UWAP, 2017) and *Paths of Flight* (Black Pepper, 2013). He co-edited (with David Macauley) the volume *The Seasons: Philosophical, Literary, and Environmental Perspectives* (SUNY Press, 2021) and (with Hannah V. Eldridge) *Rilke's 'Sonnets to Orpheus': Philosophical and Critical Perspectives* (Oxford University Press, 2019). With Dalia Nassar, he guest-edited a special section of the *Goethe Yearbook* (2015) on Goethe and Environmentalism. Fischer holds a PhD from the University of Sydney where he is also an honorary associate of the philosophy department. For more information visit: www.lukefischer.net

James Hatley is an emeritus professor in both philosophy and environmental studies at Salisbury University in Maryland. He is a co-editor of *Facing Nature: Levinas and Environmental Thought*, as well as the author of a philosophical response to the Holocaust framed by the thought of Emmanuel Levinas titled *Suffering Witness: the Quandary of Responsibility after the Irreparable*. Over the last decade, Hatley has collaborated with the Extinction Studies Working Group and the Religion and Extinction Network to produce a series of articles and book chapters addressing the quandaries of living responsibly in a time of human-caused mass species extinction.

Don Hanlon Johnson is a professor of Somatics in the School of Consciousness and Transformation at CIIS. He is the founder of the clinical master's degree program in Somatic Psychology and the author of several books and collections on the relations between direct body experiences and the major questions that challenge us now, including how we think of ourselves as earth beings nurtured within trees like these: His website is https://donhanlonjohnson.com

Alphonso Lingis is professor of philosophy emeritus at the Pennsylvania State University. Among his books are *The Community of Those Who Have Nothing in Common, Abuses, The Imperative, Dangerous Emotions, Trust, The First Person Singular, Contact, Violence and Splendor, Irrevocable,* and *The Alphonso Lingis Reader.*

David Macauley is Academy Professor and Professor Emeritus of Philosophy and Environmental Studies at Penn State University, Brandywine. He has taught at Oberlin College, Emerson College, and New York University and was a Mellon Fellow at the University of Pennsylvania. Macauley is the author of *Elemental Philosophy: Earth, Air, Fire, and Water as Environmental Ideas*; editor of *Minding Nature: The Philosophers of Ecology*, co-editor of *The Seasons: Philosophical, Literary, and Environmental Perspectives*; and co-editor of *The Wisdom of Trees*. He has published articles on ethics, aesthetics, politics, Greek philosophy, and Continental thought. Macauley is completing a book entitled *Walking the Earth: Philosophical and Environmental Foot Notes*; putting together a collection of philosophical parables and myths called *Re-storying Wisdom*; and working on a book project entitled *Discovering Beauty in Dark Times*. He lives in West Philadelphia, where he bikes, gardens, competes in distance races, and renovates a Victorian house. He enjoys running beneath trees in forests, parks, and cemeteries.

Joan Maloof, PhD, is an ecologist, activist, and writer. Her five books about trees and forests are *Teaching the Trees, Among the Ancients, The Living Forest, Treepedia,* and *Natures Temples: A Natural History of Old-Growth Forests*. Maloof's most recent book is a meta-memoir titled *Wild Old Woman* (2024). In addition to these books, she has authored numerous scholarly papers, essays, and poems. Maloof is an emeritus professor in biology and environmental studies at Salisbury University and the founder of the Old-Growth Forest Network (OGFN), a national nongovernmental organization in the United States. Her organization works to preserve the remaining old-growth forests as well as "future old-growth forests" and connects people of all generations to the forests. Visit www.oldgrowthforest.net to learn more.

Michael Marder is IKERBASQUE Research Professor in the Department of Philosophy at the University of the Basque Country (UPV-EHU), Vitoria-Gasteiz, Spain. His writings span the fields of ecological theory, phenomenology, and political thought. He is the author of numerous scientific articles and monographs, including *Plant-Thinking* (2013), *The Philosopher's Plant* (2014), *Dust* (2016), *Energy Dreams* (2017), *Heidegger* (2018), *Political Categories* (2019), *Pyropolitics* (2015, 2020); *Dump Philosophy* (2020); *Hegel's Energy* (2021); *Green Mass* (2021), *Philosophy for Passengers* (2022), *The Phoenix Complex* (2023), *Time Is a Plant* (2023), and, with Edward S. Casey, *The Place of Plants* (2023). For more information, consult his website: michaelmarder.org

Sam Mickey, PhD, is an adjunct professor in the Environmental Studies program and the Theology and Religious Studies department at the University of San Francisco. He is also a researcher and podcast host for the Yale Forum on Religion and Ecology and the author of several books of environmental philosophy, including *Coexistentialism and the Unbearable Intimacy of Ecological Emergency* (Lexington Books), *On the Verge of a Planetary Civilization: A Philosophy of Integral Ecology* (Rowman and Littlefield), and *Whole Earth Thinking and Planetary Coexistence* (Routledge). Some of his edited works include *Eco-Anxiety and Pandemic Distress: Psychological Perspectives on Resilience and Interconnectedness* (Oxford University Press), *Living Earth Community: Multiple Ways of Being and Knowing* (Open Book Publishers), and *Literature and Ecofeminism: Intersectional and International Voices* (Routledge). He enjoys spending time in the redwood forests where he lives in northern California.

Mara Miller has loved trees since infancy, when she was lucky enough to live with a majestic silver maple and weeping willows—the latter providing an emotional and aesthetic bridge to her master's studies at the University of Michigan in Japanese literati painting. The National Outdoor Leadership School taught her to understand trees environmentally, in relation to each other and the land, while a stint as consultant to Philadelphia's Shofuso Japanese House and Garden helped her understand the myriad ways Japanese culture uses and values trees and the products made from them. Since earning her doctorate in philosophy at Yale University, Mara has published *The Garden as an Art* (SUNY Press) and seventy scholarly articles in aesthetics, comparative selfhood, Japanese art, women's/gender studies, and environmental philosophy. Mara has taught Western and Eastern philosophy, Japanese literature and religion, Chinese and Japanese art history, as well as "Gardens, Landscape and Sacred Space" in East Asia and globally. She is finishing two books, *The Sky in the Garden* and *The Philosopher's Garden*.

Dalia Nassar is associate professor of philosophy at the University of Sydney and a member of the Sydney Environment Institute. Her research sits at the intersection of the history of philosophy (especially nineteenth-century German), environmental philosophy, ethics and aesthetics. She has been the recipient of grants from the Australian Research Council, the Humboldt Foundation, the Social Sciences and Humanities Research Council (Canada), and the Thyssen Foundation. Her most recent book, *Romantic Empiricism: Nature, Art, and Ecology from Herder to Humboldt* (OUP 2022), uncovers an under-studied empiricist tradition that emerged in Germany in the late eighteenth century, investigates its role in the emergence of ecology, and argues for its relevance in current environmental debates. She is the editor of a number of volumes, including *Women Philosophers in the Long Nineteenth Century: The German Tradition* (with Kristin Gjesdal, OUP 2021).

Eric W. Orts is the Guardsmark Professor of Legal Studies & Business Ethics at the Wharton School of the University of Pennsylvania. Prior to joining Wharton's faculty, he practiced law at Paul Weiss in New York City and was a Chemical Bank fellow in corporate social responsibility at Columbia Law School. He has previously held visiting appointments at UCLA, Michigan, Leuven, Tsinghua, University of California Santa Barbara, Harvard, Sydney, NYU, INSEAD, and Columbia. He is graduate of Oberlin (BA in government, minor in philosophy), the New School for Social Research (MA in political science), the University of Michigan (JD), and Columbia (LL.M., JSD). His primary research interests are in corporate governance, environmental sustainability, business ethics, and business theory. Examples include *Business Persons: A Legal Theory of the Firm* (rev. ed. 2015); *The Moral Responsibility of Firms* (co-edited with Craig Smith) (2017); and "The Climate Imperative for Business" (with Brian Berkey), *California Management Review* (2021), https://cmr.berkeley.edu/2021/04/climate-imperative. His favorite local trees in West Philadelphia are two tulip poplars (*Liriodendron tulipifera*) and a white pine (*Pinus strobus*).

Laura Pustarfi, PhD, is adjunct faculty at the California Institute of Integral Studies. Her scholarly work examines trees and plants in Western thought with particular focus on philosophical literature in order to explore an arboreal and vegetal ontology and ethics that respects plants themselves. Laura has presented at the several academic conferences including those of the International Association for Environmental Philosophy (IAEP), TORCH Oxford, the Pacific Association for the Continental Tradition (PACT), and the International Society for Environmental Ethics (ISEE). She is Director of the Psychedelic-Assisted Therapies and Research Certificate Program at CIIS and is responsible for the administration of the certificate program training mental health professionals in the field of psychedelic-assisted psychotherapy. She lives in the San Francisco Bay Area on occupied Indigenous territory of the Coast Miwok and Southern Pomo, represented by the Federated Indians of Graton Rancheria.

Musician and philosopher **David Rothenberg** wrote *Why Birds Sing*, *Bug Music*, *Survival of the Beautiful*, and many other books, published in at least eleven languages. He has more than fifty recordings out, including *One Dark Night I Left My Silent House*, which came out on ECM, and most recently *In the Wake of Memories* and *Faultlines*. He has performed or recorded with Pauline Oliveros, Peter Gabriel, Ray Phiri, Suzanne Vega, Scanner, Elliott Sharp, Umru, Iva Bittová, and the Karnataka College of Percussion. *Secret Sounds of Ponds* is his latest book. *Nightingales In Berlin* is his latest film. Rothenberg is Distinguished Professor at the New Jersey Institute of Technology. Rothenberg grew up in Connecticut climbing white pine trees, and later developed a love for the small, often very old wind-gnarled subalpine conifers known as *krummholz*. He is sad that the magnolia tree in his garden has reached the end of its days, over fifty years old, and had to be cut down.

John Charles Ryan is an international researcher in literary studies, creative writing, and environmental humanities. He is Adjunct Senior Research Fellow at the Nulungu Research Institute, University of Notre Dame, Australia. Funded by the Kone Foundation in Helsinki, his current research examines possibilities for communication and collaboration between people and trees in Northern Finland. Ryan's books include *Environment, Media and Popular Culture in Southeast Asia* (2022, Springer, co-edited) and *Introduction to the Environmental Humanities* (2022, Routledge, co-authored). He is Chief Editor of the journal *Plant Perspectives* and Managing Co-Editor of *The Trumpeter*. His connections to trees extend from North America and Northern Europe to Oceania and Southeast Asia with special affinities for the Christmas tree (*Nuytsia floribunda*) of Western Australia,

Antarctic beech (*Nothofagus moorei*) of New South Wales, the sassafras tree (*Sassafras albidum*) of the eastern United States, and the titan arum (*Amorphophallus titanum*) of Sumatra, Indonesia. For more information, see www.johncharlesryan.com.

Matthew David Segall is a transdisciplinary researcher, writer, teacher, and philosopher applying process-relational thought across the natural and social sciences, including the study of consciousness. He is an associate professor in the Philosophy, Cosmology, and Consciousness Program at California Institute of Integral Studies in San Francisco, California, and author of several books, including *Physics of the World-Soul* (SacraSage, 2021) and *Crossing the Threshold* (Integral Imprint, 2023). He feels most at home under the shade of old trees.

Index

Aboriginal ontogenesis, 167
abortion, 392
acacia trees, 95
Acts of Religion (Derrida), 126n11
Adams, Ansel, 23, 26n39, 279
Aesthetics and the Environment (Carlson), 283n3
"After Apple-Picking" (Frost), 304
Agamben, Giorgio, 12
agency, 7, 42–43, 47
Ahmed, Sara, 383
Alerce Milenario (Gran Abuelo), 185
Alighieri, Dante
   Divine Comedy, The, 78
allegory, 330
altruism, 349
Amazon forests, 216
ambience, 265, 266
American beech trees, 263
American sycamore trees, 375
Angel Oak, 21
Animal Liberation (Singer), 394, 408n43
Anthropocene, 11, 360
Antoine Roquentin (fictional character), 377–79
Anxiety of Influence, The (Bloom), 286–87n61
apples/apple trees, 259, 267, 304
Arabidopsis thaliana, 39

babies, 189
Bachelard, Gaston, 109, 146, 148–49, 149, 265, 278
backgrounding, 55, 69–70n2
Bacon, Francis
   Masculine Birth of Time, The, 62
Baluška, František, 46
bamboo
   Bambusa nana, 348–49
   discussed, 7, 283n2, 332, 336, 350, 362n16
   Rihua on, 356–57
   virtues, 337, 354–55
   Zan on, 357–58
banksia trees, 93
banyan trees, 193–94, 255
Barbour, Margaret
   "Tree Stories," 238n22
bark, 263
Barnhart, Richard, 340, 344–45
Baron in the Trees, The (Calvino), 267
Bartram, John, 412n90
Bashō, Matsuo, 270
bathing in the forest atmosphere, 266
Baudrillard, Jean, 68
Beaumont, Julia
   "Great Irish Famine, The," 238n21
"Beautiful Yuroke Red River Gum" (Bellear), 173
beautility, 256

beauty
  discussed, 283–84n13
  and functions, 251
  Greeks on, 248
  Haskell on, 255
  leaves, 261
  Maloof on, 252–53
  and seasons, 270
  and utility, 256
  wabi-sabi, 260
beavers, 310–11
Beck, Hanno
  "Kommentar," 236n15
"Becoming Bonsai, Becoming Carer" (Jimenez), 286n59
Being and Nothingness (Sartre), 379
Beiser, Frederick, 149
Bell, Clive
  Art, 288n92
  discussed, 271
Bellear, Lisa
  "Beautiful Yuroke Red River Gum," 173
  discussed, 163
Beneficent Trees, 97
Bennett, Jane, 280
Bentham, Jeremy, 252
Bergson, Henri, 52n23, 145–46, 200–201
Berleant, Arnold
  Living in the Landscape, 283n3
Berry, Thomas, 47
Beuys, Joseph, 280
"Beyond Birth and Death" (Hanh), 406n15
Bhagavad Gita (unknown), 150n13, 194
binaries, 381
biogeography, 238n23
biosemiotics, 98n8
"Birches" (Frost), 263
birds, 63, 122, 187, 193, 254, 264

black walnut trees, 349
Blake, William, 3, 272
Bloom, Harold
  Anxiety of Influence, The, 286–87n61
boab trees, 167–68, 171, 174
Bodhi Tree, 163, 194, 266–67, 275, 330
Böhme, Jacob, 81, 82
Bonfadio, Jacopo, 361n5
Bonfiglioli, Cristina, 109
Bonpland, Aimé, 214
bonsai, 258, 260, 286n59
Book of Changes (Wenwang), 275
books, 268–69
borders, 205
Botany of Desire, The (Pollan), 304
bottlebrushes, 171
boundaries, 205
bowerbirds, 286n49
Brady, Emily, 278
Braun, Alexander
  "Vegetable Individual in Its relation to Species, The," 237n17
Brecht, Bertolt
  "To Those Born Later," 10
Bridle, James
  discussed, 398
  Ways of Being, 405n10, 409n48
Brigman, Anne, 78
bristlecone pines, 4, 158, 184–85, 400
Bryant, William Cullen, 304
Buber, Martin
  discussed, 89, 90
  I and Thou, 281, 289n118
Buddha
  and Bodhi Tree, 8, 163, 194, 266–67, 327, 330
  discussed, 258
  Four Noble Truths, 350
Buddhism, 258, 316, 415
burials, 184

Burke, Edmund, 57
Burke, Tarana, 158

Cage, John
   "Child of Tree," 296
Caldas, Francisco José de, 232, 238n24
Callicott, J. Baird, 38, 408n43
calligraphy, 339, 343–44
Calvino, Italo
   Baron in the Trees, The, 267
camphor trees, 262
Candolle, Augustin de, 236n15
Cañizares-Esguerra, Jorge
   "How Derivative was Humboldt?," 238n24
carbon dioxide, 94, 123, 322, 390, 397
Carlson, Allen
   Aesthetics and the Environment, 283n3
   Functional Beauty, 284n25
cathedral trees, 65, 275
Cavarero, Adriana
   Inclinations, 284n20
cemeteries, 183, 242
Cézanne, Paul, 259, 304
Chamovitz, Daniel, 170
Changing Difference (Malabou), 72n48
chaos, 376
Chapman, John (Johnny Appleseed), 267, 304
charismatic megaflora, 32
Charleston shuffle, 21
cheeky theory, 373
chestnut trees, 372, 377–79
chiasm, 158, 282
"Child of Tree" (Cage), 296
chimpanzees, 63
Chipko movement, 273
chlorophyll, 261
Chomsky, Noam, 380, 386n36
chronodiversity, 158, 250

churches, 275, 280
Cicero, 361n5
citizens, 392
civil service system, 339
Clark, Stephen, 408n43
Clarke, Ellen
   "Problem of Biological Individuality, The," 237n19
Claudel, Paul, 197
clearing, 204
climate change, 11, 31, 320, 395, 409n48, 410n62
Clinton, Hillary, 58, 73n52
clonal trees, 4
Clouds in Each Paper, 285n38
Clunas, Craig
   Fruitful Sites, 362n18
Coccia, Emanuele, 374
   Coexistentialism and the Unbearable Intimacy of Ecological Emergency (Mickey), 72n48
Coleridge, Samuel Taylor, 152n65
columnar trees, 193–94
communion of subjects, 47
Confucianism, 332, 350–51
Confucius, 344
conifers, 222–24, 236n13
conjunctive creativity, 383
connective beauty, 255
Connolly, William, 401
consciousness, 45–46, 52n23, 119–20, 120, 124–25
contemporary art, 115
Cook, Diane
   Wise Trees, 362n16, 403n6
Cooper-Smithson, Hannah, 373, 381
Council Oak Tree, 174
creative activity, 52n23
creative potency, 92
creativity, 143
Creator Beings, 167
creaturely discernment, 315

Crisp, Peter, 165
"Criticism, Feminism, and the Institution" (Grosz & Spivak), 70n10
Critique of Cynical Reason (Sloterdijk), 373
Critique of the Power of Judgment (Kant), 227
Cron, Lisa
  Wired for Story, 267
Crossing of the Visible, The (Marion), 109
crown shyness, 266
crowned hornbills, 187–88
Crowther, T. W.
  "Mapping Tree Density at a Global Scale," 13
cryptogams, 231
cyanide, 262
cypress trees, 241–42

Daly, Mary, 60
Daoism, 332, 349–50, 351, 382
dark times, 10
Darwin, Charles
  discussed, 63, 102n41, 134, 254
  Power of Movement in Plants, The, 163
Darwin, Francis
  Power of Movement in Plants, The, 163
  Rustic Sounds, 163–64
Davis, Jack
  "Forest Giant," 173
  "Red Gum and I, The," 171–72
dead trees, 65, 261, 413n92
death of nature, 62, 71n27
Death of Nature, The (Merchant), 71n27
deforestation, 12, 13, 409n51
deformity, 248

Deleuze, Gilles
  and bonsai, 286n59
  discussed, 134, 209, 372, 374, 381
  on imagination, 148
  Thousand Plateaus, A, 197, 198
  on trees, 379–80
  wisdom of the plants, 382
Deloria, Ella
  Waterlily, 127n18
Democracy Dies in Darkness, 110
dendrochronology, 4
dendrocide, 173, 175
Dendrofemonology (Shlain), 4, 158
dendroglyphs, 173–74
Dendroids (Paine), 279
dendrophilia, 176
dendrophobia, 175, 176
Denning, Lord, 6
deodar cedar trees, 158
Derrida, Jacques
  Acts of Religion, 126n11
  discussed, 375–76, 376–77, 381, 382
Descartes, René, 134
"Dialogue of the Tree" (Valéry), 260, 286n60
Dialogues Concerning Natural Religion (Hume), 142
"Did a Fall From a Tree Kill Lucy, Our Famous Ancestor?" (Hoffman), 361n4
"Die tropischen Gebirge" (Troll), 236n15
different intentions of the eye, 281
Dillard, Annie
  discussed, 251
  Pilgrim at Tinker Creek, 316–17
directionality, 211
diversity work, 383
Divine Comedy, The (Alighieri), 78
Divine Logos, 81
Doctrine of the Mean (Xi), 340

Index | 439

Dōgen
  discussed, 296
  Shōbōgenzō, 359, 366n60
  "Verses of Praise on Portraits of Himself," 358–59
  doing nothing, 384
Dooren, Thom Van, 315, 316
Douglas, David, 318
Douglas fir trees, 41
Dreaming, 167, 168, 169, 170, 171, 173
Dred Scott decision, 391
dualisms
  Deleuze & Guattari on, 381
  discussed, 61, 62, 70n21, 80, 82
Duchamp, Marcel
  Fountain, 280
Dutton, Denis
  Art Instinct, The, 253

e-co-affectivity, 207
"Earth laws, right of nature and legal pluralism" (Pelizzon), 99n10
Earth's Wild Music (Moore), 291
Ecclesiastes, 347, 364n36
Eckermann, Ali Cobby
  discussed, 163
  "Leaves," 170
  "Story Tree," 173, 174–75
  "Today," 170–71
ecofeminism, 60–61
ecology, 62–63, 213
ecoproprioception, 207
ecosystem services, 7, 397, 411n64
"Ecosystem Services as a Contested Concept" (Schröter), 411n64
edge-to-edge patterns, 207
edges, 203–4, 204–6, 207–8
efficacious uselessness, 383
elder trees, 165
elderflora, 4, 158, 250, 391

Elderflora (Farmer), 411n65
Elkins, James
  Object Looks Back, The, 289n120
embodied history of trees, 238n22
Emerson, Ralph Waldo
  discussed, 3, 246, 253, 273, 276
  on imagination, 277
emotions, 272
empathy, 63
Empedocles, 71n27
Encounter, The (McBurney), 296
end-of-life decisions, 392
Endangered Habitat Act, 276
Endangered Species Act, 276
enlightened self-interest, 347, 348
Enneads (Plotinus), 141
environmental aesthetics, 245, 283n3
environmental personhood, 390
"Environmental Personhood" (Gordon), 403n6
environmental persons, 403n6
environmental services, 251
epizoochory, 254
Erotic Phenomenon, The (Marion), 109
"Essay on Man, An" (Pope), 128n45
Essay on the Geography of Plants (Humboldt), 238n23
ethical extensionism, 412n91
Eucalyptus globulus (Tasmanian bluegum trees), 369–70
eucalyptus trees, 369
eukaryotes, 185
eulogies, 354
evolution, 63
Ewbank, Thomas, 234–35n7
exceptional trees, 361n2
Extraordinary Attorney Woo (TV series), 399

fairy rings, 65

Farmer, Jared
  discussed, 3–4, 158, 250, 391
  Elderflora, 411n65
Fay, Neville, 334–35
Fellow Creatures (Korsgaard), 404–5n10, 409n47, 409n50
Felski, Rita, 372–73
Feminism and the Mastery of Nature (Plumwood), 69–70n2, 70n21, 71n24
Fenner, David
  Art and Philosophy of the Garden, The, 361n5
Fenner, Ethan
  Art and Philosophy of the Garden, The, 361n5
Fiedler, Carl E.
  discussed, 318, 319–20
  Ponderosa, 326n28
fig trees, 194
final good, 409n47
finding, 65
Finding Mother God (Pearson), 65–66
Finding the Mother Tree (Simard), 65–66, 95, 165, 254
"Fir" (Fischer), 92
fire, 48, 119, 120–21, 320–21, 323
Firn, Richard, 51n10
First Nature, 328
Fischer, Luke
  "Fir," 92
  "Invisible Service," 91
  Poet as Phenomenologist, The, 98n9
flesh of the world, 36
Flora Berloinensis (Willdenow), 238n24
flowers, 91, 144
Fong, Wen, 340, 345
Food and Agricultural Organization, 13
"Forest Giant" (Davis), 173
"Forest in the Library, The" (Snyder), 268

"Forest Resilience, Biodiversity, and Climate Change" (Thompson), 405–6n15
forests, 77–78
Forests (Harrison), 77
forgetting, 165
forgetting of her, 55, 62, 71n27
form
  discussed, 105, 228–29, 248, 284n14
  Humboldt on, 216, 226, 227–28, 229, 232
Foster (forest owner), xiv
Foster's Forest, xiv
Foundations of Esotericism, The (Steiner), 102n41
Fountain (Duchamp), 280
Four Causes, 360n1
Four Gentlemen, 337, 357
Four Noble Truths, 350
fragility of things, 401
Frankfurt, Harry, 394
Frazier, James
  Golden Bough, The, 275
free variation in imagination, 205
Freud, Sigmund, 363n25
"From Enlightenment Vision to Modern Science?" (Godlewska), 236n15
Frost, Robert
  "After Apple-Picking," 304
  "Birches," 263
  discussed, 24, 279
  "Sound of Trees, The," 263–64
Fruitful Sites (Clunas), 362n18
Fu, Du
  discussed, 344, 351
  "Song of My Nan Tree Uprooted by the Storm," 327–28
Functional Beauty (Parsons & Carlson), 284n25
functions, 251
funerals, 188–89

fungi, 41, 186, 187

Gagliano, Monica
 discussed, 40, 44, 292–93, 296–97, 297–98
 Language of Plants, The, 102n41
 Mind of Plants, The, 134
 Thus Spoke the Plant, 293
garden cress, 45–46
Garimara, Doris Pilkington
 discussed, 161–63
 Under the Wintamarra Tree, 161
Gateless Gate, The (Yamada), 258–59
Gautama, Siddhartha. *See* Buddha
General Morphology (Haeckel), 213
General Sherman, 8, 184
generative semantics, 380, 386n36
generative syntax, 380
generative uselessness, 383
Geographische Geschichte des Menschen, und der allgemeinen verbreiteten vierfüßigen Thier (Zimmermann), 238n23
Germany, 400
ghost gums, 170, 171
Gilbert, Kevin
 discussed, 169, 171
 "Tree," 167
gingko trees, 269
"Ginkgo Biloba" (Goethe), 25n17
Giving Tree, The (Silverstein), 257, 303
Glissant, Édouard, 373
Global Forest Resources Assessment, 13
God, 60, 71n27, 80–81
Godlewska, Anne Marie Clara
 "From Enlightenment Vision to Modern Science?," 236n15
Goethe, Johann Wolfgang von
 discussed, 85, 91, 100n18, 250
 "Ginkgo Biloba," 25n17
Goethean science, 90, 100–101n22, 100n21

Gogh, Vincent van
 discussed, 259, 279
 Starry Night, 242
 Wheat Field with Cypresses, 242
Gold Creek, 308–9, 309, 311, 317, 321
Golden Bough, The (Frazier), 275
Goldsworthy, Andy
 discussed, 24
 Wood Line, 279
Gongwang, Huang
 discussed, 354
 "Six Trees," 332
Goodall, Jane, 63
Goodpaster, Kenneth, 408n43
Gordon, Gwendolyn J.
 discussed, 390, 393, 398, 400–401
 "Environmental Personhood," 403n6
Graft (Paine), 279
Graham, Mary, 167
Gran Abuelo (Alerce Milenario), 185
Grandmother Redwood, 33, 55, 56–58, 62, 64
Grant, Iain Hamilton, 145
gravitropism, 197
gravity, 267, 304
Great Animal Orchestra, The (Krause), 291
"Great Irish Famine, The" (Beaumont & Montgomery), 238n21
Great Onslaught, The, 12
Greater Perfections (Hunt), 361n5
Green, Charmaine Papertalk
 discussed, 163
 "Honey to Lips Bottlebrush," 170, 171
Green Legacy Hiroshima, 269
Green, Sam
 32 Sounds, 296
Griffin, Susan
 "Timber," 62
Grimonprez, Mavra, 44
Grober, Ulrich, 109

Grosz, Elizabeth
"Criticism, Feminism, and the Institution," 70n10
Grotesque Pine (unknown), 352
growth-thought, 141
Grundriss der Kräuterkunde (Willdenow), 238n24
Guattari, Félix
discussed, 134, 209, 372, 374, 381
on imagination, 148
Thousand Plateaus, A, 197, 198
on trees, 379–80
wisdom of the plants, 382
Gueimeng, Lu, 352
Gunkel, David, 375

hackberry trees, 399
Hacker, Karel, 297
Haeckel, Ernst
General Morphology, 213
haiku, 259, 270
Hall, Matthew
discussed, 9, 44–45
Imagination of Plants, The, 135
Hallowell, Irving, 44
Hanh, Thich Nhat
"Beyond Birth and Death," 406n15
discussed, 285n38
Hao, Zhing, 354
Haraway, Donna, 71n32, 315
Harding, Sandra, 71n32
hardwood, 264
Harjo, Joy
"Speaking Tree," 22
"Story Tree," 173, 174–75
Harris, Randy Allen
Linguistics Wars, The, 386n36
Harrison, Robert Pogue
Forests, 77
Haskell, David
discussed, 262, 294–95, 298
Songs of Trees, The, 255, 293

Hawthorne, Nathaniel
"Young Goodman Brown," 267
Hay, John, 334, 337, 338, 360
"Healing Tree, The" (Thomas), 173, 174
Heaney, Seamus, 24, 279
heartwood, 264
heaths, 231
Hegel, Georg Wilhelm Friedrich, 137, 146, 152n63
Heidegger, Martin, 119, 204, 291, 304
Hempton, Gordon, 128n39
Heraclitus, 81, 138, 143, 144, 197
"Herschel Walker's Anti-Tree Campaign is Genius" (Milbank), 405n11
Hesse, Hermann, 3, 277
heterotrophs, 123
hibakujumoku, 269
hibakusha, 269
Hildegard of Bingen, 123
Hill, Julia Butterfly, 32, 272, 416
Hinduism, 194
hitching, 254
Hoffman, Adam
"Did a Fall From a Tree Kill Lucy, Our Famous Ancestor?," 361n4
Hoffmann, Nigel, 92
Hogan, Linda
"What Holds the Water, What Holds the Light," 311–13
Holmes, Nancy, 372
Homer
Odyssey, The, 138
homo sacer, 12
"Honey to Lips Bottlebrush" (Green), 170, 171
Hooper, Steven, 169
horizon, 204
"How Derivative was Humboldt?" (Cañizares-Esguerra), 238n24
How Forests Think (Kohn), 405n10

How I Became a Tree (Roy), 78
How to Do Nothing (Odell), 384
hub trees, 41, 42, 97
Huizi, 382, 383
Humboldt, Alexander von
  on conifers, 222, 236n13
  discussed, 215, 230, 236n15, 237n17
  Essay on the Geography of Plants, 238n23
  on form, 232
  and Francisco José de Caldas, 238n24
  "Ideas for a Geography of Plants," 221
  "Ideas for a Physiognomy of Plants," 216, 217–18, 221
  Kosmos, 213, 229, 235n11, 237n18
  at Lake Valencia, 214, 231, 234–35n7
  on landscape painting, 219–20
  and national parks movement, 234–35n7
  Views of Nature, 216
  and Willdenow, 238n24
  on willows, 224–25
Humboldt Current, The (Sachs), 235n7
Hume, David
  Dialogues Concerning Natural Religion, 142
  discussed, 143
Hunt, John Dixon
  Greater Perfections, 361n5
Hussain, Altaf, 41
Husserl, Edmund, 107, 119, 137, 205, 208
Hyperion, 7–8, 31

I and Thou (Buber), 281, 289n118
"Ideas for a Geography of Plants" (Humboldt), 221
"Ideas for a Physiognomy of Plants" (Humboldt), 216, 217, 221

If you see something, say something, 110
imagination, 100–101n22, 277–78
Imagination of Plants, The (Hall), 135
In the Beginning, She Was (Irigaray), 55, 71n27
Inclinations (Cavarero), 284n20
Indigenous invisibility, 174
individuation, 200
Indra's Net, 255
ineffable quality of understatement, 359
Ineinsbildung, 152n65
ink painting, 366n55
intelligence, 7, 39, 40, 47, 51n10
intensification, 85
inter-being, 255
interfaces, 207
interpretive semantics, 386n36
intuitive judgment, 100n18
"Invisible Service" (Fischer), 91
Irigaray, Luce
  In the Beginning, She Was, 55, 71n27
  on contemporary art, 115
  discussed, 37, 56, 59, 60, 120
  on silence, 111–13, 114–15
irises, 259, 336, 380
Irish potato famine, 238n21

Jeffers, Robinson, 256
Jenshel, Len
  Wise Trees, 362n16, 403n6
Jeremijenko, Natalie
  Tree Logic, 280
Jimenez, Jayson
  "Becoming Bonsai, Becoming Carer," 286n59
Johnny Appleseed (John Chapman), 267, 304
Johnson, Galen, 264–65
jumping genes, 63

Jung, Carl G.
  discussed, 17–18, 284n20, 330, 345
  "Philosophical Tree, The," 18

kairos, 346–47, 364n36
kami, 262, 275
Kant, Immanuel
  Cavarero on, 284n20
  Critique of the Power of Judgment, 227
  discussed, 106, 114, 126n4, 145, 405n10
  on flowers, 144
  Korsgaard on, 396
  on the sublime, 274
  "What is Enlightenment?," 105–6
Karban, Richard, 41
Keats, Jonathan, 158
Keller, Evelyn Fox, 71n32
khora, 376
ki, 49
Kiefer, Anselm, 279
Kimmerer, Robin Wall, 14, 48–49, 166
Klaver, Irene
  "Silent Wolves," 72n45
Klee, Paul, 281
Klinkenborg, Verlyn
  discussed, 349
  Wise Trees, 362n16
Kohák, Erazim, 371, 374
Kohn, Eduardo
  How Forests Think, 405n10
Kolbert, Elizabeth, 393
"Kommentar" (Beck), 236n15
Korsgaard, Christine M.
  discussed, 396
  Fellow Creatures, 404–5n10, 409n47, 409n50
Kosmos (Humboldt), 213, 229, 235n11, 237n18
Koyasan, 316

Krause, Bernie
  Great Animal Orchestra, The, 291
Krishnamurti, Jiddu, 245
Kühlewind, George
  Logos-Structure of the World, The, 99n15
Kukai, 316
Kung Fu Panda (film), 351
Kwan-yin, 354
kwela, 168

Lake Valencia, 214, 215, 231, 234–35n7
Lakoff, George, 380
landscape painting, 219–20, 228, 232
Landsdowne Sycamore, 404n9
Lane, Belden, 63–64
language
  arboreal, 86, 87, 97, 337
  discussed, 56, 85, 86, 337, 386n36, 396
  Gagliano on, 44
  Hay on, 338
  Merleau-Ponty on, 44
language of nature, 81, 82, 83, 98n7
Language of Plants, The (Gagliano & Ryan & Vieira), 102n41
Last Child in the Woods (Louv), 20
leaves, 7, 250
"Leaves" (Eckermann), 170
legal fictions, 404n8
Leibniz, Gottfried Wilhelm, 212n3
Leopold, Aldo
  discussed, 252, 256
  Sand County Almanac, 133
Levinas, Emmanuel
  discussed, 43, 107–8, 313–14, 314
  Otherwise than Being, 324n6
  Totality and Infinity, 106
libraries, 268
lignification, 87
Lingis, Alphonso, 272

Index | 445

Linguistics Wars, The (Harris), 386n36
linking postulates, 61–62
literati, 339
Littlejohn, Ronnie, 349–50
Living in the Landscape (Berleant), 283n3
Lock her up, 69
Locke, John, 394
lodgepole pine trees, 41
Logan, William Bryant, 334
logic of colonization, 61, 66, 69
logic of solids, 145
logocentrism, 375–77, 377
logos, 113, 141
Logos, 80–81, 82, 84, 85, 96
Logos-Structure of the World, The (Kühlewind), 99n15
Loose lips sink ships, 127n19
Louv, Richard
  Last Child in the Woods, 20
Lucy (primate fossil), 328, 361n4
Luna, 32, 272
lungs of the planet, 397

Macauley, David
  "Night and Shadows," 109
Machine Man (de La Mettrie), 17
Malabou, Catherine
  Changing Difference, 72n48
  discussed, 59
Maloof, Joan, 252–53, 277
Man as Plant (de La Mettrie), 17
Mancuso, Stefano, 46
Manning, Erin, 383
Manning, Richard, 310, 317
maple syrup, 263
maple trees, 263, 360
"Mapping Tree Density at a Global Scale" (Crowther), 13
Marder, Michael
  arbor sacra, 12
  discussed, 140, 144, 145, 147, 149

  on memory, 169–70
  non-conscious intentionality, 43
  Philosopher's Plant, The, 9
  on *physis*, 138, 142
  on phytophobia, 9
  plant-thinking, 148
  Plant-Thinking, 9, 52n23, 54n40, 101–2n34, 134
  Plants in Place, 9
  on Plato, 139
  on Plotinus, 141–42
  on Schelling, 146
  Time is a Plant, 9
  vegetal metaphysics, 137
Margulis, Lynn, 63, 185
Marion, Jean-Luc
  Crossing of the Visible, The, 109
  discussed, 108
  Erotic Phenomenon, The, 109
Márquez, Gabriel García
  One Hundred Years of Solitude, 267
marri trees, 172
Marsh, George Perkins, 234n7
Masculine Birth of Time, The (Bacon), 62
Matsuda, Will, 269
McBurney, Simon
  Encounter, The, 296
McClintock, Barbara, 63
Melville, Herman
  Moby-Dick, 267
memory
  in Aboriginal Australian poetry, 167, 170
  F. Darwin on, 163–64
  discussed, 39, 164, 165, 166, 175
  in "Honey to Lips Bottlebrush," 171
  Marder on, 169
  Milroy & Milroy on, 168
Merchant, Carolyn
  Death of Nature, The, 71n27
  discussed, 62–63, 71n32

Merck Corporation, 297
Merleau-Ponty, Maurice
    discussed, 8, 44, 50, 84, 281–82
    flesh of the world, 36
Merwin, W. S.
    "Place," 22
mesquite, 257
Metamorphoses (Ovid), 78, 267
metaphors, 329
metaphysics, 105, 109, 376–77, 380
#MeToo movement, 158
Mettrie, Julien Offray de La
    Machine Man, 17
    Man as Plant, 17
Mickey, Sam
    Coexistentialism and the Unbearable Intimacy of Ecological Emergency, 72n48
microbiota, 185–86
middle, 210–11
Midgely, Mary, 408n43
Milbank, Dana
    "Herschel Walker's Anti-Tree Campaign is Genius," 405n11
Miller, Elaine, 146
Milroy, Gladys Idjirrimoonya, 168
Milroy, Jill, 168
Mimosa pudica, 40, 42, 45–46
Mind Eye (Ziemska), 280
Mind of Plants, The (Ryan & Vieira & Gagliano), 134
Minter, Peter
    discussed, 163
    "Tree, The Tree, The," 170, 171–72
Moby-Dick (Melville), 267
Moderns, 117, 124
modular growth, 205
Molly (Doris Pilkington Garimara's mother), 161
Montgomery, Janet
    "Great Irish Famine, The," 238n21

Moore, Kathleen Dean
    Earth's Wild Music, 291
Moore, Marianne, 259
Moore, Ronald, 247, 255
moral agents, 410n56
moral patients, 410n56
Morris, Edwin T., 354–55
Morton, Timothy
    discussed, 265, 280
    "Treating Objects Like Women," 72n48
Mother Earth/Father Time, 62
Mother God, 66, 67, 68–69
Mother Nature, 69
mother trees
    versus beneficent trees/hub trees, 97
    discussed, 67, 68–69, 96, 164, 165
    Simard on, 66, 95
motion, 206
mountain birch trees, 40
mountains and water, 344
movement, 229, 237n18
Muir, John, 235n7, 254, 276
Mulga Seed Dreaming (Tjapaltjarri), 162
mulga trees, 161–63
"Municipal Gum" (Noonuccal), 173
Murck, Alfreda, 359
Murdoch, Iris, 255
Mustard Seed Garden, The (unknown), 357
my place in the sun, 201
mycorrhizal interchanges, 167
mycorrhizal networks
    discussed, 116
    Simard on, 63, 77, 95, 97, 165
mysterium coniunctionis, 196
Myth of the Cave, 139

Nabham, Gary, 257
Naess, Arne, 408n43

Nagel, Thomas
  "What Is It Like to Be a Bat?," 53n36
Namatjira, Albert, 170
Nannup, Noel, 169
Nassar, Dalia
  "Tree Stories," 238n22
nasty woman, 58
national parks movement, 234n7
Nature Conservancy, 311, 321
nature deficit disorder, 20
Naturphilosophie (Schelling), 137, 146, 147
Nausea (Sartre), 148, 377–79
Nealon, Jeffrey T.
  Plant Theory, 134–35
Neely, Sol, 314, 315
Neem, 257
Neidjie, Bill, 167
Nemerov, Howard, 14
Neruda, Pablo, 78
Newton, Isaac, 267, 304, 327
Nicholson, Daniel
  discussed, 227, 236–37n17
  "Return of the Organism as a Fundamental Explanatory Concept in Biology, The," 237n17
Nietzsche, Friedrich, 3, 55–56, 165, 247
"Night and Shadows" (Macauley), 109
9/11, 270
non-conscious intentionality, 43, 52n23
non-intentional consciousness, 43
nonhuman turn, 9
Noonuccal, Oodgeroo
  discussed, 171
  "Municipal Gum," 173
  "Tree Grave," 168
Norway maple trees, 401–2, 412n90
Norway spruce trees, 4

not-being, 148
Novalis, 81, 82
nurse logs, 261
Nussbaum, Martha, 272

oak trees, 186–87, 226, 275
Object Looks Back, The (Elkins), 289n120
objective immortality, 275
Odell, Jenny
  How to Do Nothing, 384
Odyssey, The (Homer), 138
Oele, Marjolein, 207
Oklahoma City bombing, 270
Old-Growth Forest Network, 32
Olympic National Park, 128n39
One Hundred Years of Solitude (Márquez), 267
ontology, 14, 60
open systems, 236–37n17
Orchid Pavilion, 342
Organism and Environment (Sultan), 215
other others, 312, 324n6
other-than-human persons, 44
Otherwise than Being (Levinas), 324n6
Otto, Rudolph, 58
overstory, 268
Overstory, The (Powers), 1–2, 32, 243, 269, 398
Ovid
  discussed, 322
  Metamorphoses, 78, 267
Owens, Delia
  Where the Crawdads Sing, 292
oxygen, 7, 94, 123, 397

Paine, Roxy
  Dendroids, 279
  Graft, 279
painting manuals, 357

Pando, 4–5
Parmenides, 71n27
Parnet, Claire, 380–81
Parsons, Glen
   Functional Beauty, 284n25
Pascal, Blaise
   Pensées, 201
Passmore, John, 408n43
pathetic fallacies, 329
patriarchy, 111
pea plants, 45–46
"Peach Blossom Spring" (Yuanming), 351
peaches/peach trees, 351
Pearson, Carol Lynn
   discussed, 57
   Finding Mother God, 65–66
   "Running Cloud Speaks," 68
Pelizzon, Alessandro
   "Earth laws, right of nature and legal pluralism," 99n10
Pensées (Pascal), 201
perdurable trees, 250, 397, 411n65
persons, 390, 394, 395, 400, 407n29
petrichor, 262
Phaedrus (Plato), 374–76, 376
phanerogams, 225
pharmakon, 375, 376
Philosopher's Plant, The (Marder), 9
"Philosophical Tree, The" (Jung), 18
philosophy, 2, 13, 137, 371
Philosophy of Organism (Whitehead), 137
photosynthesis, 7, 94, 201, 261
physician-assisted suicide, 406n25
physiognomy, 216–18, 217, 218, 231
physis
   discussed, 140, 145, 146
   Homer on, 138
   Kant on, 144–45
   Marder on, 138, 142
   Schelling on, 149

phytoncide, 266
phytophilia, 9, 10
phytophobia, 9–10
phytosemiosis, 98n8
Pierce, Charles, 409n47
Pigeon, John, 49
Pilgrim at Tinker Creek (Dillard), 316–17
pine trees, 337, 350, 352, 354, 359
pitch pine trees, 263
"Place" (Merwin), 22
placedness, 199, 200
placeology, 199
places, 206–7, 209–10
plane trees, 375, 376
plant blindness, 9, 99n16, 247
plant cognition, 40
plant-nature synecdoche, 142
plant neurobiology, 102n41
plant-souls, 147
Plant Theory (Nealon), 134–35
plant-thinking, 4, 148
Plant-Thinking (Marder), 9, 52n23, 54n40, 101–2n34, 134
Plants in Place (Marder), 9
Plato
   on beauty, 248
   discussed, 8, 61, 71n24
   and form, 105
   Phaedrus, 374–76, 376
   Republic, The, 139
   Sophist, 148
   Theaetetus, 139–40
   Timaeus, 102n41, 139, 140, 149, 376
Platonism, 376–77
Plotinus
   discussed, 147
   Enneads, 141
   Marder on, 141–42
Plum Creek Timber Company, 309, 310, 311, 318, 320

plum trees, 337, 358–59
Plumwood, Val
  discussed, 55, 61
  Feminism and the Mastery of Nature, 69n2, 70n21, 71n24
Poet as Phenomenologist, The (Fischer), 98n9
poetics of relation, 373
pohutukawa trees, 403n6
Polanyi, Michael, 372
Pollan, Michael
  Botany of Desire, The, 304
  discussed, 267, 274, 360
pollarding, 352
Ponderosa (Fiedler & Arno), 326n28
ponderosa pines, 255, 308–9, 317–18, 319, 320
Pope, Alexander
  "Essay on Man, An," 128n45
postcritical thinking, 372–73
posthuman theory, 9
Potawatomi basket makers, 49
Power of Movement in Plants, The (Darwin & Darwin), 163
Powers, Richard
  discussed, 23, 247, 255
  Overstory, The, 1–2, 32, 243, 269, 398
practical wisdom, 346
pragmatics of the useless, 383–84
Preface to the Poems Composed at the Orchid Pavilion (Xizhi), 342
prickly juniper trees, 210
Prigogine, Ilya, 376
Primm, Mahala, 310, 319, 321
Primm Meadow, 309–10, 317, 319, 320, 321
"Problem of Biological Individuality, The" (Clarke), 237n19
Prometheus, 4, 158, 411n78
Proust, Marcel, 3
purity politics, 373

Pyne, Stephen, 323
Pyrocene, 323, 324
Pythagoreans, 248

Qian, Tao, 344
quaking aspen trees, 4
Quasha, George, 207
queer use, 383
quietest place in the United States, 128n39

rainbow eucalyptus trees, 263
Rawlence, Ben
  Treeline, The, 405n10, 409n48
Ream, Cathy, 309–10, 320, 321–22
Ream, Tarn, 309–10, 320, 321
reappearing forms, 218
"Red Gum and I, The" (Davis), 171–72
redwood trees, 5, 7–8, 31–32
Regan, Tom, 38, 408n43
reincarnation, 275
relational aesthetics, 256
relationality, 41, 47, 63
relationist ethos, 167
Republic, The (Plato), 139
resistance-in-place, 384
resistant essence, 72n48
"Return of the Organism as a Fundamental Explanatory Concept in Biology, The" (Nicholson), 237n17
rhizomes, 372, 380, 381, 382
rhizosphere, 165, 169
Rich, Adrienne
  "What Kind of Times are These," 10
Richards, I. A., 329
Ricoeur, Paul, 372
Rihua, Li, 356
Rilke, Rainer Maria, 259, 266, 282

rings
  and dendrochronology, 4
  in *Dendrofemonology,* 4
  discussed, 157–58, 169, 200
  Kimmerer on, 166
  in redwoods, 5
Riverbank, The (unknown), 344–45
Roe v. Wade, 391–92
Rolston, Holmes, III, 38, 246, 408n43
Rose, Deborah Bird, 315, 316
Rothenberg, David
  Survival of the Beautiful, 286n49
Roy, Sumana
  How I Became a Tree, 78
Ruhua, Li, 332
"Running Cloud Speaks" (Pearson), 68
Rustic Sounds (F. Darwin), 163
Ryan, John C.
  discussed, 255
  Language of Plants, The, 102n41
  Mind of Plants, The, 134

Sachs, Aaron
  Humboldt Current, The, 235n7
sacred forests, 328
sacred groves, 361n6
sacred trees, 328, 362n8
sacred web of connections, 167
Sagan, Carl, 268
St. Marie, Susan, 58
Sand County Almanac (Leopold), 133
sapwood, 264
Sartre, Jean-Paul
  Being and Nothingness, 379
  discussed, 372, 374
  Nausea, 148, 377–79
Schelling, Friedrich Wilhelm Joseph von
  Beiser on, 149
  discussed, 143–44, 145, 148, 149, 152n65

Naturphilosophie, 137–38, 146–47
  on *physis,* 149
Schröter, Matthias
  "Ecosystem Services as a Contested Concept," 411n64
Schultz fire, 326n28
Schussler, Elizabeth, 9
Schutz, Alfred, 338, 356, 363n25
Scientific Revolution, 80
second faith, 372
second naïveté, 372
self-/non-self-discrimination, 349
senses, 7, 408n45
sensible ideas, 100n19
sentinel plants, 164–65
sequoias, 7–8, 184, 393, 407n37
Sessions, George, 408n43
Seven Sages of the Bamboo Grove, 335–36, 339, 350, 356
Shakers, 265
sheoak trees, 168, 169
sheoak whispers, 168
Shikibu, Murasaki
  Tale of Genji, The, 332
shinboku, 275
Shinto, 262
Shiojiri, Kaori, 41
Shlain, Tiffany
  Dendrofemonology, 4, 158
Shōbōgenzō (Dōgen), 359, 366n60
shocked recognition, 371
Shōen, Myōe, 330
"Should Trees Have Standing?" (Stone), 53n34, 390
Siegel, Samantha, 21
significant form, 288n92
silence, 103, 104–5, 111–13, 114–15, 141
"Silent Wolves" (Klaver), 72n45
Silverstein, Shel
  Giving Tree, The, 257, 303

Simard, Suzanne
  discussed, 41, 63, 77, 96
  Finding the Mother Tree, 65–66, 95, 165, 254
Singer, Peter
  Animal Liberation, 394, 408n43
sites, 196
Six Gentlemen, The (Zan), 354
"Six Trees" (Gongwang), 332
Sloterdijk, Peter
  Critique of Cynical Reason, 373
smells, 262
smooth space, 198
snags, 261
Snow White (fictional character), 304
Snyder, Gary
  discussed, 250, 276, 277
  "Forest in the Library, The," 268
Society for the Study of Ancient Groves, 328
Socrates
  discussed, 139–40, 140, 372, 376, 377, 378
  and *Phaedrus*, 374–75
softwood, 264
Sōjun, Ikkyū, 259–60
Soko Ga Japan (TV series), 362n8
Solzhenitsyn, Aleksandr, 416
"Song of My Nan Tree Uprooted by the Storm" (Fu), 327–28
song of pines, 264
Song of the Seal, The (unknown), 292
Song of the Swamp, The (unknown), 292
Song Synthesis, 339
Songs of Trees, The (Haskell), 255, 293
sonification, 293–94, 297
Sophia, 56
Sophist (Plato), 148
Soul of All, 141
"Sound of Trees, The" (Frost), 263–64

Spanish needles, 172
"Speaking Tree" (Harjo), 22
speciation, 200
species beings, 395, 402, 409n50
species loneliness, 66, 72n43
Spivak, Gayatri Chakravorty
  "Criticism, Feminism, and the Institution," 70n10
Splittereiche, 163
stamp of impossibility, 72n48
standing, 392, 393, 407n29
Standing People, xiii
Starry Night (van Gogh), 242
Steiner, Rudolf
  discussed, 147
  Foundations of Esotericism, The, 102n41
Stengers, Isabelle, 376
Stevens, Wallace
  discussed, 261
  "Thirteen Ways of Looking at a Blackbird," 247
Stillness in Motion (Ziemska), 280
stilt palm trees, 202–3
Stone, Christopher
  discussed, 393, 400, 402, 408n38
  "Should Trees Have Standing?," 53n34, 390
stories, 267–68
"Story Tree" (Eckermann & Harjo), 173, 174–75
strangler fig trees, 193
strategic essentialism, 59, 70n10
Strathern, Marilyn, 184
striated space, 198
sublime, 274
suchness, 258
sugar maple trees, 389, 390, 404n9
Sultan, Sonia
  Organism and Environment, 215
sun, 201

452 | Index

survival intelligence, 66
Survival of the Beautiful (Rothenberg), 286n49
Svalbard Global Seed Vault, 23
swamp oaks, 168
symbiogenesis, 63

Tacarigua. *See* Lake Valencia
Taegio, Bartolomeo, 361n5
Tagore, Rabindranath, 3
taking = giving, 201–2
Tale of Genji, The (Shikibu), 332
Tales of Ise (unknown), 336
Tandi, Pak, 188–89
T'ao Yuan-ming's Ode on "Homecoming" (Tsai), 332
Tarra trees, 189
Tasmanian bluegum trees *(Eucalyptus globulus)*, 369–70
tastes, 263
Taylor, Bron, 10
Te Aroha, 403n6
teeth, 238n21
terpenes, 262
Theaetetus (Plato), 139–40
Thellier, Michel, 172
Theophrastus, 8
thinking before thinking, 43
"Thirteen Ways of Looking at a Blackbird" (Stevens), 247
32 Short Films about Glenn Gould (film), 296
32 Sounds (film), 296
Thomas, Jared
"Healing Tree, The," 173, 174
Thompson, Ian
"Forest Resilience, Biodiversity, and Climate Change," 405–6n15
Thoreau, Henry David
"Autumnal Tints," 261–62
different intentions of the eye, 281

discussed, 24, 249, 257, 271, 279
Walden, 250, 273
Thousand Plateaus, A (Deleuze & Guattari), 197, 198
Three Friends of Winter, 337
Three Natures, The, 361n5
three perfections, 356
Thus Spoke the Plant (Gagliano), 293
thusness, 258
Timaeus (Plato), 102n41, 139, 140, 149, 376
"Timber" (Griffin), 62
time, 4
Time is a Plant (Marder), 9
Tjapaltjarri, Clifford Possum
Mulga Seed Dreaming, 162
"To Those Born Later" (Brecht), 10
"Today" (Eckermann), 170–71
Totality and Infinity (Levinas), 106
touch, 263
transcendentalism, 127–28n33
"Treating Objects Like Women" (Morton), 72n48
"Tree" (Gilbert), 167
tree farms, 199
tree ferns, 6
"Tree Grave" (Noonuccal), 168
tree-huggers, 401, 412n85
tree line, 409n48
Tree Logic (Jeremijenko), 280
tree marriage, 275
Tree of Jiva and Atman, 275
Tree of Life, 194, 275
tree shapes, 249, 252
"Tree Stories" (Nassar & Barbour), 238n22
"Tree, The Tree, The" (Minter), 170, 171–72
Tree told me so, The... (Ziemska), 280
Treeline, The (Rawlence), 405n10, 409n48

Index | 453

trees
  discussed, 6–7, 268, xiii
  as human property, 389, 393, 403n2
Trees and Rocks (unknown), 340
Trees of Mystery, 4
Treviranus, Gottfried Reinhold, 238n23
Trewavas, Anthony
  "Aspects of Plant Intelligence," 409n47
  discussed, 39
Troll, Carl
  "Die tropischen Gebirge," 236n15
Trump, Donald, 58, 72–73n52
Tsai, Li
  T'ao Yuan-ming's Ode on "Homecoming," 332
Tsukada, Saori, 296
Tuana, Nancy, 71n32
tubeworms, 185
Tung-po, Su, 355
Tzu, Lao, 350

Ulrich, R. S.
  "View through a Window May Influence Recovery from Surgery," 25n18
Under the Wintamarra Tree (Garimara), 161
understory, 268
unlearning, 384
unselfing, 255
uselessness, 382, 383
utility, 256

Valéry, Paul
  "Dialogue of the Tree," 260, 286n60
  discussed, 44
"Vegetable Individual in Its relation to Species, The" (Braun), 237n17
vegetal metaphysics, 137

Velasco, Julian, 258
"Verses of Praise on Portraits of Himself" (Dōgen), 358–59
Vieira, Patricia
  Language of Plants, The, 102n41
  Mind of Plants, The, 134
"View through a Window May Influence Recovery from Surgery" (Ulrich), 25n18
Views of Nature (Humboldt), 216
village pharmacy, 257
Vining, Joseph, 396
virgin forest, 62
viriditas, 123
visualization, 293

wabi-sabi, 260
Walden (Thoreau), 250, 273
Walujapi, 168
Wandersee, James, 9
Warnock, Raphael, 405n11
Washington Post, The, 110
water, 7
Waterlily (Deloria), 127n18
wattles, 171
Way of the Ancestors, 188
Ways of Being (Bridle), 405n10, 409n48
Wei, Wang, 343
weird essentialism, 72n48
Wendling, Caroline
  White Wood, 280
Wenwang
  Book of Changes, 275
Weston, Anthony, 323
"What Holds the Water, What Holds the Light" (Hogan), 311–13
"What is Enlightenment?" (Kant), 105–6
"What Is It Like to Be a Bat?" (Nagel), 53n36

"What Kind of Times are These" (Rich), 10
Wheat Field with Cypresses (van Gogh), 242
Where the Crawdads Sing (Owens), 292
Whispering Pines on a Mountain Path (Yin), 341
white pine trees, 166
White Wood (Wendling), 280
Whitehead, Alfred North
  on creativity, 143
  discussed, 47–48, 148, 152–53n90, 196, 275
  Philosophy of Organism, 137
wild, 67, 72n45
wilderness experience, 66
wildness, 67
Willdenow, Carl Friedrich
  discussed, 232
  Flora Berloinensis, 238n24
  Grundriss der Kräuterkunde, 238n24
William Tell (fictional character), 304
Williams, Delores, 66
Williams, Michael, 12
Williams, William Carlos, 259
willows, 224–27
Wired for Story (Cron), 267
wisdom, 2–3, 4, 346–47, 347, 382
wise trees, 164
Wise Trees (Cook & Jenshel), 362n16, 403n6
witches, 62
wondrous law of nature, 236n15
Wood Line (Goldsworthy), 279
Wood Wide Web, 1
Wordsworth, William, 277–78, 286–87n61
World-Soul, 141
World-Tree, 141

writing system, 339
wuwei, 347, 349–50

Xenophanes, 197
Xi, Zhu
  Doctrine of the Mean, 340
Xizhi, Wang
  discussed, 343–44, 351, 356
  Preface to the Poems Composed at the Orchid Pavilion, 342
Xuan, Qian, 343, 344
Xunzi, 350

Yamada, Koun
  Gateless Gate, The, 258–59
Yellowstone National Park, 78, 235n7
yew trees, 286–87n61
Yin, Tang
  discussed, 342
  Whispering Pines on a Mountain Path, 341
Yokawa, Ken, 45
Yosemite National Park, 235n7
"Young Goodman Brown" (Hawthorne), 267
Yuanming, Tao
  discussed, 332, 356
  "Peach Blossom Spring," 351

Zagajewski, Adam, 291
Zan, Ni
  discussed, 332, 357–58
  Six Gentlemen, The, 354
  untitled painting, 345–46
Zetian, Wu, 158
Zhou, Zhuang. *See* Zhuangzi
Zhuangzi, 382, 383, 384
Ziemska, Olga
  discussed, 24
  Mind Eye, 280
  Stillness in Motion, 280
  Tree told me so, The . . . , 280

Zimmermann, Eberhardt August Wilhelm von
  Geographische Geschichte des Menschen, und der allgemeinen verbreiteten vierfüßigen Thier, 238n23

zoning laws, 403n3

zoocentrism, 9